A Victorian Dissenter

A Victorian Dissenter

Robert Govett and the Doctrine of Millennial Reward

DAVID E. SEIP

◦PICKWICK *Publications* • Eugene, Oregon

A VICTORIAN DISSENTER
Robert Govett and the Doctrine of Millennial Reward

Copyright © 2018 David E. Seip. All rights reserved. Except for brief quotations in critical publications or reviews, no part of this book may be reproduced in any manner without prior written permission from the publisher. Write: Permissions, Wipf and Stock Publishers, 199 W. 8th Ave., Suite 3, Eugene, OR 97401.

Pickwick Publications
An Imprint of Wipf and Stock Publishers
199 W. 8th Ave., Suite 3
Eugene, OR 97401

www.wipfandstock.com

PAPERBACK ISBN: 978-1-5326-1834-5
HARDCOVER ISBN: 978-1-4982-4384-1
EBOOK ISBN: 978-1-4982-4383-4

Cataloguing-in-Publication data:

Names: Seip, David E., author.

Title: A Victorian dissenter : Robert Govett and the doctrine of millennial reward / David E. Seip.

Description: Eugene, OR: Pickwick Publications, 2018 | Includes bibliographical references.

Identifiers: ISBN 978-1-5326-1834-5 (paperback) | ISBN 978-1-4982-4384-1 (hardcover) | ISBN 978-1-4982-4383-4 (ebook)

Subjects: LCSH: Govett, Robert, 1813–1901 | Dissenters, Religious—England—History—19th century | England—Church history—19th century | Great Britain—Religion—19th century.

Classification: BR1609.5 S33 2018 (print) | BR1609.5 (ebook)

Manufactured in the U.S.A.   04/13/18

To My Wife Leslie

Contents

Acknowledgments | ix

Introduction | 1

Chapter 1: The Emergence of Victorian Dissent | 41

Chapter 2: Govett's Life in Context | 70

Chapter 3: Govett's Writings and Victorian Print Culture | 94

Chapter 4: Govett and Infant Baptism | 126

Chapter 5: Govett and Eschatological Reward | 154

Chapter 6: Govett's Afterlife in Context | 187

Chapter 7: Conclusion | 212

Select Bibliography | 223

Acknowledgments

Though my name alone appears on the cover of this book, there are a great many people who have contributed to its completion. I owe my gratitude first to my wife Leslie whose patience, sacrifice without complaint, and loving encouragement made the process of travel, countless hours of research, and writing possible.

My deepest gratitude is to my supervisor, Dr. Crawford Gribben. I have been amazingly fortunate to have a supervisor who is a leading scholar in my field of interest and who gave so freely of his time. His enthusiasm for my discoveries during the lengthy process of research kept me digging deeper for facts and his insight and guidance taught me to avoid numerous pitfalls and, hopefully, to become a better historian.

While well into the process of writing Dr. Gribben assumed a new position on the faculty of another prestigious university he graciously offered to continue in an unofficial capacity of supervision, for which I am also deeply grateful. Dr. David O'Shaughnessy subsequently agreed to assume the official role of supervisor at Trinity. My gratitude goes to Dr. O'Shaughnessy who has been consistently responsive to my submissions and has regularly provided me with recommendations that have proven extremely valuable.

No writing would be possible if it were not for the research that precedes it. Given that no scholarship previously existed on Govett there was much archival digging that needed to take place. I am grateful to the Norfolk Records Office in Norwich, England, for permitting access to their archives, as well as the leadership of Surrey Chapel, Norwich, for their kindness in providing unencumbered access to their Govett archives. Special gratitude is due to Dr. Lewis Schoettle, Schoettle Publishing Company, for providing access to his extensive Govett archives on so many trips. The hospitality that Dr. Schoettle and his wife showed me was delightful and warmly appreciated.

Particular mention must also go to Dr. Rosamunde Coding and Mr. Keith Ives who both became special friends during this study and who both contributed invaluable background to Govett's life and writings. Particular thanks is given to Dr. Timothy Stunt for his genealogical contributions, Mrs. Norma Virgoe for meeting with me to share her vast knowledge of religious worship in Norfolk, England, during the 1800s, the Stoudenmires for their tireless assistance in photographing voluminous pages of tracts and sermons, and to Mrs. Beryl Heisman, former archive librarian at Princeton University, who invested her time to find countless books for me through interlibrary loan.

I would like to acknowledge those who financially provided for my travels and assisted in the payment of tuition. I am certain that they would prefer to receive their thanks by remaining anonymous. I am also indebted to my parents for their enthusiastic belief that this endeavor would one day be a reality and to my children who were beyond patient in sharing time with this work.

And, finally, for any errors or inadequacies that may remain in this work, of course, the responsibility is entirely my own.

Introduction

WEDNESDAY, 20 FEBRUARY 1901 began as a typically cold and snowy day, not unlike many winter days in Norwich, England,[1] except that on this particular day, at 9:30 in the morning,[2] Robert Govett, pastor, theologian, and author, died in his home at 12 Chapel Loke.[3] He had just turned eighty-eight years of age. The cause of death was officially recorded as old age. Friends affirmed this ruling by remarking that he appeared to have just worn out. Yet, he had displayed his usual robustness until a few weeks before his death, when his last sermon was delivered with "virile powers."[4] Those who were present with him at his death, including his close friend William Dix, recounted that his last spoken word was at the conclusion of a prayer offered on his behalf. While appearing to be unconscious the single word he spoke was a fervent "amen."[5] The anecdote pays tribute to a man who was an enthusiast for prayer and unabashed about his theological convictions he zealously preached to his evangelical, nonconformist church, and that he wrote about with equal conviction in one hundred eighty-four published books and tracts.[6] His

---

1. See the official climatological observations made by the Royal Meteorological Society observatory at Brundall, Norfolk, 20 February 1901. Information provided by the Royal Meteorological Society, Reading, UK.

2. See the *Eastern Daily Press* obituary of Robert Govett's death (21 February 1901).

3. Certificate of Death, signed 21 February 1901, by M. M. Gardener, Deputy Registrar, in the Sub District of East Wymer, in the City and County of the City of Norwich. See Norfolk Records Office catalog reference FC76/89.

4. *The Christian* (28 March 1901). Norfolk Records Office file FC76/59.

5. Rosamunde Coding, *Book of Thanksgiving, 150 Years at Surrey Chapel, Norwich: 1854–2004* (Norwich: Surrey Cahapel, 2004) 11.

6. This number increases when including the numerous reprints over the years, which combined tracts related by topic.

theological convictions were also evident through the sustained flow of articles he published in the numerous, but diverse, religious journals that emerged during the Victorian age. In nineteenth-century evangelical print culture his theological opinions, while sometimes strongly contested, were often sought and nearly always respected. When, for example, *The Voice upon the Mountains*[7] reviewed Govett's tract *Sowing and Reaping* (1868),[8] it praised the author as a man of tremendous ability who was able to "do full justice to any subject he took in hand."[9] The *Gospel Herald* argued that his tract, *The Observance of Lent* (1869),[10] was one of the best ever published on the subject.[11] In a review of Govett's tract *Christ Superior to Angels* (1884),[12] the editors of *The Sword and the Trowel*, the evangelical journal with perhaps the largest circulation, wrote: "We may differ from some of Mr. Govett's opinions, but we never differ from himself . . . Our friend received his gospel, not of man, neither was he taught it, but he searched the Word for himself under the illumination of the Holy Ghost."[13] Nevertheless, despite his frequent contributions to the print culture of nineteenth-century evangelicalism, Govett has disappeared from contemporary scholarly literature, thus making this study of his life and contribution to millennial opinions important to the ongoing reconstruction of religious dissent in Victorian England.

Despite the initial appeal Govett had in print culture, he was never more than a minor figure in comparison to the popularity of some preachers and theologians of his day. This is because he had the misfortune of being twice buried and forgotten given that he found himself on the losing side of many theological arguments. In the first place, as a Dissenter (and a Dispensationalist at that), but one with a very small following, he was always on the margins of Victorian religious life, though he did contribute

7. *The Voice upon the Mountains; a Journal of Prophetic Testimony and Evangelical Effort* was published between January 1867 to December 1869. Its orientation was evangelistic and sought to provide information on the "personal coming, reign and kingdom of the Lord Jesus Christ." See *Waterloo Directory of English Newspapers and Periodicals, 1800–1900*, series 2 in 20 vols. (Ontario: North Waterloo Academic, 2003).

8. Robert Govett, *Sowing and Reaping* (London: Nesbet and Co., 1868).

9. *The Voice upon the Mountains: A Journal of Prophetic Testimony and Evangelistic Effort* 2 (1868), 148–49.

10. Robert Govett, *The Observance of Lent* (Norwich: Fletcher and Son, 1869).

11. *The Gospel Herald*, vol. 38.6 (June 1869), 143.

12. Robert Govett, *Christ Superior to Angels, Moses, Aaron: A Comment on the Epistle to the Hebrews* (London: James Nisbet and Co., 1884).

13. *The Sword and the Trowel; a Record of Combat with Sin and of Labor for the Lord* (October 1885), 548.

enthusiastically to contemporary periodicals and was a respected commentator on exegetical matters. As a minister he was by all accounts dedicated, but he did not pastor a large congregation as measured by some of the most popular ministers of his day, founded no particular denomination, left behind almost no structural legacy, and therefore he has not seemed all that important to religious or cultural historians of the period who have had the distractions of such matters as the Oxford Movement and the so-called "crisis of faith" upon which to concentrate. In the second place, Govett originated what has become known as "partial rapture," and argued that some of the followers of Jesus, justified by faith but failures in practical Christianity, would not receive any portion of the Millennial Kingdom. Those who forfeited this kingdom would be "left behind" to suffer in the Tribulation to come subsequent to the Rapture. This original idea lost out in dispensational theology to the much more influential interpretation of John Nelson Darby (1800–1882), which eventually achieved dominance through dissemination in the Scofield Bible and had an enormous influence on twentieth- and early twenty-first-century Dispensationalism in North America. In part, this study reveals Govett to be a forgotten contributor to the vitality of theological debate in the Victorian era. His many contributions to religious periodicals, and his book-length studies, as well as his life story, all shed light on the sheer complexity of a period that has tended to be presented by some historians in very monolithic ways.

Because of his developing idiosyncratic theological position on eschatology Govett became a rather eccentric figure. Later in life his "end-time" teaching won him very few followers. His views were subsequently rejected by more than a few major dissenters, while eventually becoming so unpopular that periodicals had to avoid giving too much space to its advocate because of the impact on readership. Moreover, while Govett was respected for his biblical scholarship, and was held in great affection by his congregation, and also by many who did not share his theological commitments, he was considered a major thinker or theologian by only a few genuinely significant figures in Victorian Britain.

At the same time, this study of Govett contributes to the demonstration of complexity to a historical understanding of Dissenting culture in the Victorian period. There existed a vitality of debate to which Govett's many contributions to religious periodicals, and his book-length studies—as well as his life story—all shed light on the sheer theological complexity of a period that has often tended to be presented in very monolithic ways by historians. As such, any biography of Govett must be constructed in the context of the age in which he lived. And, as this study will show, the theological debates in which Govett engaged cannot easily be lifted from the political, philosophical, and scientific debates of his day. Likewise, the literature and culture of the Victorians was also steeped in religious thought and practice. Therefore, to better understand Govett it is important to understand something of the age through which he lived.

This study could not have been justified had Govett's legacy not been so highly prized in his own day. Nevertheless, most residents of Norwich did not notice Govett's death, despite the contributions he had made to the city over a long life. In contrast, the congregation of Surrey Road Chapel deeply mourned the death of their beloved minister of fifty-seven years.[14] His life of devotion and commitment to his congregation had ended, but his death created a point of demarcation for his dwindling yet faithful fellowship.[15] His death ended a long and fruitful ministry, but it ushered in a legacy that continues to impact generations of Surrey Road Chapel congregants. Their devotion to their founder and former minister is evidenced by the fact that when the congregation moved to a new location on Botolph Street, in the northern half of Norwich, in 1985, they maintained the name Surrey Chapel and placed an inscription memorializing Govett in the entrance hall of their new building.[16] Further evidence of their devotion is visible just off the sanctuary in a room that bears their former pastor's name and reverently houses the fragmented remains of his once voluminous personal library. It was upon his death that Govett's books and tracts, his magazine articles, book reviews, key correspondence, and hundreds of his handwritten sermons were preserved in the chapel that Govett helped to build with his own personal funds. The total cost of construction in 1854 was £3,300, of which Govett contributed £3,000.[17] The contribution illustrates both his personal

---

14. Robert Govett is buried in Rosary Cemetery, Norwich, England, with the following inscription on his headstone: "In memory of Robert Govett, MA. For fifty-seven years pastor of the church connected with Surrey Chapel, Norwich. Who fell asleep 20 February 1901. Age 88. 'Until the Day dawn and the Day star arise.'" The years noted in connection with his service include forty-seven years at Surrey Chapel and the remainder with the congregation at Bazaar Chapel preceding the building of Surrey Road Chapel. See Coding, *Book of Thanksgiving*, 11.

15. The 1851 Census gives the attendance figures of 459 in the morning service. See Govett's obituary, *Eastern Daily Press* (21 February 1901), which noted that there were 200 congregants in 1892, and about 60 in 1900.

16. After his death this plaque was erected and placed on the wall of the original church foyer containing an inscription from 1 Peter 5:4, which reads: "And when the Chief Shepherd appears, you will receive the crown of glory that will never fade away." See Norfolk Records Office file FC76/59 (1 of 2). This sentiment reflected the church's understanding of what their shepherd had conveyed to them over the years regarding the doctrine of reward.

17. "Death of the Rev. R. Govett," *Eastern Daily Press* (21 February 1901). See also *Surrey Chapel Book of Remembrance, 1854–1954* (Norwich: Surrey Chapel, 2004)

wealth and the devotion he felt toward his flock and to the pastoral work in which he wholeheartedly engaged.

The importance of the devotion Govett and his church reciprocated cannot be overstated since without this bond and the sustained affection of a flock for its former pastor many of the facts concerning Govett's life, as well as his written work, would likely have been lost, and there would not exist the means to methodically piece together the details of Govett's life and writings. And although there exist numerous published works by which to judge his contributions to the theological debate and print culture of his day, there would be little if any context by which to judge the rationale and motivation which lay behind them.

Since his death some of the materials and formal documents relating to Govett and his ministry at Surrey Road Chapel have made their way into the hands of the Norfolk Records Office.[18] In the early 1940s German warplanes regularly bombed the area near Surrey Road Chapel because of its proximity to a railway station and large aircraft manufacturing plant.[19] Bombing was often quite dense so, in a gesture of concern, a large portion of the Govett archives was removed by Henry Frederick Weatherley, church treasurer, and stored in the basement of his house for safekeeping. In the mid-1970s most of what remained in the chapel in the form of letters and documents was given to the county of Norfolk to archive for permanent safekeeping. At the same time most of what remained of Govett's tracts and some of his personal books were once again moved to Weatherly's home. Weatherly's portion of the archive remained in his house until the early 1980s when Lewis Schoettle procured them from Weatherly's daughter for his publishing company in America, which went on to publish all but one of Govett's books.[20] Previously, David M. Panton (1870–1955), friend,

---

archived at the same location. This account differs from the *Eastern Daily Press* by recording Govett's personal contribution as £2,300 of his own money to help construct Surrey Chapel, whose total cost was £3,200.

18. There are 175 files dating from 1836 archived at the Norfolk Records Office ranging from church minutes and other legal church documents to items related specifically to Robert Govett. See Norfolk Records Office Catalog Reference FC/76.

19. Author interview with Dr Rosamunde Codling, 26 February 2011, after her consultation with older members of Surrey Chapel who were present during World War II.

20. Schoettle Publishing Company, Haysville, NC, retains approximately 1,000 of Govett's handwritten sermons from the early years of his ministry at Surrey Chapel; copies from the early years of the *Dawn* magazine; numerous tracts; book reviews which appeared in newspapers; personal Bibles and several books belonging to Govett. The one book which Schoettle did not publish is: Robert Govett, *English Derived from Hebrew with Glances at Greek and Latin* (London: S. W. Partridge & Co., 1869).

student, and successor to Govett at Surrey Road Chapel, had helped to keep the contribution of Govett's writings alive for several decades by publishing portions of his books in the monthly *Dawn* magazine—a publication that Panton established and edited until his death in May 1955. Nevertheless, the limited distribution of these sources and the ever changing theological landscape since Panton's death have contributed to the slow but inevitable decline of interest in Govett's many writings and consequently the extinction of his memory. Chapter 6 will describe the events and circumstances contributing to his disappearance.

Govett's numerous writings are largely exegetical and expository. The general characteristics of his writings were categorized by W. J. Dalby, a deacon in the Church of England, in a memoir of Govett which he published in the preface to the second edition of Govett's commentary on Galatians.[21] It is somewhat curious to note that this tribute, written twenty-nine years after Govett's death, is penned by an Anglican minister—curious, given that Govett was a nonconformist throughout most of his life.[22] In his memoir Dalby accurately described five particularly noticeable characteristics of Govett's writings. The first was his emphasis on logic. Govett was known for finding the error in the logic of others and hence pointing out the weakness in their theological writings. It was an approach he exercised most liberally— particularly in the theological journals in which his many articles appeared. Secondly, Govett was known to be independent in his thinking. He relied upon his own fresh scrutiny of Scripture and was not swayed by those who demanded his conformity to the doctrines of Protestant scholasticism. Thirdly, Govett was observed to be a systematic theologian. He used this approach to Scripture to extract important truths which often separated him from his peers. Fourthly, Govett wrote in an accessible literary style. He avoided using lofty prose or writing condescendingly to his audience or those with whom he differed. Lastly, he always sought to be faithful to Scripture, and to discover its meaning by the guidance of the Holy Spirit, as he understood it.[23] These characteristics of Govett's writings frame the context of this discussion of his approach to the biblical and doctrinal themes that

---

21. See Robert Govett, *Govett on Galatians—Moses or Christ* (London: Thynne & Co., 2nd edition, 1930).

22. "Ecclesiastical News," *The Times* (27 December 1922). W. J. Dalby, B.A. Christ's College, Cambridge, was ordained and served as deacon of St Augustine and St Mary, Coslany, Norwich.

23. W. J. Dalby, "Memoir of Robert Govett, M.A.," printed as a foreward to Robert Govett, *Govett on Galatians—Moses or Christ* (London: Thynne & Co., 2nd edition, 1930), no pagination.

occupied his attention, and they are used to form the background for many of the conclusions reached throughout this study.

Govett's writings, while always having an exegetical focus, vary in style and approach. A portion of his writings consists of commentaries on various books of the Bible rather than thematic subjects. Some of the commentaries and tracts were held in high regard at the time of their publication. It is reported by the press that C. H. Spurgeon (1834–1892), a pulpit giant of the Victorian age, speaking of Govett's commentary on the Gospel of John, said, "You may take away every book from my library but leave me Govett on John, I cannot do without that."[24] The actual words may have been somewhat embellished but the sentiment reflects the tone of a review of Govett's book in Spurgeon's *The Sword and the Trowel*.[25] Spurgeon also referenced Govett's work on Hebrews in a sermon he preached in 1891. He referred to Govett as "my good friend."[26] Likewise, Govett's commentary on Romans is instructive for understanding something of the measure of his empathy toward others. For instance, although in this commentary Govett was keen to warn the believer of the dire consequences of not living in a manner pleasing to Christ, and although his exposition of Scripture on this matter was often forcefully delivered, he never wrote in a condemning manner, or with a legalistic ring. There was a positive tone to his writings—which was especially apparent to those who were weak in their faith—which undergirded his theological passions. This was brought out when arguing his cause in reply to a letter which was printed in *The Rainbow*, in which he hoped "that we may have grace to not write bitterly of one another in the controversies which arise. Truth and love are sisters; let us not, in the fight for truth, plunge our sword into the bosom of love. The adversary will have vantage ground against us if he can say that we are just like any other men, and cannot keep our tempers when once we differ."[27] Notwithstanding, he was prepared to note when other theologians were not acting with biblically tolerant deportment. Such was the case in his commentary to the Romans. In chapter 14 he commented on the position taken by John Nelson Darby

---

24. "The Rev. R. Govett," *Eastern Daily Press* (26 February 1901). Norfolk Records Office file FC76/59.

25. *The Sword and the Trowel; a Record of Combat with Sin and of Labor for the Lord* (September 1883), 512.

26. See Spurgeon's sermon titled "Between the Two Appearings," preached the morning of 15 March 1891 at the Metropolitan Tabernacle. See also, Robert Govett, *Christ Superior to Angels, Moses, Aaron: A Comment on the Epistle to the Hebrews* (London: James Nisbet and Co., 1884).

27. *The Rainbow: A Magazine of Christian Literature, with Special Reference to the Revealed Future of the Church and the World* 2 (April 1865), 187.

(1800–1882) on "open communion." Darby refused fellowship to any who did not condemn the conduct of George Müller and his pastoral associate Henry Craik of Bristol, England.[28] Govett's response to Darby was to ask the question: "Was Christianity then a dry, contentious system, in which the chief thing was to be ecclesiastically right?"[29]

In many of his works Govett expounded upon the subject of prophecy and dealt with the particulars of anticipated future biblical events. He was especially concerned to write about Christ's Second Coming and its impact upon believers at its pending judgment. No theologian or religious scholar of his day appears to have treated the subject of judgment and its aftermath in as much published work. This focus and his scholarship in general led to Govett's unsought celebrity, for he was known throughout the United Kingdom, and at least one account declared that his repute was higher still in America.[30] Spurgeon, who grew to become one of Govett's friends and admirers, was reported in *The Christian* journal to have said, with respect to one of Govett's last books, that as a writer he was before his time, and predicted the day would come when his writings would be held "as treasured gold."[31] But contrary to the predictions of this most notable preacher, Govett's name, his writings, and their theological contributions have all but vanished from contemporary writings pertaining to evangelical millennialism and its debate in Victorian England.

Govett and His Religious Convictions

Govett was one of many writers who framed the religious debates in nineteenth-century England. He interacted through his writings with many notable theologians including John Nelson Darby, William Kelly, John Cumming, and Edward Bishop Elliott. He was not afraid to go against the grain of conventional thought, nor the expectations placed upon one who had been ordained in the Church of England once he was convinced the church was in

---

28. George Müller and Henry Craik co-ministered as pastors of Bethesda Chapel—a Brethren assembly in Bristol, England—for many years, as well as ministering to many thousands of orphans and founding the mission's Scripture Knowledge Institute at Home and Abroad. Their work was well known and respected around the world. See, for example, Arthur T. Pierson, *George Mueller of Bristol and his Witness to a Prayer-Hearing God* (London: Pickering and Inglis, 1899).

29. Robert Govett, *The Righteousness of God, the Salvation of the Believer: or, the Argument of the Romans* (Norwich: Fletcher and Son, 1891), 501.

30. Norfolk Records Office file FC76/59. *Eastern Daily Press* article published shortly after Govett's death. No date.

31. *The Christian* (28 March 1901).

error on some matter of doctrine or Scriptural interpretation. All through his adult life Govett stood firm on his religious convictions and was not hesitant to defend unpopular positions. One such position was his tenacious rejection of the Established Church's practice of infant baptism. This conviction would markedly change his life. It would result in his formal separation from the Established Church and his subsequent career as a dissenting nonconformist. This was no small stand for Govett to take considering that he came from a long line of ordained Anglicans and was directly descended from the famous eighteenth-century theologian William Romaine. The theological implications of this stand are discussed in chapter 4.

Given the vast number of books and tracts Govett published in his lifetime this study organizes the primary sources by date in the bibliography. The study also engages with a number of their themes and attempts to ascertain his motivation for choosing them. Two of the most prominent themes—baptism and eternal reward—are presented in detail in chapters 4 and 5. Furthermore, this study answers the question as to whether there can be established points of thematic embarkation whereupon Govett shifts his attention to a new or deeper area of concern in his writings. When these shifts occur it is often in response to the religious debate that sprang from the many influences upon Victorian life. One such example is his passion for eschatological issues related to the believer's conduct in this life and the coming judgment of Christ and concomitant reward.[32] Conduct, and its eschatological reward, is an evolving subject area for Govett which becomes increasingly important in his writings after the onset of his pastorate at Surrey Road Chapel. Thereafter, Govett treats this subject as an imperative upon which all else in the Christian life depends.

There does not appear to be any consistency in the means by which Govett selected topics for debate. Occasionally theological subjects appear to present themselves rather spontaneously—such as in his tract on vegetarianism.[33] At other times he doggedly pursues a subject for years. For example, he never writes about baptism until he at once forms a conviction over what he firmly holds to be biblical truth respecting believers' baptism. He concludes this while observing the act on one occasion in a Baptist church service. Once he concluded that his former position was in error he published a steady output of writings on the subject of believers' baptism in opposition to the teachings of the Established Church. Tracts on the subject began to appear in 1843. Thereafter, he continued writing on the

32. See, for example, Robert Govett, *Entrance into the Kingdom* (Norwich: Fletcher and Son, 1853).

33. See, for example, Robert Govett, *Vegetarianism: A Dialogue* (London: Campbell, 1849).

subject well into the last decade of his life. Yet, he did not write on this topic in obscurity. His written thoughts were often sought after. In 1860 C. H. Spurgeon wrote to Govett, his "dear brother," asking where he might find copies of his tracts on baptism—presumably the series of seven tracts published in 1847.[34] Spurgeon desired permission to print and distribute portions of the tracts, hoping to "disseminate a great truth which is far too much kept in the background."[35]

Many of Govett's tracts, and all of his books, passed through multiple editions. The extent to which his tracts and books were reprinted provides an understanding of the popularity of their subject matter and, to some extent, of Govett's personal convictions. Govett identifies these priorities in letters which he wrote to his congregation on his annual holiday. These letters were formally printed and distributed—usually the Sunday before his anticipated return to the pulpit at Surrey Road Chapel. They often provided a summary of the "state of the church," but they also frequently provided a window into the theological concerns of the author. Such is the perspective of the letter he wrote to his congregation on 14 January 1883, nearly forty years into his pastorate. It clarifies what Govett had felt to be the "great truths which for so many years I have been privileged to testify to you,"[36] and which he now took time to reaffirm. These "great truths" center on what he believed to be the two paramount concerns of the Christian. Both are concerns that no doubt were reflected in countless hours in study and writing since they form the foundation of much of his published works. In this letter he posits that these matters must of necessity be grounded in Scripture which is to be "our one and sufficient rule." Before he lays out the first "great truth" he asserts that God's evangelist's call is upon all who are sinners. They are to repent and turn from their wicked way and to leave their associations with the worldly. Once this is accomplished the new believers are to join the assembly of Christ. Having buttressed the great truths with this introduction Govett proceeds to the first of these truths: immersion. While the mode of baptism was important to Govett it was always fraught with theological

---

34. Presumably these were the series of seven tracts published in 1847. See *The Principal Argument from Scripture in Favour of Infant Baptism Considered; Baptism Foreshadowed by Noah's Salvation in the Ark; The Passage Through the Red Sea—a Type of Baptism; "At Any Rate, Infant Baptism is Not Forbidden;" Sin After Baptism—or a Long Neglected Command of the Lord Jesus, Recommended to Believers; Open or Strict Communion? Judgment Pronounced on the Question by the Lord Jesus Himself; The Baptismal Services of the Church of England* (Norwich: Fletcher and Son, 1847).

35. Letter to Govett from Spurgeon, 20 October 1860. Norfolk Records Office file FC76/59 (1 of 2).

36. Robert Govett, "A Letter to the Saints Assembling at Surrey Road," 14 January 1883. Norfolk Records Office file FC76/59.

conflict. He wrote that water baptism of the believer is a testimony to a believer's vast and momentous movement from death in sins to life in God. From Govett's perspective baptism also bears upon the sequence of death and resurrection. And here there is a connection between this first "great truth" (believers' baptism by immersion) and Govett's millennialism. In his letter he reveals that immersion is God's commanded mode of the believer to express faith in the Lord and Savior Jesus Christ, slain and risen, and "our faith in a resurrection yet to come."[37] Immersion, therefore, takes place in obedience to God, after evangelical conversion, which places emphasis in faith upon the future coming of Christ. This then finds an intricate and binding connection to the next great truth expressed in his letter.

The second of Govett's "great truths," and which has a future purpose in the Coming Kingdom, is the Day of Judgment and the reward that will be given to those who have been obedient to the Savior's commands.[38] Govett does not claim this to have meritorious connection between the believer and Christ. He distinguishes with Paul between the *gift* of God, which is eternal life, which is surely the believer's, and "the *prize* of our calling," of which the believer may be accounted unworthy. The believer, therefore, is to be looking for the return of the Son of God from heaven. But he cautions that not all believers will be looking and not all will be found to be at peace with Christ. Consequently some will be ashamed before Him in the Day of Judgment. The point of caution is that the Savior is coming to judge believers—not as to whether they are friends or foes of God, but concerning their service to Christ since they became His children. Govett reminds his congregation that this truth is so important a subject, but of so little regard, that he has just sent a short tract for printing with some exposition of the Scriptures upon which the doctrine rests. Lest his congregants were confused by the distinction Govett was making concerning faith resting in faith, and reward being consequent upon work, he added this statement: "While our works will not save us, we shall yet be judged according to them. Hence the deep importance of obedience to Christ's commands."[39] He goes on to explain that there will be an accounting by Christ of some who are worthy, in which case there will be an entry on the first and blest resurrection (or the "Glory of the Thousand Years," as he describes it). If any are rejected from reward, they will enter into eternal life only after the thousand-years are over. This touches upon his position that not all of the church will reign with Christ in the millennium. Not all of the church would participate in the rapture,

37. Ibid., 1.
38. Ibid., 2–3.
39. Ibid., 2.

which Govett believed was described in 1 Thessalonians 4:16. This feature becomes central to Govett's eschatology and is discussed in chapter 5 and 6. It was a unique theological position that many would come to reject.

Nevertheless, Govett believed that the same consequence was true of the non-believer. Govett's *Entrance into the Kingdom*, first published in 1853, argues that no one should misunderstand his position as to be arguing that the doctrine of reward for good works applies only to believers. This in no way—he strongly asseverated—can be used as a means of justification. The doctrine of reward, Govett avows, does affect the unbeliever (or wicked, as he refers to them), because each act of trespass on their part is "increasing their damnation."[40] Govett's two "great truths" are consistently the two most prevalent truths he expounds throughout his many years of writing and are inextricably intertwined with his futurist views of prophecy. Yet Govett does not write in a religious vacuum. He is as influenced by events taking place around him as any theologian writing and preaching in Victorian England; especially those events relating to the progression of religious dissent, evangelicalism, millennialism, and the formation and spread of the Brethren movement. This study examines Govett in the context of these theological developments. But, of course, it is important to note that the many theological terms used by necessity in this study developed–in some cases–over the span of centuries. For example, the use of terms such as "evangelical" and "evangelicalism," or "millennialism" and "millennialist" acquired definitions that are sometimes broadly used and, therefore, the meanings can tend to become unstable in modern scholarly debate.[41]

Clarification of Terms

It is important that this study of Govett be preceded by an acknowledgment and understanding of key religious terms. The religious terms are numerous and sometimes interconnected. Therefore clarification of terms is important. Two additional headings follow to provide further clarification: Eschatology and Interpretations of the Apocalypse. Govett was first and foremost an evangelical and was defined by this term long before he dissented from the Church of England. It is not easy to define an evangelical of the nineteenth century, for historians have not always been careful

---

40. Robert Govett, *Entrance into the Kingdom. or Reward According to Works* (Norwich: Fletcher and Son, 1853) Preface, no pagination.

41. Crawford Gribben, *Evangelical Millennialism in the Trans-Atlantic World, 1500–2000* (New York: Palgrave Macmillan, 2011) 3.

in distinguishing between the terms "evangelical" and "evangelicalism."[42] Some confusion has always been prevalent: Anthony Ashley-Cooper (1801–1885), 7th Earl of Shaftesbury, wrote in a letter to a friend, "I know what constituted an evangelical in former times. I have no clear notion what constitutes one now."[43]

The term Evangelicalism was coined in the mid-eighteenth century at a time when there was rekindled interest in a personal gospel experience, but it has been far from consistently defined and applied. David Bebbington correctly notes that Evangelical religion in Britain has greatly changed during the two and a half centuries of its existence even though Evangelicals have claimed that their brand of Christianity has possessed an essentially changeless content. He states: "Its [Evangelical religion] outward expression, such as its social composition and political attitudes, have frequently been transformed. Its inward principles, embracing teaching about Christian theology and behavior, have altered hardly less. Nothing could be further from the truth than the common image of Evangelicalism."[44] Those that considered themselves evangelical envisioned themselves as the true representatives of Christianity. This self-importance is exhibited by Edward Irving (1792–1834), a somewhat controversial evangelical. Irving delivered a sermon to the London Missionary Society in 1826, which highlights this self-importance. The essence of the sermon was described by Margaret Oliphant (1828–1897), in her biography of Edward Irving as "the first point upon which Irving fairly parted company with his evangelical brethren, . . . exasperated that large, active, and influential community which, as he somewhere says, not without a little bitterness, 'calls itself the religious world.'"[45] This expression of "religious world" placed its focus upon the breadth of the evangelical movement which imperiously promoted itself as exclusive of denominations that did not fit this perception of Christianity. Evangelicalism, therefore, was not a denomination but a movement whose followers crossed the divide of politics and theological systems. They were both Calvinists who believed in divine sovereignty, and Arminians who believed in salvation gained by free will. Donald M. Lewis, introducing his two-volume dictionary of evangelical biographies, attempts to show how many points the evangelicals touched and states that, "Contemporary scholars may be for-

---

42. Gribben, *Evangelical Millennialism*, 3.

43. Edwin Hodder, *The Life and Work of the Seventh Earl of Shaftesbury, K.G.* (London: Cassell, 1887) 451.

44. D. W. Bebbington, *Evangelicalism in Modern Britain: A History from the 1730s to the 1980s* (London: Unwin Hyman, 1989) 269.

45. Margaret Oliphant, *The Life of Edward Irving, Minister of the National Scottish Church, London* (London: Hurst and Blacket, 1862) 1:202.

given for being baffled by the sheer diversity of evangelicalism."[46] Because of this diversity most scholarship turns to belief—even with its limitations—to establish its criteria and definition because there remained a number of beliefs that were integral to evangelicalism.

Perhaps the most helpful historic definition is the four-fold criteria offered by David Bebbington in his work *Evangelicalism in Modern Britain: A History from the 1730s to the 1980s* (1989). As the title of his book suggests, Bebbington identifies the origin of evangelicalism in the 1730s–although many historians seek to apply the term to discussions of the Reformation.[47] His four qualities which he finds to be the "special marks" of evangelical religion are: (1) "conversionism," the belief that lives need to be changed; (2) "activism," the expression of the gospel in effort; (3) "biblicism," a particular regard for the Bible; and (4) "crucicentrism," a stress on the sacrifice of Christ on the Cross.[48] It is this definition of Evangelicalism that this study utilizes concerning Govett's personal Christian theology.

Further help in understanding the term "evangelicalism" can be obtained in definition provided by George M. Marsden in *Understanding Fundamentalism and Evangelicalism* (1991).[49] He asserts that evangelicalism in the twentieth century includes any Christian who is able to affirm the essential beliefs of the nineteenth-century evangelical consensus. These essential beliefs include: (1) the Reformation doctrine of the final authority of the Bible (2) the real historical character of God's saving work recorded in Scripture (3) salvation to eternal life based on the redemptive work of Christ (4) the importance of evangelicalism and missions, and (5) the importance of a spiritually transformed life.[50] More recently, Darryl Hart, in *Deconstructing Evangelicalism: Conservative Protestantism in the Age of Billy Graham* (2004), has written about the voluminous increase in the amount of literature on the subject just since the 1980s.[51] To this end Bruce D. Hindmarsh helps to prioritize the list by remarking that David Bebbington acknowledges three of these characteristics were not particularly

---

46. Donald M. Lewis, ed., *The Blackwell Dictionary of Evangelical Biography, 1730–1860, vol. I–II* (Oxford: Blackwell, 1995) xviii–xix.

47. Bebbington, *Evangelicalism in Modern Britain*, 1.

48. Ibid., 2–3.

49. George M. Marsden, *Understanding Fundamentalism and Evangelicalism* (Grand Rapids: Eerdmans, 1991).

50. Marsden, *Understanding Fundamentalism*, 4–5.

51. Darryl G. Hart, *Deconstructing Evangelicalism: Conservative Protestantism in the Age of Billy Graham* (Grand Rapids: Baker Academic, 2004) 28.

distinguishing. What *was* the most singularly distinguishing characteristic was its new dynamism or expansive energy for missions and service.[52]

David Bebbington places the emergence of an evangelical movement into the early 1730s. According to Bebington, this was later to become known as "evangelicalism"–the most important development of any in the history of Protestant Christianity.[53] An evangelical revival had produced a "New Dissent" with an inrush of evangelicals into the strata of dissenters who were now finding less in common with the Established Church. Its beginning occurred not in England, but in Wales. Typical of the early evangelicals was a young school master named Howel Harris, who came to faith in the spring of 1735 and thereafter enthusiastically preached his convictions. Shortly thereafter Daniel Rowland (1711–1790), a curate at Llangeitho in Carmarthenshire, had a similar conversion experience.[54] The two soon were traveling around Wales proclaiming to large audiences the "good news" of salvation. George Whitefield (1714–1770) was converted a few weeks after Easter in 1735 as an undergraduate in Oxford. Moved by an increasing zeal he soon began open air preaching in Bristol and London.[55] In 1738 John and Charles Wesley (1707–1788) identified with the evangelical movement through a conversion experience. John Wesley (1703–1791), having had his heart "strangely warmed" remarked, "One thing I know: I was blind, but now I see."[56] For Whitefield, his zeal for his new-found faith caused many clergymen in London to become concerned by his passionate preaching. By the time he left for Georgia on his first trip to America in 1738 he was already barred from many pulpits on account of his preaching the "new birth." In America, the movement which Whitefield helped to ignite was described as the "Great Awakening," but it was actually an inseparable part of the "Eighteenth-Century Revival,"[57] that was a quickening of a spiritual

---

52. D. Bruce Hindmarsh, "The Antecedents of Evangelical Conversion Narrative: Spiritual Autobiography and the Christian Tradition," in Michael A. G. Haykin and Kenneth J. Stewart, eds., *The Advent of Evangelicalism: Exploring Historical Continuities* (Nashville: B&H Academic, 2008) 328. See also Bebbington, *Evangelicalism in Modern Britain*, 35.

53. Bebbington, *Evangelicalism in Modern Britain*, 20.

54. Mark A. Noll, *The Rise of Evangelicalism: The Age of Edwards, Whitefield and the Wesleys* (Downers Grove: InterVarsity, 2003) 89.

55. Arnold A. Dallimore, *George Whitefield: God's Anointed Servant in the Great Revival of the Eighteenth Century* (Wheaton: Crossway, 1990) 21.

56. John Telford, ed., *The Letters of the Rev. John Wesley* (London: Epworth, 1931) 2:384.

57. Arnold A. Dallimore, *George Whitefield: The Life and Times of the Great Evangelist of the Eighteenth-Century Revival* (London: Banner of Truth, 1970) 1:14.

surge in Britain and beyond.⁵⁸ And it was a quickening that appeared to be needed by the dissenters as their numbers were beginning to dwindle. At the same time the number of churches was dwindling. The Baptist churches, for example, which numbered 283 congregations in 1716 were diminished to around 200 by 1751.⁵⁹ At the same time a transformation was beginning to take shape that reversed the trend.

Evangelicalism transformed the situation. In the second half of the eighteenth century the revival in England influenced "Old Dissent" to such an extent that the numbers of Independents and Baptists sharply rose. After 1750, until the turn of the century, the number of Baptist churches increased from 200 to 269. The Methodists made even greater strides. Their membership increased from 22,410 in 1767, the first year when it was recorded, to 88,334 in 1800 and 232,074 in 1830. But the Presbyterians continued to decline—so much so that by 1808 the adherents of the movement were vastly outnumbered by both Independents and Baptists.⁶⁰ Similarly, the Church of England experienced decline during the eighteenth century and kept falling relative to population until the 1830s.⁶¹ Chris Brooks in *The Victorian Church: Architecture and Society* notes that between 1801 and 1831 the proportion of the population aged fifteen and over taking communion on Easter Sunday slid from some 10 percent to just over 7 percent. Its membership had been falling in real terms from the middle of the eighteenth century. Over the same period between 1801 and 1831, in the same age-segment of the population, membership of the evangelical nonconformist churches doubled from 2.75 percent to 5.5 percent. Part of the problem was the fact that Anglicanism did not have the buildings in the new urban centers. For dissenters, a meeting-room or converted building sufficed as temporary accommodations.⁶² Govett serves as a good example of the willingness to meet in public buildings as his congregation met in one for a decade until a formal church building was permanently erected. Population continued to rise in the British Isles at a time when the birth of evangelicalism also saw great social, commercial and economic change. With the birth of evangelicalism came the beginning of the Industrial Revolution and the rise of the

---

58. Bebbington, *Evangelicalism in Modern Britain*, 21.

59. Richard Brown, *Church and State in Modern Britain 1700–1850* (London: Routledge, 1991) 111.

60. Bebbington, *Evangelicalism in Modern Britain*, 21.

61. Robert Currie, Alan D. Gilbert, and Lee Horsley, *Churches and Churchgoers: Pattern of Church Growth in the British Isles Since 1700* (Oxford: Clarendon, 1977) 139.

62. Chris Brooks and Andrew Saint, *The Victorian Church: Architecture and Society* (Manchester: Manchester University Press, 1995) 5.

commercial middle class.[63] Yet, evangelicalism in Britain did not grow in isolation from the world and the events of Europe, nor did it remain isolated from the debate and spread of millennial thought.

David Ceri Jones has recently asserted that it is now impossible to study evangelicalism in England without reference to its European context.[64] W. R. Ward's *The Protestant Evangelical Awakening* (1992) suggests that many of the features of what would eventually become evangelicalism originated in Germany at the end of the seventeenth century and the early eighteenth century.[65] The Salzburgers, Huguenots, and the Moravians came under heightened persecution from Europe's Catholic monarchies after the 1685 revocation of the Edict of Nantes (1598).[66] There ensued a crisis of confidence that provoked a migration of pietistic Christians to England and the American colonies. This exodus and loss of their spiritual distinctiveness has led Ward to conclude that the history of evangelicalism began in the 1670s[67]—rather than in the 1730s, as David Bebbington suggests.[68] In doing so, Ward moves the identity of evangelicalism from a solidly biblical and doctrinal center, espoused by both Marsden and Bebbington, to one that also invites mysticism and apocalyptic enquiry from an expanded European context. The difference in dates is further explained by Ward's account of the origin of evangelicalism based upon a three-fold critique of existing scholarly narrative. Ward's critique of the existing secondary literature claims that it is inappropriately concentrated on British and American contexts, that it had given too late a date for the emergence of evangelicalism as a distinct religious movement, and that it had not provided a sufficiently broad description of evangelical identity.[69] Within the context of a broad evangelical identity was the mounting wave of millennial debate that impacted the Established Church and dissenters alike. Additionally, it could be argued that eschatological interests helped to shape the evangelical movement throughout its history.

---

63. David Ceri Jones, "Calvinistic Methodism and the Origins of Evangelicalism in England," in Michael A. G. Haykin, and Kenneth J. Stewart, eds., *The Advent of Evangelicalism: Exploring Historical Continuities* (Nottingham: Apollos, 2008) 111.

64. Jones, "Calvinistic Methodism," 107.

65. See W. R. Ward, *The Protestant Evangelical Awakening* (Cambridge: Cambridge University Press, 1992).

66. Ward, *Evangelical Awakening*, 22. See also W. R. Ward, *Christianity under the Ancien Regime, 1648–1789* (Cambridge: Cambridge University Press, 1999).

67. Ward, *Early Evangelicalism*, 1.

68. Bebbington, *Evangelicalism in Modern Britain*, 20.

69. Gribben, *Trans-Atlantic World*, 7.

Eschatology

Govett fits easily into David Bebbington's definition of an evangelical, but he was far more. His ministry was dominated by his concern with eschatology. Govett the evangelical must, therefore, be placed into the broader spectrum of eschatology. Michael Wheeler, in *Death and the Future Life in Victorian Literature and Theology* (1990), assesses the controversial nature of the subject of eschatology in the period as evidenced in part by the diverse opinions found within the vast collection of tracts and periodicals of the day.[70] It was an age in which there was great focus upon the four last things—death, judgment, heaven, and hell. A wide range of doctrinal teachings emerged on these subjects which were rigorously defended along secular lines. Govett participated in the debate throughout his life. For instance, in the last decade of his life he wrote a book titled, *The Presence of Christ in its Effects on the Church and the World: Being the Argument of the Epistles to the Thessalonians, with Notice of Dr. Bullinger's Theory of the Hinderers, and Dr. Eadie on the First Resurrection* (1893). In this work he methodically presented his understanding of 1 Thessalonians concerning the future life of the believer. By the time of this writing Govett had become well known for his unique, yet controversial, position on what became known as the "partial rapture." Govett argued that "there is no passage so far as I am aware, that declares that all believers shall attain the Millennial Kingdom of God."[71] Not all agreed with him. However, much earlier in the debate, Govett found support for his doctrine of "partial rapture" in a letter written in 1865 to the editor of *The Rainbow* magazine, signed "A Lover of Practical Truth, Norwich."[72] He stated, "Now, believing the doctrine advanced by Mr. Govett in the main points to be true, I believe, that so far from its depreciating the blessed work of Christ, it is a truth which touches the secret walk with Christ, and if rightly secured, it brings the Christian to frequent confession of sin and prayer, and thus the heart is brought into closer communion and fellowship."[73]

---

70. Michael Wheeler, *Death and the Future Life in Victorian Literature and Theology* (Cambridge: Cambridge University Press, 1990) xii.

71. Robert Govett, *The Presence of Christ in its Effects on the Church and the World: Being the Argument of the Epistles to the Thessalonians, with Notice of Dr. Bullinger's Theory of the Hinderers, and Dr. Eadie on the First Resurrection* (Norwich: Fletcher and Son, 1893) 57.

72. There is no indication who actually wrote the article. Given the location of Norwich it could have been a member of Govett's church, but it is not likely Govett himself as he always associated his name with the articles he wrote for *The Rainbow* and other magazines.

73. "A Practical Truth," *The Rainbow: A Magazine of Christian Literature, with*

Govett's position pertaining to the Rapture of the Saints added more terminology to an age already crowded with theological meanings. Reiner Smolinski observes, in his article "Caveat Emptor: Pre- and Postmillennialism in the Late Reformation Period" (2001), that the study of eschatology is frequently blurred by a "quagmire" of terminology that can be confusing at best.[74] Contributing to the many terms are those which disseminate from the theological positions surrounding the book of Revelation and its eschatology.

Interpretations of the Apocalypse

Christian eschatology, by definition, deals with the "last things" mentioned in the book of Revelation, the only New Testament book of "apocalyptic" genre. Bernard McGinn provides assistance in distinguishing the difference by defining eschatology as covering any type of belief that looks forward to the end of history as that which gives structure and meaning to the whole. What sets off apocalypticism from general eschatology is the sense of the proximity to the end.[75] Crawford Gribben notes that evangelical eschatology can either be pessimistic or optimistic depending upon the placement of the events associated with the apocalypse.[76]

The terms premillennial, postmillennial, and amillennial are terms which are also used to articulate differing views of end-time events. The term "millennialism" (sometimes referred to as "messianism," and "chiliasm")[77] is the broader term which encompasses these three terms. Each has its basis of interpretation in the biblical text found in Revelation 20:1–3 which describes the binding of Satan in the "abyss" for one-thousand years. Millennialism and its three sub-components emerged to identify this thousand-years in an attempt to provide Scriptural context. Additionally, Douglas H. Shantz notes that millennialism represents a particular instance of apocalypticism

---

Special Reference to the Revealed Future of the Church and the World 2 (1865) 140.

74. Reiner Smolinski, "Caveat Emptor: Pre- and Postmillennialism in the Late Reformation Period," in James E. Force and Richard H. Popkin, eds., *Millenarianism and Messianism in Early Modern European Culture, Volume III, the Millenarian Turn: Millenarian Contexts of Science, Politics and Everyday Anglo-American Life in the Seventeenth and Eighteenth Centuries* (Dordrecht: Kluwer Academic, 2001) 145.

75. Bernard McGinn, ed., *Apocalyptic Spirituality* (New York: Paulist, 1979) 5, quoted in Crawford Gribben and C. F. Stunt, eds., *Prisoners of Hope? Aspects of Evangelical Millennialism in Britain and Ireland, 1800–1880* (Carlisle: Paternoster, 2004) 19.

76. Gribben, *Evangelical Millennialism*, 11.

77. The term "chiliasm" is also used to denote the thousand-year reign of Christ. The word has a Greek etymology.

that focuses on earthly utopias.[78] The three sub-components (i.e., systems) are common evangelical millennial schemes with contemporary origin and, therefore, must be applied with caution to older material on the subject since newer writings tend to be less broad in scope and meaning.[79] Furthermore, classifying millennial theories on the basis of their placement of when Christ would appear is fairly meaningless prior to 1800 since prior to that time there existed numerous competing systems that had not taken clarity of form.[80] By the time of Govett's writings these terms had been clarified and he uses them with full confidence of meaning.

By definition, generally speaking, premillennialists are those who adhere to placing Christ's Second Coming at the beginning of the thousand-years. It had its beginning in the first three centuries of the Christian era and became the dominant eschatological interpretation. Among its early adherents were such patristic writers as Irenaeus, Justin Martyr, and Tertullian. Postmillennialists are those who adhere to placing Christ's Second Coming at the end of the thousand-years (or millennium). They usually perceive that the world is living or will live in a "golden era" that will experience increased portions of grace prior to Christ's return and appearance at the Day of Judgment. It gained popularity in the seventeenth century but lost its influence in the nineteenth century—perhaps mostly as a result of the violent uprooting of European political and social institutions during the era of the French Revolution.[81] Amillennialism denies a future millennium. This interpretive system has its beginning in the fourth century with Augustine of Hippo. During this period the thousand-year reign of Christ and the church was equated with the entire history of the church on earth.[82] It should be noted that further distinctions are made by scholars regarding millennial studies—such as the distinction made by Ernest Lee Tuveson when he describes that postmillennial view as "millennialist," and the premillennialist view as "millenarian."[83] This study, however, is careful not to impose that fine a distinction—choosing instead to recognize the fluidity of terms found in various eschatological works.[84]

78. Crawford Gribben and C. F. Stunt, eds., *Prisoners of Hope? Aspects of Evangelical Millennialism in Britain and Ireland, 1800–1880*. (Carlisle: Paternoster, 2004) 19.

79. Gribben, *Evangelical Millennialism*, 11.

80. Smolinski, "Caveat Emptor," 146.

81. Robert G. Clouse et al., eds., *The Meaning of the Millennium: Four Views* (Downers Grove: InterVarsity, 1977) 11.

82. Clouse, *The Meaning of the Millennium*, 9.

83. Ernest L. Tuveson, *Redeemer Nation: the Idea of America's Millennial Role* (Chicago: University of Chicago Press, 1968) 34.

84. Ernest R. Sandeen, *The Roots of Fundamentalism: British and American*

Govett can be classified as an evangelical premillennialist, but his treatment of the book of Revelation and the apocalypse, in terms of how he understood end-time events, must be further defined. To this end, broadly speaking, there are four major schools of interpretation. The "preterist" view (from the Latin meaning "past") finds the events of Revelation to have all occurred in the past; the "idealist" view argues capaciously that the message of Revelation is timeless and is intended for every generation; the "historicist" view sees the events of Revelation as in the future—at the time they were written, but since the writing of the book have already occurred (or are currently occurring) within the history of the church. It was a school of thought which had been the most popular premillennial view held by evangelicals until the 1840s—a view that was heavily influenced by the work of Joseph Mede (1586–1683). Mede's scheme of interpretation had two key premises. First, he equated the Antichrist with the papacy. Second, he interpreted the 1,260 prophetic days mentioned in both Daniel and Revelation to mean literal years, rather than days.[85] The historicist school was most popular during the French Revolution.[86] The fourth school of interpretation, the "futurist" view, sees most of the book of Revelation—those events mentioned after the description of the seven churches in chapters 2 and 3—as prophetic and still future (i.e., end-time events).[87] Govett was a futurist and he consequently insisted in his writings that most of the events of Revelation were still to come.

These four schools of interpretation were characterized by strong opinions. This was the case with Reverend Dr John Cumming, minister of the Scottish National Church, London. In 1847–48 he delivered a series of lectures on the Book of Revelation at a large public meeting place in London known as Exeter Hall.[88] These lectures and his work *Apocalyptic Sketches* (1848) illustrate the various classes of interpretation of Revelation as they were understood in the Victorian age. According to Cumming those holding a "preterist" view included Professor Lee, "one of the best Hebrew scholars in England," and Moses Stewart, "an able scholar in America."[89] Like

---

Millenarianism, 1800–1930 (Chicago: University of Chicago Press, 1970).

85. Jonathan D. Burnham, *A Story of Conflict: The Controversial Relationship Between Benjamin Wills Newman and John Nelson Darby* (Carlisle: Paternoster, 2004) 105.

86. LeRoy Edwin Froom, *The Prophetic Faith of Our Fathers: The Historical Development of Prophetic Interpretation* (Washington, DC: Review and Herald, 1946) 2:642–49.

87. Wilfried E. Glabach, *Reclaiming the Book of Revelation: A Suggestion of New Readings in the Local Church* (New York: Lang, 2007) 8–12.

88. John Cumming, *Apocalyptic Sketches: or, Lectures on the Book of Revelation; Delivered in the Large Room, Exeter Hall, in 1847–1848* (London: Hall, 1848).

89. Cumming, *Apocalyptic Sketches*, 15.

other preterists they believed the entirety of the book of Revelation to have been fulfilled in the first few centuries of the church age. Cumming finds their position untenable and absurd. Those mentioned in his lectures who take an opposite view–the futurist view–consisted of Burgh, Todd, and Maitland. Cumming grants that they are all learned men but wrongly suggests that some are motivated by staunch sympathy with Roman Catholic beliefs. He makes this statement believing the motivation behind their writings to be motivated by love for these tenets and would seek to "justify the Church of Rome."[90] On several occasions Govett found opportunity to refute the eschatological conclusions of Cumming.[91] This study describes this heightened debate over eschatology and the Roman Catholic Church in several chapters since it is characteristic of the deeply intertwined eschatological and ecclesiastical disputes of Victorian print culture. Govett was not alone in his refutations of Cumming's evangelical beliefs. In her 1855 article written for the *Westminster Review*, George Eliot wrote a critical review of his preaching. She writes: "It is in vain for Dr. Cumming to say that we are to love man for God's sake: with the conception of God which his teaching presents, the love of man for God's sake involves, as his writings abundantly show, a strong principle of hatred."[92] Even the prophetic views of Dr. Cumming are criticized as simply the "transportation of political passions on to a so-called religious platform."[93]

Despite his prejudices and strongly expressed objections to the end-time views of others, Cumming finds a class of interpreter in which he is sympathetic—the historicists. Heading the list is Edward Bishop Elliott (a minister whom Govett also refuted in writing), author of *Horae Apocalypticae* (1846).[94] Elliott is grouped among many who believed that much of the Apocalypse has been fulfilled, or is currently being fulfilled. In this group Cumming lists Faber, Dr M'Neile, and Bickersteth.[95] Nevertheless, none of

90. Ibid., 16.

91. See Robert Govett, *The Popes Not the Man of Sin: Being an Answer to the Publication of Dr. Cumming, Dr. Morison and the Rev. E. B. Elliott on that Subject* (London: Nisbet, 1852); See also Robert Govett, *The Locusts, the Euphratean Horsemen, and the Two Witnesses; or, the Apocalyptic Systems of the Revds. E. B. Elliot, Dr. Cumming and Dr. Keith, Proved Unsound* (London, 1852).

92. Gertrude Himmelfarb, *The Spirit of the Age: Victorian Essays* (New Haven: Yale University Press, 2007) 143.

93. Himmelfarb, *The Spirit of the Age*, 137.

94. See Edward Bishop Elliott, *Horae Apocalypticae, or a Commentary on the Apocalypse, Critical and Historical: Including also an Examination of the Chief Prophecies of Daniel* (London: Seeley, Burnside & Seeley, 1846). See also Thomas K. Arnold, *Remarks on the Rev. E. B. Elliott's "Horae Apocalypticae"* (London: F. & J. Rivington, 1845).

95. Cumming, *Apocalyptic Sketches*, 18.

the four schools of interpretation developed in a theological vacuum. There was much happening in the world during the Victorian age that impacted Britain's society, culture, politics, and especially its religious views.

Historical Context

To understand Govett in these changing times this study seeks to place him in his context. Govett was born into tumultuous times in England. Politically, the aftermath of the French Revolution and Napoleonic Wars was still being felt. Around the birth of Govett, with the return of peace, the classic age of the industrial revolution was also born. Socially and economically England continued to emerge as an industrial country leading the way world-wide in the industrial revolution. The wealth of the nation increased, drawing heightened attention to the contrast between the rich and the poor. What can reasonably be argued, according to Norman Gash, is that the issues facing British society in 1815 were more than the single issue of the industrial revolution.[96] Yet, as a result, the cities soon swelled with unprecedented numbers of people. Child labor, terrible working conditions, disease, poor sanitation, and decreased agricultural production exacerbated the problems for the over-worked and financially deprived labor class. In addition to the difficulties imposed by industrialization, factors such as the post-war slump in trade and manufacturing, the increase in population, and the growth of the cities all added to an overburdening of the government that took until the mid-nineteenth century to stabilize.[97] The educational conditions of the British people had become alarmingly defective. It was found that in 1818 more than half of children were growing up without an education. Additionally, one third of men and one half of women could not sign their names.[98] Small-pox was still a deadly disease, claiming one-tenth of all deaths. In the cities, the filth of the streets and houses of the poor produced grievously high mortality.[99]

The Established Church faced increased growth in dissent.[100] English dissenters grew in power through increasing numbers, but they were not to-

---

96. Norman Gash, *Aristocracy and People: Britain, 1815–1865. The New History of England* (Cambridge, MA: Harvard University Press, 1979) 1.

97. Gash, *Aristocracy and People*, 2.

98. Robert Mackenzie, *The 19th Century: A History* (London: Nelson and Sons, 1880) 95.

99. Mackenzie, *The 19th Century*, 98.

100. See, for example, David W. Bebbington, *Victorian Nonconformity* (Bangor: Headstart History, 1992).

tally free from the Established Church since they were burdened, for example, with such requirements as giving to the support of the church. Chapter 1 develops the issues of dissent and the Victorians. Dissenters were further dismissed by the church in that their ministers were kept from performing marriage ceremonies.[101] Similarly the ministers could not be buried in the parish graveyard. And only the service of the Established Church was permitted to be read over them before they were lowered into the ground.[102] Even as late as 1879 the House of Commons spent a portion of each session debating these questions. Insult deepened with the exclusion of their sons from entering Oxford, and in the more liberal Cambridge they could study but were not permitted to matriculate toward a degree. Equal rights were not achieved until 1871.[103]

The Established Church was soon divided into three parties: High, Broad, and Evangelical. It is out of the "evangelical" movement that Govett emerged. Chapter 2 describes how Govett, within his familial setting, was no stranger to the evangelical movement within the Established Church. His great-grandfather, William Romaine (1714–1795), was a well respected evangelical minister within the Church of England and had a profound influence upon him. Chapter 2 also identifies the strong magnetism the name Romaine had upon Govett's own father. Yet, unlike his father and clergy brothers, Govett chose to dissent. The issue for Govett was a singular one: infant baptism. But in Govett's mind it soon became intermingled with thoughts of the apocalypse.

The Rise of Millennialism

The rise of millennialism and its relation to apocalyptic thought, which prophesied the final defeat of the Antichrist and the establishment of Christ's millennial reign on earth, provided a future hope—but for Britain it proved to be much more. By the mid-seventeenth century millennialism was on the rise in England.[104] Through the person and writings of Joseph Mede, it is possible to see the emerging influence of millennialism in English apocalyptic thought—an influence that extended well into the eighteenth century

101. Mackenzie, *The 19th Century*, 147.

102. Govett himself was buried in a non-denominational cemetery—Rosary Cemetery, the first in England opened in 1821 by Thomas Drummond, a local Norwich minister who provided a place where people could be buried with the religious service of their choice.

103. Mackenzie, *The 19th Century*, 143–44.

104. Jeffrey K. Jue, "'Heaven upon Earth': The Apocalyptic Thought of Joseph Mede (1586–1638)," PhD diss., University of Aberdeen, Scotland, 2003, 5.

and into its political world.[105] Those in power were perceived to be either God's representatives on earth, or working against his advancing kingdom. Thoughts of regicide focused upon replacing the royal dynasty with the rightful king. The purpose was to clear the way for the second coming of Christ who was thought by millennialists to be England's rightful king.[106] This conclusion also extended to the magisterium of the Roman Catholic Church. In the puritan apocalyptic tradition, few terms were more evocative as the term "Antichrist." The existence of the Antichrist in the world was associated with the visible presence of the Vatican and became proof to many church leaders that the end was near.[107]

While all of this was taking place, Great Britain, in the decade which began in 1730, experienced the beginning of a religious revival from which emerged the movement that became known as Evangelicalism. David Bebbington ranks it the most important development in the history of Protestant Christianity.[108] It became a multi-faceted movement that would touch the lives of millions. By the year 1830— the year in which Govett came up to Oxford—evangelical religion had put down deep roots in Great Britain. It is during the third decade of the nineteenth century that the activism of the movement enabled it to permeate British society.[109] It is in this context that Govett, immediately upon graduation, begins a long life of interaction in the religious cultures of print—a culture that forms the backdrop for this study.

By the early 1800s the political unrest across the English Channel on the Continent brought about renewed apocalyptic speculation, end-time predictions and millennial thinking. With an increased awareness of its responsibility to advance the cause of Christianity before Christ's return the evangelical church felt added concern to spread the gospel. With the French monarchy collapsing and Europe on the verge of entering into twenty years of almost continuous war, the Baptist Missionary Society was born—the first of many similar associations to be formed throughout the first quarter of the nineteenth century.[110] Religious tracts were translated and sent abroad. France was a key recipient of such tracts which were translated into

105. Ibid., 6.

106. Crawford Gribben, *The Puritan Millennium: Literature & Theology, 1550–1682.* (Dublin: Four Courts, 2000) 196.

107. Gribben, *Puritan Millennium*, 27.

108. Bebbington, *Evangelicalism in Modern Britain*, 20.

109. Alan D. Gilbert, *Religion and Society in Industrial England: Church, Chapel and Social Change, 1740–1914* (London: Longman, 1976) 3.

110. Mackenzie, *The 19th Century*, 210.

French and widely distributed, thus disseminating Britain's evangelical and millennial beliefs upon the people of France.[111]

Just prior to the dawn of the 1800s the debate over millennialism tended to divide between two schools of thought: postmillennialists and premillennialists. The contrast between the two can be simplified by observing that postmillennialists are optimistic regarding a brighter future for the world, whereas premillennialists tend to be pessimistic toward the future. In premillennialism social and world events are thought to increasingly worsen until Christ returns to claim his church.[112] Christ's return is said to precede the thousand-year reign of felicity on earth. However, the prominent view until the early 1800s remained postmillennial. Because of this optimism Britain emerged as the leading country introducing missionaries throughout the world.[113]

Nonetheless, by the second and third decade of the nineteenth century the optimism regarding a brighter future began to be replaced by a resolute adherence to a pessimistic premillennialism. Such theological pessimism can be found on the pages of the dissenting *Evangelical Magazine* (1793–1904), the *Morning Watch* (1829–1833), and Alexander Haldane's Calvinistic *Record* (1828–1923)—which took the place of the moderate *Christian Observer* as the best-selling evangelical journal of the 1830s.[114] By the fourth decade of the century the premillennial position was espoused in a dozen new periodicals and many dozens of published books.[115] Through these articles, pamphlets and books evangelical leaders emerged giving rise to debate on differing prophetic positions and expounded thought on the minutest details of Christ's Second Coming. Among those to emerge was Govett with his intricate articulation of the believer's relationship to Christ's "reward" upon his coming. For almost the entirety of the second half of the nineteenth century Govett stood out as a herald exposing the danger that would befall a Christian in the "Coming Kingdom" who does

---

111. Govett had at least three of his tracts translated into French. See *Calvinism by Calvin* (Norwich: Fletcher and Son, 1840); *Baptism Overshadowed by Noah's Salvation in the Ark* (Norwich: Fletcher and Son, 1875); *The Passage through the Red Sea a Type of Baptism* (Norwich: Fletcher and Son, 1875).

112. W. H. Oliver, *Prophets and Millennialists: The Uses of Biblical Prophecy in England from the 1790s to the 1840s* (Auckland: Auckland University Press, 1978) 21.

113. Iain Hamish Murray, *The Puritan Hope; A Study in Revival and the Interpretation of Prophecy.* (London: Banner of Truth Trust, 1971) 142.

114. Boyd Hilton, *The Age of Atonement: The influence of Evangelicalism on Social and Economic Thought, 1795–1863* (Oxford: Clarendon Press, 1988) 10.

115. LeRoy Edwin Froom, *The Prophetic Faith of Our Fathers: The Historical Development of Prophetic Interpretation* (Washington: Review and Herald, 1946–1954) 3:266–68.

not heed the warnings of Scripture regarding a believer's "work" for the Lord in this life. A detailed explanation of Govett's views on this subject is provided in chapter 5.

Relevant Eschatological Literature

Placing Govett into context also bears upon scholarship given that it largely ignores him. Given his views, some of which were considered unusual by his peers, he has been written out of the historiography. At best, later writers of nineteenth-century millennial literature have considered him idiosyncratic and have glossed over him. In recent history America has been a particularly lavish source of millennialism.[116] As evidenced from the many recent books and conferences, there has been an explosion of interest in the subject in the past several decades.[117] In this explosion Govett's name is missing. The three-volume *Encyclopedia of Apocalypticism* reflects an example of this recent historical scholarship.[118] A number of factors can be postulated to account for this immense interest. One of the best-selling books of the 1970s was Hal Lindsey's *The Late Great Planet Earth* (1970) which sold over fifteen million copies.[119] In the 1990s a series of novels by Tim LaHaye and Jerry B. Jenkins, the *Left Behind* series, began to appear: approximately 65 million copies have been sold to date.[120] The burgeoning video game industry has also captured the imagination of children and teens with its apocalyptic-style graphics and battles against evil forces. A popular theory reignited the attention of scientists as they pondered the possible end of the world in 2012 as predicted by the ancient Mayan calendar.[121] In Luke 21:9–11 Jesus predicted there would be rumors of wars and revolutions

116. Ted Daniels, *Millennialism: An International Bibliography.* (New York: Garland, 1992) x.

117. Douglas H. Shantz, "Millennialism and Apocalypticalism in Recent Historical Scholarship," in Crawford Gribben and C. F. Stunt, eds., *Prisoners of hope? Aspects of Evangelical Millennialism in Britain and Ireland, 1800–1880* (Carlisle: Paternoster, 2004) 20.

118. John J. Collins, Bernard McGinn, and Stephen J. Stein, *The Encyclopedia of Apocalypticism* (New York: Continuum, 1998). The three volumes are arranged as follows: vol. 1, *The Origins of Apocalypticism in Judaism and Christianity*, ed. John J. Collins; vol. 2, *Apocalypticism in Western History and Culture*, ed. Bernard McGinn; vol. 3, *Apocalypticism in the Modern Period and Contemporary Age*, ed. Stephen J. Stein.

119. Hal Lindsey, *The Late Great Planet Earth*. (Grand Rapids: Zondervan, 1970).

120. David E. Nantais and Michael Simone, "Apocalypse When?," *America Magazine* 189, no. 4 (2003) 18–25.

121. Bob Berman, "End of the World: 2012," *Astronomy Magazine* 35, no. 12 (2007) 14.

and that these things would come before the end came. He said that there would be earthquakes, famines, and pestilence in various places as well as fearful events and great signs from heaven. John O. B. Agbaje speculates that the deadliest earthquake in Shansi, China on 23 January 1556, that claimed the life of 830,000 people, seemed to have opened the floodgate of such natural disasters "ordained to fulfill the prophecy of the end time by Jesus."[122] Terrorism epitomized by the 9-11 collapse of the Twin Towers in New York City, major warfare in the so-called "hot spots" of conflict in the Middle East, as well as Third World countries on the verge of acquiring atomic weapons help to feed the notion that the world is not getting better and that the end must be near. The Y2K bug, which was characterized by a world-wide scare that millions of computers would crash on the first second into the new millennium, was assumed by some to be a prophetic day of reckoning.[123] Hollywood films such as *End of Days* (1999), *Stigmata* (1999), and *The Omen* (2006) are examples of the preoccupation with end-time occurrences. Natural disasters such as the 2004 Indian Ocean tsunami that killed one quarter of a million people, and the 2011 earthquake off the coast of Japan which triggered a tsunami that claimed nearly 20,000 lives, also fuel end-time concerns. Michael Barkun's *Millennialism and Violence* (1996) provides descriptions of end-of-the-world scenarios caused by predictions of nuclear war and world famine.[124] Yet, these predictions are not new. When Napoleon marched on Moscow in 1812, the Russian Orthodox Church identified him as the Beast or Antichrist.[125]

Modern scholarship, from the middle of the twentieth century, has produced a large body of work on millennialism. Here again, Govett's name is missing. The writings began to appear early in the last century but most were published from the mid-century forward and ranging across the spectrum of millennial views held by the author. For instance, William E. Blackstone took a decidedly premillennial stance in *The Millennium* (1918). Charles Feinberg, a dispensationalist, wrote *Premillennialism or A-millennialism* (1936).[126] Diedrich Hinrich Kromminga's *The Millennium*,

---

122. John O. B. Agbaje, *Prophetic Force: A Demystification of Eschatology* (Bloomington: Authorhouse, 2012) 82.

123. See Jerrry W. Rockett, *Troubles on the Horizon: Surviving Y2K* (Lincoln: iUniverse, 1999).

124. Michael Barkun, *Millennialism and Violence* (London: Cass, 1996) 2.

125. Penelope J. Corfield, "Millennialism: 'The End is Nigh,'" *History Today* 57, no. 3 (2007) 37-39.

126. Charles Feinberg was formerly dean of Talbot Theological Seminary, and one of the committee scholars responsible for the changes to the *New Scofield Reference Bible* published in 1967.

in the Church: Studies in the History of Christian Chiliasm, published in 1945 was followed three years later by his work entitled, *The Millennium, its Nature, Function and Relation to the Consummation of the World*. Both books advocate Kromminga's Reformed premillennial position. George L. Murray in *Millennial Studies* (1948) concludes after twelve years of study that the premillennial position is incorrect. He references the Scofield Bible more than any other work.[127] Ernest Lee Tuveson produced a historical study entitled *Millennium and Utopia, a Study in the Background of the Idea of Progress* (1949). The period surveyed is the later part of the seventeenth and eighteenth centuries.

A similar number of books on the topic appeared between the mid-century and its close. They all convey the author's theological position on the subject and lacked the rigor of serious scholarship.[128] By the turn of the twenty-first century Charles E. Hill had published *Regnum Caelorum: Patterns of Millennial Thought in Early Christianity* (2001), a scholarly investigation of the connection of early Christian thought between millennialism and the beliefs about the intermediate state of the soul after death. In the same time period further interest in the topic of millennialism was exhibited with the publishing of two encyclopedias on the subject. Richard A. Landes assembled the *Encyclopedia of Millennialism and Millennial Movements* (2000) which was intended to be a guide to the religious and spiritual social movements throughout history and around the world. In 2011 Catherine Wessinger served as editor to *The Oxford Handbook of Millennialism*, in which the focus was the theoretical underpinnings of the study of millennialism and its many manifestations across history and cultures.

Far fewer scholars focus on the subject of dispensational history. On this subject Govett's name also does not appear. There are many examples of popular writings on general subjects related to millennialism, but scholarship bearing upon dispensational history and the influence of its early contributors remains sketchy. Helpful works include Clarence B. Bass's *Backgrounds to Dispensationalism: Its Historical Genesis and Ecclesiastical Implications* (1960), which concentrates upon the life and theology of John Nelson Darby. Its weakness, however, is that it tends not to provide an

---

127. See George L. Murray, *Millennial Studies: A Search for Truth* (Grand Rapids: Baker Book House, 1948); See also John F. Walvoord, *The Millennial Kingdom: A Basic Text in Premillennial Theology* (Grand Rapids: Zondervan, 1959) 12.

128. See, for example, Charles Lee Feinberg, *Millennialism, the Two Major Views: The Premillennial and Amillennial Systems of Biblical Interpretation Analyzed & Compared* (Chicago: Moody, 1980); Stanley J Grenz, *The Millennial Maze: Sorting Out Evangelical Options* (Downers Grove: InterVarsity, 1992); Darrel L. Bock, ed., *Three Views on the Millennium and beyond* (Grand Rapids: Zondervan, 1999).

historical genesis and, therefore, lacks sufficient background and perspective. L. V. Crutchfield's *The Origins of Dispensationalism: The Darby Factor* (1992), reconstructs Darby's dispensational scheme from his numerous writings. Although seldom reviewed by peers, Peter E. Prosser's *Dispensationalist Eschatology and its Influence on American and British Religious Movements* (1999) must also be added because of its broadly researched connection to dispensationalism and end-time events connecting religious movements on both continents.[129] More recently, Tim Grass's *Gathering to His Name: The Story of the Open Brethren in Britain and Ireland* (2006) is helpful in understanding the origins of dispensationalism.[130]

Govett and Scholarship

There exists no comprehensive biography of Govett's life nor chronology of his work. Rosamond Codling's *Book of Thanksgiving, 150 Years at Surrey Chapel* (2004) is a fine beginning but her work, as the title suggests, is primarily concerned with the overall history of Govett's former church.[131] Furthermore, Govett's name seldom appears in scholarship pertaining to the history of evangelicalism, millennialism, or more narrowly of dispensationalism in Britain in the nineteenth century. Chapter 6 pieces together the events and circumstances that led to the current lack of attention to Govett. His scholastic demise occurred quickly upon his death and was brought about by decreasing support for his convictions about Christ's return and the consolidation and systemization of dispensationalism as it passed from Great Britain to America.

Govett was certainly not alone in his understanding of a literal reign with Christ in a future dispensation. But what makes him unique among his peers is his ardent pursuit of the question of who will be admitted into the coming thousand-year Kingdom and the grounds upon which the exclusion would be made. Historically, only a small number of theologians contemporary with Govett write concerning the loss of reward for believers in the Coming Kingdom. These include the American author and pastor who succeeded Spurgeon, A. T. Pierson (1837–1911) of Philadelphia, whose writings include such statements as: "With many disciples the eyes

---

129. L. V. Crutchfield, *The Origins of Dispensationalism: The Darby Factor* (Lanham, MD: University Press of America, 1992).

130. Tim Grass, *Gathering to His Name: The Story of the Open Brethren in Britain and Ireland* (Waynesboro, GA: Paternoster, 2006).

131. Rosamunde Codling, *Book of Thanksgiving, 150 Years at Surrey Chapel, Norwich: 1854–2004* (Norwich: Surrey Chapel, 2004).

are yet blinded to this mystery of rewards, which is an open mystery of the Word. It must be an imputed righteousness whereby we enter; but having thus entered by faith, our works determine our relative rank, place, reward."[132] A. J. Gordon (1836- 1895), also an American pastor and author, writes: "just as the Legalist resents the doctrine that good works can have no part in effecting our forgiveness, so the evangelical recoils from the idea that they can constitute any ground for our recompense."[133] In Britain contemporaries include Alexander Maclaren (1826–1910), pastor of Union Chapel, Manchester, who states: "I believe for my part that we suffer terribly by the comparative neglect into which this side of Christian truth has fallen. Do you not think that it would make a difference to you if you really believed, and carried away with you in your thoughts, the thrilling consciousness that every act of the present was registered, and would tell, on the far side beyond?"[134]

G. H. Lang (1874–1958), a prolific writer, Bible scholar and teacher among the Brethren, wrote fourteen major works on various Christian and church subjects, along with numerous booklets. Lang published most of these writings after the age of fifty—some years after Govett's death—and they reflect a keen understanding of the Kingdom. Lang was a contributor to *Dawn* magazine, whose editor was D. M. Panton (1870–1955).[135] Panton wrote numerous pamphlets, but only two short books, both on the subject of the Kingdom, its reward and exclusion. But his most significant contribution to the dissemination of this doctrine was as editor. He was editor of *Dawn* magazine from 1924 until his death in 1955. According to George H. Ramsey, writing in the final issue of *Dawn* magazine, Panton believed that God put *Dawn* into his hands for making known the truths which he learned from Govett. The last issue of *Dawn*, published shortly after Panton's death, included a brief memoir of the late editor. His words reflect the lifelong impact of his mentor Robert Govett. His words suggest that the congregation of Surrey Chapel, to which he was called to pastor upon Govett's death, continued to be taught about the future effect upon the believer of this present relationship to his Redeemer. Panton's memoir, in language typical of Govett, goes on to state that as a responsible agent of

---

132. D. M. Panton, *The Judgment Seat of Christ* (Hayesville, NC: Schoettle, 1984) 4.

133. Panton, *The Judgment Seat*, 4.

134. Ibid., 7.

135. David Morrieson Panton was a close friend of Govett's who lived with him the last two years of Govett's life. He was mentored by Govett and became pastor of Surrey Chapel on 6 October 1901.

Christ, the believer must hand in an account of his stewardship before the Judgment Seat of his Lord.[136]

Scholarship on Evangelicalism

While recent scholarship pertaining to the doctrine of reward and Christ's Judgment Seat remains obscure, evangelicalism is attracting the attention of a growing number of scholars. A generation ago the subject was sizeably overshadowed by Reformation studies.[137] But now, with work by prolific scholars such as Crawford Gribben, David Bebbington, and W. Reginald Ward, evangelical historiography has profoundly impacted the historical studies of the church from the sixteenth century to the present day.[138] While numerous writings of each of these scholars form excellent examples of noteworthy work, a few stand out as most widely cited. The importance placed upon the emphasis of eschatology in the progression of evangelical thought has seen a surge in scholarly writing which now encompasses its development in Britain and America. Evangelicalism is an international movement, but in America and other English-speaking countries it took on very different manifestations.[139] Because of the evolving evangelical paradigms, such work as Crawford Gribben's *Evangelical Millennialism in the Trans-Atlantic World, 1500–2000* (2011) has provided the reader with an understanding of the eschatological commitments that have advanced over five centuries to dominate contemporary evangelicalism in the trans-Atlantic world.[140] As

---

136. George H. Ramsey, "A Brief Memoir of the Late Editor," *Dawn* 32, no. 6 (1955) 161.

137. Stuart Piggin, "Preaching the New Birth and the Power of Godliness and Not Insisting So Much on the Form. Recent Studies on (mainly English [British]) Evangelicalism," *Journal of Religious History* 33, no. 3 (2009) 366–76.

138. See, for example, Mark Smith and Stephen Taylor, eds., *Evangelicalism in the Church of England, c. 1790–c.1900* (Woodbridge: Boydell, 2004); Khim Harris, *Evangelicals and Education: Evangelical Anglicans and Middle-Class Education in Nineteenth-Century England* (Milton Keynes: Paternoster, 2004); Mark Hopkins, *Nonconformity's Romantic Generation: Evangelical and Liberal Theologies in Victorian England* (Milton Keynes: Paternoster, 2004); Roger Shuff, *Searching for the True Church: Brethren and Evangelicals in Mid-Twentieth Century England* (Milton Keynes: Paternoster, 2005); Tim Glass, *Gathering in His Name: The Story of Open Brethren in Britain and Ireland* (Waynesboro, GA: Paternoster, 2006); Michael Harkin and Kenneth Stewart, eds., *The Emergence of Evangelicalism: Exploring Historical Continuities* (Nottingham: InterVarsity, 2008).

139. Piggin, *Preaching the New Birth*, 367.

140. Crawford Gribben, *Evangelical Millennialism*, 1. See also Crawford Gribben, *Writing the Rapture: Prophecy Fiction in Evangelical America* (Oxford: Oxford University Press, 2009).

previously noted, David Bebbington's *Evangelicalism in Modern Britain: A History from the 1730s to the 1980s* (1989) remains notable for its definition of evangelicalism and for its treatment of the subject as it both molded society in the nineteenth century and was transformed by forces at work in that society. Ward has also written several notable texts on the subject of evangelicalism. His *Early Evangelicalism: A global Intellectual History, 1670–1789* (2006)[141] involves discussions within the evangelical movements of Central Europe and the American colonies and the partisan wrangling that eventually surfaced. These works and others have helped frame historical thought pertaining to evangelicalism and millennialism.

Advancing scholarship has brought attention to evangelicalism in general and the dominance of evangelical millennialism in the trans-Atlantic world in particular. Yet within these historical studies, little attention has been allotted to the doctrine of reward. This doctrine relates to a futurist system of eschatology which contends that believers will experience certain privileges given by Christ based upon works performed in this life. These privileges are granted after the Rapture of the church (as mentioned in 1 Thessalonians 4), and prior to the one-thousand year reign with Christ (as mentioned in Revelation 20). Several unpublished works stand out as examples of scholarship pertaining to "reward" at the final judgment of Christ. An older work by James Rosscup representing an exegetical study on 1 Corinthians 3:10–17 still stands out as an important scholarly work on reward in Scripture but does not deal with it in a historical context.[142] In 2000 an unpublished work by the present author appeared which also pertained to an exegetical study on reward. In this instance the work considered the subject of reward from the context of the Pauline epistles.[143] More recently, in 2009, the present author wrote an historical study of the doctrine of reward and of Govett himself. The work is an unpublished master's thesis and lacks the thoroughness of scholarship necessary to bring Govett into a Victorian context, which is the intention of the present work.[144] No scholarly accounts of the doctrine of reward have been published within the past century—and only several popular books and a handful of modestly academic books have

---

141. W. Reginald Ward, *Early Evangelicalism: A Global Intellectual History, 1670–1789* (Cambridge: Cambridge University Press, 2006).

142. James E. Rosscup, "Paul's Teaching on the Christian's Future Reward with Special Reference to 1 Corinthians 3:10–17," PhD diss., University of Aberdeen, 1976.

143. David Seip, "Pauline Theology on Future Reward for Christians: With Particular Reference to Forfeiture," MTh diss., University of Aberdeen, 2000.

144. David Seip, "Robert Govett: His Understanding of the Millennium and its Reward, with Emphasis upon His Impact on the Early Development of Dispensationalism," ThM thesis, Westminster Theological Seminary, 2009.

recently been published on the subject. Likewise, in the same time period no scholarly analyses of Govett have been published.

Govett and the Victorian Age

A thorough study of Govett and his writings would not be complete without providing a backdrop to set his life work in the context of the Victorian era in which he lived. The Victorian age and the role of religious nonconformity created an environment which compelled much interest in the "last things," a subject of keen interest for Govett. Furthermore, Govett and the print culture of his day were strongly influenced by issues associated with religious dissent. Reflected in the contemporary scholarship regarding the Victorian age is the uniqueness of the long and religiously rich era. A plenitude of scholars write on the subjects which define the Victorians but a few stand out as being useful to this study. Valentine Cunningham has written much on the literature of the Victorians. His *Everywhere Spoken Against: Dissent in the Victorian Novel* (1975) is an older work but still valid in helping to trace religious thought through the many important novels of the nineteenth century—which in themselves helped to mold the thought and culture of the British reading public.[145] James C. Livingston has written numerous works on the Victorian age. Most notable is *Religious Thought in the Victorian Age: Challenges and Reconceptions* (2006)[146] which reconceptualizes British religious thought from the last decades of the nineteenth century to the first decade of the twentieth. Currently the most prolific scholar of the Victorian era is Timothy Larsen. Of note is his *Contested Christianity: The Political and Social Contexts of Victorian Theology* (2008), which challenges the usual assumptions about the Christians of the Victorian era from the political, cultural, and intellectual forces that helped to define nineteenth-century Christianity in Great Britain.[147] Michael Wheeler has written several works on the nineteenth century. Of particular importance to this study is his *Death and the Future Life in Victorian Literature and Theology* (1990).[148] The book centers on the four last things of Christian eschatology: death, judgment, heaven and hell. They are assessed through the literature of some

---

145. Valentine Cunningham, *Everywhere Spoken Against: Dissent in the Victorian Novel* (Oxford: Clarendon, 1975).

146. James C. Livingston, *Religious Thought in the Victorian Age: Challenges and Reconceptions* (London: T. & T. Clark, 2006).

147. Timothy Larsen, *Contested Christianity: The Political and Social Contexts of Victorian Theology* (Waco: Baylor University Press, 2008).

148. Michael Wheeler, *Death and the Future Life in Victorian Literature and Theology* (Cambridge: Cambridge University Press, 1990).

of the major novelists and poets of the age and their views of death and the life beyond. Wheeler notes that one of the most contentious eschatological issues was the question of the judgment and the elect of God.[149] In the words from the Book of Common Prayer, the dead were buried "in sure and certain hope of the Resurrection to eternal life."[150] This certain hope was a subject of great interest to Govett as confirmed in the subject of his writings from the early 1850s until his death. Tangentially Govett and the novelists shared an interest in the "last things" but he never focused his writings upon their views. His concern was to target the thoughts of the theologians.

While Govett's books and tracts were numerous on the subject of the "last things" it is equally important to note his prolific engagement with other print culture. As often as Govett wrote books and tracts, he wrote articles in numerous religious journals and magazines. On many occasions his articles appeared as a series extending for several consecutive months and later were used to create tracts that were then more widely distributed. His articles very often created lively debate. And as chapters 4 and 5 reveal, while the editors of the magazines and journals did not always agree with Govett's conclusions, they nearly always mentioned that they appreciated his thorough analysis and his scholarly presentation of the facts surrounding the subjects in hand. His writings appeared in many of the religious periodicals, and Govett was regarded as a sought-after contributor to these publications. Govett's intent to appear so frequently in this form of print culture was perhaps due to their popularity.

Fiction writer Wilkie Collins (1824–1889) described the nineteenth century as "the age of periodicals"[151] and noted that the "readership of the penny novel journals is to be counted in the millions."[152] G. Kitson Clark in *The Making of Victorian England* (1962), speaking of Great Britain, notes that it may not be too extravagant to say of the nineteenth century that in "no other century, except the seventeenth and perhaps the twelfth, did the claims of religion occupy so large a part in the nation's life, or did men speaking in the name of religion contrive to exercise so much power."[153] How this exercise of power was contrived came in large measure due to the burgeoning periodical press. Josef L. Altholz, in *The Religious Press in*

---

149. Wheeler, *Death and the Future Life*, 6.

150. See *The Book of Common Prayer, and Administration of the Sacraments* (Oxford: Bensley, Cooke, and Collingwood, 1815) 238.

151. Wilkie Collins, "The Unknown Public," *Household Words. A Weekly Journal* 439 (1858) 222.

152. Collins, "The Unknown Public," 217.

153. G. Kitson Clark, *The Making of Victorian England* (Cambridge, MA: Harvard University Press, 1962) 20.

Britain, 1760–1900 (1989), clearly sees that the nineteenth-century periodical press became the chief medium through which to communicate on "all subjects, secular and religious."[154] Altholz's work has been useful to this study in understanding the evolution of the periodical, as has *The Waterloo Directory of English Newspapers and Periodicals, 1800–1900* (1997),[155] which has helped determine the backgrounds of the periodicals in which Govett's writing appeared.

Historically the periodical is one of the best sources by which to assess the writers of the nineteenth century and their many schools of religious thought. This is certainly true of Govett. Although he published one hundred and eighty-four books and tracts his plentiful articles and letters appearing in various periodicals help to provide a more thorough assessment of his theological assertions. As such this study also engages with Govett's periodical writings to draw attention to his many doctrinal and eschatological concerns. Additionally, this study is somewhat concerned to know the cultural and religious nature of the Victorian age. For that assessment this study looks to the origin and growth of religious dissent and the many factors of life which shaped it. The periodical became an important vehicle for the dissemination of a great variety of information in this age and Govett discovered its importance for his own religious cause.

The Periodical

The role of the periodical in the cultural life of the nineteenth century has become a focus for some of the best scholarship on the period, and periodical culture has also become a growing and important field. One key reason for the attraction of these scholars is the sheer volume of publications—approximately 100,000 in Great Britain in the nineteenth century.[156] Print culture for the Victorian embodied many forms but one that demanded significant attention was the "press." Nineteenth-century British periodicals regarded the press as a phenomenon of the age.[157] The press was considered as anything published regularly: annuals, quarterlies, monthlies, fortnightlies, weeklies, and dailies. Authors were as diverse as the periodicals in which

---

154. Josef L. Altholz, *The Religious Press in Britain, 1760–1900* (New York: Greenwood, 1989) 1.

155. John S. North, *The Waterloo Directory of English Newspapers and Periodicals, 1800–1900* (Waterloo: North Waterloo Academic, 1997).

156. E. M. Palmegiano, *Perceptions of the Press in Nineteenth-Century British Periodicals: A Bibliography* (New York: Anthem, 2012) vii.

157. Palmegiano, *Perceptions of the Press*, vii.

they wrote. They might have full-time positions in the press, but they were just as likely to be freelancers who had other employment.[158] Often articles and letters which appeared in print were penned by anonymous authors or those who chose to use pseudonyms. Govett frequently interacted with authors who used pseudonyms.

Numerous bibliographies covering nineteenth-century periodicals have been carefully researched and published which draw attention to their diversity. However, these bibliographies routinely acknowledge the limitations inherent in their study. As E. M. Palmegiano notes: "Their numbers [periodicals] and their fluidity, resulting from mastheads capriciously altered, contents mysteriously labeled, and parts lost, complicate inquiry."[159] Who read the periodicals is also difficult to assess since audience surveys did not formally exist. But it may be asserted with some accuracy that the nineteenth century in Britain was uniquely the age of the periodical and that the circulation of periodicals was wider and more influential than books in Victorian society.[160] In *The English Common Reader*, Richard Alrick remarks that by mid-century, "No longer was it possible for people to avoid reading matter; everywhere they went it was displayed."[161] Perhaps for this reason and the financial accessibility of periodicals Govett found an accessible audience for his theological assertions. Regulatory reform and an increase in national literacy contributed to the sales growth of periodicals. Literacy rose from around 50 percent at the end of the 1830s to 99 percent at the end of the century.[162] It appears by the sheer volume of his articles that Govett welcomed this new medium. Yet not all who placed their thoughts in print felt the same. Kathryn Ledbetter writes that Tennyson claimed to hate periodicals but that despite this hatred he appears to have sought them out for financial gain. Nevertheless, the fortunate result was that readers around the world knew of Tennyson and he became as much a commodity as were his poems and the publishing formats in which they appeared.[163] Whether Govett was conscious of his popularity is not certain but it is evident that the periodical and Govett became cooperative

---

158. Ibid., vii.

159. Ibid., vii–viii.

160. J. Don Vann and Rosemary T. VanArsdel, eds., *Periodicals of Queen Victoria's Empire: An Exploration* (Toronto: University of Toronto Press, 1996) 3.

161. Richard D. Altick, *The English Common Reader: A Social History of the Mass Reading Public, 1800–1900* (Chicago: University of Chicago Press, 1957) 301.

162. Andrew King and John Plunkett, eds., *Popular Print Media 1820–1900* (Abingdon: Routledge, 2004) 12.

163. Kathryn Ledbetter, *Tennyson and Victorian Periodicals: Commodities in Context* (Aldershot: Ashgate, 2007) 5.

partners, as this study seeks to demonstrate. It is most likely that he chose specific periodicals for their ability to disseminate his theological views and they in turn chose him because of his proven ability to impress his readers with the thoroughness of his argument.

Govett never abandoned the publishing of his books and tracts, but added to his busy writing schedule articles submitted to numerous periodicals in which he contributed with much regularity for several decades. The periodicals in which Govett's writings appeared were those which often had eschatological topics as their focus. They were dissenting journals which formed a sub-group within the numerous religious publications available to a growing readership. While dissenting journals dealt with a broad range of religious issues, often attacking the theological positions of those religious groups and churches in which they found important differences, Govett tended instead to concentrate the bulk of his writings on proving his position by scriptural means. Where comparisons are made his tendency was to do so with reserve and respect.

The readership of dissenting journals tended to be relatively small in comparison to other religious journals, thus making it difficult to research the history of the periodical themselves. The most utilized bibliographies by researchers do not mention these periodicals. The exception is *Waterloo Directory of English Newspapers and Periodicals: 1800–1900* which contains modist background information such as purpose and audience, dates of publication, and first editor. Circulation and cumulative sales figures are typically not available. Where information is available it has been included in this study, typically as a footnote.

Conclusion

Govett's theological learning drew a number of his readers to conclude that his thoughts deserved their respect. This admiration continued throughout his lifetime. For instance, in 1869 Govett published a book entitled *English Derived from Hebrew*.[164] It was reviewed by the prophetic journal *The Voices Upon the Mountains*,[165] which remarked that the learned will "highly

---

164. Robert Govett, *English Derived from Hebrew, with Glances at Greek and Latin* (London: Partridge, 1869).

165. According to the *Waterloo Directory of English Newspapers and Periodicals: 1800–1900*, Thomas George Bell was the editor of the journal, which was published from January 1867 to December 1869. Its purpose was to promote "the Personal Coming, Reign and Kingdom of the Lord Jesus Christ." See John S. North and Brent Nelson, eds., *Waterloo Directory of English Newspapers and Periodicals: 1800–1900* (Waterloo: North Waterloo Academic, 2003).

esteem" the book. The reviewer further noted that "in every case there is the manifestation of great ingenuity, and the author's well-known talent for matters of critical study."[166] At the time of this review Govett was forty-six years of age. He was well established in his writing career which began with his first published work on Calvinism in 1840.[167] By 1869 Govett had published at least sixty-five books and tracts[168] on various theological subjects pertaining mostly to eschatological issues of concern to the Christian community in Great Britain, although his work was also appreciated in America, as this study reveals in chapter 6. Nevertheless, his conclusions were often severe causing more than a few of his readers to disagree. Yet, for several decades his contributions to print culture remained of interest to readers who found themselves in an era where the views on eschatology were numerously varied.

Eschatology in the Victorian era at times forms a complex discussion, since evangelicalism and evangelical millennialism varied in popularity and form over the span of Govett's life. The discussion is made more complex by the interjection of matters such as church dissent, national politics, emerging religious movements, scientific discoveries, and increased religious scepticism. In many ways Govett, as expressed in his numerous contributions to the print culture of his day, appears to be reacting to these important matters—matters which were heightened by the Victorian's curiosity with the "last things" (i.e., death, judgment, heaven, and hell). But no matter what the issue before him, as this study demonstrates, he always sought to return the discussion to an understanding of Scripture. For instance, in 1864 a review in the *Journal of Sacred Literature*[169] of Govett's booklet *The Righteousness of Christ, the Righteousness of God: a Refutation of the Views Generally Held by the Christians Commonly Called "Plymouth Brethren" on that Subject*,[170] stated that, "Mr. Govett quotes the opinions of Mr. Darby

---

166. *The Voice upon the Mountains. A Journal of Prophetic Testimony and Evangelistic Effort* 3 (1869) 22.

167. See Robert Govett, ed., *Calvinism by Calvin; Being the Substance of Discourses* (London: Nisbet, 1840).

168. The exact number of publications by this date cannot be precisely ascertained since twenty-four tracts and booklets known to be in existence today cannot be accurately dated.

169. According to the *Waterloo Directory of English Newspapers and Periodicals: 1800–1900*, Harris Cowper was the editor of the journal from 1861 to 1868. The journal existed from January 1848 to 1868. Its orientation was non-denominational, non-sectarian, and Protestant orthodox. See John S. North, and Brent Nelson, eds., *Waterloo Directory of English Newspapers and Periodicals: 1800–1900* (Waterloo: North Waterloo Academic, 2003).

170. Robert Govett, *The Righteousness of Christ, the Righteousness of God: A Refutation*

and the leading Plymouthists on a number of related topics, and refutes them *seriatim*, with much earnestness and acumen."[171] However, while Govett was not always agreed with he was nearly always respected on matters involving of Scriptural knowledge.

Govett's eschatological interests took him to reaches of theology on the Judgment that very few theologians of his day cared to venture. Christ's return and the believer's entrance into the thousand-year reign with Christ were of paramount importance to Govett and motivated much of his writing throughout his life. His commitment to "believers' baptism"—the topic which caused his removal from the Church of England—was inextricably tied in his mind to the believer's entrance into that Coming Kingdom. Accordingly, this study examines Govett's understanding of the "entrance into the kingdom" and "baptism," his debates in the print culture over these matters, as well as his challenging assertion (original to himself) that not all believers would enter into the thousand-year reign with Christ. The "partial rapture" theory, as it came to be known, was a large factor in his disappearance from the mainstream of dispensational thought soon after his death in 1901. This study concludes with the determinant issues surrounding the disappearance of his repute. The issues were many and complex, and they took place not in Great Britain where his writings began but in America where dispensationalism found a new and receptive home.

---

of the Views Generally Held by the Christians Commonly Called "Plymouth Brethren" on that Subject (London: Stock, 1864).

171. "Notices of Books," *The Journal of Sacred Literature and Biblical Record* 5 (1864) 478.

CHAPTER 1

The Emergence of Victorian Dissent

Govett was thirty-one years old when he acquired the label "Dissenter." It was not a title he sought but he received nonetheless as a result of his strongly held biblical beliefs which ran counter to the practice of infant baptism maintained by the Church of England. As a dissenter, Govett was identified with the membership and institutions of those religious movements that refused to conform to the Church of England. Religious debate was always present in the Victorian era. It made its way into the forefront of thought in the print culture, the pulpits, and in the development of powerful movements both outside and within of the Church of England. Religious dissent surfaced in numerous ways. Religious belief and confidence in the Bible were complicated by scientific and philosophical thought which helped fuel the crisis of faith associated with the latter part of the nineteenth century. Govett's own religious convictions often found their place in journals and books. As he engaged in the debates, his writings revealed his consciousness of the political, religious, and societal struggles of the Victorians. Dissent involved not only the organization of the church, but also involved the relationship of the believer to God. In the mindset of the dissenter both had been severely impacted in the late seventeenth century by Charles II who imposed an Act of Uniformity (1662) requiring the use of the Book of Common Prayer in all public worship. The Act further insisted that every minister be ordained by a bishop within the Church of England. This resulted in nearly 2000 clergymen leaving the church. Dissenters could not graduate from the universities of Oxford and Cambridge, and were barred from holding public or military office. In 1689 the Act of Toleration provided some relief to the dissenters but the ascendancy of

Queen Anne to the throne in 1702 and her conformist leanings led to more attacks on their persons and property.

This chapter introduces some of the key religious developments leading up to the Victorian era as well as those which helped frame it during the nineteenth century. Govett's thoughts and writings are interjected where appropriate in this chapter to give a sense for the breadth of his concerns and the issues to which he was willing to lend his voice.

The denominational debate was in some measure a debate about the locus of religious authority. Anglicanism embraced not only the authority of the Bible, but also church tradition as related to the Patristic Fathers, the three Creeds (Nicene, Apostolic, and Athanasian), the Book of Common Prayer (1662), and the Thirty-nine Articles. Nonconformists such as the Presbyterians and Baptists, for example, had their own confessions of faith which held as much authority within their denominations as the Thirty-nine Articles held among Anglicans. Some Anglicans practiced their faith through ritualism and liturgy grounded in medieval traditions, but not all. Philip Davis recalls that in a famous article "Church parties" in *The Edinburgh Review* (October 1853), W. J. Conybeare claimed that by mid-century the Church of England consisted of three main groups: Low Church evangelicals who believed in Bible-centered literalism, enthusiastic individual conversion experience, and plain services; the Anglican High Churchmen who believed in the church, its formal traditions, liturgies, and sacraments; and in between the two the Broad Churchmen who, "committed to a truly wide national establishment, responded to developments in contemporary biblical and scientific studies by being liberal in theology."[1] The Anglicans also had the distinction of functioning as a national church bequeathed with a sense of power derived from the state. Dissenters favored worship that was centered on the local church. Worship tended to be intimate and unrestricted by liturgical formality, although not always. Worship could be cold and formal. Preaching could be rationalistic and didactic—as characteristic in the example of eighteenth-century Baptist preacher John Gill.[2] Yet, such differences went deeper than doctrinal and liturgical issues. Everyday life was also affected. Govett, as a dissenter, was part of a religious community with a long history. By 1715 the number of dissenters in England and Wales was about 300,000 in a population of approximately 5.5 million.[3] The

---

1. Philip Davis, *The Victorians: 1830–1880* (New York: Oxford University Press, 2002) 103.

2. Gregory A. Wills, "A Fire That Burns Within: The Spirituality of John Gill," in Michael A. G. Haykin, ed., *The Life and Thought of John Gill (1697–1771) a Tercentennial Application* (Leiden: Brill, 1997) 204.

3. Brown, *Church and State*, 109.

principal dissenting groups were Presbyterians—who made up two-thirds of the total number—the Independents (or Congregationalists), the Baptists and the Quakers. The number of dissenters remained static or slightly even declined until the mid-eighteenth century. At the same time, dissent failed to appeal to the "working" population which potentially could have allowed the movement to grow.[4]

Evangelical Eschatology

A thorough discussion of evangelical eschatology is complex and involves far more history than this study can afford to mediate without losing sight of its intended focus. Nevertheless, it is important that this study should formulate a frame of reference that places Govett and the Victorian age within a religious tradition that shows dissent and evangelical eschatology in its rich historic light. As the eighteenth century progressed and as eschatology had become increasingly diminished in the mainstream of Christian thought, it became clear that the most natural home for millennial eschatology was within evangelical dissent[5]—even though for the first half of the nineteenth century many dissenters retained their postmillennial views. Prior to this, Anglican theologians were best known for maintaining eschatological expectations—and especially millennium.[6] But the history of millennialism presents a deeper complexity requiring clarification.

Norman Cohn in *The Pursuit of the Millennium* (1970) clarifies the complexities of eschatology and millennialism by reminding his readers that the original meaning of millennialism was narrow and precise and that Christianity has always had an eschatology in a sense of a doctrine concerning the final state of the world. Christian millennialism was simply one variant of Christian eschatology.[7] Premillennialism referred to the belief in Revelation 20:1–10 that after his Second Coming Christ would establish his messianic kingdom upon the earth and would reign over it for one-thousand years—the conclusion of which would usher in the Last Judgment. Advocates of millennial belief—or "chiliasm" as it was frequently described—surfaced almost immediately after the New Testament canon

---

4. Ibid., 110.

5. W. J. Van Asselt, "Chiliasm and Reformed Eschatology in the Seventeenth and Eighteenth Centuries," in A. van Egmond and D. van Keulen, eds., *Christian Hope in Context*, Studies in Reformed Theology 4 (Zoetermeer: Meinema, 2001) 12.

6. Gribben, *Trans-Atlantic World*, 53.

7. Norman Cohn, *The Pursuit of the Millennium* (Oxford: Oxford University Press, 1970) 15.

was formalized. The history of Christian eschatology finds its beginnings in the apocalyptic hopes of salvation cherished by the earliest Palestinian Christian communities.[8] However, this study's overview of the early years of millennial understanding begins with the second century and one of the most important biblical theologian in that period, Irenaeus.

Irenaeus believed in a future, earthly millennium, but there were those who opposed his millennial views—an opposition which he perceived emanated from both orthodox and heretical circles. Those who opposed Irenaeus's view did so most often on the ground that the righteous go immediately after death into the presence of God in heaven. The opposition appeared to also be antagonistic toward the idea of a bodily resurrection. Chiliasm did, however, fall into eventual disfavor and was considered heterodox by the church for many years. Charles Hill cites the most accepted reasons for its drift from favor: chiliasm's alleged association with Montanism (which was thought to have brought shame upon the doctrine in the eyes of the larger church), the influence of Origen's spiritualizing of eschatology and allegorizing of Scripture, the related infiltration of the church by Greek philosophy, the progressive deterioration of the church's once vibrant hope of Christ's return (a decay aided by the peace of Constantine), and the authoritative and enormously influential rejection of chiliasm by Augustine (354–430).[9]

Augustine "spiritualized" Revelation 20:1–10 to claim that its reference to the one-thousand years of Christ's reign was referring to one-thousand years of Christian history—or, the "whole period of this world's history."[10] Seven centuries after Augustine another millennial interpretation became popular. This "historicism" began with Rupert of Deutz (1075–1129). For Rupert, seals one through six in Revelation chapter 5 symbolized the period stretching from the Incarnation to the *vocatio gentium* (the calling of the Gentiles), with the seventh describing the Last Judgment. He held that the Apocalypse recounted the history of the church up until the Council of Nicea (325), with the Last Judgment constituting a future event which is not to be dated, and the half an hour's silence in heaven denoting the "future rest" of the saints after the Last Judgment.[11] And while the eschatological landscape was ever changing with thoughts of the afterlife and all of its

---

8. Brian A. Daley, *The Hope of the Early Church: A Handbook of Patristic Eschatology* (Cambridge: Cambridge University Press, 1991) 5.

9. Charles E. Hill, *Regnum Caelorum: Patterns of Millennial Thought in Early Christianity* (Grand Rapids: Eerdmans, 2001) 3.

10. Gribben, *Trans-Atlantic World*, 23.

11. Irena Backus, *Reformation Readings of the Apocalypse: Geneva, Zurich, and Wittenberg* (Oxford: Oxford University Press, 2000) 90.

complexities, Augustine's eschatology largely remained the standard until the mid-sixteenth century.

Still, throughout the first fifteen hundred years of church history the canonicity of the Book of Revelation (or, the Apocalypse) was often problematic. For example, from the late third century, the Eastern church rejected the book of Revelation and only slowly yielded to the decision of the West by admitting the book into its canon.[12] Yet the book was not only increasingly accepted as Scripture, but was also commented upon by the ante-Nicene Fathers such as Justin, Tertullian, and Lactantius each of whom were chiliasts. Richard Landes notes that prominent figures such as Jerome and Augustine did their best to delegitimize most forms of apocalyptic expectation and the chiliastic hopes it often inspired. Evidence suggests that medieval writers avoided the subject of the millennium whenever possible.[13] Desiderius Erasmus (1466–1536), while noting that the Apocalypse frequently used the term *chilias* condemned the book for its "recourse to allegory, its barbarous style, and the dubious person of its author constantly compelled to justify his authorship." Martin Luther (1483–1546) also held that the book was neither apostolic nor prophetic, because no Old Testament prophet–let alone a New Testament apostle—speaks about Christ quite so obscurely.[14] Several decades later the German evangelical theologian David Pareus (1548–1622) still felt the need to address the arguments of Erasmus and Luther in his commentary on Revelation (1618).[15] Nevertheless, by the time of his writing commentaries typically agreed that Revelation was an important part of the biblical canon, while rejecting as dangerous the millennialism that some discovered within its pages. Early reformation creeds generally rejected the millennial hope as a dangerous heresy. For instance, the Sixth Section of the Second Helvetic Confession (1566) reads: "Moreover, we condemn the Jewish dreams, that before the day of judgment there shall be a golden world in the earth; and that the godly shall possess the kingdoms of the world, their wicked enemies being trodden under foot."[16] But the millennial hope would be revived.

---

12. James Hastings, *A Dictionary of the Bible: Volume IV, Part One* (Honolulu: University Press of the Pacific, 2004) 241.

13. Richard Landes, "The Fear of an Apocalyptic Year 1000: Augustinian Historiography, Medieval and Modern," in Richard Landes, Andrew Gow, and David C. Van Meter, eds., *The Apocalyptic Year 1000: Religious Expectation and Social Change* (Oxford: Oxford University Press, 2003) 246.

14. Backus, *Reformation Readings*, 6.

15. Ibid., 33–35.

16. Peter Hall, *The Harmony of Protestant Confessions* (London: Shaw, 1842) 88.

Despite the fact that the Lutheran, Anglican, and Calvinist reformations rejected the millennial hope, a number of English and Scottish Reformed theologians revivified the belief in the first part of the seventeenth century.[17] Much of this renewal had its beginning in the 1550s when, for fear of persecution from Queen Mary, English Protestants fled into foreign exile. In Strasbourg, Geneva and elsewhere these exiled Protestants published writings which consolidated their fundamentally apocalyptic world view. Through the Geneva Bible (1560) and John Foxe's *Acts and Monuments* (1563), these early evangelicals confirmed that the one-thousand years of Revelation 20:1-10 had already been fulfilled—even though Foxe's writings presented an uncertainty about when the millennium had begun. Their writings initiated a paradigm shift that drove an English recovery of millennial belief.[18] There arose a sense of impending victory and optimism that was epitomized in the third and final edition of the Geneva Bible (1599), which included the inclusion of Franciscus Junius's (1545-1602) commentary on Revelation—replacing the original notes of John Bale and Heinrich Bullinger.[19] Junius's timetable included eschatological delay and the expectation of impending prophetic events. He was not alone in arguing for a future period of latter-day glory for the church. But neither was there yet any scholarly consensus on the matter.

Eschatological paradigms continued to surface in England and on the Continent. Crawford Gribben states that seventeenth-century British Reformed orthodox writers found in their discussions of millennial theories a liberty of conviction and expression that challenges easy assumptions of their unity and their Biblical or confessional limitations. It was in maintaining millennial theories that they displayed the greatest difference from the sixteenth-century confessions they had inherited and from their European contemporaries.[20] One such contemporary was Conrad Bröske (1660–1713), Court Preacher to Count Johann Philipp II in Offenback/Mayn. Douglas H. Shantz notes that Bröske's fame stems from a ten-year period between 1694 and 1704 in which he espoused with increased vigor his conviction that Revelation 2–3 taught that the church of Sardis stood

---

17. See Crawford Gribben, *The Puritan Millennium: Literature and Theology, 1550–1682* (Dublin: Four Courts, 2000).

18. Gribben, *Trans-Atlantic World*, 29.

19. See Arthur Sumner, T. H. Darlow and H. F. Moule, eds., *Historical Catalogue of Printed Editions of the English Bible: 1525–1961* (London: British & Foreign Bible Society, 1968).

20. Crawford Gribben, "Millennialism," in Michael A. G. Haykin and Mark Jones, eds., *Drawn into Controversies: Reformed Theological Diversity and Debates within Seventeenth-Century British Puritanism* (Göttingen: Vandenhoeck & Ruprecht, 2011) 84.

for the age of Reformation. It was thought that this age would soon be superseded by that of the Philadelphian church which was understood to refer to the millennial age.[21] Bröske drew upon the writings of Jakob Böhme (1575-1624) and the London visionary Jane Leade (1624-1704)[22] and was instrumental in assisting the so-called "Philadelphian" millennialist movement in gaining widespread support among German Pietists in the 1690s. It was Bröske's writings and the chiliastic literature published by the Offenbach press that helped nurture future millennial expectations among its readers. Still during this period of millennial revival the debates continued over the correct paradigm.

Among English dissenters, Richard Baxter (1615-1691) also reflected upon a century of eschatological study. In his published works *The Glorious Kingdom of Christ, Described and Clearly Vindicated* (1691), he surveys the confusing state of eschatological paradigms as they focused on the number of periods of time referred to in Revelation 20:1-10 and concluded that,

> Some of them say, The Thousand years are on Earth; and some say, they are only of the Souls of Martyrs and Confessors in Heaven: Some say, they are both in Heaven, or in the Air, and on Earth at once. Some say, that they shall be a Jewish Monarchy at Jerusalem, and some, that it shall be of the godly all over the World. Some say, Christ will Reign there visibly in his Humane Nature; others, that he will only sometime appear, as he did after his Resurrection: And some, that he will Rule there only by Reforming Christian Princes. Some hold but one thousand years and some two (one being after the other.) Some hold two New Jerusalems, and some but one. Some say, that the Day of Judgment is the thousand years (and yet that Scripture hath not told us how long Christ will be Judging of us.) And some, that it is only the Beginning and the End of the thousand years, that the Judgment will take up, and the rest will be in other Government.[23]

---

21. Douglas H. Shantz, *Between Sardis and Philadelphia: The Life and World of Pietist Court Preacher Conrad Bröske* (Leiden: Brill, 2008) xv.

22. See Julie Hirst, *Jane Leade: Biography of a Seventeenth-Century Mystic* (Aldershot: Ashgate, 2005).

23. Richard Baxter, *The Glorious Kingdom of Christ, Described and Clearly Vindicated* (London, 1691) 9-10. See also Reiner Smolinski, "Caveat Emptor: Pre- and Postmillennialism in the Late Reformation Period," in James E. Force and Richard H. Popkin, eds., *Millenarianism and Messianism in Early Modern European Culture: The Millenarian Turn* (Dordrecht: Kluwer Academic, 2001) 145-69.

It was, therefore, in eschatology that seventeenth-century British Reformed theologians exhibited the greatest variety of thoughts and exerted the widest differences with sixteenth-century European confessions. This diversity of tradition dispels the notion that British Reformed writers shared a common eschatology (or millennialism), or that among seventeenth-century British Reformed writers formed a unified tradition. Nevertheless, three discernible paradigms emerged from the debates of the seventeenth century—amillennialism, premillennialism, and postmillennialism. But they did not find acceptance without struggle. One subject which caught the attention of many commentators and sparked prolonged debate was that of the "Antichrist." Anthony Milton argues that the claims that the pope was the Antichrist began to intensify as early as the late sixteenth century. He asserts that it became an unchallenged orthodoxy and of substantial doctrinal importance in the Elizabethan Church. A whole range of sermons, treatises and popular manuals, written to prove the pope to be the Antichrist prophesied by Scripture, proliferated during this time. Milton estimates that between 1588 and 1628 over 100 systematic expositions of the papal Antichrist were published in England. Foxe's *Acts and Monuments* and the marginal notes of the Geneva Bible further spread these apocalyptic ideas.[24] It was from this debate that a number of millennial positions emerged but with significant disagreement. And even by mid-century the Augustinian tradition continued to find a few defenders, while the modern distinction between pre- and postmillennialism (not as yet clearly delineated traditions) also found their roots in this period.[25]

By the eighteenth century evangelicals found their millennial commitments were being fashioned by factors that included not only theological and denominational concerns, but politics as well. As the eighteenth century began to develop it was not unusual to find that premillennialists were often high Calvinists, such as the English Baptist John Gill (1697–1771), and that postmillennialists were often moderate evangelical Calvinists such as English Baptist Andrew Fuller (1754–1815). But there was never any substantial link between millennial theories and prior theological commitments. Whatever was remaining of a denominational context with millennial affiliation was finally broken in the revolutionary period of the late eighteenth century with

---

24. Anthony Milton, *Catholic and Reformed: The Roman and Protestant Churches in England Protestant Thought, 1600–1640* (Cambridge: Cambridge University Press, 1995) 93. The claim that the pope was the Antichrist reached creedal status in an expansion of the Thirty-Nine Articles (1563), in the Irish Articles (1615), and the Westminster Confession of Faith (1647), which concluded that the pope "was that man of sin . . . that exalteth himself in the Church against Christ" (see 25.6).

25. Gribben, *Trans-Atlantic World*, 48.

the collapse of the *ancien régime*.[26] Nonetheless, postmillennialism tended to dominate in the early evangelical movement as the belief in the premillennial advent of Christ (as found in the mid-seventeenth century) eventually disappeared from the mainstream of evangelical thought. Premillennialism found no place in the creed of the leaders of the eighteenth-century Revival, nor did it find a place in the men of the missionary movement which followed.[27] David Bogue (1750–1825), Congregational minister and leader in the foundation of the London Missionary Society in 1794,[28] expressed his hostility to the "aberration" of premillennialism in his *Discourses on the Millennium* (1818). In it he questions "how wise and pious men could ever suppose that the saints, whose souls are now in heaven, should, after the resurrection of the body from the grave, descend to live on earth again."[29] For its part, in reviewing Bogue's publication, the *Christian Observer* (published by The Eclectic Society, a sub-group of the Church of England, and appealing to evangelical clergymen),[30] agrees that Revelation 20 depicts a "bright" period for the church during which it will no longer struggle with opposition, and concurs with Bogue that the approach of the period will be gradual.[31] While postmillennialism dominated among British believers in the eighteenth century, premillennialism did not disappear. It was John Gill, popular Baptist theologian, who sought to bridge the two[32]—as did Sayer Rudd (d.1757), dissenting minister and sometime Baptist, before him who expounded similar views of a latter-day glory before the second coming followed thereafter by a millennium glory.[33] Like Gill, Andrew Fuller, Baptist minister and theologian, was identified as a hyper-Calvinist in his early ministry. The earliest systematic theology that the young pastor studied was

---

26. Ibid., 54–55.

27. Murray, *The Puritan Hope*, 187.

28. See Joseph King, *Ten Decades: The Australian Centenary Story of the London Missionary Society* (London: London Missionary Society, 1895).

29. David Bogue, *Discourses on the Millennium* (London: Hamilton, 1818) 17.

30. See John S. North, and Brent Nelson, eds., *Waterloo Directory of English Newspapers and Periodicals: 1800–1900* (Waterloo: North Waterloo Academic, 2003).

31. Review "Discourses on the Millennium," *The Christian Observer* 17, no. 11 (1818) 746–47.

32. See John Rippon, *A Brief Memoir of the Life and Writings of the Late Rev. John Gill, D.D.* (London: Bennett, 1838); Michael A. G. Haykin, ed., *The Life and Thought of John Gill (1697–1771): A Tercentennial Appreciation* (Leiden: Brill, 1997); William Staughton, *Gill's Complete Body of Practical and Doctrinal Divinity: Being a System of Evangelical Truths, Deduced from the Sacred Scriptures* (Philadelphia: Graves, 1810).

33. See Sayer Rudd, *An Essay towards a New Explication of the Doctrines of the Resurrection, Millennium, and Judgment* (London: Blackwell, 1734).

Gill's *A Body of Doctrinal Divinity*.[34] But Fuller abandoned Gill's premillennial vision. Fuller's eschatology is an excellent representation of the hopeful postmillennialism that was characteristic of the time of evangelical revival and the missionary zeal it fostered.[35]

Thus eighteenth-century evangelicals generally agreed that, as the Christian gospel spread throughout the world and individuals and societies came under its sway, a perfect kingdom would gradually emerge and take the place of the corrupt kingdom presently in existence. Standing out in relief against this general eighteenth-century background was Charles Wesley (1707–1788). Kenneth Newport has suggested that Wesley's journals, letters, sermons, and hymns support the view that he espoused a premillennial faith.[36] Premillennial in its modern formulation began to be articulated at the end of the eighteenth century. This perfect kingdom, described in Revelation 20, which would last for a period of one-thousand years, would prepare the people of God to meet the Lord when he returned at the millennium's close. In this context John Wesley's sermon "The General Spread of the Gospel,"[37] based on Isaiah 11:9, seems reasonably typical of his age. John's brother, Charles Wesley, however, saw things differently.[38] Newport notes that his sermon "On the Cause and Cure of Earthquakes" takes on a new and dramatic form. The earthquake that hit London in 1750, according to Charles, gave warning of impending apocalyptic doom. In the sermon he argues that the world is destined to get worse rather than better. Society will continue to spiral downward spiritually and morally until the great "eschaton," the coming of Christ, who will set all things right.[39] By the end of the eighteenth century the evolution of millennial ideas had begun to include the emergence of a premillennial interpretation of prophecy. While not settled by any means, the transition was brought into clearer focus with the onset of the French Revolution and the conclusion of the Napoleonic Wars. A growing sense of proclamation for the imminent return of Christ

---

34. John Gill, *A Body of Doctrinal Divinity: or, a System of Evangelical Truths, Deduced from the Scriptures*, 2 vols. (London: n.p., 1769).

35. Paul Brewster, *Andrew Fuller: Model Pastor and Theologian* (Nashville: B&H, 2010) 23, 160.

36. Kenneth G. C. Newport, "Premillennialism in the Early Writings of Charles Wesley," *Wesleyan Theological Journal* 32, no. 1 (1997) 104.

37. John Wesley, "Sermon LXIII, The General Spread of the Gospel," *The Works of the Rev. John Wesley, A.M.* (London: Mason, 1840) 6:261–71.

38. Newport, "Premillennialism," 105.

39. Kenneth G. C. Newport, *The Sermons of Charles Wesley: A Critical Edition with Introductions and Notes* (Oxford: Oxford University Press, 2001) 63.

began to surface in societal and religious thought.[40] With it apocalyptic and millennial images emerged in the popular writings of such authors as Blake, Coleridge, Wordsworth, and Shelley.[41] Frank Turner notes in *John Henry Newman: The Challenge of Evangelical Religion* (2002) that by the end of the second decade of the nineteenth century premillennialists and others concerned with prophecy, such as the Society for Investigating Prophecy (1826), quickly established their own literary culture, including *The Morning Watch* (1829-1833), the *Christian Herald* (1830-1835), and the *Investigator* (1831-1836).[42] Premillennialism became further established through a series of prophetic conferences held in England and Ireland. In England, Henry Drummond (1786-1860) held the first of five annual prophecy conferences at Albury Park, Surrey, in 1826. The purpose of the meeting was chiefly to study unfulfilled prophecy and the second advent of Christ from the perspective of futurist premillennialism. In September of 1830, Theodosia, Lady Powerscourt (1800-1836), the second wife of the fifth Viscount, herself having attended the Albury conferences on prophecy, held the first of a series of similar prophecy conferences at her estate in County Wicklow, south of Dublin.[43] Among those in attendance were John Nelson Darby (1800-1882) and other early founders and adherents of what would develop into the Brethren Movement.

Brethren Movement and Dispensationalism

John Nelson Darby was one of the most significant figures attending the Powerscourt conferences. He was an Irish clergyman, graduate of Trinity

40. Oliver, *Prophets and Millennialists*, 20.

41. Stefan Collini, Richard Whatmore, and Brian Young, eds., *History, Religion, and Culture: British Intellectual History 1750-1950* (Cambridge: Cambridge University Press, 2000) 205.

42. Frank M. Turner, *John Henry Newman: The Challenge of Evangelical Religion* (New Haven: Yale University Press, 2002) 39.

43. The year is incorrectly reported in several accounts concerning the first Powerscourt conference. Some report the year to be 1827. Some report the year to be 1831 based upon the *Christian Herald* publishing that date as the first Powerscourt conference. See *Christian Herald* (December 1832) 290. September 1830 is given as the date of the first Powerscourt conference in a recently discovered contemporary listing of the conference discussions. It was in September when Edward Irving visited Dublin and may have been the occasion of Darby's discussion with Irving on premillennial topics. See Tim Grass, *Gathering to His Name: The Story of Open Brethren in Britain and Ireland* (Milton Keynes: Paternoster, 2006) 26, 508-9; Crawford Gribben, Timothy C. F. Stunt, eds., *Prisoners of Hope? Aspects of Evangelical Millennialism in Britain and Ireland, 1800-1880* (Carlisle: Paternoster, 2004) 67.

College, Dublin (1815–1819), and admitted to Lincoln's Inn (1819) to practice law—a profession which he soon gave up in favor of taking clerical orders.[44] Soon after his experiences at Albury and Powerscourt he steadily elaborated the view that the predictions of Revelation would be fulfilled after believers had been "raptured" to meet Christ in the air.[45] Prior to the prophetic conferences Darby was known to hold a "historicist" view of eschatology—a school of thought which had been the most popular premillennial view held by evangelicals until the 1840s. But the very event that lent confidence to the historicist school of prophecy began to raise questions in the minds of many of its adherents. Evangelicals were no longer uniformly confident that God was working to use the forces of liberty to bring about the end of the monarchy and the traditional view that the pope was the Antichrist was now open to theological debate.[46]

The other school of premillennial thought was the "futurist" school. It was articulated in the work of Roman Catholic theologians who sought to counter the charges of sixteenth-century Protestant reformers that the pope was the Antichrist. Their writings responded to these attacks by claiming that the "beast" of Revelation could not be the pope for the beast would only be revealed in the "future." Major contributors of this position were Franciscus Ribera (1537–1591) and Francis Suarez (1548–1617).[47] One of the most influential writers of the futurist school of this period was the Jesuit, Manuel Lacunza (1731–1801), who wrote under the pen name Juan Josafat Ben-Ezra because he was fearful of the Roman Church. The reason for his fear stemmed from his writing *The Coming of the Messiah in Glory and Majesty*[48] in which he predicted that the Antichrist was not an individual, but a moral body which would spring forth from an apostate Catholic Church.

During the 1820s two of the main individuals responsible for advancing the futurist school were Samuel Roffey Maitland (1792–1866) and Edward Irving (1792–1834). Maitland was converted from the historicist school to futurist through the influence of several men, each with a connection to Trinity College, Dublin—including William [de] Burgh whose significant contributions to the early theological structuring of dispensationalism was eventually overshadowed by the popularity of Darby. In 1826 Maitland

44. Donald M. Lewis, *The Blackwell Dictionary of Evangelical Biography 1730–1860* (Oxford: Blackwell, 1995) 1:290.

45. Bebbinton, *Evangelicalism in Modern Britain*, 85.

46. Burnham, *A Story of Conflict*, 106.

47. Froom, *The Prophetic Faith of Our Fathers*, 2:489–502.

48. Juan Josafat Ben-Ezra, *The Coming of Messiah in Glory and Majesty*, translated from the Spanish, with a preliminary discourse by Edward Irving, vol. 1 (London: Seeley and Son, 1827).

published his first book on the futurist position entitled *An Enquiry into the Grounds on which the Prophetic Period of Daniel and St. John has been Supposed to Consist of 1260 Years*. In his work he refuted Mede's premise regarding the literal interpretation of the 1,260 days and further concluded that the pope could not be identified with the Antichrist since the Antichrist would deny both the Father and the Son—a position that the Roman Church never held.[49] Irving, on the other hand, held to a peculiar mix of premillennial historicism and futurism. In 1825 Irving used his growing popularity to commence a series of discourses on prophecy in his crowded church.[50] In 1827 he published a translation of a treatise in Spanish, written by the Chilean Jesuit, Manuel Lacunza entitled *The Coming of Messiah in Glory and Majesty*. According to Irving the book showed the error of the opinion that Christ is not to come until the end of the millennium. Instead he argued the present age would come to a close with the second advent, which would precede the millennium.[51] In a letter to the Reverend Edward Probym dated 10 November 1831, Irving wrote concerning a recent gathering in his home where those present spoke about the reign of Christ upon the earth which would be "for ever and ever."[52] Irving was not concerned to follow popular views. Tim Grass remarks in *The Lord's Watchman: A Life of Edward Irving (1732-1834)* that he always looked down on ministers who merely reflected popular views instead of challenging and stretching their congregations. He also always felt a sense of distance between himself and the outlook of contemporary Evangelicals.[53]

Timothy Stunt has suggested that at some point in 1827 or 1828 Darby read Irving's translation of Launza's celebrated work. Alfred-Félix Vaucher asserts wittily that if the Plymouth Brethren had been in the habit of citing their sources, Lacunza's name would have frequently occurred in their writings.[54] But it is extremely difficult to find the source of Darby's ideas. Larry Crutchfield in *The Origins of Dispensationalism: The Darby Factor* (1992)

49. Burnham, *A Story of Conflict*, 108.

50. Murray, *The Puritan Hope*, 189.

51. David W. Bebbington, *The Dominance of Evangelicalism: The Age of Spurgeon and Moody* (Leicester: Inter-varsity Press, 2005) 179.

52. Barbara Waddington, ed., *The Dairy and Letters of Edward Irving* (Eugene, OR: Pickwick, 2012) 286.

53. Tim Grass, *The Lord's Watchman: A Life of Edward Irving (1732-1834)* (Eugene, OR: Pickwick, 2012) 25.

54. Timothy C. F. Stunt, "Influences in the Early Development of J. N. Darby," in Crawford Gribben and Timothy C. F. Stunt, eds., *Prisoners of Hope? Aspects of Evangelical Millennialism in Britain and Ireland, 1800-1880* (Waynesboro, GA: Paternoster, 2004) 57.

states that there is little doubt that Darby borrowed ideas and profited from other sources. It is also true that he examined these ideas under the light of Scripture.[55] Whatever his sources, it is clear that his two pamphlets in 1829 and 1830 indicate that he had not yet totally committed to a futurist premillennial position.[56] Iain Murray notes that all the salient features of Darby's scheme are to be found in Irving including the expectation of impending judgments upon Christendom, the imminence of Christ's advent, and his consequent millennial reign upon earth.[57] In his assertion, Murray misses what was most distinctive of Darby—the pre-tribulation rapture. Nevertheless, others such as Ernest Sandeen agree with Murray that Irving had substantial influence upon early nineteenth-century millennialism. But Irving came to the end of his life in 1834 as an outcast among the millennial party—his name turned into a term of reproach among evangelicals.[58] Irving's final years were replete with controversy and heresy charges unrelated to his eschatological opinions. Mark Patterson and Andrew Walker attempt to demonstrate that essential elements of the doctrine of the pre-tribulation Rapture of the saints were first formulated by Irving and the Albury Prophecy Conferences and then disseminated through their journal *The Morning Watch*.[59] This journal, coupled with historical realities regarding both Irving and Darby suggest that Irving, not Darby as is usually asserted, was the true originator of the prophetic premillennial school known as Dispensationalism. The truth of this assertion is still being debated.[60]

The historical links between the origins of the Brethren and the excitement created by Irving's futurist teachings were evident in Darby as he emerged from the Powerscourt conferences. The developing Brethren movement identified with Darby's opinion that world history could be divided into distinct eras called "dispensations." Each dispensation was to

---

55. Larry V. Crutchfield, *The Origins of Dispensationalism: The Darby Factor* (Lanham, MD: University Press of America, 1992) 17.

56. Stunt, "Influences in the Early Development of J. N. Darby," 56–58.

57. Murray, *The Puritan Hope*, 200.

58. Sandeen, *The Roots of Fundamentalism*, 14.

59. *The Morning Watch* (or, *The Quarterly Journal of Prophecy and Theological Review*) was published between March 1829 and June 1833. The journal was published in London by Henry Drummond and Edward Irving. The periodical focused on interpretations of biblical prophecy and its fulfillment. See John S. North and Brent Nelson, eds., *Waterloo Directory of English Newspapers and Periodicals: 1800–1900* (Waterloo: North Waterloo Academic, 2003).

60. Mark Patterson and Andrew Walker, "Our Unspeakable Comfort: Irving, Albury, and the Origins of the Pre-tribulation Rapture," in Stephen Hunt, ed., *Christian Millennialism: From the Early Church to Waco* (Bloomington: Indiana University Press, 2001) 99–100.

be characterized by the way that God dealt with humanity. For the present dispensation—the church age—the believer was to understand that it would soon terminate in the calamitous event described in Revelation as the "great tribulation." A highly debatable issue in the Victorian age, Darby believed that the church would be called away into the air to meet Christ and that the so called "rapture" could occur at any moment.[61] This position was widely held by premillennialists but Darby never sought to build upon it or to articulate the Rapture in greater depth. This became an area of disagreement for Govett who would write in some detail about their differences. According to Govett, there was to be a "partial" Rapture made up of only those Christians who worked to receive the "heavenly prize" (Philippians 3:14). This distinction not only separated Govett from Darby, but as this study will demonstrate, by the turn of the twentieth century from the mainstream of "dispensationalism."

In addition to Darby's developing eschatological views, his views regarding Christ occasionally brought about debate. In this regard the question of Christ's "imputed righteousness" surfaced in Darby's writings. Govett was one who strongly disagreed with the Brethren in general, and Darby in particular, on this doctrine. Govett argued for the traditional protestant view that believers are justified by the imputation of the righteousness of Christ— a view which contrasted the general opinions among Brethren that believers are justified by the righteousness of God. Darby's numerous publications occasionally lent themselves as lighting rods for controversy and debate. For example, Govett, in 1864 published a work entitled, *The Righteousness of Christ, the Righteousness of God. A Refutation of the Views Generally Held by the Christians Commonly Known Called Plymouth Brethren on that Subject*.[62] The journal *The Voice Upon the Mountain* reviewed the booklet in its December 1868 issue but declined to take a stand on any side of the issues mentioned in Govett's booklet—admitting that much has already been written and "much heat stirred up" and strong words expressed on all sides. The argument in Govett's booklet is presented in reply to Darby's writings. The reviewer admits to seeing truth expressed on each side, but concludes with, "We can have no hesitation in saying, that the book is written with Mr. Govett's usual ability; but we refrain from giving an opinion as between him and Mr. Darby."[63] Implications connected with dispensationalism surfaced

61. Bebbington, *The Dominance of Evangelicalism*, 185–86.

62. Robert Govett, *The Righteousness of Christ, the Righteousness of God. A Refutation of the Views Generally Held by the Christians Commonly Known Called Plymouth Brethren on that Subject* (London: Stock, 1864).

63. *The Voice upon the Mountains. A Journal of Prophetic Testimony and Evangelistic Effort* 2 (1868) 162.

in other issues as well. For example, futurists, and particularly dispensationalists, generally regarded politics as a perilous snare.[64]

As the Brethren movement grew and Darby's popularity spread through his increasing list of publications it became accepted in the minds of his followers that he was the undeniable founder of Brethrenism. He was its energizing spirit but there were those who disputed Darby's rightful designation as founder and originator of the Brethren doctrines. One who is not given proper credit for his influence upon the infancy of the movement was William [de] Burgh (1801–1866), a graduate of Trinity College, Dublin, later a lecturer at Trinity, who was the same age as Darby.[65] Burgh was highly regarded among the circle associated with Darby. It was tempting from the beginning to give undue credit to Darby for developing the positions of the Brethren. William Kelly (1821–1906), also a Trinity College graduate and close friend and admirer of Darby, gives enthusiastic credit to Darby in his booklet entitled *God's Principle of Unity*.[66] Frederick Whitfield (1827–1904), a Trinity College graduate and hymn-writer who was associated with the Brethren, published a very critical reply to Kelly's booklet in an effort to correct the perception it had created. In response Whitfield notes that Burgh was first to receive "these grand and glorious truths," and that "his books were purchased, and literally devoured by the Brethren." He continues, "here then was the first dawning of the light, and not where Mr. Kelly places it."[67]

---

64. Bebbington, *The Dominance of Evangelicalism*, 187. Bebbington uses Govett as an illustration of one who held strong opinions concerning the effect of politics upon a Christian's spiritual life. See *Baptist Magazine* (July 1868) 461–64. See also Robert Govett, *The Christian and Politics* (Norwich: Fletcher, 1850). But Bebbington incorrectly suggests that Govett "embraced" Darby's doctrine. There is no evidence that Govett was directly influenced by the Brethren or Darby. Bebbington also incorrectly identifies Govett as a Baptist minister. It is occasionally suggested by others as well that Govett pastored a Baptist church. He did not. Govett remained a non-denominational dissenter from the point in time that he left the Church of England in 1844. Surrey Chapel, Norwich, remains non-denominational to this day. See also A. D. Bayne, *A Comprehensive History of Norwich: Including a Survey of the City and its Public Buildings* (London: Jarrold and Sons, 1869) 720. Surrey Road Chapel is incorrectly listed there as a Baptist church in Norwich.

65. For William [de] Burgh's dates see A. P. Burke, ed., *A Genealogical and Heraldic History of the Landed Gentry of Ireland*, by Sir Bernard Burke, 9th ed. (London: Harrison, 1899).

66. William Kelly [signed WK], *God's Principle of Unity* (London: Morrish, n.d.).

67. Timothy Stunt remarks that there appears to be no extant copy of Frederick Whitfield's *The Plymouth Brethren A Letter to Rev. Osmond Dobree, B.A., Guernsey, Containing Strictures on Mr. William Kelly's Pamphlet Entitled "God's Principle of Unity"* (London: Shaw, 1863). The cited quotations are to be found in an extract from this "truthful and telling pamphlet" reproduced in *The Quarterly Journal of Prophecy* 15 (1863) 197. There is at least one piece of circumstantial evidence for the truth of

Yet, despite the many controversies surrounding Darby no one disputes the strength of his personality and the sway he exhibited upon those who would become the early leaders of the Brethren Movement.

Darby and the Oxford Movement

The Oxford Movement, or that of the Tractarian Movement as it is also known, typifies from another perspective the earnest struggle of religion and doctrine in the Victorian era. It had its origins in the early 1830s at the time Govett was attending Worcester College, Oxford. Its start is usually marked by John Keble (1792–1866) preaching his Assize Sermon at Oxford in 1833, followed thereafter by the movement's central publications, the *Tracts for the Times*. Much transpired prior to the twelve years of the existence of the Oxford Movement and much was the outcome, but the vast amount of scholarship pertaining to the history of the movement is not consistent in its emphasis. Owen Chadwick in *The Spirit of the Oxford Movement, Tractarian Essays* (1990) makes note of "a very striking thing— the people who resent it, or dislike it, or hate it, write their memoirs; the people who loved it and owed their soul to it and regarded it as the highest ideal of life they had ever known—are silent."[68] Overall, it would appear that the best manner in which to assess the movement is as a history of controversies. And while the origin of the Oxford Movement might be in doubt and much of what is known about the movement centers upon theology, its origins are viewed by some to remain decidedly political. Chadwick notes that it is "safe to say that the movement would not have taken the form

---

Whitfield's claim that Burgh's work was highly regarded among the Brethren. Thomas Lumisden Strange (1808–1884) who was still associated with the Plymouth Brethren in 1852, when he reviewed Elliott's *Horae Apocalyticae*, nowhere refers to the writings of Darby but alludes to his fellow futurists as "those who with myself follow Mr. Burgh in his able commentary on this subject." Thomas Lumisden Strange, *Observations on Mr. [E. B.] Elliott's Horae Apocalypticae: Offered towards Refutation of the Historical System of Interpreting the Apocalypse*, 2nd ed. (London: Campbell, 1852) 62. For the Brethren phase in Strange's own fascinating pilgrimage, see T. L. Strange, *How I Became and Ceased to Be a Christian* (London: Trübner, 1881) 11–12. See also Timothy Stunt, "Trinity College, John Nelson Darby and the Powerscourt Milieu," in Joshua Searle and Kenneth G. C. Newport, eds., *Beyond the End: The Future of Millennial Studies* (Sheffield: Sheffield Phoenix, 2012) esp. 64.

68. Owen Chadwick, *The Spirit of the Oxford Movement, Tractarian Essays* (Cambridge: Cambridge University Press, 1990) 137–38. See also Benjamin O'Connor, "An Introduction to the Oxford Movement," in Kenneth L. Parker, and Michael J. G. Pahls, eds., *Authority, Dogma, and History: The Role of the Oxford Movement Converts in the Papal Infallibility Debates* (Palo Alto: Academica, 2009) 12.

which it took without the impetus of ecclesiastical and secular politics."[69] Having said this he is also quick to note that the Oxford Movement was of great importance to the religion of the English, as well as to the Church of England itself and especially to the "high church group" which gave birth to the movement and transformed it over time.[70] And by the end of 1835, John Keble, Richard Froude, Edward Pusey, and John Newman were united in a mutual cause as friends with great fears and hopes for the future of their "party." It soon became organized around the able leadership of Pusey. Nevertheless, as Peter B. Nockles notes, many of the work on the movement have been focused on these four leaders and its historiography presupposes that the Oxford Movement represented a dominant group within Anglicanism from 1833 onward.[71]

In a tangential way Darby is also recognized as having a connection to the formative days of the movement. The start of the Oxford Movement was also the time of the Powerscourt conferences in Ireland, the early stages of development of Darby's futurist premillennial theology, and the beginning of his meetings with like-minded men in Dublin—men who would form the nucleus and early development of the Brethren Movement. While Darby and other key figures in the Brethren Movement had decidedly moved away from the Established Church, it was also experiencing a profound internal debate that sought to reshape its priorities. One of the men who became a close associate to Darby, Benjamin Wills Newton (1807–1899), also holds a place of importance among a group of radical evangelicals at Oxford who opposed the Oxford Movement.[72] Much is documented about the events which took place between Newton's entrance into Exeter College in 1824 and the actual beginning of the Oxford Movement in 1833. Unlike the struggle between the Church of England and the dissenters, or the eschatological historicists against the futurists, or the place of the emerging Dispensationalists in contrast to Reformed theology, the Oxford Movement sought to engage in a battle against the state on political grounds. And if there was a "first shot fired" it most likely came from the Reform Act of 1832. Even with its good intent its result was to weaken the Tory traditions upon which ecclesiastical authority politically rested. It became politically necessary that the clergy of the Church of England should look to leaders who would declare that the authority of the church rested not upon the state, but upon

69. Chadwick, *The Spirit of the Oxford Movement*, 2.

70. Ibid., 1.

71. Peter B. Nockles, *The Oxford Movement in Context: Anglican High Churchmanship 1760–1857* (Cambridge: Cambridge University Press, 1994) 2.

72. Timothy C. F. Stunt, *From Awakening to Secession: Radical Evangelicals in Switzerland and Britain 1815–35* (Edinburgh: T. & T. Clark, 2000) 194.

divine authority—upon the bishop or the vicar whose authority came from apostolic commission. Even if the church were disestablished, even if there were a complete separation between church and state, the church would still have a claim upon the allegiance of Englishmen because the church was the commissioned agent of Christ and his apostles to the people of England.[73] But a political impetus does not create religious thought. It gives opportunity and purpose, and created a sense of outrage that was especially acute. In this heightened environment Darby emerged.

It was in 1830 when Darby arrived at Oxford to give a series of lectures. It is reported that Newton, among numerous others, fell under the spell of his compelling personality.[74] William Kelly recounted some years later the impact on the lives of those present during Darby's visit with the words of Wigram, "may he give me to follow and serve Him at all cost!"[75] The events of the previous years, including the opposition of the authorities to certain aspects of evangelical piety, the increased fascinations with prophecy, and heightened high-churchmanship served to prepare for the arrival of Darby and the success of his message. Timothy Stunt notes that the formal break with Newton and the Establishment did not occur for some time, but there can be little doubt that Darby's personality played a decisive part in drawing Newton and others at a later stage into another ecclesiastical connection, "especially at Plymouth."[76]

All that has been mentioned occurred at a time when Great Britain was embarking on a new era marked by the 63-year reign of Queen Victoria that began in 1837. It was marked by a period in British history that also saw the rise of agnosticism and religious doubt. New challenges surfaced in part by conventional religious tenets being confronted by scientific breakthroughs and Charles Darwin's theory of evolution. Simultaneously, a number of skilled and prolific theological writers emerged in the Victorian era. And while Victorian society witnessed a new resurgence of evangelicalism it also ushered in debate over doctrines of original sin and the four last things. A great deal of turbulence was brewing beneath the surface of Victorian society. Traditional religious beliefs were contested leading to the emergence of a number of ideas surrounding new theological interpretations. Struggles within the Established Church continued to lead to wider issues of dissent and had implications extending beyond the discipline of

---

73. Owen Chadwick, *The Mind of the Oxford Movement* (Stanford: Stanford University Press, 1960) 13.

74. Stunt, *From Awakening to Secession*, 218.

75. W. G. Turner, *John Nelson Darby* (London: Hammond, 1944) 70.

76. Stunt, *From Awakening to Secession*, 219.

church history. Thoughts soon found their expression in the explosion of print culture with the proliferation of prophetic journals and novels which reflected the religious mood of the nation.

Romanticism

David Bebbington in *The Dominance of Evangelicalism: The Age of Spurgeon and Moody* acknowledges that it is often recognized that the Romantic spirit affected religion.[77] For example, Mary Hermann writes that many of the trends of the Roman Catholic Church had Romantic proclivities.[78] In the Church of England the Oxford Movement of the 1830s was also thought to have a Romantic influence and one of its leaders, John Henry Newman, was said to acknowledge his debt to Sir Walter Scott, a Romantic Prose writer of some renown.[79] What is not widely understood is that Romantic leanings strongly affected the evangelical movement, so much so that by the middle of the nineteenth century there were significant numbers of Evangelicals professing ideas with a distinctly Romantic influence. Edward Irving was preeminent among them. Simultaneously, John Nelson Darby was formulating doctrine under Romantic influence.[80] Still, as Bernard M. Reardon points out, any discussion of the Romantic movement will soon be faced with the problem of definition because romanticism, like religion itself, is notoriously difficult to define. Nevertheless, there can be no real question but that the first four decades of the nineteenth century constitute a romantic era. To a greater or lesser degree, so was the entire century part of the Romantic era.[81] Reardon further remarks:

> The variety and multiformity of Romantic thought and art are manifest. The Romantic scene, historically speaking, is immensely colorful and invariably fascinating to observe; but it is appallingly cluttered—a treasure-house in disorder. Can we venture to say that behind all this teeming confusion there are principles which, when grasped, yield us coherence, a true pattern of consistency?[82]

77. Bebbington, *The Dominance of Evangelicalism*, 149.

78. Mary Hermann, *Catholic Devotion in Victorian England* (Oxford: Clarendon, 1995) 142.

79. Bernard M. G. Reardon, *Religious Thought in the Victorian Age: A Study from Coleridge to Gore* (London: Longman, 1980) 92–93.

80. Bebbington, *The Dominance of Evangelicalism*, 151.

81. Reardon, *Religious Thought in the Victorian Age*, 1–2.

82. Ibid., 2.

The central theme in the history of Evangelical theology from the 1820s onward is its attempt to come to terms with the impact of Romanticism. Romanticism replaced the Enlightenment's stress on reason with an emphasis on will and emotion.[83] At the same time, the understanding of a static universe operating according to a set of fixed laws began to yield to an understanding of a world of change.[84] The most significant early adoption of an aspect of Romantic thought by the religious community was by Evangelicals in the area of eschatology. Probably the most significant of Edward Irving accomplishments was on the topic of the Second Advent. In 1827 he translated the work of a Chilean Jesuit which he titled *The Coming of Messiah in Glory and Mystery*. The work predicted the imminent personal return of Christ which was a belief that, at the time, was not widely held among Evangelicals. Irving abandoned the post-millennialism views held by his contemporaries, arguing instead that Christ would usher in the millennium and would reign upon the earth. Such a premillennial view appealed to the Romantic notion of the dramatic and spread among Evangelicals as the century progressed. A version of Irving's eschatological teachings was dispensationalism which was disseminated by John Nelson Darby who viewed the church as a divine insertion in the divided periods of world history. He believed the church would soon be caught up to meet the Lord in the air.[85]

It is said that the essence of romanticism lies in the feeling that the finite is not self-explanatory and self-justifying, but that behind it and within it there is always an infinite beyond, and that "he who has once glimpsed the infinity that permeates as well as transcends all finitude can never again rest content with the paltry this-and-that, the rationalized simplicities, of everyday life."[86] In Romantic thought there is the repeated coincidence of the finite and the infinite. For instance, William Wordsworth wrote in *The Excursion*: For I must tread on shadowy ground, must sink/Deep, and aloft ascending breathe in worlds/To which the heaven of heavens is but a veil.[87] Likewise, Wordsworth writes in the 1850 version of *The Prelude*: Faith in life endless, the sustaining thought/Of human being, eternity and God.[88] Reardon notes that although the Romantic spirit longs for ultimate reconciliation and peace it is won only out of ceaseless striving

83. David W. Bebbington, "Evangelicalism," in David Fergusson, ed., *The Blackwell Companion to Nineteenth-Century Theology* (Chichester: Wiley-Blackwell, 2010) 244.

84. David W. Bebbington, "Evangelicalism," 244.

85. Ibid., 245.

86. Reardon, *Religious Thought in the Victorian Age*, 3.

87. William Wordsworth, *The Excursion* (London: Moxon, 1836) xii.

88. William Wordsworth, *The Prelude*, in *The Complete Poetical Works of William Wordsworth* (Boston: Houghton Mifflin, 1919) 3:315.

and struggle.[89] The Romantic understanding of Christianity incorporates the idea that eternal life has to be understood to be lived here and now. Eternity itself is a dimension of the present order of things. Basic Christian values are seen as rooted in this world. Jesus Christ is to be viewed as the man in whom all men may see their own idealized reflection.[90] To this end, Govett methodically wrote of the importance of integrating a clear comprehension of the future promise of reward, the Coming Kingdom, eternal life, and to the premillennial return of Jesus—all of which were to be understood as a dimension of the present order of life. Life was to be lived with a goal toward the attainment of these eventual realities. Govett taught that the soon return of the Lord was to be rehearsed each day in the mind and life of every believer.

Victorians and the Last Things

Eschatology was a highly controversial subject in the Victorian age as the religious tracts and numerous periodicals reveal. Michael Wheeler writes that the absence of definitive and coherent teaching on judgment, heaven, and hell in the New Testament led to a wide range of doctrinal positions, each based upon a few individual texts that were defended on sectarian lines. His contention is widely evident in the large collection of theological writings of the day. However, it was generally not the case that evangelical defenses of judgment, heaven, and hell referred to only a few biblical texts. Govett, as later chapters in this study affirm, drew upon a particularly wide range of biblical references in his articulation of these themes. Adding to the confusion surrounding the debates over doctrinal issues was the introduction of Higher Criticism which brought into question claims of the New Testament concerning the future life. This reopened the debate on the nature of religious belief and some of its key questions among theologians and secular writers. The concern increasingly became how to find a discourse that could convey an idea of the transcendent in an increasingly scientific-materialistic world.[91] As such, between the late eighteenth and the mid-nineteenth centuries the sciences, including geology, paleontology, and zoology opened up a vast and unfamiliar history of the earth, of the animal kingdom, and the human race itself. According to James C. Livingston, the coming of the Darwinian revolution and the cumulative force of all these sciences

---

89. Reardon, *Religious Thought in the Victorian Age*, 5.
90. Ibid., 10–11.
91. Wheeler, *Death and the Future Life*, xii.

transformed the vision of humanity's place in natural history.[92] Yet, despite such a world, the Bible still loomed uniquely large in Victorian culture. For example, the Bible continued to be the fundamental textbook in schools and the source through which people gained basic literacy skills. Children learned to read in Sunday schools and other religiously sponsored venues. The Bible was also central to Victorian literature. Timothy Larsen writes that there are only two kinds of eminent Victorian authors—the kind who have had a whole book written about their use of Scripture and the kind who are ripe for such attention.[93] Charles Dickens (1812–1870) serves as a reminder that the centrality of the Bible in the Victorian age is abundantly revealed in its literature. In his final will, Dickens urged his offspring not to be bound by any dogmatic scheme but to take their rule of life directly from the New Testament.[94] In the wake of Scriptures holding a central place in Victorian culture their preoccupation with death, judgment, heaven, and hell continued to dominate British literature as well as the arts.

Deathbed scenes were a familiar convention to the Victorians, not only in their prose, but also in their narrative and lyric poetry.[95] The deathbed also helped to form a transitional link with the "bed" that is the grave, and the "intermediate state" between the moment of death and the last judgment.[96] Of course, a distinction must be drawn between the deathbed scenes depicted in Victorian fiction and the complexities of the theological battles regarding the end-times which took place in the religious periodicals. Nevertheless, the subject of death and dying was quite prevalent in the culture of the day. For example, Edward Bickersteth, in 1863, making frequent use of the image of "sleep," wrote that the intermediate state is the period between the death of the saint and the second coming.[97] Govett also references the imagery of sleep and its connection with the Second Coming of Christ in his commentary on First and Second Thessalonians. He references 1 Thes-

---

92. James C. Livingston, *Religious Thought in the Victorian Age: Challenges and Reconceptions* (London: T. & T. Clark, 2006) 150.

93. Timothy Larsen, *A People of One Book: The Bible and the Victorians* (Oxford: Oxford University Press, 2011) 2.

94. Ibid., 3–4.

95. The writings of Garrett Stewart are excellent examples of the Victorian themes of death, dying, bereavement, and mourning. See Garrett Steward, *Dickens and the Trials of Imagination* (Cambridge MA: Harvard University Press, 1974); Garrett Stewart, *Death Sentences: Styles of Dying in British Fiction* (Cambridge, MA: Harvard University Press, 1984); Garrett Stewart, *Novel Violence: A Narratography of Victorian Fiction* (Chicago: University of Chicago Press, 2009).

96. Wheeler, *Death and the Future Life*, 70.

97. E. H. Bickersteth, *The Blessed Dead: What Does Scripture Reveal of their State before the Resurrection?*, 2nd ed. (London: Shaw, 1863) 12.

salonians 4:16 regarding "the dead in Christ rising first" at Christ's Second Coming and states, "Theirs [believers] then, is not a descent from heaven with Christ into air. They are *sleeping* [italics his], and with a shout Christ *wakes them*, as he did Lazarus."[98] For both Bickersteth and Govett, lying in the grave did not represent the final state of the body. However, numerous other variations of understanding of the intermediate state were also being developed, as well as the different kinds of anticipations of the collective future that were characterized by millennialism and judgment. These represented events many Victorians believed to be imminent and which were represented in fiction, poetry, and the visual arts.

A sense of urgency was developing which was reflected in the writings of poets such as Matthew Arnold. Along with Tennyson and Browning, his work was regarded as preeminent among Victorian poets. Nevertheless, Arnold prided himself more for his work as a religious critic than for his poetry.[99] The developing urgency was also found in the visual arts. Ushering in the subject in the decades immediately preceding the Victorian age was the artist John Martin (1789–1854). Several of his paintings represented the apocalypse.[100] For instance, Martin's *The Destruction of Pompeii and Herculaneum* was the subject of a poem by his friend Edwin Atherstone, as well as Edward Bulwer's novel, *The Last Days of Pompeii*. Furthermore, Martin's *The Fall of Nineveh* appeared in the first of six books of a poem by Atherstone, and Martin's *The Last Man*, in this pre-Victorian era, was preceded by literary works on the same subject by Thomas Campbell and Mary Shelley.[101] Thomas Campbell's poems often used the metaphor of death such as in *The Last Man* and *The River of Life*.[102] Mary Shelly, likely wrote her apocalyptic novel of a future world ravaged by a plague, *The Last Man* (1826),[103] from her own experiences with death. Shelley's mother died when she was eleven

---

98. Robert Govett, *The Presence of Christ in its Effects on the Church and the World: Being the Argument of the Epistles to the Thessalonians, with Notice of Dr. Bullinger's Theory of the Hinderers, and Dr. Eadie on the First Resurrection* (Norwich: Fletcher and Son, 1893) 57.

99. James C. Livingston, *Matthew Arnold and Christianity: His Religious Prose Writings* (Columbia: University of South Carolina Press, 1986) ix.

100. See Michael J. Campbell, *John Martin, 1789–1854: Creation of Light* (Madrid: Royal Academy of Fine Arts, 2006).

101. Wheeler, *Death and the Future Life*, 84–85.

102. Thomas Campbell, *The Complete Poetical Works of Thomas Campbell, with A Memoir of His Life* (Boston: Phillips, Sampson, 1857).

103. Mary Shelley, *The Last Man: In Three Volumes* (London: Colburn, 1826).

days old. She lost three children before she gave birth to her last and only surviving child. Her husband later drowned while sailing.[104]

In his abridged work *Heaven, Hell and the Victorian* (1994), Wheeler asserts that Tennyson's *In Memoriam* (1850) was the most important poem of the Victorian period on the subject of death and the future life.[105] Dickens also writes on the subject in his novel *Our Mutual Friend* (1864), with a central theme of rebirth and resurrection. For example, the River Thames, and repeated references to water, become part of a major theme of rebirth and renewal. Water is seen as a sign of new life.[106] To a certain extent this theme is also apparent in his work *Great Expectations* through Pip's pursuit of identity and homecoming.[107]

One significant reason for the Victorian's fascination with death and the after-life was due to the death rate. Cholera epidemics were often devastating. In 1840 the annual death rate per 1,000 persons in England and Wales was 22.9; by 1880 it had fallen to 20.5, and in 1900 it was still 18.2; by 1935 it had decreased to 11.7. In 1840 there were 154 infants under a year old who died out of 1,000 live births, and this figure remained fairly constant until 1900.[108] Grief at the death of a beloved family member was traumatic for both unbeliever and believer alike. Pat Jalland notes that the difference between the two was that Christians trusted that their faith offered consolation and hope of a future life. This stemmed from a belief in the resurrection of the body and Christ's promise of life after death. Many Victorian Christians extended this doctrine to mean that they would be reunited with their departed family and friends in heaven.[109]

Death was a primary concern of evangelical theology. Evangelical revival had influenced the "ideal" of the deathbed scene in the first half of the nineteenth century. Thousand of tracts and journals attested to the

---

104. See Anne K. Mellor, *Mary Shelley: Her Life, Herr Fiction, Her Monsters* (New York: Methuen, 1988).

105. Michael Wheeler, *Heaven, Hell and the Victorians*, abridged ed. of *Death and the Future Life in Victorian Literature and Theology* (Cambridge: Cambridge University Press, 1994) 2.

106. See Charles Dickens, *Our Mutual Friend* (Chicago: Belford, Clarke, 1884).

107. See Charles Dickens, *Great Expectations: Volume 1* (New York: Gregory, 1861).

108. Geoffrey Rowell, *Hell and the Victorians; a Study of the Nineteenth-Century Theological Controversies Concerning Eternal Punishment and the Future Life* (Oxford: Clarendon, 1974) 12. See also Anthony C. Thiselton, *Life and Death: A New Approach to the Last Things* (Grand Rapids: Eerdmans, 2012); Douglas Davies, *Theology of Death* (London: T. & T. Clark, 2008).

109. Pat Jalland, *Death in the Victorian Family* (Oxford: Oxford University Press, 1996) 265.

zeal to save souls by showing people how to die.[110] At the heart of the evangelical death scene was the traditional belief that most people were doomed at death to eternal physical punishment in hell. But for the non-evangelical Christian, belief in a literal interpretation of hell diminished during the nineteenth century, while evangelicals continued to produce popular literature on the perpetual punishment awaiting the damned.[111] Govett was one such evangelical. His writings routinely warned of the consequence of life without Christ.

Memoirs of the life and death of a recently deceased evangelical Christian were typically included at the front of the early issues of the monthly *Evangelical Magazine*[112] published between 1793 and 1893. The *Christian Guardian and Church of England Magazine* (1809–1849),[113] as in the *Evangelical Magazine*, opened with a six-page memoir which extolled the virtues of deceased clergy–usually those who died in the seventeenth century and represented a period of greater piety.[114] Yet, despite the vast attention paid by the British in their literature and arts on the four last things, by the middle of the century some Victorians had shifted their attention to new-found doubts about the Christian faith. Many scholars have written on the subject of this so called "crisis of faith," (sometimes referred to as the "loss-of-faith") noting that it permeated society at every level. But the subject is complex with recent scholarship emphasizing a resurgence of faith over its decline. Timothy Larsen notes that the nineteenth-century crisis of faith is a motif that has become vastly overblown. There was a crisis of faith, but its sense of proportion is often lost.[115] This study will address some of

---

110. Jalland, *Death in the Victorian Family*, 21.

111. Ibid.

112. The *Evangelical Magazine* was published under that name until 1812. After that date the name was changed to the *Evangelical Magazine and Missionary Chronicle* until 1893. It then was published under the name *The British Missionary* until 1966. It was a leading Dissenter and Evangelical publication which enjoyed the widest circulation of any religious miscellany. See John S. North, and Brent Nelson, eds., *Waterloo Directory of English Newspapers and Periodicals: 1800–1900* (Waterloo: North Waterloo Academic, 2003).

113. *The Christian Guardian and Church of England Magazine* was first published as *The Christian Guardian; a Theological Miscellany* from 1802 to 1808. Its stated purpose was to disseminate the knowledge of genuine Christianity among those persons, whose "necessary engagements in worldly business deprive them of leisure for the perusal of larger compositions." See John S. North, and Brent Nelson, eds., *Waterloo Directory of English Newspapers and Periodicals: 1800-1900* (Waterloo: North Waterloo Academic, 2003).

114. Jalland, *Death in the Victorian Family*, 22.

115. Timothy Larsen, *Crisis of Doubt, Honest Faith in Nineteenth-Century England* (Oxford, Oxford University Press, 2006) 1. See also Joss Marsh, *Word Crimes:*

its complexities in a later section on Victorian doubt. Still scholars such as Frank M. Turner have emphasized a crisis of faith in their writings. Turner draws attention to political reaction, denominational rivalry, and evangelicalism as the underlying causes for this crisis and states that "these forces of intensified religiosity sowed the dragon's teeth that generated the soldiers of unbelief."[116] Krishen L. Kalla writes that, "The *Origin of the Species* by Charles Darwin, destroyed the old theological conception of God which bishop Paley taught. Fitzgerald, Clough, J. Thomson and Matthew Arnold wrote of their loss of faith. George Eliot's "unbelief," the atheism of Charles Bradlaugh, the agnosticism of Huxley, Leslie Stephen, John Morley and W. K. Clifford are all too obvious incidents of the age."[117] Still others discovered, or rediscovered, their faith. One such person of note was William Hone, an English writer, satirist and bookseller known mostly for his victorious court battle against government censorship in 1817. He spent most of his life as a writer of religious doubt but late in life experienced a full-fledged conversion of faith. He writes in a letter to a friend, which appeared in print after his death, "It has pleased the Almighty to have dealings with me for several years, until, by His Holy Spirit, I have been brought from darkness to light; to know Him, through faith in Christ."[118]

Leading up to the mid-century, religion offered considerable solace to a majority of people. But evidence of its erosion in the three or four decades after 1860 was for some a crisis born of the polarizing oppositions between science and faith, naturalism and supernaturalism, order and chaos.[119] The public read novels of faith and doubt in which science was but one force which drove some readers toward unbelief.

Historical research, biblical criticism, and philosophical speculation also contributed to this cultural movement. *Robert Elsmere* (1888), a novel by Mrs. Humphry Ward (Mary Augusta Ward) remains one of the most notable novels of the time on faith and doubt. Ward writes, "Evolution—once a germ in the mind—was beginning to press, to encroach, to intermeddle with the

---

Blasphemy, Culture, and Literature in Nineteenth-Century England (Chicago: University of Chicago Press, 1998).

116. Frank M. Turner, "The Victorian Crisis of Faith and the Faith That Was Lost," in Richard J. Helmstadter and Bernard Lightman, eds., *Victorian Faith in Crisis: Essays on Continuity and Change in Nineteenth-century Religious Belief* (Stanford: Stanford University Press, 1990), 14.

117. Krishen L. Kalla, *The Mid-Victorian Literature and Loss of Faith* (New Delhi: Mittal, 1989) 3.

118. William Hone, "The Late Mr. William Hone," *Notes and Queries*, vol.93 (August 1851) 106.

119. K. Theodore Hoppen, *The Mid-Victorian Generation 1846–1886* (Oxford: Oxford University Press, 1998) 502.

mind's furniture."[120] Yet, Timothy Larsen cautiously notes that while there was a crisis of doubt in the Victorian Secularist movement,[121] far more Secularist leaders became Christians than Christian ministers became skeptics. Larsen contends that so much attention has been paid to the lives and thought of figures who lost their faith that the intellectual cogency of Christianity for many Victorians has been obscured. He writes, "Victorians who had fully imbibed, and indeed widely disseminated, all the latest ideas from German biblical criticism to Darwinism yet who ultimately came to the conviction that faith was more intellectually compelling than doubt."[122]

This emerging crisis of faith (or doubt) was clearly on Govett's mind when he wrote a letter on 5 December 1872, addressed to his "brethren in Christ." He writes, "The days are darkening around us,—the evil days of which the Scriptures gives us warning. Faith seems to be dying out in many hearts." And then he adds, "Against this sad state of soul, the remedy taught us by the Holy Ghost, is constant exhortation."[123] While Govett as author and preacher saw this apparent crisis he did not capitulate to it. Govett took his own advice of a remedy and spent his life in "constant exhortation"—both in his sermons and his published writings. His letter ends with an admonition to labor to enter into the rest to come, because "dangers encompass us" and the loss of the promised heavenly rest is "fearfully possible." Govett was referring to the "Millennial Kingdom" which he believed Christ would usher in at his Second Coming. To combat the dangers which encompassed the Victorian Christian meant—for Govett—an habitual working to gain a future salvation. Govett understood that Scripture spoke of two kinds of salvation. In *The Believer's Standing in Grace and Under Responsibility; or Sins Before Faith and Sins After Faith* (1872), Govett traces the New Testament mention of the two salvations. The first is that which is possessed already by faith, and which ends assuredly in everlasting life as described in Ephesians chapter 2. But Govett finds that there is a future salvation which "looks onward to the day of Christ's appearing" to possess it. Because of this distinction, and because of the dangers of falling away

---

120. Hoppen, *The Mid-Victorian Generation*, 504.

121. See Edward Royle, *Victorian Infidels: The Origins of the British Secularist Movement, 1791–1866* (Manchester: Manchester University Press, 1974); Edward Royle, *Radicals, Secularists and Republicans: Popular Free Thought in Britain, 1866–1915* (Manchester: Manchester University Press, 1980).

122. Larsen, *Crisis of Doubt*, vii.

123. Robert Govett, *Seek the Sabbath Rest to Come* (Norwich: Fletcher and Son, 1872). This tract began as a pastoral letter to a "brethren in Christ," written from Clevedon on 5 December 1872—presumably while on holiday. The tract was later combined with several others and published by Schoettle Publishing in 1989, under the title *Reward According to Works*.

from the faith which, leads to its forfeiture, Govett admonishes the believer to "work out your own salvation with fear and trembling."[124] Throughout his life he persevered with his message of pursuing the second salvation. The reason appears to be clear, that he was keenly aware of the dangerous times of faith in which he was living. In his commentary on the Gospel of John he asks these questions: "Why are the masses slipping away?" "Why will they not come to church and chapel?" He laments that many will come out to hear some novelty, and most seem to think that the great evil of the day is religious ignorance. But Govett is mindful of the rich religious heritage of the Victorians, and concludes that the crisis of faith confronting the Victorians is not knowledge. Rather it is the natural tendency of man choosing to go on in sin.[125]

Govett labored all his life to warn Victorians against this natural tendency toward sin. By example, he exhibited a life of deep theological convictions. His was a life steeped from birth in religious heritage. He was born into a long line of Anglican preachers which began with his great-grandfather, William Romaine, the prominent evangelical preacher and friend of John Wesley and George Whitefield. As we have already noticed, Govett had been educated at Oxford, ordained into the Church of England but shortly thereafter when at odds with the church's stance on infant baptism, stood upon his convictions and was promptly removed from the church by his bishop. But, although labeled a dissenter he was able to find common ground among evangelical believers. It is also important to restate that his convictions concerning eschatological doctrines were based upon scholarly study of the Bible and were presented boldly in his writings. These attributes made him a favorite contributor of a wide array of religious journals. And while more than a few editors admitted to disagreeing with him on some of his theological positions, he was frequently respected for the care with which he approached his arguments.

---

124. Robert Govett, *The Believer's Standing in Grace and Under Responsibility; or Sins Before Faith and Sins After Faith* (Norwich: Fletcher and Son, 1872) 34.

125. Robert Govett, *Exposition of the Gospel of St. John, vol. I–II* (London: Bemrose and Sons, 1881) 1:116–17.

CHAPTER 2

Govett's Life in Context

ROBERT GOVETT HAS BECOME lost among an impressive list of nineteenth-century British divines. While scholarship on the period continues to expand, producing voluminous writings on more recognizable figures like that of John Nelson Darby and movements like that of the Brethren, Govett and others of note have been relegated to the margins of church history. Nevertheless, the nineteenth-century evidence, when more closely examined, reveals Robert Govett's importance within the religious history of Britain.

Govett's Beginnings (1813–1833)

Robert Govett was born on 14 February 1813, in Staines, Middlesex. He was the eldest child born to Robert Govett, Sr and Sarah Romaine.[1] Sarah was an only child of William and Martha Romaine. She grew up in a privileged home, the granddaughter of William Romaine (1714–1795), the renowned eighteenth-century evangelical clergyman in the Church of England. Her father, William Romaine, Jr, was also an Anglican clergyman. Likewise, her husband, Robert, Sr, was an Anglican clergyman who became the vicar of Staines—serving in that parish for forty-nine years until his death at the age of seventy-eight.[2] No record of Sarah's date of death remains,[3] but she most likely predeceased her husband and died in

---

1. See P. Hutchinson, "Govett Family," *Notes and Queries* 12 (1867) 274. The article provides a genealogy of Robert Govett Sr and his siblings.

2. *Ecclesiastical Directory: Containing a Complete Register of the Dignities and Benefices of the Church of England* (London: J. G.& F. Rivington, 1836) 183. See also *Trewman's Exeter Flying Post or Plymouth and Cornish Advertiser* (5 October 1809); "Death Notice," *The Times* (9 October 1858).

3. Sarah (Romaine) Govett is buried along-side her husband in St Mary's cemetery,

the early 1850s.⁴ Robert Sr was the eldest of five siblings—one brother, who predeceased him, and three sisters. Most of the siblings, including himself, were financially very well-off.⁵

Robert Sr and Sarah had eleven children—eight boys and three girls—of whom Robert was the eldest by two years.⁶ Remarkably, five of the eight sons were ordained into the Church of England.⁷ The Govett family was profoundly influenced by Sarah's heritage and the Romaine name which Robert Sr adopted in 1827.⁸ Robert was seventeen at the time. There is no record of Robert ever using the new surname but the second son, William Govett—one of the three sons not to become a minister— did use the new surname as is evident from recorded wills and newspaper articles about his activities.⁹ The third oldest son, Thomas Govett, was given the middle name of Romaine.¹⁰ The closeness of Robert Sr to the name of the renowned evangelical Romaine is exhibited in the Sessional Papers of the House of Commons which records on 9 March 1838, that Robert Sr was appointed

---

Staines. The memorial is a raised cruciform copestone (location F22) which reads: "Here side by side rest the remains of the Reverend Robert Govett, M.A.. 49 years vicar of this parish who died AD 1858 aged 79 and of Sarah his wife. Erected in the memory of a beloved father and mother by their eleven children." No dates are given for Sarah.

4. Martha Romaine—Sarah's mother—died in 1853. She left a very thorough will, bequeathing property and funds to Robert Govett Sr and grandchildren, but no mention of her only child Sarah—suggesting that Govett's mother died prior to 1853. See Middlesex County, probated will, Martha Romaine, proved 2 February 1853.

5. "Devon Lent Assize," *Trewman's Exeter Flying Post or Plymouth and Cornish Advertiser* (25 March 1852).

6. Joseph Foster in *Alumni Oxonienses: The Members of the University of Oxford 1715–1886*, lists Decimus Storry Govett and Adolphus Frederick Govett as twins, but this is incorrectly stated. They were separated in birth by three years with a sister–Martha Clementina Govett–being born in between. See Joseph Foster, *Alumni Oxonienses: The Members of the University of Oxford 1715–1886* (London: Parkey, 1887) 35.

7. Govett's siblings were: William Govett Romaine, born 1815; Thomas Romaine Govett, born 1816; John Clement Govett, born 1817; Henry Govett, born 1819; Sarah Louisa Govett (no date); Jane Octavia Govett, born 1826; Charles Albert Govett, born 1827; Decimus Storry Govett, born 1828; Martha Clementina Govett, born 1831; Adolphus Frederick Govett, born 1831.

8. Joseph Foster, *Men-At-the-Bar: A Biographical Hand-list of the Members of the Various Inns of Court* (London: Reeves and Turner, 1885) 399. See also, W. R. Williams, "Romaine, William Govett (1815–1893)," Reverend Lynn Milne, *Oxford Dictionary of National Biography*, Oxford University Press, 2004 (http://www.oxforddnb.com/view/article/ 2007, accessed 15 Aug 2011).

9. Foster, *Men-at-the-Bar*, 399.

10. See "Ecclesiastical Intelligence. Preferments and Appointments," *The Hull Packet and East Riding Times* (24 May 1850). See also *Liverpool Mercury etc.* (29 February 1848).

trustee in the "cleaning and preserving in good condition" the monument to the Reverend William Romaine who died in 1795.[11]

Robert never married, although he makes a rather tender request in his will that he be buried in the Rosary Cemetery, Norwich, "as near as may be to the burial place of my deceased friend Miss Sarah Stacy."[12] Sarah was seven years younger than Robert and was twenty-five years old at the time of her death.[13] He was granted his request and was buried in the same plot as his friend. His lack of a wife and children may in part explain why he was able to focus so much of his life on reading and writing and may suggest how it was that he was able to turn out such a voluminous number of published works. It appears that most all of his siblings did marry, many of them into prominent families with established names.[14] The Govett brothers were also very accomplished in their own right. Prominent among them was the second oldest brother, William Govett Romaine. Born in 1815, he graduated from Trinity College, Cambridge, with a B.A. in 1837 and an M.A. in 1859. He was appointed Deputy Judge-Advocate to the Army of the East during the Crimean War.[15] Thomas Romaine Govett matriculated in 1841 from Magdalen Hall, Oxford, and was appointed rector of Alby, Norfolk in 1853, and later in 1883, of Trimingham, Suffolk. Thomas married Sarah Frances Bignold of Norwich in 1848. Sarah was a niece to the wife of Edward Bickersteth (1786–1850). The significance of this marriage will be suggested in the following section. John Clement Govett, M.A. was the curate at Staines and St Mark's Tey, and later became vicar of Pentesbright, Essex, and rector at Shepperton, Middlesex.[16] Henry Govett graduated with a B.A. from Worcester College, Oxford, in 1841, and later became arch-

---

11. *Accounts and Papers, Great Britain, Parliament, House of Commons*, vol.76 (London: His Majesty's Stationery Office, 1902), 16.

12. The Last Will and Testament of Robert Govett proved 5 June 1901, Norwich.

13. Sarah Elizabeth Stacy, born 20 August 1820: died 28 December 1845. She was buried in Rosary Cemetery, Norwich. Sarah's sister Fanny Sophia Stacy, who died on 4 August 1921, is also buried in the same plot.

14. See, for example, *The Observer* (8 May 1848), regarding the marriage of Thomas Romaine Govett to Sarah Frances Bignold, of the prominent Norwich Bignold family. See also, *The Times* (28 January 1861), concerning the marriage of William Govett Romaine, Esq., in the Chapel of the British Embassy, Paris, to Phebe Tennant, daughter of Henry Tennant, Esq., of Cadoxton Lodge, Glamorganshire.

15. See Colin Robins, *Romaine's Crimean War: The Letters and Journal of William Govett Romaine, Deputy Judge-Advocate to the Army of the East 1854-6* (Gloucestershire: Sutton, 2005).

16. On 27 April 1854, John Clement Govett married Marianne Leslie daughter of Reverend Edward Leslie, Rector of Annahilt, Ireland. See *The Belfast News-Letter* (1 May 1854).

deacon of Taranaki, New Zealand. He died in New Zealand after residing there for fifty-nine years.[17] Charles Albert Govett became a solicitor. He and his brother William Govett Romaine remained very close. During the Crimean War Charles acted in financial matters on behalf of William.[18] His wife died at the age of twenty-six.[19] They were married just over two years.[20] Decimus Storry Govett graduated from Wadham College, Oxford, in 1850 with a B.A. and an M.A. in 1859.[21] In 1882 he became the archdeacon of Gibraltar. The youngest brother, Adolphus Frederick Govett graduated from University College, Oxford, with a B.A. in 1852, and an M.A. in 1860. He had an aptitude for business and founded the firm of Govett, Sons and Company near London. For thirty years he was a director of the Old London and South-Western Railway. He owned a grouse moor near Ballater on which he shot grouse with King George V. Upon his death in April 1928, being just shy of his ninety-seventh birthday, the King sent forward a telegram expressing his grief at the death of "his old friend, Mr. Govett."[22] Not much is known about Robert Govett's sisters except the announcement of the wedding of the oldest.[23]

Very little is recorded concerning Robert Govett the younger's life before entering Oxford. It seems likely that his was a stable upbringing—one of relative affluence and social connections—given that his father remained the vicar of Staines until his death in 1858 and the fact that he went up to Oxford.[24] Many of his siblings remained in Middlesex and surrounding London counties throughout their lives (or ventured back), thus renewing and sustaining their friendships. Some of these friendships would become useful

---

17. *The Times* (24 November 1903). See also Joseph Foster, *Alumni Oronienses: The Members of the University of Oxford 1715–1886* (London: Parkey, 1887) 35. See also "University and Clerical Intelligence," *The Morning Chronicle* (19 June 1841).

18. Robins, *Romaine's Crimean War*, 228, 235.

19. See *The Morning Chronicle* (29 June 1853).

20. See *The Times* (17 February 1851).

21. See also Robert Barlow Gardiner, ed., *The Registers of Wadham College, Oxford (Part II), From 1719–1871* (London: Bell and Sons, 1895) 440.

22. "Obituary. Mr. A. F. Govett," *The Times* (21 April 1928).

23. The oldest of the sisters, Sarah Louisa, was married to an attorney, Phillip Wright (Trinity College, Cambridge), of Birkenhead, Cheshire, on 25 April 1848. See *The Times* (28 April 1848).

24. Robert Govett Sr. and his siblings had a substantial sum of money that was passed down to them. In 1852, his sister Sarah Govett pressed charges of fraud in the courts to recover a large sum of money. The account and background into the Govett family's financial well-being is described. See "Devon Lent Assize," *Trewman's Exeter Flying Post or Plymouth and Cornish Advertiser* (25 March 1852). See also Martha Romaine's Last Will and Testament, proved in London, 2 February 1853.

74 A VICTORIAN DISSENTER

later in life for Robert when he relocated to Norwich to assume the curacy of a church. Robert and most of his brothers graduated from Oxford—although their father graduated from Cambridge.[25] However, they graduated from different colleges. Robert graduated from Worcester College, Oxford, with a B.A. in 1834, and was made a fellow in 1835 until his removal from the Church of England in 1844. He received his M.A. in 1837.[26]

Govett's Early Ecclesiastical Career (1833–1843)

It is in 1833 that the historical records begin to frame a picture of Govett's academic accomplishments and the ecclesiastical assignments that preceded his secession from the Established Church. On 29 May 1836, Govett, with his B.A. from Worcester College, Oxford, in hand was formally ordained as deacon in the Church of England by the Bishop of Oxford in the Cathedral Church of Christ in Oxford.[27] On the first of December of that same year Govett signed a formal declaration that he would conform to the liturgy of the United Church of England and Ireland as it then existed by law. The document was administered by John Eveleigh, Clerk and Vicar of Darenth in the county of Kent, diocese of Canterbury, which declared that Govett was to be licensed to perform the office of assistant curate in the parish church of Bexley, and in Bexley Heath Chapel, in the county of Kent.[28] Just eight days later he was officially granted by the Archbishop of Canterbury a license to perform the office of stipendiary curate in the parish church of Bexley, and in Bexley Heath Chapel. Govett was granted a yearly stipend of one hundred pounds to be paid quarterly and was further directed to reside at Bexley Heath.[29] This appointment brought Govett back to the London area where he was once again close to family and life-long acquaintances. The next year, on 21 May 1837, having received his M.A., Govett was for-

25. Joseph Romilly, *Graduati Cantabrigienses: Sive Catalogus Exhibens Nomina Eorum* (London: Deighton, Bell, 1856) 158. Note that *The Clergy List for 1841* (London: Cox) wrongly lists Robert Govett senior as having graduated from Worcester College, Oxford. Robert Sr. graduated from Sidney Sussex College, Cambridge in 1801 and 1804 with a B.A. and M.A., respectively.

26. Robert Govett's Master of Arts is conferred and announced in the paper. In the announcement he is listed as a Fellow of Worcester College. See *Jackson's Oxford Journal* (20 May 1837).

27. Norfolk Records Office file FC76/89. Official certificate from the Bishop of Oxford ordaining Govett as Deacon in the Church of England. (29 May 1836).

28. Norfolk Records Officee file FC76/89. Official Declaration of Licensure. (1 December 1836).

29. Norfolk Records Office file FC76/89. Official notice of position of Stipendiary Curate at Bexley (13 December 1836).

mally ordained a priest in the Church of England by the Bishop of Oxford in the Cathedral Church of Christ in Oxford.[30] Five years later he was on his way to Norwich to become the curate of St Stephen's church.

It was during this time of various appointments that he published his first two books. The first of these was a book published in 1840 pertaining to discourses on "grace" delivered by Calvin and others.[31] In it he attempted to strike a balance between the "dispensing power of the Most High" and the equally established proof of the responsibility of man.[32] He acknowledged that his conclusions had been heavily influenced by Dr Edward Williams (1750–1813), an independent minister, and his book on grace entitled, *An Essay on the Equity of Divine Government and the Sovereignty of Divine Grace* (1809), which Govett felt was the one volume that satisfied the difficulties of the subject.[33] At a very basic theological level the incubation of his life-long intense interest in the subject of the doctrine of eschatological reward emerged in this writing. While grappling with the issue of God as a sovereign on the one hand—doing what he pleases with gifts he possesses—he looked to God as a "Judge to judge," and on the other hand stated that God is "rewarding the recompense of a man's hands unto him."[34]

His second book entitled *Isaiah Unfulfilled*[35] was published in 1841. His stated purpose in writing the book was to add a new dimension to the celebrated work on Isaiah which was published in 1778, by Reverend Dr Robert Lowth (1710–1787).[36] While Govett acknowledged the contribu-

30. Norfolk Records Office file FC76/89. Official certificate from the Bishop of Oxford ordaining Govett as Deacon in the Church of England. (21 May 1837).

31. Robert Govett, *Calvinism by Calvin; Being the Substance of Discourses. Delivered by Calvin and Other Ministers of Geneva on the Doctrines of Grace. With an Introductory Essay, by the Rev. R. Govett, Jun.* (London: Nisbet, 1840). Note that the title page mentions Govett as Assistant Curate of Somers Town, St Pancras. No official ecclesiastic lists mention this appointment, but a letter of recommendation written on his behalf on 18 March 1841, substantiates this information.

32. Govett, *Calvinism by Calvin*, 4.

33. See Edward Williams, *An Essay on the Equity of Divine Government and the Sovereignty of Divine Grace* (London: Burditt, 1809). His book strove to bring Calvinism in harmony with the evangelical preaching of the day. See also, J. E. Lloyd, "Williams, Edward (1750–1813)," Reverend S. J. Skedd, *Oxford Dictionary of National Biography* (Oxford: Oxford University Press, 2004); online edition, May 2006, accessed 9 Sept 2011 (http://www.oxforddnb.com/view/article/29497).

34. Govett, *Calvinism by Calvin*, 9–10.

35. Robert Govett, *Isaiah Unfulfilled: Being an Exposition of the Prophet; with New Version and Critical Notes to which are Added Two Dissertations One on the "Sons of God" and "Giants" of Genesis VI and the Other a Comparative Estimate of the Hebrew and Greek Texts* (London: Nisbet, 1841).

36. Robert Lowth, *Isaiah. a New Translation: with a Preliminary Dissertation, and*

tion of Lowth's celebrated work and humbly admitted his own "inferior" learning, he was grieved to see that Lowth paid so little attention to the connection of Isaiah to the New Testament writers and their arguments that are derived from the scriptural quotations they took from Isaiah. In his book Govett exposed his mastery of biblical Hebrew. It was quite a daring undertaking considering that Govett was in his late twenties at the time of his book's printing while Lowth was a well-seasoned theologian when his own book appeared in print. But the real significance of Govett's book with regard to this study was in what it revealed about Govett's evangelical millennial theology, for Govett brought into the open his prophetic views as a futurist. He believed the prophecies in the Book of Isaiah would be fulfilled literally and argued that the reader of his book would arrive at the conclusion that the greater part of Isaiah's prophecies were yet to be fulfilled. In addition, he believed that those prophecies which were acknowledged to have been accomplished had only initial fulfillment.[37] What was not yet made known was whether he had become a premillennialist. That question would be sufficiently answered by 1843.

By January 1841 Govett had determined to seek a clerical appointment in Norwich. It is conceivable that Govett achieved this appointment on his own, but it is also very possible that he achieved it with the intervention of his friend Edward Bickersteth (1786–1850), rector of Watton-at-Stone, Hertfordshire (bordering greater London), and fellow evangelical. While no communication between the two men exists to prove his involvement, there is communication that demonstrates Bickersteth's keen interest in Govett's well-being and future in the Church of England. Furthermore, Bickersteth was well-connected in Norwich, having family members in prestigious positions in the community, as well as a personal friendship with the Bishop.[38] In 1812 Bickersteth had married Sarah Bignold, eldest daughter of

---

Notes Critical, Philological, and Explanatory. by Robert Lowth, D.D.F.R. Ss. Lond. and Goetting. Lord Bishop of London (London: printed by J. Nichols; for J. Dodsley in Pall-Mall, and T. Cadell in the Strand, 1778). See also, F. L. Cross and E. A. Livingstone, eds., The Oxford Dictionary of the Christian Church. (New York: Oxford University Press, 2005) 1005.

37. Govett, Isaiah Unfulfilled, 123.

38. In February 1848 Bickersteth's son was admitted to Deacon's orders by the Bishop of Norwich. Note: Bickersteth's son Edward was baptized by his father (Robert Govett's friend) on Sunday, 28 July 1850. His godfather was one of his uncles, the Reverend T. R. (Thomas Romaine—uncle by way of his wife, a Bignold) Govett, M.A. and John McGregor, Esq., better known as "Rob Roy," who had been a bosom friend of his father's at Trinity College, Cambridge. See Samuel Bickersteth, Life and Letters of Edward Bickersteth Bishop of Tokyo (London, Sampson Low, Marston, 1899) 8. Samuel Bickersteth's book pertains to the son (Edward Henry) grandson of Robert Govett's Bickersteth. Edward (the grandson) married his cousin Rosa (p. 4), daughter of Sir

Thomas Bignold,[39] a prominent Norwich businessman and descendant of a respected Norwich family. Bickersteth was at the time a solicitor and in partnership in Norwich with Sarah's brother, another Thomas Bignold. It was during the ensuing three years while Bickersteth practiced as a lawyer in Norwich that his religious interests developed.[40] Whether Bickersteth had a direct hand in helping Govett become curate of St Stephen's Church, Norwich, is not known. What is known is that the extended Bignold family had a connection with St Stephen's Church. In May 1848, Govett's clergyman brother Thomas Romaine Govett married Sarah Frances Bignold, the second daughter of Sir Samuel Bignold, Esq. of Surrey Road, Norwich,[41] a niece to Bichersteth's wife Sarah. Thomas and Sarah were married in St Stephen's Church, and since Govett at the time was no longer in the Church of England, his father officiated the service.[42] Govett also maintained a business relationship with a Bignold—Edward S. Bignold—throughout his years as pastor of Surrey Chapel.[43]

Another circumstance of friendship suggests that events may have helped lead Govett toward a curacy in Norwich. Through a mutual friend, William Cox, Govett made known his interest in becoming the curate of St Stephen's Church in Norwich. The vicar of St Stephen's and curate of St Saviour's, Stephen Oakeley Attlay, first wrote back to Cox asking him to warn Govett of the difficulties of the assignment. When it appeared that Govett was still very much interested the vicar wrote directly to Govett. In his letter dated 7 January 1841, the vicar wrote to Govett to announce that the curacy of his parish would be open as of 5 April and added, "if you have courage to enter upon a wide sphere of usefulness with little that is earthly to cheer and

---

Samuel Bignold, M.P. for Norwich.

39. Samuel Bickersteth, *Life and Letters of Edward Bickersteth Bishop of Tokyo* (London, Sampson Low, Marston, 1899) 8.

40. John Wolffe, "Bickersteth, Edward (1786–1850)," *Oxford Dictionary of National Biography* (Oxford: Oxford University Press, 2004); online edition, May 2008, accessed 5 Aug 2011 (http://www.oxforddnb.com/view/article/2345). See also Thomas R. Birks, *Memoirs of the Rev. Edward Bickersteth, Late Rector of Watton, Herts* (London: Seeleys, 1951) 1:392.

41. *The Observer* (8 May 1848).

42. Thomas Romaine Govett and Sarah Bignold were married in May 1848. Robert Govett had been removed from the Church of England by the Bishop in 1844. St Stephens was Robert Govett's former church. See "Births, Marriages, and Deaths," *The Observer* (8 May 1848).

43. Surrey Chapel utilized Edward S. Bignold as its solicitor. Norwich Records Office file FC76/89. The file contains correspondence from Edward S. Bignold, 19 November 1890, Lady's Lane, Norwich. It may also be worth noting that Govett's nonconformist church was later built in 1854 on Surrey Road—the same road Sir Samuel Bignold, who was a conspicuous land owner, lived on.

support you."⁴⁴ He concluded his lengthy letter with remarks regarding the Bishop. He remarked that he saw "our kindhearted Bishop this morning" and told him that he was in communication with Govett about his curacy—detailing Govett's experience for the Bishop. The Bishop had responded by saying that he would be pleased to accept such a man provided he bring to him satisfactory testimonials from the Bishop of London.

On 18 March 1841, four ministers of the Church of England in the diocese of London, where Govett was assistant minister of Somers Chapel, Somers-Town, in the Parish of St Pancras, in the county of Middlesex, served notice as references to the Bishop of Norwich. They affirmed that they had personally known Govett for the space of two years and during that time they believed Govett to be living "piously, soberly, and honestly." They also vouched in their letter that Govett—as far as they knew—had not, "held, written, or taught anything contrary to the doctrine of the Church of England." Nevertheless, within three years, Govett would stand against the church's doctrine of infant baptism which would lead to the swift removal of his license to preach.⁴⁵

On 8 May 1841, Govett received his formal license as Stipendiary Curate of Saint Stephen's Church, Norwich, by nomination of Attlay, Clerk and Incumbent of Saint Stephen. He was to receive the yearly stipend of fifty pounds paid to him by the Incumbent. He was addressed as "Robert Govett the Younger" due to his father also being a licensed clergyman in the Church of England.⁴⁶ That same day Govett signed an official document directed to the Bishop declaring that he would conform to the Liturgy of the Church of England as it was established by law.⁴⁷ This, of course, meant that he would conform to the position held by the church on the Sacrament of Baptism—a conformity he would challenge within two years.

Within two years questions surfaced in his mind regarding some of the theological assertions made by the Established Church respecting the position of a bishop. This prompted Govett to write to his old friend Edward Bickersteth, rector of Waton At Stone. On 4 January 1843 a very earnest

---

44. Norwich Records Office file FC76/89. Letter from S. O. Attlay, Vicar of St Stephen's and Curate of St Saviour's, Norwich, to Govett (7 January 1841).

45. Norfolk Records Office file FC76/89. Letter written on 18 March 1841, by Thomas Watson, Minister of St Philips, Clerkenwell; T. Jones, Vicar of Bedfont, Middlesex; Reverend Thomas J. Judkin, Somers-Town, St Pancras; William Rupells, Rector of Shepperton.

46. Norwich Records Office file FC76/89. Official notice of position of Stipendiary Curate of Saint Stephen (8 May 1841).

47. Norfolk Records Office file FC76/89. Official declaration by Govett to the Bishop of Norwich of conformity to the church (8 May 1841).

response was returned by Bickersteth.[48] Bickersteth drew his friend's attention to the writings of Richard Hooker (1554–1600) to help satisfy his concerns over eight specific spiritual and ecclesiastical issues.[49] Bickersteth's advice to Govett was to read Richard Hooker whose work was " to me satisfactory." Of particular focus was Bickersteth's recommendation that Govett read Hooker's third book on *The Laws of Ecclesiastical Polity* (1593) and its discussion of the church's power to decree rites.[50] One of the matters troubling Govett was the church's position on the power imputed to bishops to execute their offices, and the belief that the Holy Spirit was a gift given to bishops upon ordination. To address this concern, Bickersteth again turned Govett to Hooker's *Laws of Ecclesiastical Polity*, Book 5 (1597), Section 77, which deals with divine appointments and ministerial commission.[51]

While Bickersteth's letter contained a multifaceted response on a number of subjects related to the church, it is apparent that the greatest worry to Bickersteth was Govett's insinuation that he had thoughts of leaving the Church of England. Govett also confirmed this to be the primary issue as he wrote on the outside of the envelope, "Bickersteth on my leaving the Church of England." It is to this subject that Bickersteth began his letter with the words: "your letter has given me great sorrow." He added that Govett appeared to him to be "a scrupulous and not a tender conscience."[52] No mention was made to Govett wrestling with infant baptism, and therefore it must be concluded that this was a concern yet to be heightened in his conscience. The state of Govett's conscience may be further clarified in a sermon he preached shortly after receiving Bickersteth's letter. Only one of the sermons preached by Govett while he was still an Anglican is extant. It was preached on Good Friday morning on 14 April 1843—three months after receiving Bickersteth's letter. He preached on Hebrews 10:12, which

48. Norfolk Records Office file FC76/59 (1 of 2). Letter from Edward Bickersteth, Rector of Watton-At-Stone, Hertsfordshire, to Govett (4 January 1843).

49. Richard Hooker (1554–1600) is described in a book on his life written by Philip Secor as one whose understanding of the Church of England was rooted in the belief that the parish priest's pastoral responsibility for his parish was of prime significance, and the "Church could no more be divorced from its social context than from its foundation in Christ." See Philip B. Secor, *Richard Hooker: Prophet of Anglicanism* (Kent: Burns & Oates, 1999) vii.

50. This book is thought to be the first major work in the fields of theology, philosophy, and political thought to be written in English. See Philip B. Secor, *Richard Hooker and the Via Media* (Bloomington: Author-House, 2006) ix.

51. See *The Works of Mr. Richard Hooker, Containing Eight Books of the Laws of Ecclesiastical Polity, and Several other Treatises* (Oxford: Vincent, 1843) 2:84.

52. Norfolk Records Office file FC76/59 (1 of 2). Letter from Edward Bickersteth, Rector of Watton-At-Stone, Hertsfordshire, to Govett (4 January 1843).

speaks of the cleansing sacrifice of Christ. His question to the congregation was, "do we desire to be consecrated of God to serve him?" And then he concluded his sermon with the reminder that he [Christ] is coming again and the admonition that the congregation be "fitted" for his approach.[53] Govett's aim, it appears, was an admonition he preached to himself as well to live in such a way that makes a true believer fit (or worthy) of Christ's appearing. It is easily assumed that Govett's questions to a dear friend in the ministry were a serious attempt to be "found worthy of Christ."

There was yet another issue that grieved Bickersteth which he mentioned before responding to Govett's eight questions, and that was Govett's position on the "future" fulfillment of Revelation. He added, "I do grieve also that you have joined the school of Maitland, Todd, Burgh and McCausland."[54] Bickersteth was 17 years Govett's senior. A staunch evangelical, he was deeply concerned for unity in the church.[55] After 1830 he moved away from the postmillennialism characteristic of the early missionary movement in favor of a conviction that the premillennial advent of Christ was to be imminently expected.[56] He had changed his position from postmillennial to premillennial but had not embraced a futurist understanding of the teachings of Revelation—perhaps for reasons which concurred with other prominent figures within the Established Church who believed that the futurist position was a rival system harming the church.[57] Nevertheless, the overall tone of his letter is one of helpfulness and empathy for a "dear brother." And while Bickersteth was not persuaded by Govett's view of Revelation as a futurist—having made up his mind on the position a long time previously—he wrote that he promised to "read carefully" Gov-

---

53. Norfolk Records Office file FC76/91. Good Friday sermon preached at St Stephens, Norwich (14 April 1843).

54. All four men were futurist premillennialists. Their views differed from Bickersteth who, while changing his views over time to a premillennial position, never embraced a futurist view of Revelation. See, for example, the following works: Charles Maitland, *The Apostle's School of Prophetic Interpretation: With its History Down to the Present Time* (London: Paternoster-Row, 1849); James Henthorn Todd, *Six Discourses on the Prophecies Relating to Anti-Christ in the Apocalype of St. John, Preached before the University of Dublin, at the Donnellan Lecture* (Dublin: University Press, 1846); William De Burgh, *An Exposition of the Book of Revelation* (Dublin: Times, 1834); Dominick McCausland, *The Latter Days of the Jewish Church and Nation, as Revealed in the Apocalypse* (1841).

55. See Thomas R. Birks, *Memoir of the Rev. Edward Bickersteth, Late Rector of Watton, Herts*, 2 vols. (London: Seeleys, 1851).

56. Wolffe, "Bickersteth," *Oxford Dictionary*.

57. For example: *The Churchman's Monthly Review and Chronicle* (September 1843) 635, which charged the futurists as having "the same fondness for Rome and hatred for Protestantism."

ett's recently published work on Revelation which he purposed to send to his friend. The work was originally entitled *The Revelation of St. John, Literal and Future: Being an Exposition of that Book: To which are Added Remarks in Refutation of the Ideas that the Pope is the Man of Sin, and that Popery is the Apostacy Predicted by St. Paul, with a Special Reference to Doctor O'Sullivan on the Apostacy* (1843).[58] Here then was to be the first published expression of Govett's premillennial futurist view of prophecy, as well as a clear statement, in opposition to many others at the time who believed the Pope to be the Antichrist. The book received a very thorough review in the *Monthly Review*.[59] And on a rather curious note, the article compared the findings of his book with that of a contrasting work on the Apocalypse, then also appearing in print, written by Thomas Rawson Birks (1810–1883), curate to Govett's friend Bickersteth, entitled *First Elements of Sacred Prophecy* (1843).[60] What first appeared surprising to some readers was that Govett's book was written by a minister of the Church of England. According to the book reviewer, "it [the book] must excite interest and stimulate curiosity; for it advances hypothesis, and follows a mode of interpretation that are to a great extent quite new, or which at least have never till recently been put into a systematized and combined order."[61]

58. See Robert Govett, *The Revelation of St. John Literal and Future: Being an Exposition of that Book: To which are Added Remarks in Refutation of the Ideas that the Pope is the Man of Sin and that Popery is the Apostacy Predicted by St. Paul. With a Special Reference to Dr. O'Sullivan on the Apostacy* (London: Hamilton, Adams, 1843). See also *Report of the Great Protestant Meetings, Held in Hope Street Gaelic Church, Glasgow, on Thursday the 17th, and Friday the 18th September, 1835: At which the Rev. Mortimer O'Sullivan, and Other Gentlemen, Engaged to Prove, by Authentic Documents, What are the Real Tenets of the Church of Rome, as Now Held by the Roman Catholic Bishops and Priests of Ireland* (Glasgow: Scottish Guardian, 1835).

59. *The Monthly Review* (1749–1845) was an English periodical founded by Ralph Griffiths, a Nonconformist bookseller. It was the first periodical in England to offer reviews. See "Article 10: 1. The Revelation of St John, Literal and Future; Being an Exposition of That Book, by the Rev. R. Govett, Junior, A. M. Hamilton, Adams, and Co.," *The Monthly Review* (February 1844) 283–97. See also William S. Ward, *Index and Finding List of Serials Published in the British Isles 1789–1832* (Lexington: University of Kentucky Press, 1953).

60. Thomas Rawson Birks was a Church of England clergyman and theologian, and was for some years a tutor and then curate to Edward Bickersteth, Govett's friend, the rector of Watton-At-Stone, Hertfordshire. Like Bickersteth he held a premillennial position, but differed with Govett on a literal futurist understanding of the Apocalypse. While curate to Bickersteth he wrote his views in a series of treatises. The first of these was *First Elements of Sacred Prophecy* (1843). See T. R. Birks, *First Elements of Sacred Prophecy: Including an Examination of Several Recent Expositions and of the Year-Day Theory* (London: Painter, 1843). See also Donald M. Lewis, ed., *The Blackwell Dictionary of Evangelical Biography, 1730–1860*, 2 vols. (1995).

61. *The Monthly Review* (February 1843) 283.

82   A VICTORIAN DISSENTER

Twelve months from the date of Bickersteth's letter to Govett, he found himself standing before the Bishop of Norwich for the purpose of explaining his position on infant baptism. There is no progression of written thought that can be traced which gives rise to Govett's epiphany-like conclusion that infant baptism, as conducted as a sacrament of the Established Church, was biblically errant. What is known is that Govett attended a "believers' baptism" at St Mary's Baptist Church, in Norwich one Sunday evening. The minister was William Brock, the popular but somewhat outspoken Baptist minister.[62] Brock was known for his social and political involvement in Norwich, almost as much as his Bible preaching. It was facetiously noted that he both preached from the Bible and *The Times* newspaper.[63] The most accurate account of Govett's doctrinal conversion is recounted by Reverend T. Phillips during his remarks as main speaker at Govett's funeral service. Phillips noted that Govett had spoken to him some years previously about his being baptized. Govett recounted that while a curate at St Stephen's he was led to pay a visit one Sunday evening to Reverend William Brock's church. On that occasion there was a baptism after the sermon at which time Govett at once remarked to himself, "That's it, without a mistake: that's the New Testament." On the following Tuesday evening Govett was himself baptized.[64] On the evening that Govett was baptized by Brock, six others were baptized who were parishioners of Govett's church. As recorded at the time, these were "six young ladies whom he had persuaded unhappily to follow his errors."[65]

A short time later, on 27 January 1844, Govett met with the Right Reverend Dr Bishop Edward Stanley, Bishop of Norwich over the matter of his ecclesiastical stand on baptism. On the same day Govett wrote a letter to an unnamed person in authority over him in the church hierarchy to inform him of his interview with "his Lordship" and his resulting desire not to participate in the services the following day, the grounds of which would create "much displeasure in many minds." On a practical note, Govett reminded the recipient that a quarter's balance was due to him.[66] Just

62. See J. H. Y. Briggs, *The English Baptists of the Nineteenth Century, a History of the English Baptists Volume 3* (Didcot: The Baptist Historical Society, 1994).

63. C. B. Jewson, *Simon Wilkin of Norwich* (Norwich: University of East Anglia, 1979) 99.

64. Govett article *Eastern Daily Press* (26 February 1901).

65. "Surrey Chapel and Its Pastor: A Unique Ministry," *Eastern Daily Press* (12 March 1912).

66. Norfolk Records Office file FC76/89. Letter from Govett to an unnamed recipient. Written on 27 January 1844.

six days later Govett received an official letter from the Bishop in the wake of their meeting.[67]

In response to this meeting a very brief letter was penned by Govett to the Bishop which read: "Being now convinced that not a few points are unscriptural in the Church of England service for the baptism of infants, I write to inform you that I cannot conscientiously use that service by the prayer-book any more." Afterwards he dated in pencil at the top of the letter the words: "in February 1844." This must have been delivered on the first day of February since the Bishop's final reply is dated 2 February 1844.

On 2 February 1844, the Bishop of Norwich wrote a letter to Govett in response to their meeting of 27 January 1844, and the letter Govett delivered to him on 1 February. In it he stated that he was resigned to the fact that Govett had decided on "quitting the Church of England," the grounds for which he believed were "singularly weak and irrational." Interestingly, the letter also indicated that the Bishop had become aware that Govett was "fitting up the Bazaar[68] for future purposes." This strongly suggests that Govett, sometime prior to meeting with the Bishop, had already made up his mind about leaving the Church of England. It is in this letter that the Bishop stated that he would only unwillingly perform the painful duty of revoking Govett's licence. The Bishop concluded by stating that he believed Govett would one day regret that he became instrumental in "increasing the divisions and schisms" in the Church of Christ resulting from his most "injudicious conduct."[69] It should be noted that although Govett was removed from his office by the Bishop of Norwich in 1844, it was not until 16 February 1878 (at the age of 65) that Govett signed a Deed of Relinquishment in accordance with the Clerical Disabilities Act of 1870 to declare that he relinquished all rights and advantages of the Office of Priest in the Church of England.[70]

Immediately upon receiving his letter from the Bishop revoking his license to preach, Govett began using the commercial building known as the Bazaar, located on St Andrews Street, Norwich, as a meeting place for worship. The government required a census of all places of worship in 1851

---

67. Norfolk Records Office file FC76/89. Letter from the Right Reverend Edward Stanley, D.D., Bishop of Norwich (2 February 1844).

68. The Bazaar was a public commercial building on St Andrews Street, Norwich, used primarily for commerce but could be let for meeting space and, in Govett's case, worship services.

69. Norfolk Records Office file FC76/89. Official letter from the Right Reverend Edward Stanley, Bishop of Norwich, to Govett (2 February 1844).

70. Norfolk Records Office file FC76/89. Official Deed of Relinquishment registered in the Diocese of Norwich by the Deputy Registrar (15 November 1878).

and the form which Govett himself completed and returned supplies a sense of what the attendance looked like during the years in which Govett utilized this space. The completed census form mentions the start date of the chapel services as 1 February 1844—the date of the Bishop's letter. The place of worship was classified as simply "Christian—having no denominational name." The average Sunday morning attendance was reported to be 459 people. There were also afternoon and evening services held which brought the total number of people worshiping on an average Sunday (in 1851) up to 849 people. The room in the Bazaar which Govett's church rented seated a total of 550 people, and it was clear that within a few years of steady growth they would need to relocate.[71] And although it has been occasionally reported that Govett affiliated himself with the Baptists and even the Brethren movement, in fact, the congregation never attached itself to any of the existing denominations.[72]

This move to a new church building occurred in 1854. But in the intervening decade, while at the Bazaar and before the new church was built, much occurred in the life of Govett. During these years he began his prolific flow of published books and tracts; he began his life-long interest in the doctrine of believers' baptism—beginning with his first baptismal tract published in 1844;[73] and he also began his discovery of the importance of the doctrine of eschatological reward for believers. The first evidence of this latter subject appears in a letter on 30 March 1849, when Govett wrote to his congregation from Brighton in his annual pastoral letter. In it he mentioned for the first time the word "reward" in the context of the future judgment. He wrote, "And how glorious that reward, which if we faint not, awaits us at the coming of our Lord and Savior."[74] It is around this time that Govett published his first work on the treatment of the subject of reward.[75]

---

71. Janet Ede and Norma Virgoe, *Religious Worship in Norfolk: The 1851 Census of Accommodation and Attendance at Worship* (Cambridge: University Press, 1998) 138. See also Rosamunde Codling, *Book of Thanksgiving: 150 Years at Surrey Chapel Norwich, 1854–2004: The Anniversary of the Opening of the First Surrey Chapel Building, A Book of Thanksgiving* (Norwich: Surrey Chapel, 2004) 5. It was noted that the Bazaar was divided into two compartments—one being used for the Chapel, and the other for the "School of Design."

72. See, for example, A. D. Bayne, *A Comprehensive History of Norwich: Including a Survey of the City and its Public Buildings* (London: Jarrold and Sons, 1869) 720. This source wrongly lists Surrey Road Chapel as a Baptist church.

73. See Robert Govett, *Not Water Baptism But the Gifts of the Holy Spirit the Baptism of Christ* (Norwich: Fletcher, 1844).

74. Norfolk Records Office file FC76/95.

75. See Robert Govett, *Reward According to Works* (Norwich: Fletcher and Son, 1850). This was first published as a 20 page tract. In 1853, Govett expanded the tract

One other significant development which occurred during this decade was Govett's ultimate realization that he was called to be a minister, and furthermore, the pastor of Surrey Chapel. He could have easily pursued a career in academia while an Anglican, or sought the pastorate of a large nonconformist chapel back home in the greater London area after his secession.[76] However, once content with his decision to be the minister of Surrey Chapel he never wavered from it. Yet, coming to that decision was a process that took several years. It began with one of his yearly holidays. Govett, like many other pastors of his day, took extended trips of weeks, sometimes months, intended as holidays to refresh their body and soul. While away, just prior to his return, Govett routinely wrote to his congregation to announce his pending return. Many of Govett's annual letters are extant and reveal much of his pastoral thoughts and difficulties with health. It was an occasion in which he also took note of congregant issues within his church in order to instruct and encourage the membership. Often the encouraging remarks centered around the importance of loving each other in Christ and living in anticipation of the Lord's imminent return. Typical of these letters was the pastoral letter of 30 January 1851, in which he drew attention to the Great Exhibition of 1851 and the boasting of the nation around the Crystal Palace which was being built to house the technology and industrial advancements of thousands of exhibitions from nations around the world.[77] Govett wrote, "let us remember that our hopes embrace a far vaster and more glorious mansion built for us by the hand of God."[78]

But this particular letter also reveals that Govett had been absent from his congregation for two years. The first indication of this separation was mentioned in his pastoral letter of 14 January 1848. Health issues plagued Govett throughout his life, making frequent mention of it in his pastoral letters written to his congregation over many years as their shepherd. Taunton, England, is the location Govett sought for his recuperation and respite that year. Lodging was provided to him and at first the tone of his letter suggests that he believed his return to the Bazaar was to occur soon. But as time

---

into a 389 page book. See also, Robert Govett, *The Order of Reward: or the Parable of the Labourers in the Vineyard Explained* (Norwich: Fletcher and Son, 1846).

76. Govett's scholarship was recognized by the leading members of both English universities. His works attained wide recognition in America. Spurgeon also highly esteemed his works. See "Surrey Chapel and Its Pastor: A Unique Ministry." *Eastern Daily Press* (12 March 1912).

77. J. R. Piggott, *Palace of the People: The Crystal Palace of Sydenham, 1854–1936* (London: C. Hurst, 2004) 2.

78. Norfolk Records Office file FC76/95. Pastoral Letter from Govett to his congregation assembled at the Bazaar, Norfolk. Written at Brighton (30 January 1851).

went on and relapses of his health condition occurred he took up temporary preaching in several local churches while doubts regarding his future continued. Over time an interim pastor was selected for the Bazaar at Govett's encouragement as, in turn, his annual letters began to suggest that God was leading him to permanently stay in Taunton. It was consequently curious that in January 1851, in the letter written from the southern coastal town of Brighton, he ended his letter expressing his hope to be with his congregation the following Lord's day, for the Lord had made it clear to him that he was to "return" as their "servant in the Lord." Thereafter, during the many remaining years as the congregation's pastor, there was never again any indication of an extended absence except for normal holiday, nor doubts about where the Lord would have him serve. This is substantiated in a letter to the editor of the *Eastern Daily Press*, Norwich, written by a long-time member of Surrey Road Chapel, who recalled the "bitter farewell to many" of Govett and his "mistaken path of Providence."[79] As the congregation grew it made plans, early in 1853, to construct a building of their own in which to worship. The new chapel was to seat 1,500 persons.[80] It would become one of the largest dissenting chapels to be built in Norwich at that time. Govett filled the new church Sunday upon Sunday with those who hung upon his words as "upon the voice of direct inspiration."[81] This degree of attention is substantiated by reports that C. H. Spurgeon regarded Govett as one of the foremost of biblical commentators.[82] Surrey Road Chapel was dedicated on 21 December 1854.[83] For a period of time it was known as Ebenezer Chapel, but was later just referred to as "Surrey Road." When it opened it had been paid for almost exclusively by Govett who on 2 February 1853 had inherited a good portion of his maternal grandmother's estate.[84]

---

79. Norfolk Records Office file FC76/91. Letter to the editor of the *Eastern Daily Press*, Norwich, by an original member of Surrey Road Chapel and who knew Govett from the beginning of his ministry in Norwich, thanking the paper for its article on the late Reverend R. Govett which appeared on 21 February 1901. Forwarded to the paper by J. Cawston (25 February 1901).

80. Obituary notice, *Eastern Daily Press* (21 February 1901).

81. Norfolk Records Office file FC76/91. Article in the *Eastern Evening News* (published in Norwich) regarding the death of Robert Govett, Norwich (21 February 1901).

82. Norfolk Records Office file FC76/91. Article in the *Eastern Evening News* (21 February 1901).

83. Norfolk Records Office file FC76/59 (1 of 2). The printed hymn sheet for the morning and evening services for the official opening of Ebenezer Chapel (as Surrey Chapel was first known), on Surrey Road. The date indicated is 21 December 1854.

84. See Last Will and Testament of Martha Romaine, Robert Govett's maternal grandmother, proved 2 February 1853. See also, *Eastern Daily Press* article, 21 February 1901, which reports that Surrey Road Chapel was almost entirely built out of Govett's

Govett: His Family Relationships and Friendships

It was the source of these funds that gave rise to an area of some misunderstanding over Govett's financial well-being and to speculation surrounding his relationship with his family. Conjecture regarding Govett's defection from the Established Church in 1844 continued to produce misstatements bearing upon the financial sacrifice that resulted. Certainly there was the loss of an estimated £300 per year after the loss of his fellowship at Worcester College.[85] But beyond this amount there is no evidence of a further downturn of loss. It was further conjectured that his immovable stance on baptism caused a great divide between him and his family members that resulted in a substantial diminution of his inheritance. For example, the obituary notice in the *Eastern Daily Press* on 21 February 1901, made the statement that it was an open secret that he had suffered heavily by his defection from the Church of England and that a large sum of money which otherwise would have come to him was willed to other family members.[86] But the facts do not substantiate this claim. Both his maternal grandmother's will (who died in 1853) and that of his father (who died in 1858) indicate that he was provided with generous bequests. In the case of his grandmother's will he was mentioned separately and preferentially over the other grandchildren. The grandmother, Martha Romaine, was very wealthy, having income from banks, government securities from England and Wales, goods, chattel, and bonds, and several estates. Govett was to receive a tenth of the annual dividends and allotments from her considerable sources of income over the span of his life, a sum which was to pass to his children should he ever marry. Income from this source began to be made available prior to the final completion of Surrey Chapel and appears to be the source which enabled him to give additional personal funds for its completion. His father's will mentions him in proper first born order leaving him not only a portion of his wealth but his estate in Baxton, Devon for his sole use and that of his children after him should he ever marry.[87] Consequently there is no evidence of estrangement. As further evidence, the inscription on Robert Govett Sr and Sarah Govett's tombstone reads that it was erected in the memory of a beloved father and mother by all

---

own pocket. It reports a variance in amounts from other reported sums when it states that he headed the subscription list with £1500 and later contributed about £1500 more. Money coming from other sources amounted to only £300.

85. Codling, *150 Years at Surrey Chapel*, 4.

86. Obituary notice, *Eastern Daily Press* (21 February 1901).

87. See Martha Romaine's will, proved 2 February 1853, and Robert Govett senior's will, proved 26 October 1858.

eleven children.⁸⁸ Govett received income from Surrey Chapel not from a stipulated salary (at least until 1875), but from contributions made directly to him through a box placed formally in the church and designated for distribution to the pastor. General contributions to the church were made in a similar manner in a separate box.⁸⁹

Part of this misreporting of financial sacrifice and familial strife was perhaps due to a certain mystique that surrounded Govett's personality. It has been reported that Govett was a recluse and spent his time in private reading and writing. This may not be the case, as the editor of the *Eastern Daily Times* contradicted that assessment when he reported that those who knew Govett well found him to have "a large and generous heart," and that he was often found helping in the City Mission, as well as frequently inviting the City missionaries from the mission to his tea gatherings. The editor further exclaimed that Govett "was gracious and received all who came to his home for fellowship with gratitude."⁹⁰ There remained longstanding local interest in Govett's theological stand on baptism—perhaps due to his ongoing commitment to writing tracts on the subject. The articles which appeared in the local papers for several days after Govett's death all mentioned the cause of his separation from the Church of England, which, after fifty-seven years, still appeared to be a matter of fascination. He is described in one account as a "Dissenter of Dissenters."⁹¹ This description is unjustly harsh, as evidenced from the tone of the many articles he wrote, which often contained respectful words for those with whom he differed theologically. Furthermore, he held on to old Anglican friendships throughout his life. For instance, he left all of his unpublished manuscripts and the rights to all of his books and tracts in his will to an old friend, and presumably former parishioner, whom he knew from his days as curate at Bexley, Kent. It was

---

88. Information provided in correspondence received from St Mary's Church, Staines, on 6 December 2011. The memorial inscription found on the tombstone at the grave of Robert Govett Sr (Location F22, St Mary's Church cemetery), was documented and made public in 1984 by volunteers of the West Middlesex Family History Society, Middlesex.

89. Norfolk Records Office file FC76/59 (1 of 2). Accounting ledger of income "receipts" for Surrey Road Chapel for the years 1875 and 1876. See also, Codling, *150 Years at Surrey Chapel*, 14.

90. Norfolk Records Office file FC76/91. Letter to the editor of the *Eastern Daily Press*, by an original member of Surrey Road Chapel and who knew Govett from the beginning of his ministry in Norwich, thanking the paper for its article on the late Reverend R. Govett, which appeared on 21 February 1901. Forwarded to the paper by J. Cawston (25 February 1901).

91. Norfolk Records Office file FC76/91. Article in the *Eastern Evening News* (21 February 1901).

reported in the *Eastern Daily Press*, Norwich, that Govett's funeral service was held at Surrey Road Chapel and the 1,500 seat chapel was fairly well filled with "various denominations being represented."[92]

There is strong evidence that the extended family remained close from generation to generation based upon the broad distribution of assets disclosed in the family's probated wills. Likewise, the affluence of the extended family gave rise to an occasional lawsuit by outsiders over the years. Each instance demonstrated the collective commitment of the extended family whose solicitor relatives represented them in court while others acted as character witnesses for the defendants.[93]

Govett and his siblings also gave the appearance of being close-knit. For example, a copy of Govett's book *Isaiah Unfulfilled* which has been preserved in the Govett library at Surrey Chapel has a handwritten inscription on the inside fly sheet that reads: "Thomas Romaine Govett, June 1841, the gift of William Romaine." It is a gift from the second oldest brother (a solicitor), to the third oldest brother, who was then age twenty-five and a young member of the clergy.[94] Yet, reciprocally, when it came to the question of Scriptural interpretation Govett did not allow family relationship to cloud his theological judgment or create compromise. By way of illustration, on 30 January 1900, Govett's brother, Decimus Storry Govett, fifteen years his junior, archdeacon in the Church of England, preached a service of intercession entitled "God First Not Last, The Lesson of War." Govett was in possession of a copy of the eight-page sermon leaflet and in his typically careful review of its theological content wrote comments across the title page and portions of the inner pages. D. S. Govett called attention to the sinful state of the nation of Great Britain, to which Govett affirmed represented, "the sin of the nation justly stated." But his notes warned his brother that Paul and the other apostles did not reference other nations as such, "save those whom they could reach to repent and be forgiven." Then he leveled a greater criticism of his brother's sermon with the remark, "Does the name of Christ appear in it?"[95] It is not known

92. Govett article *Eastern Daily Press* (26 February 1901). The article was published a day after the funeral of Govett.

93. See, for example, "Devon Lent Assize," *Trewman's Exeter Flying Post* or *Plymouth and Cornish Advertiser* (25 March 1852).

94. Affection within the family is also exhibited in the dedication page of a book written by Thomas Romaine. It reads: "This little book is, with dutiful affection, dedicated to his Beloved Father, the vicar of Staines for almost half a century, by his son, T. Romaine Govett. Alby Rectory, Norfolk (20 February 1858)." See Thomas Romaine Govett, *Scripture Illustrations. By an Eye-Witness* (London: Wertheim, Macintosh, and Hunt, 1858).

95. Norfolk Records Office file FC76/92. This was a reprint of a sermon preached

whether his comments were ever shared with his brother, or kept private. What is known is that he kept his brother's sermon.

In his last will and testament Govett left his piano and music to his oldest sister Sarah Louisa Wright, and to each brother and sister the "option of taking any one volume out of my library."[96] His money and his home were divided among friends and the church, but were not bequeathed to his family. Interestingly, on 27 March 1901, Govett's brother, Decimus Storry Govett, then archdeacon of Gibraltar, wrote a response to a letter he received from William Dix, executor and long time friend of Govett, which had enquired whether Decimus would be interested in having a book from his brother's library. Decimus was interested in having a book by Tennyson should the library contain one (but did not request any theological books). He was also interested in any recent photographs of his brother.[97] Govett's funeral service suggests the possible estranged relationships at the end of his life since no siblings attended his service. However, by the time of his death only three brothers remained alive—two in England and one in New Zealand. The only relative present at Govett's funeral service was Colin Romaine.[98] The precise relationship of Romaine to Govett is not known, but he was a man of some leisure and social prominence who resided at the Priory, Old Windsor, Berkshire.[99] It should be noted, however, that one of Govett's sisters died on 21 February (just one day after Govett), and the wife of one of his brothers on 23 February, making it seemingly impractical for some of the surviving family members to attend.[100]

New friendships and acquaintances outside of the Established Church were formed over the years. His popularity was growing so that by late in 1859 he was invited by Reverend Thomas Dugard to preach to a new Free Church congregation in temporary facilities in Hackney, on the east side of London. Dugard had seceded from the Church of England in 1858 taking with him from the Haggerstone Church, where he had been curate, a "large

---

by Govett's brother, D. S. Govett, M.A., Archbishop. "God First Not Last, The Lesson of the War." A sermon preached in Gibraltar Cathedral at the Service of Intercession, 30 January 1900, by Decimus Storry Govett, M.A., Archdeacon, "published at the request of many and the expense of one, Mr. Adamson, Church Street, Gibraltar. For the War Fund."

96. See Robert Govett the younger's will, proved 3 June 1901, Norwich.

97. Norfolk Records Office file FC76/89. Letter from Govett's brother Decimus Storry Govett, Archdeacon of Gibraltar, later to become Dean of Gibraltar, fifteen years his younger, to William Dix, esq. (27 March 1901).

98. Govett article *Eastern Daily Press* (26 February 1901).

99. *The London Times* (19 March 1924). Death notice of William Colin Campbell Romaine.

100. Govett article *Eastern Daily Press* (26 February 1901).

body of friends and followers."[101] The occasion of the invitation was the active canvassing for contributions toward the completion of a new 4,000 person church building. On this occasion Govett preached from Galatians 1:8, 9.[102] The subject he chose was the revision of the Prayer Book, especially referencing the baptismal services, the Catechism and the Confirmation services. Govett insisted in his sermon that the Prayer Book required baptism upon a "promised" faith—which he believed was unknown in the New Testament. As a dissenter Govett was free to contend that infant baptism was in itself inconsistent with justification by faith and preached that it implied a justification without faith. He managed to also bring to bear in his sermon another subject becoming of primary importance to him—the doctrine of the final perseverance of the regenerate. To this he added that the doctrine was overthrown if the Established Church and its infant baptism services were right.[103] For Govett it was a matter of standing for what he believed to be biblical truth.

Later in life he began a friendship with a writer and part-time theologian by the name George H. Pember. Pember, a man described as being of independent means, was a member of the Brethren movement. He wrote on several subjects of mutual theological interest to Govett—one being the coming of the Kingdom and Christ's return. In 1886 Pember published a book entitled *The Antichrist Babylon and the Coming of the Kingdom*.[104] Govett, in keeping with the importance he placed upon the understanding of the Kingdom, wrote a note to Pember correcting what he believed to be a mistake made in the book where Pember inadvertently wrote the word "kingdom" when (in Govett's estimation) the word should have been "kings." Pember wrote a respectful letter in response thanking Govett for "setting him right" with the correction and promising to correct the mistake in future publications.[105] The importance of this respectful relationship will become relevant when their common interest in the subject of "partial rapture" is described in chapter 6 which articulates Govett's impact upon

---

101. "Free Church Movement In Hackney," *The Harbenger: A Magazine of the Countess of Huntingdon's Connexion* (November 1859) 271.

102. Galatians 1:8–9 (NIV) reads: "But even if we or an angel from heaven should preach a gospel other than the one we preached to you, let him be eternally condemned! As we have already said, so now I say again: If anybody is preaching to you a gospel other than what you accepted, let him be eternally condemned!"

103. Norfolk Records Office file FC76/59 (1 of 2). Undated newspaper article.

104. George H. Pember, *The Antichrist Babylon and the Coming of the Kingdom* (London: Hodder & Stoughton, 1886).

105. Norfolk Records Office file FC76/89. Letter from G. H. Pember to Govett (2 February 1887).

the eschatology of the modern evangelical church, and postulates why his theological views fell out of favor.

Govett: Author and Pastor of Surrey Chapel (1855–1901)

Interaction between Govett and other theologians and religious writers—whether in a letter or a printed document—in an effort to correct a biblical inconsistency (or just plain error) was to become a lifelong habit. After the opening of Surrey Road Chapel in December of 1854, the remainder of Govett's life was committed to preaching to his congregation and utilizing his private time in habitually digesting the religious dialogue as it made its way into the print culture. Govett was an energetic writer in the period between 1855 and his death in 1901. A great portion of his writings were occupied by prophecy in general, and the doctrine of eschatological reward and that of infant baptism more specifically, while more obscure topics such as Swedenborgianism, Christadelphianism, vegetarianism, and the septenary arrangement of Scripture were integrated along the way.[106] The remainder of this study provides the understanding of these years in the context of the religious world around him and its connection to the development of his thinking.

As the volume of Govett's writings increased so did the opportunity for critical review of his work. When he was not producing tracts or books, he was often opposing the theological views of others in the numerous prophecy journals of his day. Many who read his work agreed with his theological positions, but others strongly opposed him—especially pastors and scholars within the Church of England. Nevertheless, times were changing within religious culture in Great Britain and Govett was a visible contributor to the discussions surrounding those changes. Unsettled times coupled with thoughts of the end of the age spawned more writing and more theological debates. Evangelical millennialism was on the rise. Dispensationalism was spreading. Futurists within the eschatological debate did not fade away as some predicted, but continued to exert influence upon the discussions of Christ's soon return. The Millennial Kingdom, to be ushered in by a great series of apocalyptic events, was increasingly on the minds of evangelicals in Great Britain, as it had been for many generations of believers before

---

106. See Robert Govett, *The Son of God (in Matthew): A Word about Swedenborgianism* (Norwich: Fletcher and Son, nd); Robert Govett, *Christadelphians, Not Christians*, 2nd ed. (Norwich: Fletcher and Son, 1874); Robert Govett, *Vegetarianism: A Dialogue* (London: Campbell, 1849); Robert Govett, *The Septenary Arrangement of Scripture: Reissued from Dr. Kitto's "Journal of Sacred Literature"* (London: Campbell, 1860).

them.[107] This was the religious climate into which the young Govett stepped upon graduation from university and into the pulpit—an eschatological debate that had actually begun in earnest in the sixteenth century.[108] And by the age of forty, when he published *Entrance into the Kingdom. or Reward According to Works*, he had become fully immersed with the development of his original thoughts on the Millennial Kingdom.

---

107. Gribben, *Evangelical Millennialism*, 2.
108. Ibid., 16.

CHAPTER 3

Govett's Writings and Victorian Print Culture

THE DEVELOPMENT OF GOVETT'S writings concerning the "last things" in general and "judgment in the life to come" in particular remained topics of interest throughout his lifetime. He was not alone in these preoccupations. Victorian culture brought the topics nearly to a point of obsession. Anthony C. Thiselton in *Life After Death: A New Approach to the Last Things* (2012) draws attention to the death rate prior to 1900 and notes that it was very different from today when society has the luxury of postponing questions about death and beyond. For the Victorians, the death of children and friends was a regular experience. The fate of unbelievers also dominated the debate of the nineteenth century. Govett frequently engaged in that debate, along with the likes of John Henry Newman and E. B. Pusey who also spoke of the subtle danger of the enemy.[1] To sway from the position of orthodoxy could have severe consequences. F. D. Maurice, for instance, was dismissed from his Chair at King's College, London, around 1853, for arguing against eternal or everlasting punishment.[2] Govett also felt the sting of dissent on occasion, but as it concerned his stance on infant baptism it had consequences that affected his ordination and changed the direction of his life.

---

1. See, for example, John Henry Newman, *Parochial and Plain Sermons,* 8 vols. (London: Longmans, Green, 1894) 1:255.

2. Anthony C. Thiselton, *Life after Death, a New Approach to the Last Things* (Grand Rapids: Eerdmans, 2012) 149.

Govett's Dissent

As we have already seen, February 1844 marked an end to Govett's preaching in the Church of England. His decision to resign was immediately followed by his Bishop's written response. Bishop Stanley of Norwich accused Govett of acting irrationally in simply "quitting" the church. But Govett's decision to do so was prompted by deep conviction—primarily over the church's doctrinal stance on infant baptism. Most troubling to Bishop Stanley in removing Govett's license to preach was that his actions would increase divisions and schisms in the church. He points out that Govett would someday regret adding to the problems. Looming in the back of Bishop Stanley's mind was likely the divisions created over the issue of liberalizing subscription to the Thirty-nine Articles. Three years after the accession of Queen Victoria to the throne in 1837 the issue of subscriptions became acute. It came before the House of Lords by means of a petition presented by Archbishop Whately who proposed that the Articles be made to harmonize with the beliefs of the clergy. James C. Livingston speculates that not much would have come of the proposal had it not been for a speech given by Bishop Stanley who spoke on the "elasticity" of the Church of England. Stanley concluded that not all clergy agreed with every part of their subscription and that giving the clergy this latitude was sound. This started a wave of concern through the church and provoked Tractarians to defend the Catholic interpretation of the Articles through John Henry Newman's Tract XC.[3] Bishop Stanley's intervention into the debate is brought out in an article titled, "Catholic Convert Club," an 1840 article from the *Bengal Catholic Expositor*.[4] The article reports that his only anxiety over the question of subscription to the Thirty-nine Articles is "to raise the church in the estimation of the public" and that the church has a "sort of elasticity" that may be shaped to meet the views of many who dissent from its articles and liturgy.[5] Perhaps Stanley's flexibility in this matter would have extended to Govett's situation had the latter not been led by his convictions to resign his license. Yet, Bishop Stanley's concern over schism

---

3. James C. Livingston, *The Ethics of Belief: An Essay on the Victorian Religious Conscience* (Tallahassee: American Academy of Religion, 1974) 2.

4. "Catholic Convert Club," *Bengal Catholic Expositor* 3, no. 24 (1840) 356. The magazine published only 8 volumes. *The Bangel Catholic Expositor* was first published in Calcutta 6 July 1839. Although the periodical was published in India, it is thought to have been circulated in England. The publication continued as *The Catholic Herald* on 13 March 1841, and again was changed 1 January 1842 to *The Bangel Catholic Herald*. It ceased publication in 1864. See John S. North, and Brent Nelson, eds., *The Waterloo Directory of English Newspapers and Periodicals, 1800–1900* (Waterloo: North Waterloo Academic, 2003).

5. "Catholic Convert Club," *Bengal Catholic Expositor* 3, no. 24 (1840) 356.

was apparently not shared by Govett, who later defended his actions in *Are Dissenters from the Church of England Guilty of Schism?* (1872). In this tract, Govett asks "are not Evangelical Dissenters, in assembling together as believers, really on the Scriptural foundation?" He cautiously added, "While right in our general position, as taking no name but Christ's, we may be wrong in our individual spirits, as being deficient in Christian affection towards those that are Christ's."[6] Nevertheless, Govett stuck by his decision to resign from the Church of England, and immediately published his first tract opposing infant baptism (1844).[7] Yet, while Govett left the Church of England on scriptural principles pertaining to the mode and meaning of the sacrament of baptism, by the 1890s he revealed a broader concern. He found the Church of England itself to be unscriptural. In his commentary on Colossians he opposed the state church with the accusation that "no one country, no one city, forms an assembly. The Church of England, the Church of Rome, is an unscriptural expression, because, it supposes that every Englishman and every Roman is a child of God."[8]

The decision to leave the Church of England also appears to have liberated him to express himself prolifically in print. After 1844, and throughout the remainder of the decade, Govett published no fewer than twenty-one books and tracts. Included in the writings were numerous tracts on select New Testament parables as well as a few on the subject of baptism.[9] An 1846 tract is the first to outline his convictions about the millennium and the Rapture of the church, subjects that would become deeply important to Govett. The title he chose for this first tract on the subject was *Will All Believers Enter the Millennial Kingdom? A Reply to the Rev. R. A. Purdon's Attack in "The Last Vials."*[10] While belief in the Rapture was not an issue

6. Robert Govett, *Are Dissenters from the "Church of England" Guilty of Schism?* (Glasgow: MacLehose, 1872) 14–15.

7. Robert Govett, *Not Water Baptism but the Gifts of the Holy Spirit the Baptism of Christ* (Norwich: Fletcher, 1844). See also Robert Govett, *The Gifts of The Holy Ghost and Miracle Essentially Connected with Justification by Faith* (Norwich: Fletcher, 1844).

8. Robert Govett, *Christ the Head; the Church His Body: Its Dangers, Duties, Glories: or, the Argument of Colossians* (Norwich: Fletcher and Son, 1890) 239.

9. Govett published seventeen identified tracts throughout his lifetime specifically on the error of infant baptism and numerous other books and tracts which contain mention of his position on the doctrine.

10. *The Last Vials; Being a Series of Essays Upon the Subject of the Second Advent* was a monthly periodical that began in February 1846, published in London. Robert A. Purdon was a frequent contributor. The magazine was published monthly in London from February 1846 to 1879. Its stated purpose was to make available prophetic and religious writings. See John S. North, and Brent Nelson, eds., *The Waterloo Directory of English Newspapers and Periodicals, 1800–1900* (Waterloo: North Waterloo Academic, 2003).

important to orthodoxy at this time, his understanding that not all believers will be raptured prior to the Tribulation would become increasingly controversial by the end of the century.[11] By 1853 this subject of "partial rapture" was fully developed and presented in *Entrance into the Kingdom. or Reward According to Works*.[12] It marked the substantial introduction of a previously unknown doctrine. The subject was ardently contested in journals throughout the remaining century, forcing Govett to regularly, yet tirelessly, defend his position. It became one of the pivotal reasons for the eventual eclipse of his reputation. Even the general subject of the millennium drew ongoing debate as theologians debated the historicist and the futurist positions. Govett, being decisively aware of the millennial debate, drew precise attention to it in his commentary of the gospel of John. Writing concerning the exegesis of John 4:23, which speaks of a time (or hour) that has come in which "true" worshipers will worship the Father in spirit and in truth, Govett uses this text to refute the objections made by "our anti-millenarian friends." He defends millennialism with a question: "Would you cast us back in your millennial scheme upon a dispensation worn out and repealed?"[13] Yet the millennial debate did not end quickly and only intensified. For instance, in 1867 an unnamed author identifying himself as "a lover of truth" wrote "What is the Millennium, and How Cometh It?," an article which appeared in the *Earthen Vessel*.[14] It drew attention to the intensifying eschatological debate which by mid-century had centered upon what the author identified as a millennial controversy that "waxed stronger and stronger" and dividing Christendom into larger numbers of "tribes" than ever. He notes sarcastically that a long column of writers of prophecy "have made good work for the publishers."[15] This evidence of skepticism occasionally accompanied the prophetic controversies that routinely appeared in print.

11. Robert Govett, *Will All Believers Enter the Millennial Kingdom? A Reply to the Rev. R.A. Purdon's Attack in "The Last Vials"* (London: Nisbet, 1846).

12. Robert Govett, *Entrance into the Kingdom. or Reward according to Works* (Norwich: Fletcher and Son, 1853).

13. Govett, *Exposition of the Gospel of St. John*, 145.

14. *The Earthen Vessel and Christian Record and Review*, later to be changed to *The Earthen Vessel and Gospel Herald* (1887–1919), was originally published in 1845 in London. Its orientation was for Baptists and Calvinists. The *Introductory Address* (p. 5) of the magazine noted that the *Vessel* "is for the gathering in, and gathering up, 'the small and despised:'—'the outcasts of Israel:'—the halt, the lame, the satan-hunted, and sin distracted souls:—such as composed David's ragged regiment; such as are in distress, in debt and discontented; that they may find contentment only in David's Son our Lord, who pays all their debt and makes them free men in his kingdom forever."

15. "What is the Millennium, and How Cometh It?" (A letter signed: A lover of truth), *The Earthen Vessel, and Christian Record* 23 (1867) 235.

One such controversy was over the historicist position versus the futurist. Govett firmly sided with the futurists. And while he was at odds with the historicists his views were often included in their published works. For example, Michael Paget Baxter (1834–1910), publisher of the *Christian Herald*, clergyman of the Church of England, historicist and frequent predictor of the date of Christ's return, described Govett as an "eminent and voluminous expositor."[16] Govett is referenced no less than twelve times in his 1887 work in regard to such issues as the vials and the trumpets presented in the book of Revelation.[17]

Crawford Gribben reminds his readers that the historicist consensus was interrupted by the sudden popularity of prophetic "futurism."[18] Futurism tended to reflect an increasing popularity of premillennialism. Isaac Newton, in the late seventeenth century, and Edward Irving, in the early nineteenth century, for example, had preferred premillennialism to postmillennial historicism. Dispensationalism caused further loss of popularity in historicism as Darby advanced dispensationalism's tenets accentuated by a distinction between Israel and the church. The tenets of dispensationalism, while not entirely unique to Darby, are nonetheless historically ascribed to him. Before long, Darby's tenacity and overbearing personality allowed the developing dispensational premillennialism to become widely disseminated. Perhaps the most innovative feature of Darby's eschatology was the "secret rapture" of the church by Christ at his Second Coming. It has proven to be one of the most controversial tenets. Attempts have been made in recent years to link this teaching to the utterances of a Scottish Irvingite girl named Margaret MacDonald.[19] In 1830 MacDonald was reported to have received prophetic visions and claimed she was given the revelation that the church would be raptured before the appearance of the Antichrist.[20] While Darby's critics have promoted this assertion with considerable energy, their case has remained unconvincing.[21] Mark Sweetnam

---

16. The 1887 editions of the *Christian Herald* claimed that it circulated over 250,000 copies per week.

17. Michael Baxter, *Forty Coming Wonders; Between 1890 and 1901, as Foreshadowed in the Prophecies of Daniel and Revelation* (London: Christian Herald, 1887) 282.

18. Crawford Gribben, "Evangelical Eschatology and the Puritan Hope," in Michael A. G. Haykin, and Kenneth J. Stewart, eds., *The Emergence of Evangelicalism: Exploring Historical Continuities* (Nottingham: InterVarsity, 2008) 383.

19. See Mal Couch, ed., *Dictionary of Premillennial Theology: A Practical Guide to the People, Viewpoints, and History of Prophetic Studies* (Grand Rapids: Kregel, 1996).

20. Couch, *Dictionary of Premillennial Theology*, 244.

21. See Dave McPherson, *The Three R's: Rapture, Revisionism, Robbery: Pretribulation Rapturism from 1830 to Hal Lindsey* (Simpsonville: P.O.S.T., 1998); *The Rapture Plot* (Simpsonville: Millennium III, 1994); *The Great Rapture Hoax* (Fletcher: New

in "Theological Roots of the Scofield Reference Bible" warns that "we should be very careful of the blame by association that is at the root of some efforts to link Darby's unconventional understanding of Christ's return to some unpalatable sources."[22]

With its dissemination "Darbyite" theology severed an important link between nineteenth-century evangelicals and the majority of their post-Reformation precursors. This new premillennialism declared that there could be no expected fulfillment of prophecy before the "secret rapture"—not even the emergence of the Antichrist.[23] In his lectures on the Second Coming, Darby speaks of the Rapture as being set before the church as an elementary and foundational truth. He states in his lecture on 1 Thessalonians that the Second Coming of Christ forms the constant topic of Scripture, and "enters as a present expectation into the whole structure of the habits of thought of those who were taught by the apostles." He laments how its loss was the sign of the church's decline and its sinking into worldliness and the world.[24] In his lecture on the book of Romans chapter 11, which he believes concerns the nation of Israel in the Coming Kingdom, Darby notes that of the two great subjects, besides the salvation of individuals, of which the Scriptures speaks—namely, the church and the government of the world—the latter leads directly to the Jews as its center just as the church is of the heavenly glory under Christ, "under whom as their head all things in heaven and earth are to be gathered together in one." Darby believed that this government would extend over the whole earth and that the royal nation, seat, and center of government will be the Jewish people.[25] According to Larry Crutchfield, Darby's real prophetic concern was how the church related to prophecy—believing it to be connected only with earth, and therefore applying primarily to the nation of Israel. Crutchfield asserts that Darby's views pertaining to the Rapture of the church and the first resurrection were merely parenthetical statements of what will happen to the true church while the "real business of prophecy is being conducted in other more earthly contexts."[26]

Puritan Library, 1983).

22. Mark S. Sweetnam, "Theological Roots of the Scofield Reference Bible: British and Irish Roots," in R. Todd Mangum and Mark S. Sweetnam, *The Scofield Bible: Its History and Impact on the Evangelical Church* (Colorado Springs: Paternoster, 2009) 72.

23. Gribben, "Evangelical Eschatology and the Puritan Hope," 383–84.

24. John Nelson Darby, *Lectures on the Second Coming* (London: Morrish, 1909) 1–7.

25. Darby, *Lectures on the Second Coming*, 90–97.

26. Crutchfield, *The Origins of Dispensationalism*, 158.

The Rapture of the church and the future of the Jews were also tenets of faith shared by Govett who himself helped popularize futurist hermeneutics in his numerous contributions in journals and published books throughout the latter half of the nineteenth century. But, while Darby's prophetic interests were principally centered upon conditions on earth and Israel, Govett's interests were centered fundamentally upon the raptured church and its relationship to Christ in heaven. Concerning the Rapture being "secret," as Darby claimed in his writings, Govett was not content to allow that term to stand without further description and Scriptural understanding. The term received Govett's careful attention in *The Rainbow* in 1864 through his article "Will the Rapture be Visible or Secret?"[27] He asks the question, "how often do Christians fail to see, that in most of the questions on which opposite sides are taken among believers each party holds a portion of truth, and that the true unity of God's plan comprehends all the parts?" Benjamin Wills Newton (1807–1899), briefly an influential leader in the Brethren movement and even more briefly close friend of Darby's, had asked the question: "Will the Second Advent of our Lord and Saviour, for which we wait, be secret, or in manifested glory?"[28] Govett responded, "The Second Advent of our Lord will be both secret and in manifested glory. Its time and aspect of secrecy will come first, and then its outburst of glory."[29] Govett finds Newton, and by association Darby, guilty of error in wrongly distinguishing between the Savior's "coming" and "manifestation."[30] It should be understood that there are no acknowledgments in any of Govett's writings that point to Darby as his source of enlightenment on any subject of "dispensational" truth. On the contrary, Govett was often at odds with Darby on central issues of Christian teaching.[31] For example, according to Darby's theory, the righteousness of God by which a sinner is justified consists of the essential righteousness of the "Father," displayed in the exaltation of Christ to his right hand in heaven,

---

27. Robert Govett, "Will the Rapture be Visible or Secret?," *The Rainbow: A Magazine of Christian Literature, with Special Emphasis to the Revealed Future of the Church and the World* 1 (1864) 257–65. *The Rainbow: A Magazine of Christian Literature, with Special Reference to the Revealed Future of the Church and the World*, was a monthly magazine published in London from January 1864 to December 1887. See John S. North and Brent Nelson, eds., *The Waterloo Directory of English Newspapers and Periodicals, 1800–1900* (Waterloo: North Waterloo Academic, 2003).

28. See Benjamin Wills Newton, *The Second Advent of Our Lord Not Secret but in Manifested Glory* (London: Houlston & Wright, 1862) 3.

29. Govett, *Will the Rapture be Visible or Secret*, 258.

30. Ibid., 259.

31. See "Reviews," *The Voice of Truth; or, Strict Baptist Magazine* 2 (1864) 183–85, 213.

on account "of the glory and honor he had brought by the person and government of him who sent him."[32] Govett disagreed.

The Antichrist Controversy

Indeed, Govett disagreed with many theologians on other important eschatological issues such as questions surrounding the Antichrist. Because of his futurist position he was not prepared to accuse the pope of being the Antichrist as the historicists of his day identified him. But he was prepared to speculate that when the Antichrist did appear he would be a "Roman." This interpretation of Scripture drew criticism from both futurists and historicists. Govett's opinion is expressed, for example, by E. G. Lea in a letter to *The Rainbow*, which agreed with Govett that Rome has had in the past, and will have in the future, a large and important place in prophecy, but he was not prepared to agree with him that the Antichrist who is to come will of necessity be a Roman.[33] Earlier Lea had written that he was glad to see that Govett had received the language of the Apocalypse in its description of the Antichrist, according to its "true grammatical sense." He would prefer, however, that Govett endeavor to divest himself of the Roman "figment" in his interpretation of prophecies relating to the Antichrist.[34] Still, Govett's writing devoted to a futurist perspective was highly valued in such magazines as *The Rainbow* which sought to print prophetic-related material. In 1870, after it had reviewed Govett's tract entitled *The Kingdom of God Future*, the magazine commented: "'R.G.' is not a novice, but an old student of, and a very voluminous writer of prophecy; and this thick pamphlet, price two shillings, proves that our friend Mr. Govett has not yet tired of the work of exposition. The writer has proved his general position that the Kingdom of God is future, and for that reason we commend his work to notice."[35] In contrast, Thomas Rawson Birks (1810–1883), Church of England clergyman and Cambridge theologian, writes concerning prophecy and its understanding by the church in *First Elements of Sacred Prophecy* (1843) that the church since the time of the Reformation has followed certain maxims of interpretation including that the visions in the book of Daniel began at

---

32. "Reviews," *The Voice of Truth; or, Strict Baptist Magazine* 2 (1864) 183–85.

33. E. G. Lea, "Mr. Govett on the Antichrist," *The Rainbow: A Magazine of Christian Literature, with Special Reference to the Revealed Future of the Church and the World* 2 (1865) 425–26.

34. "Questions for Mr. Govett," *The Rainbow: A Magazine of Christian Literature, with Special Reference to the Revealed Future of the Church and the World* 2 (1865) 329.

35. "Literature," *The Rainbow: A Magazine of Christian Literature, with Special Reference to the Revealed Future of the Church and the World* 7 (1870) 528.

the time of the prophet. He further contends that the events predicted in the book of Revelation begin from the time of prophecy—or within the first century—and that the little horn of Daniel chapter 7 denotes the Papacy. In addition, there are maxims which he concludes are received from the most learned of the Protestant commentators in England from the time of Joseph Mede to the time of his present book, which include the understanding that the two beasts in Revelation 13 denote the civil and ecclesiastical Latin empire, and that a prophetic "day" denotes a natural year, and a prophetic "time" three hundred and sixty natural years. But all of these maxims were rejected by several contemporary writers which he lists as DeBurgh, Maitland, Todd, Dodsworth, Tyso, MacCausland, and Govett.[36] Birks distinguishes the position of the Established Church and what he considers its rival system as the "Protestant" and the "Futurist" interpretations.[37] Furthermore, *The Churchman's Monthly Review and Chronicle*[38] utilized Birks's *First Elements of Sacred Prophecy* to elaborate on its position that found the Tractarian and the Futurist movements were co-equal assailants against the church. It charges the Futurists as having "the same fondness for Rome and hatred for Protestantism."[39]

In the same year in which Birks's book appeared in print *The Churchman's Monthly Review and Chronicle*[40] reviewed Govett's book *The Revelation of St. John, Literal and Future*.[41] The reviewer begins with the claim that the general view of the Apocalypse, as a prophetic history extending

36. Toward the close of the nineteenth century the tension between the futurists and the historicists was still prominent in the Christian journals. C. H. Spurgeon's journal the *Sword and the Trowel* reviewed G. H. Pember's book *The Antichrist, Babylon and the Coming of the Lord*, 2nd ed. (London: Hodder and Stoughton, 1888). In the review it states, "In fact, like DeBurgh, B. W. Newton, and Mr. Govett, of Norwich, he is a 'futurist,' while Elliot, of the 'Horae Apocalypticae;' Cumming, and our good friends Mr. and Mrs. Guinness, have preferred the more modern system, generally known as the 'Historico-Prophetic.'" See *The Sword and the Trowel* (January 1889) 36.

37. Thomas Rawson Birks, *First Elements of Sacred Prophecy: Including an Examination of Several Recent Expositions, and the Year-Day Theory* (London: Painter, 1843) 1–3.

38. *The Churchman's Monthly Review and Chronicle* was a monthly magazine published in London between January 1841 and December 1847. See John S. North, and Brent Nelson, eds., *The Waterloo Directory of English Newspapers and Periodicals, 1800–1900* (Waterloo: North Waterloo Academic, 2003).

39. *The Churchman's Monthly Review and Chronicle* (September 1843) 635.

40. *The Churchman's Monthly Review and Chronicle* (April 1843) 264–78.

41. Robert Govett, *The Revelation of St. John, Literal and Future: Being an Exposition of That Book: To which are Added Remarks in Refutation of the Ideas that the Pope is the Man of Sin, and that Popery is the Apostasy Predicted by St. Paul, with a Special Reference to Doctor O'Sullivan on the Apostasy* (London: Hamilton, Adams, 1843).

from the time of the Apostles until the end of the world, prevailed almost without contradiction for many centuries. He finds that in the ninth century and following, as the church became increasingly corrupt, pious men began to see a correlation between the Church of Rome and the visions of prophecy that predicted similar features to the harlot city of Babylon. He holds that once more, after the Reformation took its course, the Apocalypse became a compounding object of interest. Looking back to the early writers the Reformed churches made a connection between the corruption of the dark ages and the papal encroachment upon the symbols of Babylon. Under Mede and other writers a fuller school of historical interpretation arose which was prevalent through the first part of the nineteenth century.[42] Additionally, the French Revolution revived a particular resurgence of interest in prophecy in the church. The church saw what it perceived to be the judgment of God upon the corruption on Christendom and the continued idolatries of the Church of Rome. The previous Protestant writers of prophecy were reconfirmed as events seemed to affirm the visions of the Apocalypse. In the same year as the publication of Birks's book a contributor to *The Churchman's Monthly* noted that for the past twenty years (1820s–1830s) the Church of Rome has "sprung up into new and vigorous activity . . . hence there has once again been a renewed attempt to overturn those views of the Apocalypse which have prevailed for centuries among protestant Christians."[43] The unnamed contributor's position was that the Futurist movement is anti-protestant in its interpretation because it refuses to recognize that the Apocalypse is a catholic history of the church through all ages. On this basis the article introduces Govett as a young writer who is an "estimable clergyman" who is far removed from a "Popish or a Tractarian creed," and is "sincere and honest in the expression of views which he believes to be true and important."[44] But the reviewer believes Govett's work to be based on a false principle and injurious and will spread to threaten the life of the church. He further states that Govett's work follows Burgh more closely than any other Futurist writer although Govett's work is more "labored and full," and, in his estimation, has its considerable share of defects common to this school.[45] At the time of the appearance of this article Govett was thirty years of age and still ordained in the Church of England. Because of his age the author scolds Govett for lecturing writers who have far greater learning and experience and who have spent more years

42. *The Churchman's Monthly Review and Chronicle* (April 1843) 264–66.
43. Ibid., 267.
44. Ibid., 268.
45. Ibid.

in studying prophecy than Govett had lived. He finds that Govett lectures them in a tone of superior wisdom which would be much better spared even if true.[46] Typical of even those who disagreed with Govett this author finds some things commendable with *The Revelation of St. John, Literal and Future*. Differing with Govett's futurist stance he nonetheless finds Govett's comments on the first resurrection worthy of commendation since, on the whole, they are "valuable and sound, and some of them original."[47] Still the reviewer is disposed to think that the futurist position, which he refers to as a novel theory, has almost reached its limit. There will return a fresh confirmation of the views of Protestant interpreters who long announced that a revival would take place before the final judgment is poured out upon the earth and "popery" finally overthrown.[48] He concludes his article with the hope that Govett's diligence and research may "before long be redirected into a profitable direction in such dangerous times."[49]

Nearly forty years later Birks remarked in his 1880 publication, *Thoughts on the Times and Seasons of Sacred Prophecy*,[50] "I believe we have now, in 1880, reached the last night watch of the great Saturday of the world's history." In his work he references the two works of E. B. Elliott and Grattan Guinness, the *Horae Apocalypticae* (5th edition, 1862), and the *Approaching End of the Age Viewed in the Light of Prophecy and Science* (2nd edition, 1879) respectively. Birks concluded that they may be said conjointly "to indicate a penultimate stage of prophetic exposition."[51] In the eighth edition of Guinness's work published in 1882, he included an appendix which contained responses to the first edition. Govett had responded to that work with a sixty-page refutation entitled, *How Interpret the Apocalypse? As Naturalists? or as Supernaturalists?: A Refutation of the Historic Interpretation, with Especial Reference to the Rev. G. Guinness' "Approaching End of the Age."*[52] This was reprinted in the appendix.[53] In it Govett is described as an author

---

46. Ibid.

47. *The Churchman's Monthly Review and Chronicle* (April 1843) 277.

48. Ibid.

49. Ibid., 278.

50. Thomas Rawson Birks, *Thoughts on the Times and Seasons of Sacred Prophecy* (London: Hodder and Stoughton, 1880).

51. Birks, *Thoughts on the Times*, 3.

52. Robert Govett, *How Interpret the Apocalypse? As Naturalists? or as Supernaturalists? A Refutation of the Historic Interpretation, with Especial Reference to the Rev. G. Guinness' "Approaching End of the Age"* (Norwich: Fletcher and Son, 1879).

53. H. Grattan Guinness, *The Approaching End of the Age Viewed in the Light of History, Prophecy, and Science*, Appendix D, "Containing Answers to Futurist Objections," 8th ed. (London: Hodder and Stoughton, 1882) 699–761.

who largely writes on prophetic subjects. But Govett's response is dismissed as a reiteration of old futurist objections to the historicist system which have been satisfactorily answered many times. Guinness's stance is one from the historicist school which held that the Apocalypse contains a threefold series of facts which have elapsed since John saw its visions. They include: the facts about the Roman Empire and its course through history; the facts about the Papal dynasty and its rise in power; and, the facts concerning the Church of Rome, its decadence, and loss of influence over the continental nations, including the facts of the Reformation and the total withdrawal from the Roman Catholic Church of all the Protestant nations.[54] As such the futurists and the historicists were strongly invested in the prophetic understanding of the Antichrist. One historicist was Robert A. Purdon, a frequent contributor to *The Rainbow*. He wrote to express his opinion on a number of issues related to the Antichrist. On one such occasion, in August 1865, his letter was published to refute Govett's understanding of the Antichrist. He partially agreed with Govett on some grounds—such as the means by which the Antichrist will die. On other issues related to the Antichrist he disagrees with Govett's assessment—such as whether the Antichrist is an ordinary man until he becomes the Antichrist.[55] Speculating on the identity of the Antichrist, Purdon writes in *The Rainbow* that Louis Napoleon could very well be the Antichrist (in opposition to Govett's denial) although he agrees with Govett that the Antichrist is still future.[56] On another occasion Purdon writes to complain that Govett's recent letter in the magazine was a waste of space and could have been used for more important prophetic debate. Govett had written to defend the view that Louis Napoleon was not the Antichrist based on the "spelling of his name."[57]

Surprisingly, this was a continuation of the dispute started ten years earlier in the *Last Vials*. Purdon speaks of the league that was formed in 1576 between Catherine de Medicis and the Princes of Lorraine for the destruction of Protestantism in France, and concludes that the Huguenots were left stronger than before because under the providence of God they possessed honest hearts and vigorous hands. "Faith stood its ground in defiance of every Popish combination."[58] Purdon held that the Lord had

54. Guinness, *The Approaching End of the Age*, Appendix D, 704.

55. *The Rainbow: A Magazine of Christian Literature, with Special Reference to the Revealed Future of the Church and the World* 2 (1865) 372.

56. *The Rainbow: A Magazine of Christian Literature, with Special Reference to the Revealed Future of the Church and the World* 2 (1865) 93–94.

57. *The Rainbow: A Magazine of Christian Literature, with Special Reference to the Revealed Future of the Church and the World* 2 (1865) 139–40.

58. Robert A. Purdon, "The Great Popish League," *The Last Vials: Being a Series of*

raised up another league far more powerful and wide-extended than the one begun in 1576—since the one begun in that year was confined to a single territory and was France against herself. This new threat was Louis Napoleon, Emperor of France, who had in one year advanced to "universal empire, with a rapidity which has never yet been approached by any monarch in the world."[59] He builds his case for the identification of the Antichrist. Purdon is confident that the old "year-day" interpreters of prophecy, who identify "Popery and Antichrist," appear to have agreed upon one point with reference to the general prophecies of the Old Testament. He contends that the extensive prophecies found in Isaiah and Ezekiel (and other prophets) concerning the mention of nations were long ago fulfilled. In doing so, these writers have confined unfulfilled prophecy almost entirely to the future fall of the Roman Catholic Church, and of the Pope. Govett is singled out as asserting that the greater part of the Old Testament prophecies are yet to be fulfilled. He calls attention to Govett's book on Isaiah published in 1841. Purdon states that "this opinion, we need hardly say, has not the slightest foundation."[60]

While it is true that journal articles abounded and made their impact upon Victorian culture and its thoughts of the end-times and speculations surrounding the Antichrist—such as those written by *The Voice Upon the Mountains* in the mid- to late 1860s[61]—some of the most influential writings were book-length studies of the subject. One such published work was that of James Henthron Todd (1805–1869), a graduate and Fellow of Trinity College, Dublin, whose book was based upon the lectures he delivered in the chapel of Trinity College during the Michaelmas term 1841. He chose as his subject the biblical prophecies relating to the Antichrist. In his lectures he attacked the view which was then held by many Irish protestant clergy that the pope was the Antichrist. These lectures were subsequently published under the title *Six Discourses on the Prophecies Relating to Antichrist in the Apocalypse of St. John*. His theological position is best described in his own words stated in the Preface:

Essays upon the Subject of the Second Advent, no.1, tenth series (1855) 1.

59. Ibid., 2–3.

60. Robert A. Purdon, "The Restoration of the Gentiles," *The Last Vials: Being a Series of Essays Upon the Subject of the Second Advent*, no.6, tenth series (1855) 1–2. See Robert Govett, *Isaiah Unfulfilled: Being an Exposition of the Prophet; with New Version and Critical Notes to which are Added Two Dissertations One on the "Sons of God" and "Giants" of Genesis VI and the Other a Comparative Estimate of the Hebrew and Greek Texts* (London: Nisbet, 1841) 123.

61. See *The Voice upon the Mountains. A Journal of Prophetic Testimony and Evangelistic Effort* 2 (1868); and vol. 3 (1869).

The author of the following pages does not think so ill of the Reformation, and is too deeply convinced of the truth of that Protestantism which is professed by the Church of England, to suppose for a moment that its cause can suffer any thing by renouncing error or embracing truth. The real question therefore should be, not what interpretation of prophecy is most useful or effective in controversy, but what interpretation is most in accordance with the plain words of holy Scripture, and most likely to represent exactly the mind of the Holy Ghost. The Pope-Antichrist argument is, no doubt, an effective weapon with the ignorant or the weak-minded, who look not beyond the surface, and are led away by words, rather than by things.[62]

Another book-length study worthy of note was John Kitto's (1804–1854) *Cyclopaedia of Biblical Literature* published in 1845 in two volumes. The work was well regarded but contained only a brief article on the Antichrist mentioning its theological debate by simply stating that the meaning of the word has been greatly modified by the controversies of various churches and sects.[63] By the end of the century the dividing lines of prophetic thought respecting the coming of the Antichrist had become sufficiently delineated for Sir William Smith (1813–1893) to publish a dictionary on the Bible that included a ten-page comprehensive investigation of the subject. By its second edition in 1893 the *Dictionary of the Bible Comprising its Antiquities, Biography, Geography, and National History* had expanded from its original two volumes to three. The expanded article on the Antichrist took up a discussion of four classes of writings on the controversial subject. It defined the classes as those who regard the Antichrist as an individual who is yet future; those who regard him as a polity now present; those who regard him as an individual whose time has already passed; and those who consider that nothing is meant beyond anti-Christian and lawless principle, not embodied either in an individual or in a special polity.[64]

Govett unequivocally believed that the Antichrist was an individual who was yet future. His position made him a frequent target of authors holding a historicist understanding of end-time events. Yet, Govett was

---

62. James Henthorn Todd, *Six Discourses on the Prophecies Relating to Antichrist in the Apocalypse of St. John. Preached before the University of Dublin, at the Donnellan Lecture* (London: F. & J. Rivington, 1846), xxi–ii.

63. John Kitto, ed., *The Cyclopaedia of Biblical Literature* (New York: American Book Exchange, 1881) 1:162.

64. Sir William Smith, and J. M. Fuller, eds., *A Dictionary of the Bible Comprising its Antiquities, Biography, Geography, and National History*, 2nd ed. (London: Murray, 1893) 1/1:142.

not the only target of the historicists who found themselves on the defensive as a result of an increasing volume of futurist writings upon which to cite. In 1875 Burlington B. Wale wrote *The Closing Days of Christendom*. It was a book on end-time prophecy which favored the views of the historicist. In 1883 the book was enlarged in its second edition by one hundred and fifty pages in which Wale, by his own admission, does not hesitate to express his "growing conviction in the general accuracy of the views propounded."[65] Govett, as well as other futurists to include Maitland, Todd, and DeBurgh, are all accused by Wale and fellow historicists of strongly sympathizing with the "Romanizing party in the Church of England."[66] The accusations against the futurist position were made primarily on the basis of refusing to believe that the Antichrist had come and was to be found in the Catholic Church. Govett, his works, and his futurist views, are cited by Wale nearly two dozen times. Unabashed by the growing criticism toward his futurist position, Govett held firm to his convictions. Just a few years after Wale's book appeared, Govett published a tract entitled *The Future Apostasy* in which he wrote:

> A conclusive proof that Romanism is not the evil thus depicted by the Holy Ghost, arises from the fact, that the Church of Rome *holds every article of the faith which is mentioned by the Apostle* [referring to 1 Timothy 3:14 to 4:8]. It believes that Jesus is God manifested in the flesh, that he died, rose, and ascended, with every other point of the faith that Paul has specified as that mystery of godliness, from which the apostates of the latter day should fall away.[67]

Govett often wrote opposing the Catholic Church on grounds that it contains profound errors of doctrine.[68] But here he finds justification to defend the church on the basis of its belief in the incarnation and ascension of Christ. Whatever Govett thought of the church's sins, he never regarded it as apostate. It could not become apostate, and could not be the source of the Antichrist, so long as it held to its creeds and so long as it professed to

---

65. Burlington B. Wale, *The Closing Days of Christendom as Foreshadowed in Parable and Prophecy*, 2nd ed. (London: Partridge, 1883), Preface to the 2nd ed., no pagination.

66. Wale, *The Closing Days of Christendom*, 379.

67. Robert Govett, *The Future Apostasy* (Norwich: Fletcher and Son, 1850) 2.

68. See, for example, Robert Govett, *The Locusts, the Euphratean Horsemen and the Two Witnesses; or, the Apocalyptic Systems of the Revds. E. B. Elliot, Dr. Cumming and Dr. Keith, Proved Unsound* (London: Nisbet, 1852).

be Christian. The church's great sin, asserts Govett, is in setting up a code of laws of human origin and enforcing them as if they were Christ's.[69]

Unorthodox Paths

Since its inception the church has always reacted strongly to unorthodox doctrine and heretical religious practice. Whenever unorthodox practice established a foothold in religious thought and began gathering committed disciples to its teaching the orthodox community tended to quickly react. Such was the case with "Christadelphianism," a religious sect that held unorthodox views on the Trinity. It made its way to England from America in the 1840s. As the religious movement began to spread in England, *The Voice Upon the Mountains* extended an invitation to Govett in 1868 to write a series of informative articles,[70] concerning the Christadelphian Ecclesia movement which was then taking hold in the larger towns—especially in the Midland districts. In his first article Govett described the movement as a sect. It arose through the mission of John Thomas, a medical doctor in America. At that time it was described as Millenarian Unitarian and concerned itself with the future Kingdom of God. The teachings contained many accepted theological points through which some adherents were attracted. But all who joined them were required to give up the essentials of the faith concerning the Trinity. Jesus was not co-eternal and equal with the Father, but was created of the Father by operation of "Holy Spirit" (not *the* Holy Spirit) upon Mary. The movement taught that the Holy Spirit is not a person in the sense as being co-equal with God the Father, but the "vehicular effluence of the Father." Jesus was of two natures—that of sinful or mortal flesh, and his present one which is holy or "spiritual flesh." On this latter matter Govett described the sect as believing that Christ rose and ascended, and was "perfected and accepted by a spirit-birth in the fulness of the Godhead," and then added, "if any one knows what that means."[71] There is no recent scholarship that includes a thorough analysis of Christadelphianism. Most of the writings stem from the nineteenth and early twentieth-centuries. Bryan R. Wilson writes that the Christadelphians consider themselves to be those who have been given

---

69. See, for example, Robert Govett, *The Popes Not the Man of Sin: Being an Answer to the Publications of Dr. Cumming, Dr. Morison, and the Rev. E. B. Elliott, on that Subject* (London: Nisbet, 1852).

70. Robert Govett, "The Christadelphian Ecclesia," *The Voice upon the Mountains. A journal of Prophetic Testimony and Evangelistic Effort* 2 (1868) 52–55.

71. Robert Govett, "The Christadelphian Ecclesia," *The Voice upon the Mountains. A Journal of Prophetic Testimony and Evangelistic Effort* 2 (1868) 52.

the opportunity of becoming "a people prepared for the Lord."[72] They were as opposed to Protestantism as to Catholicism.[73]

Later, in the June issue of *The Voice Upon the Mountains*, Govett wrote a second article on Christadelphianism,[74] opposing the sect's position that Satan is a personal agent or supernatural power of evil. The devil, according to the Christadelphians and to Robert Roberts (1839–1898) in his fifth lecture,[75] is a "personification of sin in its several forms of manifestation."[76] In July *The Voice Upon the Mountains* published a letter by George Lloyd[77] in response to an article in the same journal written by Govett on the subject of Christadelphianism.[78] Lloyd claimed that Govett had ably handled the errors of the sect and believed that the heresy is a "masterpiece of Satan" recognizing that the time is short. Therefore, the most effective way to "injure" truthful doctrine is to corrupt it quoting Scripture that in the latter times some shall depart from the faith, giving heed to seducing spirits. Given the prophetic nature of this heresy Govett's series of articles demonstrated the zeal he had concerning the exposition of Scripture in calling attention to error wherever he found it.

---

72. Bryan R. Wilson, *Sects and Society; A Sociological Study of the Elim Tabernacle, Christian Science, and Christadelphians* (Berkeley: University of California Press, 1961) 219. See also John Thomas, *Who are the Christadelphians? A Question for the Serious Consideration of All Who Desire to Return to Apostolic Faith and Practice* (Birmingham: Davis, 1869).

73. Charles C. Walker, *Rome and the Christadelphians: Being a Reply to "Christadelphianism" by J. W. Pointer* (Birmingham: Christadelphian, 1923) 10. See also Frank C. Jannaway, *Christadelphian Facts Concerning Christendom* (London: Jannaway, 1921).

74. Robert Govett, "Christadelphianism. Is Satan a Real Person?," *The Voice upon the Mountains. A Journal of Prophetic Testimony and Evangelistic Effort* 2 (1868) 65–67.

75. Robert Roberts, *The Twelve Lectures on the Teaching of the Bible in Relation to the Faiths of Christendom; to which are Added Five Additional Lectures, on the Devil, Judgment to Come, the Promises to the Fathers, the Covenant with David, and the Signs of the Times*, 5th ed. (Birmingham: Roberts, 1869). After Thomas's death, Roberts surfaced as a significant apologist for the movement, but not successor. See Robert Roberts, *Christendom Astray: Popular Christianity, both in Faith and Practice*, publishers forward (London: Dawn, 1965) 11–14. See also Irving Hexham, Stephen Rost, and John W. Morehead II, eds., *Encountering New Religious Movements: A Holistic Evangelical Approach* (Grand Rapids: Kregel, 2004) 179–82.

76. Robert Govett, "Christadelphianism. Is Satan a Real Person?," *The Voice upon the Mountains. A Journal of Prophetic Testimony and Evangelistic Effort* 2 (1868) 65.

77. *The Voice upon the Mountains. A Journal of Prophetic Testimony and Evangelistic Effort* 2 (1868) 85.

78. See Robert Govett, "The Christadelphian Ecclesia," *The Voice upon the Mountains. A Journal of Prophetic Testimony and Evangelistic Effort* 2 (1868) 52–55.

Several other letters appeared in the same issue thanking the journal for publishing Govett's articles on Christadelphianism.[79] They wrote comments such as "I am very thankful to the Lord for the clear and strong statements ... to the signs of these evil days," and, "I rejoice to see Mr. Govett's contributions to *The Voice* ... His papers are very valuable ... surely we ought to be very thankful that this new and most abominable sect is being thus exposed."[80]

In the July 1868 issue of *The Voice Upon the Mountains*, Govett wrote a third article condemning the sect and this time he dealt with its false teaching pertaining to the eternal existence of man.[81] The systemic false doctrine is epitomized in Govett's quote from one of Roberts's lectures which reads: "No amount of theorizing can persuade a good man that God is the merciful being of order and harmony brought before us in the Bible, if he is told, that with all His foreknowledge and omnipotence, He is to permit nine-tenths of the human race to be consigned to an eternal existence of blaspheming torture indescribable."[82] Govett strongly disagreed with such sentiment. His position was clearly affirmed some years later when he wrote that God disposes of all things according to His open will. "He elected from all eternity whom He would; not on foreseen grace, but according to His own counsels of renewing the souls of whom He would."[83] Through the teachings of its founder John Thomas, Christadelphians also denied the existence of Satan and his evil spirits. And from this rises the denial of the intermediate state of souls, and the future eternal existence of men, and of heaven and hell.[84]

Govett's articles on Christadelphianism, which appeared in the 1868 issues of *The Voice Upon the Mountains*, were subsequently published by Govett in tract form in 1869. A notice of the tract appeared in the March 1869 issue of *The Voice* which read: "This is a most valuable tract. It is a revised copy of Mr. Govett's articles in *The Voice Upon the Mountains*, and the testimony for truth which it contains was loudly called for by the rapid

---

79. Ibid.

80. *The Voice upon the Mountains. A Journal of Prophetic Testimony and Evangelistic Effort* 2 (1868) 86.

81. See Robert Govett, "The Christadelphianism. Man's Eternal Existence," *The Voice upon the Mountains. A Journal of Prophetic Testimony and Evangelistic Effort* 2 (1868) 86–89, 96–98.

82. See Roberts, *The Twelve Lectures on the Teaching of the Bible*, 68.

83. Robert Govett, *Exposition of the Gospel of St. John, Vol. I–II* (London: Bemrose and Sons, 1881) 259.

84. Robert Govett, "The Christadelphianism. Man's Eternal Existence," *The Voice upon the Mountains. A Journal of Prophetic Testimony and Evangelistic Effort* 2 (1868) 86. Article continued in vol. 2 (1868) 111–13.

spread of the Christ-dishonouring heresies which it postulates."[85] It notes that the portion of the tract which refers to "man's eternal existence" is especially valuable when so many are accepting the theory of the non-eternity of future punishment.

Another sect of some concern to the Victorian era religious community was that of Swedenborgianism, which had roused the interest of William Blake (1757–1827) toward the end of the eighteenth century.[86] It began as a religious movement based upon the writings of Emanuel Swedenborg (1688–1772), a Swedish scientist and theologian who claimed divine inspiration for his writings. During his life little effort was made to establish an organized religion. However, fifteen years after his death the Swedenborgian church movement (also known as the New Church) was founded in England.[87] Govett, reflecting upon both the Swedenborgian and Christadelphian sects of his day, was concerned about their influence upon the unbeliever. Paramount to his trepidation was their denial of the divine nature of the Savior being the Son of God and the Son of Man, and being pre-existent with the Father. He noted: "That those who reject this entirely, as did "the Men of Intelligence" of that day, and the Unitarians, Spiritualists, Swedenborgians, and Christadelphians of this day, are under death and the curse, afar from God; and under greater wrath, because of their unbelief in the testimony of God. Nor can they, by any obedience of theirs, escape from death to life."[88] According to Swedenborg, the Lord was continually putting forth his humanity received from Mary, until at length on the cross the last remains of it were removed, and His body was God. Govett retorts, "There was therefore no 'Son of God' it was only the Father."[89] Moreover, Swedenborg denies that the Christ can ever visibly come again. Christ has put off His body. He will not visibly come to reign and to judge.[90] Govett sought

---

85. See "Notice of Books," *The Voice upon the Mountains. A Journal of Prophetic Testimony and Evangelistic Effort* 3 (1869) 36. See also Robert Govett, *Christadelphians, Not Christians* (London: Nisbet, 1869).

86. Blake attended the organizational meeting of the New Jerusalem church, which based its doctrines on Swedenborgianism. But by 1790 he had rejected its doctrines in a poem entitled *The Marriage of Heaven and Hell*.

87. See Emanuel Swedenborg, *The True Christian Religion: Containing the Universal Theology of the New Church*, 3 vols. (New York: American Swedenborg, 1873).

88. Robert Govett, *Exposition of the Gospel of St. John, Vol. I–II* (London: Bemrose and Sons, 1881) 284.

89. See Robert Govett, *The Son of God (in Matthew): A Word about Swedenborgianism* (Norwich: Fletcher and Son, nd) 2. In this tract Govett calls attention to Swedenborg's system, which denies the Trinity of Persons in the Godhead.

90. Robert Govett, *Exposition of the Gospel of St. John, Vol. I–II* (London: Bemrose and Sons, 1881) 287.

to correct what he perceived to be incorrect biblical teaching concerning the person of Jesus Christ and his humanity. In *The Trinity, the Christ, and Antichrist: or, Thoughts On the First Epistle of John* (1874) Govett refuted the position of Swedenborg, who believed that it was in error to hold that the Lord took upon himself a human soul as well as human body.[91] In the same work Govett refutes the similar position of the Plymouth Brethren. He quotes from James C. L. Carson's *The Heresies of the Plymouth Brethren* (1870) which affirms that those in the Brethren movement believe that the humanity view of Christ, held by the "mass of Christians," is a "fearful heresy."[92] Govett continued his concern for the apostasy he saw in Swedenborgianism with the publication two years later of *Christ's Resurrection and Ours; or, I Corinthians XV. Expounded*. In it he attempts to debunk the denial of the Swedenborgians, the early Quakers, and the "Spiritists." Govett contends that the denial of the resurrection, which is fundamental to the Christian faith stems from ignorance of God's power, and from unbelief in the Scriptures.[93] A review of this book in *The Evangelical Magazine and Missionary Chronicle* criticizes Govett's work for having been cleverly written, but along too narrow a line of exegesis. Purdon comments that "the tone of confidence with which the writer draws out the whole programme of the future . . . does not convince us."[94] Govett appeared never to decline to write with full conviction in expressing his thoughts. But, on the balance of evidence, it would be difficult to claim that he ever intentionally attacked to cause personal harm. Rather his desire was to place Scriptural truth (as he interpreted it) above all other concerns. At times his candor attracted as many admirers as detractors, but his writings continued to center upon Christ's Second Coming and end-time events. He wrote in the context of

---

91. Robert Govett, *The Trinity, the Christ, and Antichrist: or, Thoughts on the First Epistle of John* (Norwich: Fletcher and Son, 1874) 98. See also William Mason, *The Indestructibility & Non-materiality of the Body of the Lord, When Taken Down from the Cross: The True Doctrine of Swedenborg* (London: Newbery, 1845) 19.

92. Robert Govett, *The Trinity, the Christ, and Antichrist*, 98–99. See also James C. L. Carson, *The Heresies of the Plymouth Brethren* (London: Houlston & Sons, 1870) 182. In this work Carson affirms the correctness of Govett's position on Christ's humanity by quoting him on several occasions.

93. Robert Govett, *Christ's Resurrection and Ours; or, I Corinthians XV. Expounded* (Glasgow: MacLehose, 1876) 2.

94. See "Literary Notices," *The Evangelical Magazine and Missionary Chronicle* 7 (1877) 97. The magazine was published in London from 1793 to 1812. Its orientation was primarily nonconformist, non-denominational. It was regarded as a leading dissenter and evangelical publication, which enjoyed the widest circulation of any religious miscellany of its day in England. See *Waterloo Directory of English Newspapers and Periodicals, 1800–1900*, series 2 in 20 vols. (Ontario: North Waterloo Academic, 2003).

an eschatological system in which he strongly believed and was prepared to debate when he perceived error. At the very least the theological, social, and political world around him stirred the debates in which he was more than willing to engage. The Victorians were obsessed with eschatological issues in their pursuit of human destiny and faith. Their literature strongly reflected these concerns.

Govett and Victorian Doubt

The search for answers for the meaning to life, death, and destiny was, of course, not unique to the Victorians. Tina Pippin asserts that one of the most famous English poems written about death in any period comes in the eighteenth century from Thomas Gray (1716–1771). His *Elegy Written in a Country Churchyard* (1751) gives a view of a public graveyard and the nature of death in eighteenth-century England.[95] In the poem the narrator moves from the sensations of his surroundings to his own thoughts of the dead.[96] But the Victorian era brought an enhanced sense of the aura of death—an assault upon loss as witnessed in deathbed scenes, elaborate funerals, mourning dress, and piously inscribed gravestones, in reaction to secular fears of extinction.[97] G. H. Lewes (1817–1878), English philosopher and literature critic, declared that literature was not only the creation of one man but also the expression of the intellectual life of a nation.[98]

After 1870, even though many of the characteristics of the era persisted, their dominance and coherence broke down. Religious doubt began to frame the mind of the Victorians and led to many of the great debates of the time. What made religious doubt most painful to the Victorians was the particular direction in which it headed. Walter E. Houghton writes, "as the Christian view of the universe receded, another took its place—the scientific picture of a vast mechanism of cause and effect, acting by physical laws that governed even man himself."[99] This religious doubt spurred Govett to

---

95. Tina Pippin, "Death and the Afterlife," in Andrew W. Haas, David Jasper, and Elizabeth Jay, eds., *The Oxford Handbook of English Literature and Theology* (Oxford: Oxford University Press, 2007) 711.

96. See Thomas Gray, *An Elegy Written In a Country Churchyard* (Philadelphia: Lippincott, 1883).

97. Davis, *The Victorians*, 459.

98. George Henry Lewes, *Life and Works of Von Goethe* (New York: Bigelow, Brown, 1902) 1:209. See also, Hock Guan Tjoa, *George Henry Lewis, a Victorian Mind* (Cambridge, MA: Harvard University Press, 1977) 60.

99. Walter E. Houghton, *The Victorian Frame of Mind, 1830–1870* (New Haven: Yale University Press, 1957) xv, 66.

persist in the representation of fundamental truths regarding Christian faith and the necessity of a personal acceptance of Jesus Christ as Savior. And, while he was always preoccupied with the prophecy surrounding the "Coming Kingdom," he never lost sight of the fundamental need of every believer to be certain of his or her salvation in Christ. He preached this concern and wrote about it throughout his ministry. For example, the earliest extant sermon preached by Govett is dated Sunday, 19 March, 1843. He preached it in the afternoon service at St Stephen's, Norwich, while a curate in the Church of England. It is interesting to note that Govett must have found the sermon to be of particular worth to congregations in general since he preached the sermon again in a morning service on 12 May, 1847, at the Bazaar in Norwich, after he dissented. The sermon was entitled "Wisdom Justified" and was based upon Matthew 11:19. The concluding words of the sermon spoke to the core of his foundational concern for his congregation when he said: "Brethren, my heart's desire and prayer for you is that you may be saved." His sermons are replete with this overriding theme. For instance, on Sunday, 21 October, 1855—nearly a year after the congregation moved into their permanent church building on Surrey Road— Govett preached a sermon to his congregation entitled "Means and Sovereignty." In it he proclaimed that:

> The Gospel is a system of means provided by God that man may escape from his position of guilt. The blood of Jesus cleanses from all sin. It is a mode of deliverance from the tremendous dangers of the wrath of God ... These means are thrown open with the utmost freedom to all that will fulfill the simple conditions of faith and repentance. Every asker shall receive.[100]

In this regard, Govett's published works further reveal his concern and passionate appeal for personal salvation. His commentary on the Gospel of John contains many references to faith in Christ and is especially useful in defining his view on "limited atonement"—a doctrine which he rejected. Referencing John 4:39-42 he declared that Christ is the Savior of the world and that he came to save not only the Jews but also the Gentiles. He states: "This is an answer to any who should say, that the mission to the Gentiles was an after-thought, forced on Christ, by the unsuccessfulness of His appeal to Israel. Jesus is 'Saviour of the world.' This, then overthrows the idea of a limited atonement; as if Christ died for the elect alone, and as if He must have suffered more had more been saved."[101] He justified his position

---

100. Sermon numbered "217." See Norfolk Records Office Catalog Reference FC 76/90.

101. Govett, *Exposition of the Gospel of St. John*, 173.

by adopting the understanding that Jesus is presented to every sinner (not to elect sinners alone) as Savior. That is to say, Christ died to save everyone that, obeying God's command, comes to him. He further held that it cannot be known that they are elect sinners until they have come.

Surrounded by an intensifying Victorian crisis of faith, Govett wrote on two fronts. On one front he sought to combat doctrine which he viewed as antithetical to sound teaching and to correct the thinking of theologians whose writings could confound their readers, or worse, lead them spiritually astray. On a second front he concerned himself with attending directly to the spiritual life of the individual believer. Here he found himself more directly confronting the Victorian crisis of faith. Yet, it was a crisis brought on by many factors. As such, the term "Victorian crisis of faith" is a label that is far from monolithic and covers a broad range of experience and debate. Bernard Lightman contends that a reasonable place to start in understanding the types of crises of faith is in observing the novels which focused on faith and doubt. Lightman states that scholars agree that Mrs. Humphrey Ward's *Robert Elsmere* (1888) contains a significant portrait of the Victorian crisis of faith. Concurring, John Wolffe, in an extensive examination of all the major novels of faith and doubt finds that *Robert Elsmere* is the great classic novel of Victorian doubt.[102] But even this telling novel has its foundation in the broad range of issues which preceded religious doubt. The effects of war, a shift in populations to urban centers, industrial revolution, economic and social changes all had their effect upon religion. There was the question of providing for the spiritual needs of the new urban populations and the growing separation of the classes. There was the question of education for the new, migrating population. And behind it all was the rising tide of economic liberalism, the demand for the removal of restraints and for better social conditions.[103] And as in any period of time its literature and art serve a double importance, since they do not only reflect the conditions of the time, they also mold them. Leonard Elliott-Binns, English historian and theologian, in *Religion in the Victorian Era* (1966—an older but often cited work) asserts that great literature is never content merely to reflect life, it must "impress" life.[104]

---

102. Bernard Lightman, "Robert Elsmere and the Agnostic Crisis of Faith," in Richard J. Helmstadter and Bernard Lightman, eds., *Victorian Faith in Crisis: Essays on Continuity and Change in Nineteenth-century Religious Belief* (Stanford: Stanford University Press, 1990). See also Robert Lee Wolff, *Gains and Losses: Novels of Faith and Doubt in Victorian England* (New York: Garland, 1977).

103. L. E. Elliott-Binns, *Religion in the Victorian Era*, 2nd edition (London: Lutterworth, 1966) 20.

104. Elliott-Binn, *Religion in the Victorian Era*, 338–41.

Nevertheless, while the crisis of faith was a real concern for the Victorians the nineteenth century was also marked by a revival of religious activity that was unmatched since the days of the Puritans. Josef L. Altholz notes that the most important thing to remember about religion in Victorian England is that there was an awful lot of it. He writes, "Above all, religion occupied a place in the public consciousness, a centrality in the intellectual life of the age, which it had not had a century before and did not retain in the twentieth century."[105] The Victorian religious revival declined in the latter decades of the century for both the middle class and the intellectual and professional classes. As evidence of this, Govett's own church experienced a significant decline in attendance as well as baptisms by the last decade of the nineteenth century.[106] In contrast to the end of the century, the 1850s had exhibited a time of relative religious calm in which churchgoers had little with which to concern themselves except the growth of the Catholic Church, opposition to dissent, and the increasing absence of the poor from the churches.[107] But then in 1859 there came another challenge to faith with the appearance of Charles Darwin's *Origin of Species*. For many years scholarship made the claim that Darwinism directly challenged the faith of the Victorians and the very accuracy of Genesis chapter 1 with its argument for the existence of God. It did not. Yet some have claimed Darwin personally caused the Victorian crisis of faith.[108] Giles St Aubyn takes up this misconception in *Souls in Torment: Victorian Faith in Crisis* by noting that many blamed Darwin for unsettling their faith but ignored the fact that Christian doubt preceded Darwin's writings.[109] Recent scholarship has reconsidered the impact of Darwin's writings on the Victorians. For example, M. A. Crowther notes that the publication of Darwin's *Origin of the Species* was not such a huge blow to the church as some have imagined, neither did it have the effect of undermining faith.[110] Govett himself rarely mentioned

---

105. Josef L. Altholz, "The Warfare of Conscience with Theology," in Gerald Parsons, ed., *Religion in Victorian Britain* (Manchester: Manchester University Press, 1988) 150.

106. A record of baptisms kept from 1885 to 1890 records the annual number of those receiving believers' baptism. The largest number occurred in 1887 with 138 baptisms. The smallest number occurred in 1890 with only one baptism recorded. A handwritten notice indicates: "An opening to every believer wether he joined us or no." See Norfolk Records Office Catalog Reference FC 76/89.

107. Altholz, "The Warfare of Conscience with Theology," 150.

108. Alister E. McGrath, *Darwinism and the Divine: Evolutionary Thought and Natural Theology* (Chichester: Wiley-Blackwell, 2011) 145.

109. See Giles St. Aubyn, *Souls in Torment: Victorian Faith in Crisis* (London: Sinclair-Stevenson, 2011).

110. M. A. Crowther, "Church Problems and Church Parties," in Gerald Parsons,

Darwin in his writings. Religious periodicals devoted some space to refute Darwin but had their attention mostly on other matters—partly because the ideas he postulated were already being discussed before he published the *Origin of the Species*.[111] Alvar Ellegård reminds his readers in *Darwin and the General Reader: The Reception of Darwin's Theory of Evolution in the British Periodical Press, 1859–1872*, that there was nothing new which arose on the matter of Darwin and the Bible concerning man's early history. Darwin on this point did little more than give powerful support to the uniformitarian view of geology, with which religious people were confronted since at least the early 1830s, when Sir Charles Lyell (1797–1875) had published his *Principles of Geology*. Both Lyell and Darwin, in their correspondence, were careful not to hurt religious susceptibilities and went out of their way to reconcile them when they could.[112] In February 1858 the *North British Review* published: "The writings of Moses do not fix the antiquity of the globe. If they fix anything at all, it is only the antiquity of the species."[113] Illuminating further complexities of the age, Mark Knight and Emma Mason in *Nineteenth-Century Religion and Literature: An Introduction* write that the publication of *Essays and Reviews* in 1860, which disseminated the insights of German Higher Criticism to its British audience, had a significant effect on Evangelicals' consciousness and elicited a far stronger reaction from them than the publication of Charles Darwin's *Origin of the Species*.[114]

It is also noteworthy that the criticisms of the Broad Church toward the evangelicals on the basis of this new historical and scientific evidence, which contributed to the question of date and authorship of many of the Scriptures, was in full sway even before the *Origin of Species*.[115] When *Essays and Reviews* was published in 1860 it included the writings of seven clergymen (six of whom were Church of England) and in their writings they introduced German biblical criticism.[116] In 1862 Bishop John Wil-

---

ed., *Religion in Victorian Britain: IV Interpretations* (Manchester: Manchester University Press, 1988) 5.

111. Crowther, "Church Problems and Church Parties," 5.

112. Alvar Ellegård, *Darwin and the General Reader: The Reception of Darwin's Theory of Evolution in the British Periodical Press, 1859–1872* (Stockholm: Almqvist & Wiksell, 1958) 159. See also Charles Lyell, *Principles of Geology: Being An Inquiry How Far the Former Changes of the Earth's Surface Are Referable to Causes Now in Operation, Volume I*, 3rd ed. (London: Murray, 1835).

113. "Scottish Natural Science," *North British Review* 55 (1858) 80.

114. Mark Knight and Emma Mason, *Nineteenth-Century Religion and Literature: An Introduction* (Oxford: Oxford University Press, 2006) 131.

115. Crowther, "Church Problems and Church Parties," 23.

116. See Frederick Temple et al., *Essays and Reviews* (1860). Other contributing authors of the essays include Rowland Williams, Baden Powell, Henry Briston Wilson,

liam Colenso (1814–1883), a bishop in the Church of England, wrote *The Pentateuch and Book of Joshua Critically Examined*, in which he denied the Mosaic authorship of the Pentateuch.[117] Colenso had been raised an evangelical but began to question some of the doctrines of his faith after his future wife introduced him to the teachings of (John) Frederick Denison Maurice (1805–1872), a less-than-orthodox Church of England clergyman. He took up Maurice's extreme teaching which doubted the eternal aspect of punishment and the divine revelation and the nature of man's knowledge of God.[118]

Adding to the complexities of the age, in the mid-1860s more discussion took place surrounding the understanding of man's created relationship with God. Jesus appeared as non-miraculous in Ernest Renan's *Vie de Jesus* (1863).[119] One's true loyalty to Jesus was questioned by Sir John Robert Seeley in his anonymous work entitled *Ecce Homo: A Survey of the Life and Work of Jesus Christ* (1865).[120] Then there were the forces at work outside of orthodox faith. *Evidence as to Man's Place in Nature* (1863), written by Thomas Henry Huxley and *The Antiquity of Man*, written by Sir Charles Lyell. Additionally, in 1871, Charles Darwin's *The Descent of Man* introduced more debate over the biblically understood uniqueness of man. It was during this far from monolithic period that Govett undertook his most ambitious writing project—a four-volume work on the Apocalypse. It was a project that took him four years to complete.[121] While he does not specifically mention these cultural underpinnings of the 1860s, he does emphasize the futurist aspect of the Apocalypse and repeatedly points to its "soon-coming" urgency. It was necessary that the unbeliever take serious reflection upon the consequence of unbelief, and the believer likewise give heed to the ensuing loss that awaits one who is found less than committed to serving Christ upon his return. Govett's concern for the spiritual condition of the believers in his own church extended as far as to carefully select the

---

Charles Wycliffe Goodwin, Mark Pattison, Benjamin Jowett.

117. John William Colenso, *The Pentateuch and Book of Joshua Critically Examined* (London: Longman, Roberts and Green, 1862).

118. See George W. Cox, *The Life of John William Colenso, Bishop of Natal*, 2 vols. (London: Ridgway, 1888); Peter B. Hinchliff, *John William Colenso, Bishop of Natal* (London: Nelson, 1964); Jeff Guy, *The Heretic: A Study of the Life of John William Colenso, 1814–1883* (Johannesburg: Ravan, 1983).

119. Ernest Renan, *Vie de Jesus* (Paris: Levy frères, 1863).

120. John Robert Seeley, Sir, *Ecce Homo: A Survey of the Life and Work of Jesus Christ* (London: Macmillan, 1865).

121. Robert Govett, *The Apocalypse: Expounded by Scripture, Vol. I–IV* (London: Nisbet, 1861–65).

hymns they sang. He published a hymn book with 521 personally selected hymns which emphasized the doctrines of salvation and future position in Christ upon his return. To further limit the encroachment of the "world" into the church services, Govett forbade the use of all musical instruments during the services.[122] Outside of the worship service Govett also held acute opinions regarding believers separating themselves from the world—especially in light of the changing social and political conditions taking place in Great Britain. In *The Sermon on the Mount Expounded* (1861) Govett insisted that Christians should not be magistrates. This he states in reference to Matthew 3:1 concerning "judging one another." He carefully writes that Christ does not condemn judging as a magistrate since according to the need for justice it is lawful and necessary. The question which arose in Govett's mind was that while judgment from the bench is necessary to the world, is it necessary "to be wielded by the disciple?"[123] A decade earlier he had taken up the broader question of believers involving themselves in politics. He wrote a tract in 1850 entitled *The Christian and Politics* in which he concluded that to the extent that the Christian is a politician, his heart is engaged with the things of the world. He asks, "Have not the love and zeal of the Nonconformists sadly declined since they have come forward to take a prominent part in the world's strifes and partizanships?"[124]

The Encroachment of Science

Nevertheless, as the 1870s unfolded, debate was still taking place which impacted the way Victorians preserved a traditional Bible-centered faith. A reasonably educated person was confronted with a choice—either to deny the increasing findings of biblical criticism and natural science, or to maintain that faith in the face of enhanced debate.[125] It was Andrew Dickson White (1832–1918), co-founder of Cornell University, who in 1876 from the other side of the Atlantic Ocean, published *A History of the Warfare of Science with Theology in Cristendom* which brought further attention to the conflict arising between science and theology in Great Britain. His extreme

---

122. Robert Govett, *Gospel Hymns*, 5th ed. (Norwich: Fletcher and Son, 1889). See Govett archives at Surrey Chapel. A fourth edition with publication dated of 1881 is the earliest known copy of Govett's hymn book and is in private ownership. The wooden pitch pipe used by Govett to guide the congregation in singing is in the possession of Surrey Chapel.

123. Robert Govett, *The Sermon on the Mount Expounded* (London: Nisbet, 1861) 236–46.

124. Robert Govett, *The Christian and Politics* (Norwich: Fletcher, 1850) 8.

125. Altholz, "The Warfare of Conscience with Theology," 151.

position accuses Christians of narrow-mindedness in opposition to science since the days of Roger Bacon (1214–1294), which White claims has led to much social harm. He curiously asserts that two-thirds of the death of sixty thousand children who died in England and Wales in 1868 and 1869 of scarlet fever would have survived had Roger Bacon not been hindered by the church from his pursuit of science. His questionable indictment further claims that putting together all the efforts of all the atheists who ever lived would not do as much harm as "narrow-minded Christianity."[126] Notwithstanding, Alister McGrath in *Science and Religion: A New Introduction* notes that the encounter between Christian religion and the natural sciences was set by two works. One was Andrew Dickson White's work just mentioned and the second was John William Draper's *History of the Conflict Between Religion and Science* (1874). Draper notes that "On every occasion permitting its display [antagonism between religion and science] it may be detected through successive centuries."[127] McGrath writes in reference to White and Draper, "The crystallization of the 'warfare' metaphor in the popular mind was unquestionably catalyzed by such vigorously polemical writings . . . The Victorian period itself gave rise to the social pressures and tensions which engendered the myth of permanent warfare between science and religion."[128] It is now understood that the idea that science and religion were at a permanent impasse was merely a reflection of agendas and concerns of a specific period. Each generation has given careful thought to the rising questions of life—both scientific and religious.[129] Such was the fervor of the time as religious thought gave way to science and the providence of God to mechanistic explanations of the universe.

There were numerous challenges to the church in the latter half of the nineteenth century—Darwinian theory was but one of them. It was the idea that humans evolved by natural selection that caused some adherents of the church to question their once tenacious hold on God as creator of the universe. Theism itself came under scrutiny by an atheistic mind-set that was now scientifically supported. Into this fray came the philosophy of German-born Frederich Nietzsche (1844–1900), which empathically stated that God was now dead. In 1882 he wrote, "The belief in God is overthrown. The belief in the Christian ascetic ideal is now fighting its last fight. Such a

126. Andrew Dickson White, *A History of the Warfare of Science with Theology in Cristendom* (London: King, 1876) 94.

127. John William Draper, *History of the Conflict Between Religion and Science* (New York: Appleton, 1898) 218.

128. Alister E. McGrath, *Science and Religion: A New Introduction*, 2nd ed. (Chichester: Wiley-Blackwell, 2010) 9–10.

129. McGrath, *Science and Religion*, 11.

long and solidly built work as Christianity—it was the last construction of the Romans."[130] In *Antichrist* he further noted that "The eternal accusation against Christianity I shall write upon all walls, wherever walls are to be found—I have letters that even the blind will be able to see... I call Christianity the one great curse, the one great depravity."[131] For Nietzsche man was now left to find his own way. Govett must have sensed this hopelessness as his writings continued to point away from the increasing abstractions of this life and onto the joyous certainty of a life to come—such as is found in his tract *The Kingdom of God Future*.[132]

Yet, as religious doubt became a spreading concern for the church in nineteenth-century Britain, it also tended to galvanize cultural debate and scientific inquiry. It did so just as the nation's empire was reaching political and administrative control over nearly one quarter of the world and its leading intellectuals were confronting the church and struggling to accept radical scientific discoveries.[133] John Henry Newman (1801–1890), while a Church of England clergyman, explained in his *Parochial and Plain Sermons* (1834–1843), "We are in a world of mystery, with one Light before us. Take away this Light and we are utterly wretched."[134] Newman retained his faith, but many other Victorians did not. Matthew Arnold wrote in his poem *Stanzas From the Grande Chartreuse* (1855), "Wandering between two worlds, one dead,/The other powerless to be born."[135] It expressed the feelings of many Victorians who were experiencing the tangled times of a world from which the God who created it was being expelled by some with differing views.[136] By the end of the century the English novelist William Hurrell Mallock (1849–1923) expressed the sentiments of a nation still in the grips of the conflict between science and religion, and still seeking an understanding of death and what lies beyond. In *Lucretius on Life and Death* (1900) Mallock recounts the Roman poet and philosopher (ca. 99BC–ca. 55BC) as expressing the view that science is that which accomplishes the great "deliverance." It does so by demonstrating two truths—first, that no

---

130. Friedrich Nietzsche, *The Gay Science* (Mineola: Dover, 2006) 175.

131. Friedrich Nietzsche, *Ecce Homo & the Antichrist* (New York: Algora, 2004) 174.

132. Robert Govett, *The Kingdom of God Future* (London: Nisbet, 1870).

133. Christopher Lane, *The Age of Doubt: Tracing the Roots of Our Religious Uncertainty* (New Haven: Yale University Press, 2011) 2.

134. John Henry Newman, *Parochial and Plain Sermons* (London: Longmans, Green, 1918) 2:215.

135. Matthew Arnold, *The Poetical Works of Matthew Arnold* (New York: Crowell, 1897) 428.

136. George Levine, *Realism, Ethics and Secularism: Essays on Victorian Literature and Science* (Cambridge: Cambridge University Press, 2008) 3.

god, or gods exist; and secondly, that even if they did exist, they would be "absolutely impotent to wreak their malice on us after death, because after death there will be nothing left of us for them to torture."[137] And in the absence of God, as some had concluded, the Victorians were living in tumultuous times. Christopher Lane reminds his readers that traditions appeared to be losing their grip, and fundamental questions loomed about the well-being of the country and the future of the world. Religious doubt affected the very fabric of British social and cultural life but it also assisted the nation to find what it believed and why it believed it.[138]

While the debate between religion and science intensified in the latter half of the century the Victorians continued to ponder their obsession with the four last things—only now with greater difficulty since the line between religion and science was increasingly blurred. The four last things were accentuated in much of what Govett wrote because he reasoned that these issues impinged upon the urgency of living in such a manner as to gain reward in the Coming Kingdom—a theme of utmost importance to Govett. For example, of the four last things, Govett speaks to the issue of "death" in *Eternal Suffering of the Wicked*.[139] In one of his sermons preached in 1843 and later published as *A Treatise on Hades, or the Place of Departed Spirits* Govett speaks on hell.[140] In a sermon preached on 23 January 1859, he addresses one of the four last things with the topic of eternal punishment.[141] Regis Martin, in his book *The Last Things: Death, Judgment, Hell, Heaven* (1998) writes that eschatological forgetfulness, especially on the part of Christians, will simply force the world to look elsewhere for information and consolation about the End.[142] In recognition of the truth of this statement Govett continued his theological fight to educate Christians about the eternal danger of eschatological malaise or just simply misunderstanding Scripture. For example, in 1868 Govett wrote an article in *The Voice On the Mountains*, as a response to an article written in the September issue of the

---

137. William Hurrell Mallock, *Lucretius on Life and Death, in the Metre of Omar Khayyam, to which are Appended Parallel Passages from the Original* (London: A. & C. Black, 1900) xiv.

138. Christopher Lane, *The Age of Doubt: Tracing the Roots of Our Religious Uncertainty* (New Haven: Yale University Press, 2011) 3.

139. Robert Govett, *Eternal Suffering of the Wicked* (London: Nisbet, 1871) 119.

140. Robert Govett, *A Treatise on Hades, or the Place of Departed Spirits* (Edinburgh: Johnstone, 1843).

141. Robert Govett, *Eternal Punishment: A Sermon Preached Jan. 23rd, 1859* (Norwich: Fletcher and Son, 1860).

142. Regis Martin, *The Last Things: Death, Judgment, Heaven, Hell* (San Francisco: Ignatius, 1998) 18.

prior year by an author who identified himself as "Mr. Goodridge." Govett's concern was that the doctrines contained in the article were not scriptural. Engaging himself in a debate over perceived theological error was typical for Govett. In this instance he believed that the author confused the understanding of the "church" and the "Body of Christ" by separating their meaning when, according to Govett, the Greek proved that they were not distinguishable when referring to true believers who make up the church. Govett further opposed Goodridge on the position of the "miraculous gifts" given at Pentecost. Contrary to the author who believed that the gifts were for Israel alone–existing only during the early days of the church–Govett wrote that he felt a particular interest in the topic, having believed and taught for years that the miraculous gifts ought to be prayed for and possessed by all believers in Christ.[143] Writing in opposition to others during the long years of the Victorian crisis of faith required a bold confidence. Govett consistently demonstrated that confidence. For instance, in *Eternal Suffering of the Wicked* he defended in minutia the biblical meaning of the word "eternal" as literally meaning "everlasting." In addition to numerous biblical references and interpretations from the original languages to prove his understanding of the word, he drew his defense from several lexicon writers, books of the Apocrypha, and various ancient writers including Aristotle, Philo, Polycarp, and Eusebius.[144] While he often debated in the religious journals with pastors and concerned believers, Govett was also not fearful of taking on biblical scholars. He was confident in his assertions and unabashed about who he debated. There were many who disagreed with him, as the next chapter will explain because he believed that baptism represented more than a sacrament stemming out of church tradition. It had a more important eternal context and, therefore, its observance and its mode were both essential to the believer. One who disagreed with him was Henry Alford (1810–1871), dean of Canterbury and biblical scholar who contended that to maintain that immersion is necessary in baptism, is the "merest trifling." Govett, in his commentary on Colossians counters Alford's justifications with these words: "by such changes (of details) you make void the word of God to keep human traditions."[145] Govett resolutely believed that proper observance of baptism was linked to the capacity of a believer being admitted into the Millennial Kingdom. This assertion can

---

143. *The Voice upon the Mountains. A Journal of Prophetic Testimony and Evangelistic Effort* 2 (1868) 4–5. Govett's argument is continued in two more issues of the journal: vol. 2 (March 1868) 26–27; vol. 2 (April 1868) 41–42.

144. Govett, *Eternal Suffering of the Wicked*, 6.

145. Robert Govett, *Christ the Head; the Church His Body: Its Dangers, Duties, Glories: or, the Argument of Colossians* (Norwich: Fletcher and Son, 1890) 125.

be affirmed by a respondent, Arthur A. Rees, to Govett's letter which appeared in the December 1864 issue of *The Rainbow*. Rees refutes Govett's assertions that a majority of believers will be excluded from the Millennial Kingdom on the mere basis of not receiving baptism. Rees, and others, maintained that Govett confused real believers with false professors, and the "reward of the kingdom" with simply admission into it or exclusion from it.[146] With so much at stake in the future and so much attention paid by the Victorians over what to believe about the four last things, Govett was not willing to trivialize any scriptural matter with which he engaged—notwithstanding baptism.

---

146. *The Rainbow: A Magazine of Christian Literature, with Special Reference to the Revealed Future of the Church and the World* 2 (1865) 42–43.

CHAPTER 4

Govett and Infant Baptism

No record is available to explain why Govett chose to attend Saint Mary's Baptist Church in Norwich on a Sunday evening in 1843. Perhaps it was out of curiosity to hear the church's charismatic and frequently outspoken minister Reverend William Block. What is known is that Govett witnessed baptism by immersion which made an indelible mark upon his conscience regarding the mode and scriptural intent of baptism. The event so moved him that he returned the following Tuesday to be himself baptized by immersion.[1] What stirred in his conscience was significant enough to compel him to relinquish his license to preach in the Church of England and to embark upon a lifelong endeavor to encourage others to see baptism in the same scriptural light. Yet, as Victorian readers would soon discover through his writings, his evolving understanding of baptism was not totally in keeping with the historical arguments which long centered upon the theological propriety of infant baptism and which continued to swirl around him throughout his lifetime.

It is well documented that Govett left the Church of England over the issue of infant baptism.[2] A clear explanation can be found in his *To Churchmen: Why Does the Church of England Baptize Infants?* The tract is not dated but is assumed to have been published sometime between 1844 and 1850.[3] The focus of the tract was on the twenty-seventh of the Thirty-

---

1. Govett article *Eastern Daily Press* (26 February 1901). See also "Surrey Chapel and Its Pastor: A Unique Ministry," *Eastern Daily Press* (12 March 1912).

2. See Norfolk Records Office file FC76/89. Official letter from the Right Reverend Edward Stanley, Bishop of Norwich, to Govett (2 February 1844).

3. The range of dates between 1844–1850 is set by comparing the advertisements of the publisher at the end of some tracts to determine when the first time a title appears in the advertisement. This technique is only partially effective and serves to narrow down possible first dates of publishing. Many of the extant tracts are second editions

nine Articles of the Church of England. The Article reads in part: "The baptism of young children is in any wise to be retained in the church, as most agreeable with the institution of Christ."[4] To refute this position Govett draws attention to two Scripture verses in the New Testament where Jesus institutes baptism. The first is Mark 16:15–16, which states "Go into all the world and preach the good news to all creation. Whoever believes and is baptized will be saved." The second is found in Matthew 28:19–20, which states "Go and make disciples of all nations, baptizing them in the name of the Father and of the Son and of the Holy Spirit." As a consequence of these two extracts from Scripture Govett finds that the command is first to "believe" and then afterward to "baptize." He pointedly asks: "Can infants do that?"[5] The Church Catechism addresses that question by asking, "Why then are infants baptized, when by reason of their tender age they cannot perform them [repentance and faith]?" The answer the Catechism gives is because "they promise them both [repentance and faith] by their sureties: which promise, when they come to age, themselves are bound to perform."[6] Govett's response to the church's position was to challenge his readers to consider if the promise of sureties that the child shall believe when he comes of age is allowed by Christ. If it is not, then his determination was that the Church of England does not have lawful grounds for baptizing infants.[7] He further concludes that infants are unable to furnish these requisites and should be excluded from baptism. Finding infants to be properly excluded from baptism he asserts that the baptism that is appointed by Christ is the immersion of a believer into the name of the Father, Son, and Holy Spirit.[8] Nevertheless, Govett's determinations regarding the explanation from Scripture did not originate with him.

---

and later and thus forcing a fair amount of speculation for some.

4. Edward Welchman, *The Thirty-Nine Articles of the Church of England, Confirmed by Text of Holy Scripture, and Testimonies of the Primitive Fathers: To which are Added, Short Notes, in Illustration of the Articles* (London: SPCK, 1842) 63.

5. Robert Govett, *Why Does the Church of England Baptize Infants?*, Tracts to Churchmen 5 (Norwich: Fletcher and Son, ca. 1844–1850) 1.

6. W. A. Hammond, *The Catechism of the Church of England, or an Instruction to be Learned of Every Person Before He be Brought to be Confirmed by the Bishop* (London: Printed For J. G. F. & J. Rivington, 1844) 33.

7. Govett, *Why Does the Church of England Baptize Infants?*, 2.

8. Ibid., 4.

Historical Debate

The theology of baptism as a doctrine of the church, its proper mode, and what it is intended to signify, has been discussed over many centuries of history. The debate continued throughout Govett's life. As with the historical discussion of dissent and that of evangelicalism in the introduction and chapter 1, it is important to this study to also place baptism into historical context. It is important because Govett was very much aware of this context and referenced it in his books and tracts. He also frequently made reference to the erroneous comfort that his opponents drew from history as they sought to justify their position from the vantage point of the past. A summary of the history of the shifting debate over baptism now follows. In its presentation it seeks to bring to light a number of important considerations transpiring from the time of the Reformation—including the inception of the Anabaptist movement and the fresh controversies which sprang from it. While Govett based his interpretation of the doctrine of baptism from the perspective of Scripture, and endeavored to base his refutations upon it, he also used history to point to relevant errors found in his opponent's arguments.

According to Everett Ferguson the earliest certain literary reference to infant baptism was provided by Tertullian in the third-century in which he opposed the practice.[9] In Tertullian's own words: "According to the circumstances and nature, and also age, of each person, the delay of baptism is more suitable."[10] Since that time the subject has been the focus of much attention within the Christian church. Anthony N. S. Lane notes that Tertullian indicates that although infant baptism may have been practiced it was not the only form of initiation being proposed.[11] Joachim Jeremias in *Infant Baptism in the First Four Centuries* states that the way in which the solidarity of the family was taken for granted explains further why no reason was found for emphasizing or justifying especially the baptism of children.[12]

---

9. Mark Dever, *The Church: The Gospel Made Visible* (Nashville: B&H, 2012) 103. See also Everett Ferguson, *Baptism in the Early Church: History, Theology, and Liturgy in the First Five Centuries* (Grand Rapids: Eerdmans, 2009) 362. See also Ernest Evans, *Tertullian's Homily on Baptism: Edited with an Introduction, Translation and Commentary by Ernest Evans* (London: SPCK, 1964).

10. Tertullian, "Chapter 18: Of the Persons to Whom, and the Time When, Baptism is to be Administered," in *The Writings of Q. S. F. Tertullianus*, trans. Sydney Thelwall (Oxford, 1842) 1228.

11. Anthony N. S. Lane, "Dual-Practice Baptism View," in David F. Wright, ed., *Baptism: Three Views* (Downers Grove, IL: InterVarsity, 2009) 152.

12. Joachim Jeremias, *Infant Baptism in the First Four Centuries* (Eugene, OR: Wipf and Stock, 2004) 23.

During the Victorian era a notable book on the history of infant baptism, although written a century earlier, was still valued. It was written by the Reverend William Wall, vicar of Shoreham, Kent; and although many years ahead of the historical starting point of this section it is intended to serve as an introduction to briefly demonstrate the importance of baptism as considered in the minds of the Victorians and Govett. Wall's book was first published in 1705. It was quickly republished in 1707 and again in two volumes in 1720. After the lapse of a century it was again republished in 1819.[13] Wall's premise is articulated in the preface of his book and is based upon an argument from silence—i.e., that the church accepted the practice of infant baptism because there is no evidence to the contrary. He bases this upon the logic that at the time of the death of the apostles, and for a generation or two after, the Christian faith and practice had been propagated into many countries. In so doing the Christians must have easily known whether the practice of infant baptism was in use at the time. If the baptizing of infants was the order and it was a rite in which the "whole body of the people" was involved, such a thing could not have been forgotten in such a short period of time, nor altered without a great deal of traceable writing.

> In a point of doctrine delivered by tradition a mistake may happen; or in the account of some matter of fact done by some particular man; but for a rite of universal concern, a whole church cannot forget it, much less all the churches in several parts of the world, in so short a time. We Englishmen, cannot be ignorant whether, infants were usually baptized in England or not in Queen Elizabeth's days, which is the same distance: the man that thinks this possible, is one that is not used to consider.[14]

Wall's argument had its basis in history, and it is upon that history that this study now draws; beginning with the Reformation. It was not until the Protestant Reformation that antipaedobaptism began to noticeably rise. In the year 1533, the year the English Protestant John Frith (1503–1533) was martyred, he wrote a short tract entitled *A Mirror or Looking Glass, Wherein You May Behold the Sacrament of Baptism Described* (referred to as *A Declaration of Baptism*).[15] In it he takes into account the rise of antipaedobaptism. By then it had existed in Germany for about eleven years, and had

---

13. William Wall, *The History of Infant Baptism: In Two Parts*, 4th ed. (London: F. C. and J. Rivington, 1819).

14. Wall, *The History of Infant Baptism*, v.

15. See John Frith, "A Mirror or Looking Glass, Wherein You May Behold the Sacrament of Baptism," in Thomas Russell, ed., *The Works of the English Reformers: William Tyndale and John Frith* (London: Palmer, 1831) 3:284–96.

recently spread to Holland. In his tract he notes that the antipaedobaptists affirm that children may not be baptized until they become "a perfect age" because they yet have no faith. His retort was that infants may be baptized, because they are partakers of the promise, although they as yet have no faith. His justification is the reference to Jesus in Luke 18:16, where Jesus welcomes the children to come to him.[16] Simultaneously, Martin Luther (1483–1546) continued to affirm the scriptural mandate for infant baptism. In his Small Catechism, Luther asks the question "who should be baptized?" His response: "All who would be saved."[17] To the more specific question of infant baptism he remarks: "Most certainly infants are to be baptized; and that on account of many and weighty reasons."[18] Of the five specific reasons given, the first mentioned is that of Christ declaring it in the gospel of Mark 10:14–16 ("Of such is the kingdom of heaven"). As a footnote to his reasons he adds that children were to receive circumcision, the token of the covenant which God made with Abraham, and the seal of the righteous faith. "So now children ought to be baptized, and receive the token of the new covenant, the seal of the same righteousness of faith."[19] John Calvin (1506–1564) also affirmed infant baptism in *Institutes of the Christian Religion*. He addresses the argument made by antipaedobaptists that infants are incapable of being taught anything of the instruction of scripture, nor have they "inwardly conceived a faith to which they can give outward testimony." His justification is that

> Of those whom the Lord recalls in infancy from this mortal life, he makes some directly heirs of the heavenly kingdom . . . Moreover, if we confess (something it is certainly necessary to confess) that even from this age vessels of mercy are chosen by the Lord [Romans 5:1], we cannot deny faith to be the sole path to salvation [Habakkuk 2:4] . . . No distinction of age is established when it is said, "This is life, to know the one true God, and him who sent, Jesus Christ [John 17:3].[20]

In summary, Calvin is saying that all God's elect enter into eternal life through faith, at whatever point of age they are "released from their prisonhouse of corruption." For the very same reason that God offered the

---

16. Frith, "A Mirror or Looking Glass," 288.

17. Martin Luther, *Luther's Small Catechism Developed and Explained*, 6th ed. (Philadelphia: Lutheran, 1893) 96.

18. Luther, *Luther's Small Catechism*, 97.

19. Ibid., 98.

20. John Calvin, *Institutes of the Christian Religion, 1536 Edition*, trans. Ford Lewis Battles (Grand Rapids: Eerdmans, 1986) 4.15.18 (100–102).

Jews through circumcision that he would be their God even through their offspring (Leviticus 26:12), Calvin notes that today God promises the same to Christians through baptism—not only to adults but also to infants. For this reason Paul also calls them "saints" (1 Corinthians 7:14) just as the infants of the Jews could have been called "saints" in contrast to the unclean and profane Gentiles.[21]

Baptism was thought to purge original sin. This was the position of both Luther and Calvin. Huldrych Zwingli (1484–1531) also defended infant baptism, but for different reasons. The contemporary debate on the issue typically centered around the issue of baptizing an infant who had no faith, and therefore, could not publicly demonstrate it. The answer usually related to the question of original sin. The argument that baptism cleansed one's soul of original sin can be traced back to Augustine.[22] However, Zwingli, along with his contemporary Desiderius Erasmus (1466–1536), resisted the notion of original sin and leaned toward an understanding that infants lacked any original sin whatsoever that needed to be forgiven. In light of Zwingli's position on original sin, by the late 1510s he had his apprehensions about continuing the practice of infant baptism. His initial finding was similar to that of his successor Calvin in the correlation between Old Testament circumcision and New Testament baptism. Both were a sign of belonging to the community. The fact that the child was not conscious of this belonging was irrelevant. But Zwingli took his argument a step further. He began with the assumption that "Baptism is a sign which pledges us to the Lord Jesus Christ,"[23] yet concluded with Erasmus that in so far as sin was inherited it was inherited only as a "tendency" to sin. Zwingli uses the term *Erbbreston*, denoting a residual inclination to sin, instead of the term *Erbsünde* (hereditary sin).[24] By this means sin is reduced from an ontological condition to a volitional action, and thereby undercuts the rationale for infant baptism. If a person is not born into sin, then the need to wash away sin becomes unimportant. And while Erasmus claimed that "I cannot depart from the consensus of the church, nor have I ever departed,"[25] Zwingli and his followers felt no such constraint. Baptism became for Zwingli an

---

21. Calvin, *Institutes*, 102.

22. Alister E. McGrath, *Historical Theology: An Introduction to the History of Christian Thought*, 2nd ed. (Chichester: Wiley & Sons, 2013) 168.

23. G. W. Bromley, ed., *Zwingli and Bullinger* (Philadelphia: Westminster, 1979) 131.

24. Carter Lindbergh, *The European Reformations*, 2nd ed. (Chichester: Wiley-Blackwell, 2010) 194.

25. John B. Payne, *Erasmus: His Theology of the Sacraments* (Richmond: Knox, 1970) 153.

external sign which consequently did not wash away original sin, but was symbolic of an initiation into the church and a pledge to lead a life of discipleship in Christ. Only when the baptized was granted faith did baptism with the Spirit–which initiated him into the Church universal–accompany the outward sign.[26] Carter Lindberg notes that what was at stake for Zwingli was "first his opposition to what he believed was the externalization and mechanization of the gospel by the sacramental theology of both Roman Catholic and Lutheran theology, and then his opposition to what he believed was their assumption of the possibility of a pure church."[27] Nevertheless, Zwingli opposed conflict within the church, and as such, found the emerging Anabaptist movement in his city troublesome.

Although Zwingli's Zurich was not the only root of Anabaptism, it was a major venue and the rise in numbers of Anabaptists there was a matter of critical concern to him. In Zwingli's view these evangelicals not only brought the gospel into disrepute, they undermined government and would cause harm to both religious life and society. The center of his concern was their disputing infant baptism. Reformers such as Luther and Calvin understood that there was one universal church and one creed. They believed that the people must live and worship in harmony within their local community. Clashing with this view, the Anabaptists largely withdrew from society by establishing local congregations who saw themselves as being set apart from the state.[28] Their position is clearly outlined in two letters to Thomas Müntzer (1489-1525) from Conrad Grebel (1498-1526). Both Müntzer and Grebel were staunch Anabaptists. Written on 5 September 1524, the letters represent thoughts from the early beginnings of evangelical Anabaptism and make clear both the widespread sense of unity among the dissenters from the territorial or magisterial Reformation of Luther and Zwingli and the early distinctions that were apparent within the Radical Reformation itself.[29] Grebel to Müntzer writes, "On the matter of baptism thy book pleases us well, and we desire to be further instructed by thee. We understand that even an adult is not to be baptized without Christ's rule of binding and loosing. The Scripture describes baptism for us thus, that it signifies that, by faith and the blood of Christ, sins have been washed away for him who is baptized."[30]

26. Robert C. Walton, *Zwingli's Theocracy* (Toronto: University of Toronto Press, 1967) 171.

27. Lindbergh, *The European Reformations*, 195.

28. Ibid., 190.

29. George H. Williams, Angel M. Nergal and Juan de Valdés, eds., *Spiritual and Anabaptist Writers* (London: Westminister, 1957) 73-85.

30. Williams, *Spiritual and Anabaptist Writers*, 80.

Despite this brief glimpse of historical clarity, Franklin H. Littell calls attention to several serious impediments which have historically blocked the path of those who have sought to study the life and thought of the Anabaptists. First, information has been notoriously scarce and has rested for the most part on hostile polemics. Much of the present evidence calls into question four centuries of partisan interpretation which has largely been presented by defenders of state-church Protestants. Littell accordingly notes that in addition to Martin Luther and Ulrich Zwingli such traditional authorities routinely cited are Justus Menius (1499-1558) and Heinrich Bullinger (1504-1575)–all of whom were hostile to the radical groups. Recently published material is changing this perspective, but the problem of definition continues to exist because the term "Anabaptist" has been very loosely applied to a wide range of groups which broke away from state-church Protestantism.[31]

The word "Anabaptist" is a Latin derivative of the Greek *anabaptismos* (re-baptism). Lutherans and Zwinglians applied the term in the beginning to those who separated themselves from the state churches. According to Austin P. Evans, as for the radicals themselves, "They repudiated the name, insisting that infant baptism did not constitute true baptism and that they were not in reality rebaptizers. They preferred to be called by the term Brüder (Brethren) but this label was never widely adopted. The term Anabaptist was so conveniently elastic that it came to be applied to all those who stood out against authoritative state religion."[32] Baptism became important simply because it was the most obvious dividing point. The underlying reason the name "Anabaptist" was used by the authorities was because it allowed for an excuse to use force to put an end to radicals. The use of the term also afforded those in opposition to impose the death penalty. This was accomplished by implication drawn between the Anabaptists and the Donatists in the fifth-century, who held similar views, and on whom an ancient law was used to impose the death penalty. The Donatists were declared to be heretics and subversives because of their practice of "rebaptism" for believers only. In doing so, they had defied the ecclesiastical and imperial authority of Rome. Their defiance was in direct disobedience of the Justinian Code—a series

---

31. Franklin H. Littell, *The Anabaptist View of the Church: A Study in the Origins of Sectarian Protestantism* (Paris, Arkansas: Baptist Standard Bearer, reprinted 2000) xiii. For a substantial bibliography of early scholarship on the subject of Anabaptists, see William R. Estep, *Anabaptist Story: An Introduction to Sixteenth-Century Anabaptism*, 3rd ed. (Cambridge: Eerdmans, 1996). For a careful compilation of many of the earliest written works on the subject of infant baptism, see Hendrik F. Stander and Johannes P. Louw, *Baptism in the Early Church* (Leeds: Carry, Reformation Today Trust, 2004).

32. Austin Patterson Evans, *An Episode in the Struggle for Religious Freedom: The Sectaries of Nuremberg, 1524-1528* (New York: Columbia University Press, 1924) 14.

of laws compiled by Emperor Justinian (527–565). Their persecution was not only brought about by their practice of rebaptizing any Catholics who joined their ranks, but also by reason of the accusation that among their number were disturbers of the civil peace. And while the Anabaptists were also accused of disturbing the peace, their most serious offence was that of upsetting the whole structure of the church, state, and society.[33] By and large the early Anabaptists were bound together with two ideas: a pure church of believers and the baptism of believers. On many other points there was often great division, such as the sleep of the soul between death and resurrection, a millennial reign of Christ, and final restoration of believers to Christ.[34] Before long the Anabaptists migrated from the continent to England and brought their theology with them. The Anabaptists in England were more difficult to identify than those of their brethren on the continent. Rather than their followers separating themselves through the practice of rebaptism, they were encouraged instead to protest against what they perceived to be spiritual decline within the Established Church.[35] Opinions vary regarding the extent of influence which the Anabaptists exerted upon the rise of English Separatism. Kenneth Latourette holds to the understanding that it is undeniable that the Anabaptists contributed to the English Separatist movement.[36] There is also some belief that Robert Browne of Norwich, the father of English Separatism, was attracted to Anabaptism through Dutch Mennonite refugees.[37]

With their arrival in England the Anabaptists soon experienced hostility. Anti-Anabaptist rhetoric served to define orthodoxy under the reign of Edward VI (1547–1553), England's first monarch raised as a Protestant. In a sermon preached before Edward VI on 29 March 1549, Hugh Latimer spoke of the parable of the wicked judge found in the gospel of Luke and stressed that it was good and lawful for God's people to use the law against their adversaries. Latimer notes that "I should have told you here of a certain sect of heretics that speak against this order and doctrine; they will have no magistrates nor judges on the earth."[38] Though the Anabaptists were small

---

33. Roland H. Bainton, *The Reformation of the Sixteenth Century* (Boston: Beacon, 1985) 98.

34. Philip Schaff, *History of the Christian Church*, 8 vols. (New York: Scribner's Sons, 1907) 7:79.

35. Hans Jürgen-Goertz, *The Anabaptists* (Oxon: Routledge, 1996) 33.

36. Kenneth Scott Latourettte, *A History of Christianity, Volume II, Reformation to the Present*, rev. ed. (New York: Harper & Row, 1975) 815.

37. William R. Estep, *The Anabaptist Story: An Introduction to Sixteenth-Century Anabaptism*, 3rd ed. (Cambridge: Eerdmans, 1996) 273.

38. George Elwes Corrie, ed., *Sermons by Hugh Latimer* (Cambridge: Cambridge

in number during the reigns of Henry VIII and his young son Edward VI there were government initiatives against them. This and the large number of published articles written against Anabaptists substantiated that the small but vocal group of believers was of considerable concern to both secular and church leaders.[39] Even in cases of heresy public debates frequently centered upon the practical and political questions of who had the authority to define heresy and enforce the law.[40] More than anything else, English evangelicals associated Anabaptism with anarchy. This fear of anarchy was exacerbated by the fact that Edward was a young king whose authority as a child, and as the head of the Church of England, was much less stable than that of his father.[41] Accordingly, the Anabaptists were forced underground and compelled to either abandon their passion for a reformed Christianity or assemble their own communities.

Numerous books have been written on Anabaptism and its early movement. Some research embraces history from a theological and ecclesiastical perspective, some from a cultural and social history perspective.[42] Complicating the historical assessment of Anabaptism is that research on Reformation history has tended to center upon the reformers themselves and their appraisal of the Anabaptists as adversaries. Much of the research has a tendency to validate the personal religious experiences of the writer. This is true not only of Anabaptism in general but also of the specific theological battle over infant baptism. Sides were clearly demarcated. For example, in 1642 William Kiffin, the Baptist pastor of Devonshire-square Chapel in London, took part in a debate held in Southwark in which he boldly announced: "We hold, that the baptism of infants cannot be proved lawful by the testimony of Scripture, or by Apostolical tradition. If you, therefore, can prove the same either way, we shall willingly submit unto you."[43] In addition,

---

University Press, 1844) 1:151.

39. Carrie Euler, *Couriers of the Gospel: England and Zurich, 1531–1558* (Zurich: TVZ, 2006) 204.

40. Ethan H. Shagan, *Popular Politics and the English Reformation* (Cambridge: Cambridge University Press, 2003) 21.

41. Euler, *Couriers of the Gospel*, 204.

42. See, for example, Hans-Jurgen Goetz, *The Anabaptists* (London: Routledge, 1996); C. Arnold Snyder and Linda A. Huebert Hechi, eds., *Profiles of Anabaptist Women: Sixteenth-Century Reforming Pioneers* (Waterloo: Wilfrid Lauier University Press, 1996); J. Denny Weaver, *Becoming Anabaptist: The Origin and Significance of Sixteenth-Century Anabaptism* (Scottdale: Herald, 1987); Kenneth Ronald Davis, *Anabaptism and Asceticism; a Study in Intellectual Origins* (Scottdale: Herald, 1974; Claus Peter Clausen, *Anabaptism; a Social History, 1525–1618: Switzerland, Austria, Moravia, South and Central Germany* (Ithaca: Cornell University Press, 1972).

43. J. Jackson Goadby, *Bye-Paths in Baptist History* (London: Stock, 1871) 142. See

no less than a hundred tracts and books came off the English presses in the seventeenth century to prove infant baptism wrong.[44]

In 1705 William Wall, the vicar of Shoreham, Kent, produced a monumental work in defense of infant baptism. It was written in response to several books on infant baptism. Beginning in 1703 the author David Russen wrote an anti-Anabaptist tract entitled *Fundamentals Without Foundation, or A True Picture of the Anabaptists*.[45] This, in turn, was answered in 1704 by the Baptist Joseph Stennett in *An Answer to Mr. David Russen's Book*.[46] Wall then answered both men with *A History of Infant Baptism*. Wall surfaced again in 1705 and 1706 when John Gale, a Baptist minister, wrote a series of letters in defense of his position against infant baptism. The letters were published in 1711 as *Reflections On Mr. Wall's History*.[47] The basis of Wall's three-volume work is not to build upon the commission of Christ to baptize in Judea during his mortal life, or to baptize the heathens as commanded to take place after his death. The position of finding Scripture to support their cause was largely the strategy of both sides of the argument for and against infant baptism. But proofs drawn from Scripture created great hindrance in the debate. Wall's argument was based upon the evidence presented from those Christians who lived closest to the times of the apostles. Wall claims that there was no particular direction given concerning what the disciple was to do in reference to the children of those that received the faith.

> And among all the persons that are recorded as baptized by the apostles, there is no express mention of any infant; nor is there, on the other side, any account of any Christian's child whose baptism was put off till he was grown up, or who was baptized at man's age (for all the persons that are mentioned in Scripture to have been baptized were the children of Heathens, or else of

---

also William Orme, *Remarkable Passages in the Life of William Kiffin* (London: Burton and Smith, 1823) 102.

44. William H. Brackney, *The Baptists* (Westport: Praeger, 1994) 57.

45. David Russen, *Fundamentals Without Foundation: or, a True Picture of the Anabaptists in Their Rise, Progress and Practice, to which is Added a Letter from the Reverend Mr. James Brome to the Author* (London: Printed For R. Bassett, 1703).

46. Joseph Stennett, *An Answer to Mr. David Russen's Book, Entitul'd, Fundamentals Without a Foundation, or a True Picture of the Anabaptists, &c. Together with Some Brief Remarks on Mr. James Broome's Letter Annex'd to that Treatise* (London: Brown, S. Crouch, and J. Baker, 1704).

47. Oscar Burdock, "William Wall," in H. C. G. Matthew and Brian Howard Harrison, eds., *Oxford Dictionary of National Biography: In Association with the British Academy: From the Earliest Times to the Year 2000* (New York: Oxford University Press, 2004) 56:918.

Jews, who did not believe in Christ at that time when those their children were born).[48]

The debate continued into the nineteenth century as the republication of Wall's treatise in 1819 demonstrates. Written in the spirit of Church of England history, William Goode in 1849 published a work in defense of the church's practice of infant baptism. Its popularity caused a second edition to be published in 1850.[49] Looking back to the earliest days of the Church of England, Goode draws attention to the Twenty-seventh Article indicating that the church has decidedly spoken on the matter of baptism. The Article reads in part: "Baptism is not only a sign of profession, and mark of difference, whereby Christian men are discerned from other that be not christened; but is also a sign of regeneration or new birth."[50] It goes on to read that "faith is confirmed and grace increased by the virtue of prayer to God."[51] According to the Twenty-seventh Article the church repudiates the doctrine of those who hold baptism to be only a sign. Additionally, Goode contends that the church has a promise from Scripture that God is willing not only to be its God, but also the God of its seed. The infant, therefore, is subject to the same secret election as the adult. And while it is unknown to man whom God will elect, the church follows the outward word which is committed to it. Under that promise, the church "baptizes our little ones as the ancients circumcised theirs."[52] It was assumed that the Anabaptists baptizing only adults could not know any more fully the state of their mind or the certainty of their election than the church in baptizing infants.[53] Civility at times was replaced with guile as seen in the refutation offered by an unidentified author to Reverend John Deck, curate of St John's, Hull. Deck had preached two sermons opposing infant baptism which were refuted in a pamphlet. The author notes that Deck charges Baptists with giving such an interpretation of Scriptures as inevitably to involve the "damnation of infants." "Calmly, yet indignantly, we denounce such conduct as at once disingenuous, and dishonourable... What then are we to think of a Clergyman professing to 'speak the truth in love' who unscrupulously represents us as believing that the commission, or any part of it, has a reference to

---

48. William Wall, *The History of Infant Baptism: In Two Parts*, 4th ed. (London: Printed for F. C. and J. Rivington, 1819) 1:iii.

49. William Goode, *The Doctrine of the Church of England as to the Effects of Baptism in the Case of Infants*, 2nd ed. (London: Hatchard and Son, 1850).

50. Welchman, *The Thirty-Nine Articles of the Church of England*, 63.

51. Goode, *The Doctrine of the Church of England*, 4.

52. Ibid., 176.

53. Ibid., 312.

infants, and then holds us up to the religious public as the abettors of infant damnation."[54] Thus the attacks against the Anabaptists and their refutations were often strident and not always accurately presented.

The debate persisted within the Church of England as well— most notably as a result of growing Tractarian frustration with the English Reformation. Tractarian doctrinal positions were at odds with those of the older Anglican High Churchmen. This was most apparent in the doctrines of baptism and the Eucharist. The Tractarians held to a narrow view of apostolic succession combined with an understanding that only the Anglican, Roman Catholic and Eastern Orthodox churches were considered to be part of Catholic Christendom. The Tractarian position on the doctrine of baptismal regeneration and Christ's real presence in the Eucharist was described in ways that were significantly advanced over the older High Churchmen.[55] Nevertheless, belief in baptismal regeneration was common to both older High Churchmen and Tractarians. Evangelicals such as John B. Sumner (1780–1862), Archbishop of Canterbury, differed markedly from High Churchmen on the spiritual effects which they believed inseparably accompanied baptism.[56] Much of the debate came to a head in 1847–1850 during the Gorham controversy. George C. Gorham (1787–1857) was being examined for a post by Bishop Henry Phillpotts who subsequently found Gorham's views in opposition to baptismal regeneration. Among those who opposed Gorham was an ecclesiastical lawyer and member of the Oxford Movement. Sumner, like William Goode, did not entirely share Gorham's covenant theology, yet they denied that his views were heretical as Phillpotts had argued. Sumner reiterates his position in his works on apostolic preaching. In it he affirms that the church had long considered baptism as conveying regeneration, but he counters the position by stating "If there is a distinction between special grace and common grace, and none are regenerate but those who receive special grace, and those only receive it who are elect; baptism is evidently no sign of regeneration, since so many after baptism live profane and unholy lives, and perish in their sins."[57] Belief in baptismal regeneration was common among both the old High Churchmen and the Tractarians. Bishop Christopher Bethell (1773–1859), who was identified with the High Church party wrote in his 1821 publication *A General View of the Doctrine*

---

54. Anon., *A Refutation of Infant Baptism, as Advocated by the Rev. John Deck, Curate of St. John's, Hull* (Hull: Hunter, 1843) 3–4.

55. Nigel Yates, *Anglican Ritualism in Victorian Britain 1830–1910* (Oxford: Oxford University Press, 1999) 47.

56. Nockles, *The Oxford Movement in Context*, 230.

57. John B. Sumner, *Apostolic Preaching Considered in Examination of St. Paul's Epistles* (New York: New York Protestant Episcopal, 1830) 91–92.

of *Regeneration in Baptism* that he agreed with Edward Pusey's *Scriptural Views of Baptism* as purported in his Tract 67. Bethell notes that the work is "highly satisfactory to me to find views which I had long ago taken."[58] Even so, Bethell took exception to Pusey's "evangelical phraseology" and complained that he added to the sacrament of baptism the language of the Calvinistic divines concerning the necessity of a change of affection and inward feeling.[59] According to Charles Cruttwell, although Pusey's mind was steeped in the early church fathers and depicted the supernatural grace of baptism in his writings, his mind was "steeped in its awfulness, and too little on its aspect of help and comfort."[60] Some within the church felt so strongly about its position on baptism that seceding was the only option. Joseph C. Philpot (1802–1869) was one of them. On 28 March 1835, he felt compelled to write to the Provost of Worcester College and resign his Fellowship. He began by stating that he could no longer in good conscience continue as a minister or a member of the Established Church.[61] He found a coldness of spirit and ritual of doctrine that bothered his conscience and so, after several years of contemplation, he came to the conclusion that he was compelled to secede from the Church of England because he could find in her "scarce one lark of a true church." In his words: "She tramples upon one ordinance of Christ by sprinkling infants, and calling it regeneration . . . and profanes the other, by permitting the ungodly to participate."[62] He found the Church of England to be in opposition to the true church as described in Scripture, finding that she embraced those of immoral character whom she christens, confirms, and buries. And she pronounces upon all she executes these offices that they are "regenerate" because of the baptismal service which renders that all of their sins are forgiven. Philpot was not alone in his concern over the ordinances of the Church of England. Among those prepared to secede over the practice of baptism was Govett.

---

58. Christopher Bethell, *A General View of the Doctrine of Regeneration in Baptism*, 2nd ed. (London: Printed for J. G. & F. Rivington, 1836) xxi.

59. Nockles, *The Oxford Movement in Context*, 231–32.

60. Charles Thomas Cruttwell, *Six Lectures on the Oxford Movement and its Results on the Church of England* (London: Skeffington & Son, 1899) 67.

61. Joseph C. Philpot, *A Letter to the Provost of Worcester College, Oxford: On Resigning His Fellowship, and Seceding from the Church of England*, 6th ed. (London: Fowler, 1835) 8.

62. Philpot, *A Letter to the Provost of Worcester College*, 12.

Govett's Baptismal Beliefs

In the year that Philpot resigned his fellowship from Worcester College, Govett was awarded a fellowship from the same college. He did not keep his fellowship long before it was revoked when he, like Philpot, resigned from the Church of England. For Govett the reason was singular—the practice of infant baptism. But he saw in that one sacrament much of the same Scriptural and spiritual corruption as did Philpot. And, like Philpot, Govett felt he had to separate himself from the church's errors and worldly system. But for Govett it came to be more. Believing that only adults had Scriptural grounds for baptism—and that only after a salvation experience—he sought to prove that baptism for believers was not only fitting and proper as a sign, but necessary in order to enter the Kingdom of Heaven (or, in Govett's understanding, the millennial reign). Baptism held a dual purpose for Govett. In one sense it was a sacrament and was to be obeyed on that ground. In another sense obedience in its observance was to bring about a prize. That prize, as the apostle Paul described it, was entrance into the Kingdom. This duality did not immediately surface in his writings on baptism but became very apparent later in life. At first he was content to simply defend adult baptism and demonstrate from Scripture why infant baptism was wrong. In defense of his position, he wrote a tract entitled *The Principal Arguments from Scripture in Favour of Infant Baptism Considered* in which he acknowledges his own spiritual journey. The difficulty, he confesses, was largely that the reasons for or against infant baptism were "nicely balanced" on both sides of the doctrine.[63] The tract is written for those who can find ground on both sides and are confused about what to believe. Concerning the subject of believers' baptism, he lays out a series of scriptural passages which were commonly considered. But, he asserts, this evidence is overbalanced in their minds in favor of infant baptism by several principal arguments which can be reduced to this assumption: Circumcision and Passover under the law related to baptism and the supper of the Lord under the gospel. The conclusion deduced is, that just as infants under the law had a right to circumcision, so infants under the gospel have a right to baptism. "On the truth or falsehood of this principal, the whole question turns."[64] Using the depth of his understanding of Scripture and his known persuasive power of deduction, he concludes that the supposed scriptural grounds utilized to prove infant baptism not only give no evidence, but positively decide against it.[65]

63. Robert Govett, *The Principal Arguments from Scripture in Favour of Infant Baptism* (Norwich: Fletcher and Son, 1847) 1.

64. Govett, *The Principal Arguments*, 6.

65. Ibid., 16.

In one of a series of tracts written by Govett shortly after leaving the Church of England he dealt squarely with his disapproval of the Baptismal Service itself as found in the Established Church. It was in *The Baptismal Service of the Church of England Considered* (1847) that Govett writes that the orthodox Baptismal Service begins and ends with two great and sound truths: the first, that all are born in sin; and the second, that the believer professes to follow Christ and to be like him in life. But agreement with the church ends there as he concludes that between these two truths lies a mass of "most pernicious doctrine." In typical fashion, the evidence presented is done so in civil tones, "not as rejoicing in the discovery of error and evil, but as desirous to exhibit to Christians of the Church Establishment, the perilous errors to which they give their sanction, by continuing to profess themselves members."[66] Three errors were of special concern to Govett regarding the Baptismal Service. The first error is of grave concern and it pertained to the liturgy of the church which teaches baptismal regeneration. The church taught that all who receive baptism according to the ritual of the Prayer Book are by baptism regenerated, and born anew.[67] Govett never appeared to doubt that what the church intended to mean by "regeneration" and "born again" was precisely what Scripture meant and he also understood it to mean—that the regenerate man is a believer, and the believer a regenerate man. The disagreement with the church converged upon its teaching that holds to regeneration taking place at baptism. "Before it [the Baptismal Service], the child or adult is in the flesh, partaker of the condemned and corrupt nature. After it, he is God's adopted child, a member of Christ, heir of the Kingdom of Glory to come."[68] Also opposing this doctrinal position at the time were many evangelical ministers within the Established Church who held that baptism did not regenerate the soul. However, they continued to consent to administer the sacrament because they maintained what was called the "hypothetical principle." In contrast to the High Churchmen who held that in all cases, baptism administered in accordance with the Prayer Book, produced regeneration, the evangelical clergy affirmed that regeneration occurred only in certain cases. They claimed that "the church accepts the profession of character (made by the candidate for baptism) as real, and

---

66. Robert Govett, *The Baptismal Services of the Church of England Considered* (Norwich: Fletcher and Son, 1847) 3.

67. John Stephens, "The Ministration of Private Baptism of Children in Houses," *The Book of Common Prayer: With Notes, Legal and Historical* (London: Harrison and Son, 1850) 2:1305.

68. Govett, *The Baptismal Services*, 7.

then promises her blessings on that charitable assumption."[69] In Govett's point of view, even the very supposition is unscriptural.

The second error of special concern for Govett was the question of sponsorship, or the appointment of those who made promises on behalf of the child. The term used in the service was "godfather" and "godmother." They were to be presented with the child in various numbers depending upon whether the child presented was male or female. But no matter how much an adult believed, or however much the parents might desire the ordinance, if they thought the command of "godparents" to be unscriptural and refused to comply, they could not receive baptism according to the Prayer Book. Govett rejected this sponsorship condition on the grounds that it was yet another tradition of men and found there to be no authority for it in the New Testament.[70]

The third error of special concern for Govett was the matter of the Baptismal Service as being considered a "covenant." This was professed to be true by both the High Churchmen and the evangelicals in respect to the belief that in the act of baptism God and man become covenanting parties. God promises and man pledges.[71] In the Book of Common Prayer it specifically reads, "Wherefore, after this promise made by Christ, this infant must also faithfully for his part promise by you, that he will renounce the devil and all his works."[72] Govett denounces this aspect of the doctrine by drawing the correlation to the covenant on Sinai. It also offered promises on God's part and condition of obedience on man's part. In Govett's estimation, the service for baptism contains a formal covenant of works and without it the promised blessings will not be given to the baptized. The unscriptural aspect of this correlation is in its denial of the gospel. Under this belief, grace ceases and Christ's power is denied. Thus the ordinance itself becomes a type of vehicle by which men are saved. In his typical fashion of focusing upon the gospel as his foremost source Govett asks, "Alas! alas! Should we be silent when the gospel is thus set aside?"[73] This was not an issue that surfaced in his own day. It stretched back to the reformers who also affirmed that the act of infant baptism regenerated the child by removing its imputed

---

69. Ibid., 8.

70. Robert Govett, *The Baptismal Services*, 10–15. See, for example, John Spurgin, *Church of England. Six Observations with Notes, Explanatory of the Office for the Public Baptism of Infants*, rev. ed. (London: Wertheim, 1884) 18.

71. Robert Govett, *The Baptismal Services*, 16. See Paul K. Jewett, *Infant Baptism & the Covenant of Grace* (Grand Rapids: Eerdmans, 1978).

72. R. P. Blakeney, *The Book of Common Prayer in its History and Interpretation*, 3rd ed. (London: Miller, 1870) 581.

73. Govett, *The Baptismal Services*, 16–24.

sins. Govett opposed this position by bringing attention to the error of the High Churchmen and the Ritualist, Rome and the Greek Church on the ground that they assumed the Holy Spirit to be tied to both the water and the form. "They exalt, as saving powers things seen and material; the powers of man and of the priest."[74]

Govett held a high view of Scripture over the acclaim of man or his institutions. This was never so apparent than in his response to several of the doctrinal positions of Darby. Disagreement over doctrine—especially infant baptism—could get contentious but Govett was never known to be deleterious in his writings. Govett, refuting Darby, wrote in the opening of his commentary on the book of Colossians that Darby was honored of the Lord in his setting forth the glorious standing of the church as the Body of Christ. He credits Darby by saying that he revealed much research in a paper that he had written pertaining to how the true doctrine concerning the church was lost immediately after the apostolic age, but that he left much for further students of the Word of God. However, he then directly accuses Darby of being wrong with regard to baptism, and to justification, and furthermore that he "refused to own the judgment of the saints before Christ in the day of His coming" regarding what the apostle Paul says in 2 Corinthians 5.[75] Govett was equally respectful of Daniel Wilson (1778–1858), Bishop of Calcutta, who had written a commentary on the book of Colossians and with whom he had disagreed on the matter of infant baptism.[76] He finds that Wilson is "often times at variance with his own self," citing that he opposes Puseyism and its false doctrines and rites but defends infant sprinkling.[77] Govett was curious about how Wilson could be wrong on the matter of infant baptism and simultaneously speak out so boldly against the "Romish spirit and tendency" of the Tractarians. Govett retorts, "If Christ instituted the sprinkling of infants, show us the command, or the example of it." He noted that Wilson would not be able to find any New Testament example. "For this rite, then, as a tradition of men, its defenders are obliged to fall back on Ecclesiastical History."[78]

Others publically found Govett to be in error on his deductions from Scripture. John Cox was one who openly disapproved of Govett's handling

74. Robert Govett, *The New Life, with its New Birth and Kingdom: Part I–II* (Norwich: Fletcher and Son, 1885) 11.

75. Robert Govett, *Christ the Head; the Church His Body: Its Dangers, Duties, Glories: or, the Argument of Colossians* (Norwich: Fletcher and Son, 1890) 1.

76. Daniel Wilson, *Expository Lectures on St. Paul's Epistle to the Colossians* (London: Hatchard and Son, 1845).

77. Govett, *Christ the Head*, 125.

78. Ibid., 126.

of Scripture. His point is made in *The Primitive Church Magazine*[79] where he refutes Govett's position in support of mixed communion and questioned how he could hold that position while denying infant baptism.[80] In another example of opposition, a reader identifying himself as "A. Watcher" wrote to *The Rainbow* to refute a previous letter submitted by Govett on the subject of adult baptism by immersion. Watcher suggests that Govett is wrong in his assertion that the gospel of John 3:5 refers literally to water baptism, holding instead that it is merely figurative language.[81] This verse is a very important point of doctrine for Govett because upon it hangs the locus of his position on the Kingdom of Heaven being made available solely to earnest believers who have submitted to believers' baptism. In his commentary on the gospel of John, concerning this same verse, Govett precisely articulates the position. He contrasts verse 3 with verse 5 to prove that each is referring to a matter of baptism which is distinctly different from the other. Verse 3 refers only to the requirement of being born (or, regenerated) by the Spirit in order to enter the Kingdom of God. Upon Nicodemus's objection to a "second birth," Jesus adds a second imperative in verse 5. Now, it would be observed, Nicodemus must not only be regenerated by the Spirit, Jesus now adds "born out of water." According to Govett the result is a stronger statement, i.e., the birth out of water added on the one side, introduces "the entry" into the Kingdom on the other. "Here then is the proof, that this second sentiment means more than the first. A new weight is put into each scale.[82] While Watcher finds these verses figurative, Govett affirms them to be decidedly literal—"The water then, we affirm, is literal water."[83] Over the years Govett continued to develop his argument for this connection to the Coming Kingdom, but he never lost sight of the importance of refuting the Established Church's position on infant baptism. Elsewhere Govett says "All baptism before faith is sinful. It does not give life."[84] And he sought other

---

79. *The Primitive Church Magazine, Advocating the Constitution, Faith, and Practice of the Apostolic Churches* (1838–1869) was published to advocate the practice of strict communion and to "bring to the text" infant baptism and mixed communion. See *Waterloo Directory of English Newspapers and Periodicals, 1800–1900*, series 2 in 20 vols. (Ontario: North Waterloo Academic, 2003).

80. John Cox, "Divine Testimony and Human Inference," *Primitive Church Magazine, Advocating the Constitution, Faith, and Practice of the Apostolic Churches* 11, no. 124 (1854) 151.

81. *The Rainbow: A Magazine of Christian Literature, with Special Reference to the Revealed Future of the Church and the world* 2 (1865) 94–95.

82. Robert Govett, *Exposition of the Gospel of St. John, Vol. I-II* (London: Bemrose and Sons, 1881) 80.

83. Govett, *Exposition of the Gospel of St. John*, 81.

84. Ibid., 192.

venues to expound his beliefs. For example, on Thursday evening, 20 September 1850, Govett delivered a lecture "upon the baptismal service of the Church of England in the chapel in Baker Street."[85]

In his tract *An Appeal to Evangelical Clergymen and Churchmen* he declares that there are two great systems in his day that struggle for mastery: the religion of tradition (or, that which "springs in great part from man") wrestles against the religion of the record (or, Scripture). It becomes a struggle of sacramental religion against personal—formal against vital godliness."[86]

His tract is addressed to evangelical clergyman within the Established Church who hold to justification without works, and who acknowledge the doctrines of God's election and the perseverance of the elect, but he cautions them that they are being deluded by the Roman Catholic Church. In Govett's estimation, the progress of "Romanism" in England was owing to the body of men known as Puseyites who propound the sacramental theory of Rome. And he notes that the origin of Puseyism, while its profound cause is the hatred of unrenewed nature to the gospel of God, in some of the churches there persisted a doctrine that was antagonistic and destructive to it. "In infant baptism lies concealed the root of the sacramental delusions of Rome."[87] Directing the focus of his writing to evangelical clergymen he challenges them to either give up the sovereign discriminating regeneration of the Holy Spirit, or surrender infant baptism. The Seventeenth Article asserted God's predestination, and effectual calling of his elect at his own good pleasure. They either give up the perseverance of the elect, or infant baptism since in their baptismal services they pronounced all infants regenerate. Yet, inconsistently, these clergy renounce as evil and unscriptural the *opus operatum* (work done in respect to baptism) of the Roman Catholic Church, but pronounce a rite upon a child who knows nothing of its effect. Govett becomes more abrupt when he recalls to his reader that it is a rite performed

---

85. "Local and General Intelligence," *The Hull Packet and East Riding Times* (20 September 1850). Presumably this was the chapel at the corner of Baker Street and Prospect Street in Hull. Andrew John Jukes (1815–1901) was its pastor. Jukes was initially a curate in the Church of England but became convinced of Baptist teaching and underwent adult baptism at the George Street Chapel, Hull. After leaving the Church of England, he joined the Plymouth Brethren and founded the independent chapel in Baker Street.

86. Robert Govett, *An Appeal to Evangelical Clergymen and Churchmen*, 2nd ed. (London: Yapp, ca. 1845) 3. See also Robert Robert, *Infant Sprinkling No Baptism: Being a Refutation of Mr. C. Paget's "Godly Practice of Infant Baptism,"* (London: Houlston and Wright, 1858).

87. Govett, *An Appeal to Evangelical Clergymen*, 5.

often by ungodly men before ungodly men and women. "Do you not own as your watchword—'The Bible alone?'"[88]

In the final decades of Govett's life he was still teaching his understanding of the error of sprinkling infants. For example, he finds it necessary to interject it into his commentary on the gospel of John, when he expounds verses 1–3 of chapter 4 where he makes mention of the Pharisees hearing that Jesus was gaining and baptizing more disciples than John the Baptist. He writes: "Observe how these simple words correct an error quite natural to those who sprinkle infants. They propose to constitute disciples by a ceremony, without any knowledge on their part of the principles of the teacher; a thing which is quite contrary to the idea of a disciple. 'Make disciples (they would say) by baptizing.' But that is not Christ's plan."[89] Govett believed that with Jesus the reality preceded the sign. Jesus "made the disciple" by instruction and persuasion, before He immersed him. This, then, was to be the rule for the church: first must come conviction and faith, then the immersion of the candidate.

As Govett searched the Scriptures he found more than firm ground for refuting infant baptism, and he also discovered, in his opinion, incontrovertible evidence for the necessity of believers' baptism as one of the prerequisites to entrance into the Kingdom (or, millennial reign). An unclouded example of his belief is captured in a letter written to his congregation just before his return from holiday in January 1883.

> Immersion of the believer is a testimony to a man's vast and momentous movement from death in sins to the life of God, and bears also on its face death and resurrection; and this is God's commanded mode of our expressing faith in the Lord Jesus, our Saviour slain and risen, and of our faith in a resurrection yet to come.[90]

Here he combines the testimony of baptism and the believer's faith in the resurrection. However, Govett's assertions must not be confused. He is not claiming that justification and forgiveness follow upon baptism. He is very clear on this point when he states that this doctrine is an error of both the Church of Rome and the Church of England.[91] Furthermore, he affirms that, "Baptism is set as the pale of distinction and separation between those

---

88. Ibid., 21.

89. Govett, *Exposition of the Gospel of St. John*, 131.

90. Robert Govett, *A Letter to the Saints Assembling at Surrey Road* (14 January 1883). Norfolk Records Office file FC76/60.

91. Govett, *An Appeal to Evangelical Clergymen*, 7.

outside the church, and those within."[92] On this he is in agreement with the Baptists. However, the strict Baptists excluded from the Lord's table and from church fellowship all who were not immersed into the name of the Father, Son, and the Spirit. Govett disagreed with this stance. But the greater point of difference was on the meaning of Jesus's words to Nicodemus the Pharisee in John 3:5, where he states, "Verily, verily, I say unto you, except a man be born out of water and the Spirit, he cannot enter into the Kingdom of God." Govett is convinced that its reference is not to the church but to the individual believer. He holds to the understanding that Jesus's words, "Verily, verily, I say unto you," denotes something not left to man's "deficient eyesight" and "failing hand and heart"; but to God's presiding government, and full determination. To this, Govett adds, "He [the believer] cannot enter [the kingdom], for God shall bar the door—not against probation in the church, but against *reward* in the *glory* [kingdom]."[93] For Govett, being born of the Spirit secures the believer in salvation, but forsaking water baptism denied a believer entrance into the future Kingdom. Govett stood apart from the Baptists on this understanding of exclusion.

There were those whose theological positions on immersion and resurrection differed from his. In his book *Christ's Resurrection and Ours*, which is an exposition of 1 Corinthians 15, Govett identifies verse 29 as troublesome to expositors and notes that it is one of the most difficult passages in Scripture. The verse reads: "Now if there is no resurrection, what will those do who are baptized for the dead? If the dead are not raised at all, why are people baptized for them?" Govett warns that this verse yields a vast variety of interpretations, "most of them very wild and farfetched."[94] The controversy occurs when the expositor misses the distinction the apostle Paul is making between himself and Christians in general. He is making an argument to put down a new act of baptism introduced at Corinth, of which he did not approve and by which he intended to expose its folly and inconsistency. The parties used immersion but denied resurrection. This position sets aside Richard Baxter's question "to what purpose do we in baptism profess our belief of the resurrection,"[95] and Edward Robinson's remark, "if the

---

92. Govett, *How Long is Baptism to be Observed?* (Norwich: Fletcher and Son, 1873) 5.

93. Govett, *How Long Is Baptism*, 13.

94. Robert Govett, *Christ's Resurrection and Ours; or, I Corinthians XV. Expounded* (Glasgow: MacLehose, 1876) 54.

95. See Richard Ingham, *A Handbook on Christian Baptism: Its Subjects* (London: Stock, 1871) 121.

dead do not rise, why expose ourselves to so much danger and suffering in the hope of a resurrection?"[96]

Govett, drawing on Colossians 2:12, states that baptism, according to the mind of God, must be done through immersion. In immersion there are both burial and resurrection. But in pouring water on the face, or sprinkling, Govett asserts there is neither burial nor resurrection. In John chapter 3 there is representation of both death and birth. Neither of these is seen in sprinkling or pouring. "Baptism by immersion is as peculiar to this dispensation, as is the Lord's Supper."[97] Govett finds in Colossians 3:1–4 that the argument of the apostle Paul turns on baptism–of which he had previously spoken in Colossians 2:20 as being the visible association with Christ. "This is true of immersed believers only, not of infants unpossessed of faith, and merely sprinkled."[98]

The most distinct of his tracts pertaining to the believer and his visible association with Christ is found in *Baptism in Relation to the Coming Kingdom and to Eternal Life*.[99] His thesis is that the baptism of the believer by immersion and entrance into the future Kingdom are necessary and explicable as found in Scripture. The believer of Christ has his eye and heart set upon two distinct things: the Kingdom of God and eternal life. These are viewed as distinct. The Kingdom of God is temporary (lasting one-thousand years, or the millennium) while eternal life is without end. The Kingdom of God is a prize to be received according to the work of each believer. The prize is not the present kingdom of grace, but the kingdom of millennial glory. In Govett's understanding of Scripture the title to eternal life is already possessed by the believer while the title to the Kingdom of God is to be sought by baptism and a new life. There is no evidence that any of Govett's contemporaries held similar views of Scripture pertaining to baptism and the millennial reign; and as has been cited there were those who vigorously opposed him in writing. When he found it necessary he refuted them in writing, but his writings never reveal a sense of aloneness in his biblical assertions. Nor is there an air of defensiveness present. If he sensed the uniqueness of his positions that others noticed, he did not reveal it.

He found many to hold opinions replete with common mistakes about both baptism and the Kingdom. The mistakes concerning baptism center

---

96. Edward Robinson, *Greek and English Lexicon of the New Testament* (Boston: Crocker and Brewster, 1836) 126.

97. Govett, *Christ the Head*, 118.

98. Ibid., 189.

99. No date can presently be determined for this tract. It does not appear within the collection of Baptismal tracts published in 1847. The assumption is made that the tract appeared sometime after that date.

upon the translation of the word from the Greek. In his opinion the word is consistently translated to mean "immersion" and, therefore, the sprinkling and pouring of water on the faces of infants is a ritual created by man and is displeasing to God because it turns back to the law under Moses in the Old Testament and, thereby, to the union of church and state. On the matter of the Kingdom, its force in many passages is lost by supposing that "eternal life" and the "Kingdom" mean the same thing.[100]

On the matter of the universal church, Govett wrote *The Church the Body of Christ, and House of God, in Relation to Baptism*, largely to refute a number of positions held by Darby—positions held similarly by the Church of England. Curiously, the reason Darby gives for leaving the Church of England was not that the world was in the church but that he found the system he was "mixed up with" to be the world and not the church of God. "I find no such thing as a 'National Church' in Scripture—was the Church of England ever God's assembly in England?"[101] Govett shared the same sentiment. He agreed with Darby on the definition of the church (as presented by the apostle Paul in Ephesians 2:5 and 2:8) being the saints called out from the world, its sinfulness and its destiny, in order to be God's holy and saved ones. And he agrees with Darby that the church of God, the body of the church, and the Household of God as defined by Scripture consist of the same persons—believers saved in Christ. But he questioned how Darby could hold to the practice of infant baptism when "sprinkled infants are not believers."[102] In order for Darby to justify his views of the church with his views on the doctrine and practice of infant baptism he was compelled to present a new theory which makes a distinction between the church as the body of Christ, and the church as the house of God. Darby was forced to say that one could belong to the House of God through "ordinances" (such as baptism), but one could only belong to the Body of Christ if the person was an elect child of God. Words to this effect are found written by Darby in the Brethren oriented journal *The Present Testimony* when he wrote, "The thought, that admission into the house conferred the privileges of the body, has been the root of the systematic corruption of Christianity."[103] Govett observes that the real ground of ad-

---

100. Robert Govett, *Baptism in Relation to the Coming Kingdom and to Eternal Life*, Part I (London: Holness, nd) 4.

101. *The Claims of the Church of England Considered: Being the Close of a Correspondence Between the Rev. James Kelly, of Stillogen, Ireland, and John N. Darby* (London: Broom, 1842) 18–21.

102. Robert Govett, *The Church the Body of Christ, and House of God, in Relation to Baptism* (Norwich: Fletcher and Son, 1873) 2, 7.

103. John N. Darby, "The House of God—The Body of Christ—The Baptism of

mission into God's assembly was originally regeneration by the Holy Spirit. After that, he was visibly introduced into the Household of God by immersion in water, and then hands were laid on the believer by the apostles in order to communicate the baptism of the Spirit.[104] As to the mode of baptism, it was originally immersion. As regards to its subject, baptism in apostolic times was always applied knowingly to believers alone. It did not produce faith, it manifested it. Before it was administered, a credible profession of faith was required. But Govett was perplexed by Darby's practice of sprinkling infants in baptism when he was confident that Darby believed in the scriptural significance of baptism—that significance being the receiver alive in Christ, born again from the dead, and saved. Yet Darby will not grant that baptism is a sign of being taken out of Adam. He states in *The Present Testimony* "Baptism is not a sign of being, or of being made, a member of Christ."[105] For Govett, immersion is a sign of being taken out of Adam, and of being knit to Christ in resurrection.

In Govett's view, baptism is the exhibition of new life. It is a new birth emerging out of water. For Darby it is a change of "place," not a change of "state" achieved by receiving life.[106] But Darby believed that infant baptism is correctly administered where there is no faith and no spiritual life. He writes "In the Christian order of things we have admission to the Christian system by ordinances recognized, and even outward privileges enjoyed, and yet no divine life, or union with Christ."[107] Govett would not support a view that leads to accepting that God's church is made up of believers and unbelievers; of those who were dead in sins alongside those who were living in Christ. Darby spoke frequently, as did others, of the "professing church" and "professing believers" within the House of God as something distinct from

---

the Holy Ghost," *The Present Testimony, and Original Christian Witness Revived. In which the Church's Portion and the Hope of the Kingdom, Etc.* 11 (1859) 40. No name is assigned to the article but Darby was a frequent contributor to the journal and the style and theory are to be also found in Darby's *Synopsis of the Books of the Bible*, 5 vols. (London: Morrish, 1857–1864). *The Present Testimony* was published in London between 1848–1871. It appears to be a renewal of the *Christian Witness* which was oriented to the Plymouth Brethren. See *Waterloo Directory of English Newspapers and Periodicals, 1800–1900*, series 2 in 20 vols. (Ontario: North Waterloo Academic, 2003).

104. Govett, *The Church the Body of Christ*, 17–18.

105. *The Present Testimony, and Original Christian Witness Revived. In which the Church's Portion and the Hope of the Kingdom, Etc.* 15 (1867) 5.

106. See *The Present Testimony, and Original Christian Witness Revived. In which the Church's Portion and the Hope of the Kingdom, Etc.* 11 (1859) 6–7.

107. *The Present Testimony, and Original Christian Witness Revived. In which the Church's Portion and the Hope of the Kingdom, Etc.* 15 (1867, 4–5.

the Body of Christ—believers and unbelievers joined together.[108] Govett emphatically denies that Scripture ever speaks of owning two churches. This distinction holds the germ of understanding of Govett's fusing together baptism by immersion, performed upon true professing believers in Christ, and his emphasis upon the believer's entrance into the Coming Kingdom. Just as there was only one true baptism, there was also one true believer who qualified for entrance into the Coming Kingdom. Baptism alone does not produce salvation just as professing belief in Christ does not qualify the believer for the Kingdom of God. Just as God's church (the House of God, as Govett defines it) on earth are to be made up of only true believers, saved first by faith, then by sign of baptism by immersion, so too the Millennial Kingdom of God will be made up of only those who truly yielded their lives to serve a living Lord. In his tract *Infant Baptism and the Abrahamic Covenant* he concludes with these words of caution: "Search and look; for of these things you must give account! How sad to find, in the day that shall try your work, that you have built up hay and stubble on the true foundation,—to see your work burned, and to feel that you have suffered loss!"[109]

Govett searched 1 Corinthians 10 which speaks of believers accounted unworthy of the Millennial Kingdom. They are "castaways," not from eternal life, which is a "gift" of God; but from the "prize" of their calling. While most theologians today are uncertain as to the human authorship of Hebrews, Govett was very certain that the author was the apostle Paul. Govett states that Paul clearly indicates in the book that he feared loss of the "prize."[110] In Hebrews 6, Govett also discovers the possibility and the danger of believers falling away from grace back to law and justice. But the chapter also adds that Paul did not suppose that the awful consequences he describes applied to any true believers.[111] Baptism is the first and total bathing to which the Savior refers. It answers to the total uncleanness of man by nature.[112] In this regard Govett raises another point of doctrine, that of feet washing. In John 13:7 Jesus is reported as saying, "You do not realize now what I am doing, but later you will understand." It assumes that behind the outward act lay concealed something deeper, something yet to come. And in verse 10 Jesus remarked, "A person who has had a bath needs only to wash his feet; his whole body is clean. And you are clean, though not every one of you." To this Govett

108. Govett, *The Church the Body of Christ*, 35.

109. Robert Govett, *Infant Baptism and the Abrahamic Covenant* (Norwich: Fletcher, 1846) 31.

110. See 1 Cor 9:24–27.

111. Govett, *The Church the Body of Christ*, 35.

112. Robert Govett, *Sin after Baptism; or a Long Neglected Command of the Lord Jesus, Recommended to Believers* (Norwich: Fletcher and Son, 1845) 9.

answers that former sins were forgiven forever when by faith the believer was united with Christ. Baptism proclaimed this truth to the believer and others. That act continues to endure. The past is behind and blotted out. But since that day the believer continues to offend in his behavior and thoughts. "You need then a second and supplementary washing, that you may be wholly clean. Such is the washing of your feet. The first washing was *total*; for sin entirely possessed you by nature. This second washing is *partial*, as your sins now are occasional."[113] His rationale for this scriptural finding is that the believer sins only occasionally after faith. He is as one who coming up out of a bath is totally clean and only needs to wash his feet to remove the dust. The symbolism of feet washing was intended to teach that daily sin demands a daily cleansing, even after the believer's old sins are purged and put away. The intercession of Jesus and his ceaseless washing are continually needed. The washing of feet is found by Govett to be of the level of an ordinance conveying important lessons regarding the standing of believers. The most obvious lesson the ordinance carries with it is humility. Yet, he finds that it carries with it a far higher meaning than any self-devised display of humility can do. It teaches the receiver that sins and errors build upon the believer even while God's past forgiveness is unaltered.[114] Feet washing is urged upon the believer, not for the lesson of humility alone, but for the day in which will appear the reward of a crown of glory.[115]

Conclusion

Much history on the subject of baptism precedes Govett's writings. This chapter has attempted to provide a summary of the historical context of the doctrine. During Govett's lifetime the debate over baptism was engaged mostly on the level of proving the appropriateness of one mode of baptism over another—the scriptural support for infant baptism over and against adult, believers' baptism. Govett took the debate to new levels by not only vigorously affirming the biblical validity of believers' baptism, but by holding to a doctrine that excludes true believers from the Coming Kingdom if they failed to receive water baptism. Prominent names who wrote to affirm infant baptism, he occasionally challenged—especially if his tracts were used or alluded to. This was the case, for instance, with Catesby Paget who wrote *The Godly Practice of Infant Baptism: Defended on New Testament Ground Alone* (1858). Govett writes that Paget has done injustice to

113. Govett, *Sin after Baptism*, 10.
114. Ibid., 21.
115. Ibid., 24.

the arguments he professes to cite by not properly quoting his words.[116] Nevertheless, his primary concern over baptism was not to condemn infant baptism on scriptural grounds but to pronounce that believers' baptism was more than merely a command by Christ as an outward sign of an inward spiritual regeneration. It was a necessary action as one of the qualifications to enter the future Kingdom of God. His tract, by an otherwise misleading title, *He that is Baptized with the Spirit Needs No Baptism of Water*, speaks to the necessity of water baptism in order to secure the Kingdom.[117] Baptism is to be entered into advisedly and with humility of thought regarding the pursuit of the Kingdom which it introduced.

It is to this relationship of pursuit of the Kingdom—a subject in which Govett spent notable time and passion—that this study now turns. In his tract *Baptism, the Kingdom of God, and Eternal Life*, published posthumously, Govett writes "What then shall become of the First Resurrection and its reward? They will indeed appear, as all believers must, before the Judgment Seat of Christ: but they will not enjoy the Thousand Years. They will be dismissed to the corruption of the tomb, according to their present sowing to the flesh."[118] In Govett's eyes the pursuit of the Kingdom is of paramount importance, because not to do so could initiate unalterable consequences of exclusion upon the appearance of Christ at the Rapture. When Govett first began writing on the subject he was unique in his presentation. But, common to many of his writings, controversy soon followed.

---

116. Robert Govett, *Infant Sprinkling No Baptism: Being a Refutation of Mr. C. Paget's "Godly Practice of Infant Baptism"* (London: Houlston and Wright, 1858) 3.

117. Robert Govett, *"He that is Baptized with the Spirit Needs No Baptism of Water,"* 2nd ed. (Norwich: Fletcher and Son, 1873).

118. Robert Govett, *Baptism, The Kingdom of God, and Eternal Life* (Norwich: From Mr. A. J. Tilney, n.d., posthumous) 31.

CHAPTER 5

Govett and Eschatological Reward

IN THE VICTORIAN ERA authors such as Alfred Lord Tennyson (1809–1892) devoted much of their writing to exploring the concept of death, attempting to understand the death of close friends and loved ones. Tennyson wrote a lengthy elegy titled 'In Memoriam A. H. H.' (1850) in which he works through the grief of losing his close friend Alfred Henry Hallam. Tina Pippin, in assessing the meaning of the poem, remarks that Tennyson does not allow for any positive assurance that there is happiness after death. Rather, he struggles to understand the complicated intertwining of religion and science that emerged in the Victorian era. In the end, the poem yields to doubt winning out over faith.[1] Pippin wrongly reads back in history and loses sight of the consoling nature of Tennyson's words which manage to overcome doubt with faith. For example, one of the first books that Queen Victoria reached for after the death of Prince Albert in December 1861, in her search for spiritual consolation, was Tennyson's *In Memoriam*. Helen Rappaport writes "For a while, it would be virtually her only reading, apart from the Bible and religious books. She soon adopted the poem as the literary emblem of her own grief. Tennyson's work, she felt, offered her very personal comfort and hope that in afterlife, she would be reunited with Albert."[2]

Nevertheless, doubt was a continuing concern for many Victorian believers. Govett knew this well. In response to this concern he regularly encouraged his congregation to hold firm to their faith. In his annual pastoral letter of 1854 Govett reminded his congregants that "Our hope is in the return of the Lord Jesus. Our desire should be, to be with him in the glory,

---

1. Pippin, "Death and the Afterlife," 721.
2. Helen Rappaport, *Queen Victoria: A Biographical Companion* (Santa Barbara: ABC-CLIO, 2003) 353.

and to appear before his presence without reproof or shame."[3] Rather than succumb to the crisis of faith that was often present in the Victorian era, Govett fostered an attitude of unwavering hope and reassured his flock at Surrey Chapel that the Lord was certain to come even if he appeared to tarry. Govett was optimistic about what lay ahead for the believer who lived a life pleasing to God. But living that life was a process that began with a realization that the millennial life to come was never to be attained if one did not first recognize one's separation from God and desire to be restored. That restoration comes about through repentance of sin, a surrender of self-righteousness, and an acceptance of salvation offered through Christ's death on the Cross. Govett writes, "First believe, then be baptized–rejoice then in your salvation." But there is a continuance that follows. The believer is then to look beyond a world that is being destroyed and look instead to the new heavens and earth of God's promise, "under the better covenant established on better promises."[4]

As previously stated, Govett was a futurist. His views of a future promise spring from an understanding that most of the book of Revelation is yet future and that there awaits the believer a thousand-year reign with Christ on earth before the ushering in of eternity.[5] Aside from the preeminence of the feature of baptism in Govett's writings, the greatest single topic which consumed his thinking was the subject of entrance into that thousand-year reign. Between 1861 and 1865 Govett wrote a four-volume work entitled *The Apocalypse: Expounded by Scripture*, under the pseudonym Matheetees (disciple or learner).[6] The volumes are written from his usual futurist position of interpretation. In 1861 Govett's first volume was reviewed in the *Quarterly Journal of Prophecy*. The reviewer stated: "This work has yet reached only to the end of the third chapter of the Apocalypse; and while it contains some good illustrations of particular passages, contains also a good many things with which we do not accord."[7] What the periodical observed was his well-crafted understanding from Scripture of what takes place at

---

3. Norfolk Records Office file FC76/95. Pastoral Letter from Govett to his congregation assembled at the Bazaar, Norfolk. Written at Brighton (17 May 1854).

4. Robert Govett, *Types of the Righteousness of Christ* (Norwich: Fletcher and Son, 1873) 19–20.

5. For an understanding of Govett's futurist position see Robert Govett, *Leading Thoughts on the Apocalypse* (Norwich: Fletcher and Son, 1885); and *How Interpret the Apocalypse? As Naturalists? or as Supernaturalists? A Refutation of the Historic Interpretation, with Especial Reference to the Rev. G. Guinness' "Approaching End of the Age"* (Norwich: Fletcher and Son, 1879).

6. The choice of this pseudonym is short-lived. He never explains why he chose to use it.

7. See "Reviews," *The Quarterly Journal of Prophecy* 13 (1861) 401.

the Rapture and extends into the Kingdom of God–a theme that permeated his writings. For Govett, the Rapture and the Kingdom were important subjects of demarcation for the believer and nonbeliever alike. David M. Panton (1870–1955), who studied Govett's theology closely, provides some clarity on this matter. "Even a casual study of the Word of God reveals that a new horizon now opens on the redeemed soul. If life is by faith, *reward* is consequent on *works* done after faith."[8] Arthur T. Pierson (1837–1911), a contemporary of Govett who followed Spurgeon as pastor of the Metropolitan Tabernacle, provided a little more clarity in 1894:

> With many disciples, the eyes are yet blinded to this mystery of rewards, which is one of the open mysteries of the Word, and some cannot see how rewards can have any place in an economy of grace. But we must not confound salvation and recompense. It must be an imputed righteousness,—exceeding far that of the most proper Pharisee—whereby we *enter* the Kingdom of Heaven; but, having thus entered by faith, our *works* determine our relative rank, place, reward, in that Kingdom. Eternal life is God's gift to be had for the asking; but he who receives the gift, and does work, sowing and reaping for God, receiveth also wages and gathereth fruit unto life eternal.[9]

Reward, then, is something to be sought-after and is directly connected to the Kingdom, which he asserts is both referred to as the Kingdom of Heaven and the Kingdom of God. He argues that the two terms generally mean the same thing in Scripture. Except in just a few exceptions the terms mean the "Millennial Kingdom."[10] Every believer is to seek this future Kingdom. And in that coming Kingdom the Lord will award to each believer according to his quality of life as measured by the Lord. The full surrender to Jesus now, or the neglecting of him, will be followed by answerable results.[11] It is through resurrection that Christ will reign in the Coming Kingdom and the believer with him. Reigning (as described in Revelation 20:6) occurs after the Savior's judgment has been adjudicated upon the believer which pronounces the extent of faithful. Govett is confident that there is no manifestation of resurrection until after Christ has descended in person to call

---

8. Panton, *The Judgment Seat of Christ*, 4.

9. Arthur T. Pierson, *The New Acts of the Apostles, or the Marvels of Modern Missions, a Series of Lectures Upon the Foundation of the "Duff Missionary Lectureship"* (London: Nisbet, 1894) 417.

10. Robert Govett, *The Kingdom of God Future* (London: Nisbet, 1870) 11.

11. Govett, *The Kingdom of God Future*, 96.

his people up to himself. The believer's state in the Kingdom demands the appearing of the Savior in person.[12]

Two years after its first review of *The Apocalypse: Expounded by Scripture*, the *Quarterly* reviewed volume 2 and had this to say: "The author holds, according to the futurist theory, that the prophetic portion of the book of Revelation, from chapter 4 to the end, is yet unfulfilled, and will only begin to receive its fulfillment when 'the Jew is brought back to his own land, and the temple and its sacrifices restored,' at the commencement of the dispensation of judgment."[13] The review also noticed that Govett holds that at the end of the present dispensation of "mercy and mystery" only believers who have been found worthy to escape those events that will occur on Earth shall be secretly caught up to the Lord. The editor remarks, "'Matheetees' seems to be an independent inquirer, who gives careful attention to the exact meaning of the original according to the best critical authorities, is earnestly desirous of eliciting and submitting to whatever may appear to be the true teaching of Scripture, and refuses to be trammeled by any existing system, however imposing."[14] There is no evidence in his writings that he was directly influenced or persuaded by any theologian espousing doctrine. But he does occasionally cite a scholar who affirms his position.[15] On the contrary, he was often at odds with them. The review also finds that Govett does not engage much in controversy with those who differ with him; but when he does, it is "always with fairness and directness"—a comment which was fairly typical of his treatment toward those who differed with him.[16]

Govett on Exclusion

What makes Govett's views on the Kingdom of Heaven of particular interest to those in the church who read him in the second half of the nineteenth century is the position he held on "exclusion" from that kingdom. Many

---

12. Ibid., 41.

13. See "Reviews," *The Quarterly Journal of Prophecy* 15 (1863) 191–92.

14. Ibid., 191.

15. For example, in *Isaiah Unfulfilled: Being an Exposition of the Prophet* (1841) Govett references several theologians in support of his position: Robert Lowth (1710–1787), biblical critic and Bishop of London is referenced for his "celebrated" book on Isaiah in the preface; Edward Gresswell (1797–1869), biblical scholar, to whom his readers are directed on page 159; Michael Dodson (1732–1799), biblical scholar, is referenced on page 169; James Begg (1808–1883) was a Free Church of Scotland minister, whose work is praised on page 177; Benjamin Kennicott (1718–1783) is also referenced on page 371.

16. "Reviews," 191.

could affirm with Govett that there was to be reward for believers in the life to come. For example, as often as Govett disagreed with Darby on points of doctrine, they could both agree upon what Darby said regarding reward in heaven: "They [believers] must not act on the principle of getting reward here, but wait for the time when they are to meet the Lord . . . This is not a question of salvation, but of reward for service."[17] Yet, there were others who disagreed—sometimes strongly. Even the *Quarterly Journal of Prophecy*, which was routinely in agreement with Govett's scholarship and pleased to report his latest works, had difficulty on this issue. The journal appears not to hold to a "futurist" position on prophecy, as it says in Govett's review, not because of the "impossibility or mad absurdities involved in it," but because the journal can see "no ground for the secret Rapture of the saints which seems essential to the scheme."[18] And concerning Govett's position on exclusion, in particular, the reviewer states:

> There are a good many points of detail in this work on which we do not agree with the author; and there is one in particular which we think ought to be noticed, because we are persuaded it is both false and in no small degree dangerous—viz., the division of believers into overcomers and overcome; the former of whom shall have special rewards and share in the millennial kingdom, while the latter, though certain to be saved at last, shall be excluded from it, and for one thousand years reap the bitter fruits of their evil works, and may even possibly be hurt of the second death, for to escape from the lake of fire does not belong to every believer; or, being judged according to their works, shall suffer punishment during the millennium, some even in the lake of fire.[19]

This statement, while in strong disagreement, very perceptively verbalizes Govett's position of the grounds upon which "exclusion" of believers may occur at the Rapture; denying some believers entrance into the Kingdom of God. The position was extremely troublesome to many theologians who otherwise agreed with Govett from a futurist perspective. Their concern was over an interpretation of the Rapture that would limit Christ from receiving the church in its entirety. On the subject of the Rapture, and Govett's unique interpretation of its nature, he found particularly strident opposition. However, Govett was no stranger to opposition and controversy. There were those who opposed him on other points of doctrine as

---

17. John N. Darby, *Notes On the Gospel of Luke* (Glasgow: Allan, 1869) 164–65.
18. "Reviews," 191.
19. Ibid., 192.

well and could become vociferous and extremely cutting in their response. For example, a letter to the editor of the *Church of England Chronicle*, from P. E. Wilson of St George's, Bloomsbury, took exception to what Govett said in his commentary of the Gospel of St John regarding the miracle of water into wine at Cana, Galilee.[20] He begins his letter by saying: "Allow me to draw attention to a remarkable instance of the ignorance and prejudice that still exist amongst educated and *well-educated* (?) persons on the subject of Temperance." And he concludes with, "Who Mr. Govett is, and what influence he may have, I know not. That he lives in the country (probably in a very secluded part of it) might be gathered from his remarks as well as from the address of his publisher."[21] Also in reference to *The Exposition of the Gospel of St. John* is, according to the *Westminster Review*, "the work of an amateur theologian, a devoted Trinitarian, but deficient in knowledge of the subject which he has selected for critical elucidation."[22] In contrast subscribers to religious journals were more likely to read the kind of sentiment *The Rainbow* expressed: "Mr. Govett's knowledge of Scripture is something extraordinary."[23] Michael Baxter, Irvingite and editor of the *Christian Herald and Signs of Our Times*, notes that Govett is an "eminent and voluminous expositor."[24] Nevertheless, not everyone who heard or read about Govett's position on "exclusion" from the Kingdom responded positively. Some, such as Herbert Bennett, thought his views to be so startling and strange that he could not bear to write a few lines in reply to Govett's article. "Indeed, so greatly hath my mind been exercised before God about putting this number [*The Voice*] into the hands of the Christians in my town, lest I should be the means of making the hearts of God's children sad."[25]

While there is evidence that Govett began to consider the concept of "exclusion" early in his ministry, it was 1853 when he fully developed the theology surrounding the Rapture and the Kingdom to include exclusion of the believer with the publication of *Entrance into the Kingdom, or Reward*

---

20. Robert Govett, *Exposition of the Gospel of St. John*, vol. 1 (London: Bemrose & Son, 1881).

21. *The Church of England Temperance Chronicle* 10, no. 1 (1882) 15.

22. "Contemporary Literature," *The Westminster Review*, American ed., 116 (1881) 253.

23. *The Rainbow: A Magazine of Christian Literature, with Special Reference to the Revealed Future of the Church and the World* 2 (1865) 192.

24. Michael P. Baxter, *The Wonders of Prophecy Between 1896 and April 23, 1908: As Foreshow in the Prophecies of Daniel and Revelation* (London: Christian Harold Office, 1894) 282.

25. Herbert Bennett, "Exclusion from the Kingdom," *The Voice upon the Mountains. A Journal of Prophetic Testimony and Evangelistic Effort* 3 (1869) 22.

According to Works.[26] Prior to this work the possibility of a believer being excluded from the Rapture was unfamiliar in published works. And for most of the second half of the century Govett was the only theologian publishing this position. Toward the end of the century and early into the twentieth century others such as J. A. Seiss, G. H. Pember, D. M. Panton, and G. H. Lang also began to write on the subject.[27] It is known, for example, that G. H. Pember, English theologian and a member of the Plymouth Brethren, sought Govett's advice on the subject.[28] Today, the reporting of the history and development of the "exclusion" model of the Rapture is fragmented and frequently misreported. Paul Lee Tan reports that this position was a restrictive view of the Rapture that was first articulated in the mid-nineteenth century by a small group of pretribulationists in England, and that their main publication was *Dawn*.[29] The date and source are both inconsistent with facts. He further reports that the first proponent of the modern theory of partial Rapture was Govett, but its ablest proponent was G. H. Lang.[30] He is correct in stating that Govett was the first proponent, but appears more speculative in asserting that Lang was the ablest in presenting the doctrine. Both Govett and Lang were well regarded for their writings, but if we are to compare the two by volume of publication on the subject and frequency of appearances in religious journals (not intending to imply here any standing associated with his contribution), Govett was far more prolific. Tan's explanation of partial Rapture appears to come in part from John F. Walvoord in his book *The Rapture Question* (1979) which also gives Govett credit for originating the theology of partial rapture.[31] But both Tan and Walvoord wrongly identify Govett's book *Entrance into the Kingdom, or Reward Ac-*

---

26. Robert Govett, *Entrance into the Kingdom, or Reward According to Works* (Norwich: Fletcher and Son, 1853).

27. See Joseph A. Seiss, *The Apocalypse: A Series of Special Lectures on the Revelation of Jesus Christ, With Revised Text*, 8th ed. (New York: Cook, 1901); George H. Pember, *The Great Prophecies of the Centuries Concerning Israel and the Gentiles* (London: Hodder & Stoughton, 1895); David M. Panton, *Rapture* (London: Thynne, 1922); George H. Lang, *Firstborn Sons, Their Rights and Risks: An Inquiry as to the Privileges and Perils of the Members of the Church of God* (London: Roberts, 1936).

28. See Norfolk Records Office file FC76/89. Letter from G. H. Pember to Govett (2 February 1887).

29. The first publication of *The Dawn: An Evangelical Magazine* was in April 1924, published in London by Thynne & Jarvis. The editor was D. M. Panton.

30. Paul Lee Tan, "Partial Rapture," in Mal Couch, ed., *Dictionary of Premillennial Theology: A Practical Guide to the People, Viewpoints, and History of Prophetic Studies* (Grand Rapids: Kregel, 1996) 347–48.

31. See John F. Walvoord, *The Rapture Question* (Grand Rapids: Zondervan, 1979) 97.

cording to Works as his first writing on the subject. It is not. Several tracts on the subject precede *Entrance into the Kingdom*, but one in particular may have formed the basis of the book cited.[32] Nevertheless, their review of the partial Rapture theory, while revealing a few inaccuracies, merely affirms the importance of further scholarship.

It should also be mentioned that the term "partial rapture" which is the contemporary expression now used by writers[33] was not the expression used when the theory first appeared in writing. Govett was never inclined to describe the phenomenon which was to occur at the Rapture as a "partial rapture." He used the expression "exclusion." But his focus remained on the importance of living in ways prescribed by Christ so as to avoid "exclusion" at the Rapture. Furthermore, the editors in the journals in which Govett's writings appeared also preferred to refer to his position as "exclusion." When he spoke of the Rapture as a doctrine, he used the expression "the doctrine of reward."

A thorough assessment of Govett's writings reveals that he never wavered on his understanding of Scripture regarding who qualifies for the Millennial Kingdom, what takes place at the Rapture, and how the "works" of a believer affect entrance into the Kingdom. In the last decade of his life he wrote, "there is no passage, so far as I am aware, that declares that all believers shall attain the millennial kingdom of God."[34] And he acknowledges that the truth of exclusion would never be popular; a reality he often personally witnessed, as this chapter demonstrates. He admits in the 1850s and 1860s that the promulgation of the doctrine of exclusion boasted no great advocates. It rested only on the proofs of Scripture in an age when the world was creeping in on the reliance of Scripture and numbing its influence, as evidenced by the many issues surrounding faith which occurred in the Victorian era.[35] The origin of the doctrine, he humbly notes, is introduced by "one little known," but he confidently trusts that the magnitude of the truth and its impact upon the church of God is certain to speedily redeem the doctrine from all obscurity. Its genesis, contrary to the speculation which

32. Robert Govett, *Reward According to Works* (Norwich: Fletcher and Son, 1850).

33. See, for example, Thomas Ice and Timothy J. Demy, eds., *The Return: Understanding Christ's Second Coming and the End Times* (Grand Rapids: Kregel, 1999); Robert H. Sundry, *The Church and the Tribulation: A Examination of Posttribulationism* (Grand Rapids: Zondervan, 1973).

34. Robert Govett, *The Presence of Christ in its Effects on the Church and the World: Being the Argument of the Epistles to the Thessalonians, with Notice of Dr. Bullinger's Theory of the Hinderers, and Dr. Eadie on the First Resurrection* (Norwich: Fletcher and Son, 1893) 57.

35. Preface to the first edition of *Entrance into the Kingdom, or Reward according to Works* written by Govett on 21 June 1853.

arose in his day, originated from a study of Scripture and not as a consequence of any theoretic inquiry.[36] Nevertheless, there were some in his day who questioned the soundness of his scriptural interpretations—especially on the subject of the Coming Kingdom and, in particular, his position on the "exclusion" of some believers at the Rapture.

Govett's scriptural discovery of "exclusion" and his passionate defense of it brought opponents who were convinced of its error. Much of the debate on the subject occurred in English periodicals, as the next section reveals. But Govett's postulation of "exclusion" also made its way to America where it began to be referred to as the "partial rapture theory." No evidence has been found that America gave original ownership of the theory to Govett or, for that matter, to any other single individual. The focus appears to be simply centered upon a concern for the theory itself. Still, if Govett was the originator, as he claims to be, it is apparent that knowledge of his doctrine was widespread enough to not only make its way to America on the heels of Dispensationalism, but also make its way into published debate. Opposition to the doctrine came from at least one prominent American leader in the Dispensational movement, Cyrus I. Scofield (1843–1921), the author of the *Scofield Reference Bible*, published in 1909 by Oxford University Press. Scofield's theology was heavily influenced by John Nelson Darby, who did not believe in the exclusion of believers at the Rapture. In 1899 Scofield took a public stand against the partial rapture theory in the *Record of Christian Work*.[37] He remarks that the partial rapture theory claims that only a prepared number of believers will be raptured to meet the Lord in the air, the rest being left to undergo the Great Tribulation, and that this understanding was not generally held by premillennialists. He notes that the theory rests chiefly on 1 Corinthians 15:22–23 which reads that "all will be made alive in Christ," and 1 Corinthians 15:51–52 which reads "we shall all be changed in the twinkling of an eye." In these two Scriptures Scofield proposes that the language eliminates the idea of a partial rapture. He contends that partial rapture overlooks "the great truth of the unity of the body of Christ . . . To look for him is the normal attitude of the believer."[38] Scofield also refer-

---

36. Preface to the second edition of *Entrance into the Kingdom, or Reward According to Works* written by Govett on 28 January 1867.

37. The *Record of Christian Work* was first published in America in 1881 under the name *The Evangelistic Record*. As its name suggests and first issue reveals, its intent was the "communication of a long-cherished belief that the special Christian work which is being so actively prosecuted today, ought to be represented by at least one periodical." See, *The Evangelistic Record* 1, no. 1 (1881) 1.

38. C. I. Scofield, "Biblical Notes and Queries," *Record of Christian Work* 18, no. 1 (1899) 32.

ences the parable of the foolish virgins in Matthew 25:1–12 as an example of Scripture that has been "wrestled" to support the partial rapture theory. He does not mention by name who wrestles the parable to support partial rapture, but he may have had in mind Govett who, early in his writing career, wrote a tract titled *All Believers Interested in the Parable of the Virgins: Matthew XXV*, and a second tract titled *Supplement to the Ten Virgins*.[39] Both tracts are written in support of the doctrine of exclusion. For Scofield any attempt to use this parable in support of exclusion spoils grace and discredits the finished work of Christ in that some sins are not washed away in the blood of Christ.[40]

After Govett's writing on the subject ceased upon his death in 1901, public opposition to his doctrine of exclusion continued. Reference to Govett by name was still missing, perhaps forgotten by many, but it can be reasonably assumed that there were sufficient numbers of Christians who believed in Govett's theological conclusions to warrant continued debate. For example, in 1918 Arthur W. Pink authored the book titled *The Redeemer's Return*.[41] In it he concludes that the partial rapture theory is a deceit of Satan "in which today is unsettling so many of the Lord's dear people."[42] He bases his conclusion on the involvement of "reward"—the very object that Govett found to be a strength. For Pink the pursuit of reward takes the focus off of Christ's return and onto self. Among the numerous reasons for finding fault with this "theory" is that it causes confusion. He writes:

> The leading advocates of the partial rapture theory teach that all believers who fail to come up to the standard necessary for participation in the Rapture will not only be left behind on earth to suffer the judgments of the Great Tribulation but that such will have no part or place in the Millennial Kingdom, and therefore that they will not be raised from the dead until *after* the thousand years. Now apart from the fact that *there is no Scripture* which teaches a resurrection of *saints* at the *close* of the Millennium, we affirm that such a theory as the above involves confusion of the worst kind.[43]

---

39. Robert Govett, *All Believers Interested in the Parable of the Virgins: Matthew XXV*, 1 (Norwich: Fletcher, 1846). See also Robert Govett, *Supplement to the Ten Virgins* (Norwich: Fletcher, 1846).

40. C. I. Scofield, "Biblical Notes and Queries," 32.

41. Arthur W. Pink, *The Redeemer's Return* (Swengel: Bible Truth Depot, 1918).

42. Ibid., 255–56.

43. Ibid., 256.

Pink accused partial rapturists of confusing entrance into the Kingdom with positions of honor in it. Contrary to Govett, Pink believed that all believers will partake of the Millennial era and will reign with Christ because the epistles plainly teach that all believers will be raptured at the time of the Lord's return. For instance, he notes that comprehensive assurances are found in the Corinthian epistles addressed to a church whose moral condition was the worst of all the churches addressed by the apostle Paul "as if to anticipate this modern heresy of limiting the Rapture to spiritual believers."[44]

An entire chapter is reserved in Pink's book for the subject of partial rapture. In it he assumes that Scriptures cannot support both the partial rapture theory and a complete rapture of the church simultaneously. Since the Rapture is a matter for the church, Pink holds that the "Church Epistles" must settle the debate. But he finds that the verses which are made the occasion for controversy are found, for the most part, in the Gospels, in Hebrews, or in the Apocalypse. Govett must be included in this group who wandered far beyond the epistles as he found ample proof of scriptural texts even in the Old Testament. However, in the epistles, the very verses Govett found to affirm his doctrine, Pink finds that they repudiate it.[45]

Scriptures were consistently the centerpiece of Govett's defense no matter the theological subject he was espousing and no matter the reader's assessment of its soundness. Aside from his unique position on the exclusion of believers at the Rapture, he found himself occasionally defending other unique eschatological positions. He was no stranger to intervening in the many eschatological arguments of his day when he found plausible proof from Scripture to defend his case. For example, in an 1873 issue of *The Last Vial* an article appeared on the subject of Napoleon III's death and the speculation as to the right understanding of the "Latter-day prophecies" and the mystery that hung over the entire Napoleonic question of Antichrist. A question arose in theological discussions concerning the ascent of the "beast" out of the Abyss (or, Bottomless Pit) in Revelation. The author questions whether it is possible that the soul of one man is able to rise from the Abyss and enter into the body of another man. "This idea is not put forth as original. It has been entertained long ago by others, or at least by Mr. Govett, who very likely was the first to think of it. But we are bound to refer to it as a fair solution of the difficulty."[46] Here again, Govett is given credit for originality in addition for his handling of a difficult subject.

44. Ibid., 260.

45. Ibid., 243.

46. "The Ascent From the Pit," *The Last Vials: Being a Series of Essays upon the Subject of the Second Advent*, no. 3, 28th year (1873) 41.

From the mid-twentieth century Govett, if known at all, was known exclusively for his position on "partial rapture" as it is now ascribed. As previously noted, the single work most cited is his *Entrance into the Kingdom, or Reward According to Works*, published first in 1853, which is characteristically assumed to be his first published work on the subject. However, what has been forgotten is that the first work dedicated to the subject of exclusion from the Kingdom was his 1850 tract, similarly titled, *Reward According to Works*,[47]—although the description of exclusion is suggested in earlier works such as his *A Treatise on Hades, or the Place of Departed Spirits* (1843).[48] Govett knew there would be some who would accuse him of muddling the doctrine of salvation and the perception of gaining eternal life through self-works. As a result, his first tract begins with an affirmation that all believers are justified without works by faith in the righteousness of Christ Jesus— attained only by the free grace of God electing them from eternity past. Upon establishing this he declares that the Bible provides most distinctly another truth that the believer will have to give account of himself to Christ on his appearing. At that occasion reward or dishonor will follow.[49] The criteria to be used by Christ to provide recompense are the believer's "works." Govett's confidence in this assertion is based upon Romans 14:11 which declares that Jesus has stated that every knee will bow and every tongue will confess to God. Everyone will give an account of himself to God.[50] In addition, the rule for distribution of Christ's rewards is according to works. This Govett concludes is established by 1 Corinthians 3:6, 8 where Paul mentions that each believer will receive his own reward according to his own labor.[51]

Govett anticipates as a rhetorical question what later would be borne out as a repeated challenge to his doctrine: "How can these statements be reconciled with other scriptures, which assert, that the believer shall never

---

47. Robert Govett, *Reward according to Works* (Norwich: Fletcher and Son, 1850). Like many of Govett's tracts this was republished several more times throughout his life. Question arises regarding the reliability of the publication date being earlier than his 1853 works. But it can be traced back to at least as early as 1852 and its listing in the following publication: *Norton's Literary Gazette, and Publishers' Circular*, vol. 3/1 (New York: Norton, 1852) 184. Also listed in Norton's publication was Govett's *The Saint's Rapture to the Presence of the Lord Jesus, with Appendix in Refutation of Dr. Cumming's Tract Entitled "The Pope the Man of Sin"* (London: Nisbet, 1852), which similarly contains "exclusion" language.

48. Robert Govett, *A Treatise on Hades, or the Place of Departed Spirits* (Edinburgh: Johnstone, 1843).

49. See, for example, Govett's handwritten sermon numbered 307, entitled "The Millennium," from Rev 20:1–6. Preached 5 August 1855. Schoettle Publishing archives.

50. Robert Govett, *Reward according to Works* (Norwich: Fletcher and Son, 1850) 3.

51. Govett, *Reward According to Works*, 4.

come into judgment, and that the believer enters into eternal life as a free gift from God?" The answer put forth is that it is commonly known that eternal life is a free gift, and that the "saved" will enter it by God's grace.

> But two objects are set before our eye—Eternal Life, and the Millennial Kingdom. Eternal life is the free *gift*. But the kingdom is the *prize* to be striven for: Phil. 3. Even in the kingdom there will be degrees, and in these different degrees will consist the differences of reward: and the appearing before Christ will be with a view to the apportionment of these. Life eternal is a bounty purchased by Christ, bestowed by God in his sovereignty. But equity will take the oversight and distribution of reward in its several degrees.[52]

Govett, in his first tract on reward and exclusion, next articulates reward to be recompensed in proportion to difficulties overcome in this life and to suffering for Christ as well as acting for him. For Govett, reward is not interpreted in Scripture as being available in the Kingdom for actions to which even the fallen sons of men are competent to perform.[53]

Fifteen years later Govett published another tract on exclusion titled *Will All Believers Enter the Millennial Kingdom? A Reply to the Rev. R. A. Purdon's Attack in "The Last Vials"* (1865). While intending to convey the scriptural truth concerning "exclusion," it also served as a reply to R. A. Purdon's attack on the doctrine which was placed in *The Last Vials*. Purdon was the magazine's editor and was known as an eminent expositor, a clergyman of the Church of England, who had published in London a sixteen-page prophetic pamphlet every month since 1845 under the title *The Last Vials*. Michael Baxter identifies him as one of great ability and genius in the interpretation of prophecy and of "frequently striking eloquence of expression." He was one of the first to proclaim distinctly and emphatically that Louis Napoleon was the person who would be revealed as the Antichrist.[54] Despite Purdon's reputation and Govett's concession that they agreed upon on many essential doctrinal points, he felt the need to refute Purdon's position on reward at the Judgment and to set the record straight regarding his misrepresentations of Govett's published statements on the subject. The subject of the exclusion of believers in the Millennial Kingdom was of momentous importance to Govett. Purdon thought that every believer, in spite of imperfection or sinful practice would still enter into the Mil-

---

52. Ibid., 6.

53. Ibid., 10–11.

54. Michael P. Baxter, *Louis Napoleon the Destined Monarch of the World* (Philadelphia: Claxton, 1867) 228.

lennial Kingdom. Govett believed Scripture taught that exclusion of some believers was the result of either no good works at all, or of the commission of sinful ones. It was in the June 1865 issue of *The Last Vial* that Govett claimed Purdon contrived to make him look very foolish.[55] First, Purdon stated many of Govett's views but omitted the proofs of Scripture by which he substantiated them. Second, in some cases, Purdon had added to Govett's views which resulted in absurd conclusions for which he made Govett appear responsible—accusing him of doing away with free grace and introducing into Protestantism "some of the worst and most dreary fictions of the Church of Rome: (Purgatory)."[56] Purdon then seized upon a statement made by Govett in *The Rainbow* accusing him of saying that those who have not received baptism by complete immersion in water would be shut out from the millennial reign. Govett's actual words were: "I gather that some will *see* the kingdom who have regeneration alone, *and not baptism*. But they will not *enter* the kingdom . . . Moral excellency *without baptism would not wholly exclude from all part of the kingdom.*"[57] Here Govett's position on entrance into the Millennial Kingdom becomes somewhat murky and invites frequent questions and criticism in contemporary print culture. He explains his position on exclusion and baptism thoroughly in *Entrance into the Kingdom, or Reward According to Works* (1853). His underlying premise begins with making a distinction between the Kingdom of God and eternal life. The two are to remain separate but linked. The Kingdom of God is the millennial reign. Eternal life is subsequent to it. On this matter he is not afraid to bring to public notice those who get this wrong—such as the Tract Society, Albert Barnes, and John Calvin.[58] For Govett, those who are regenerated by faith and the Holy Spirit but are not baptized by immersion with water may "see" the kingdom, but may not "enter into" it. Much as Moses was permitted to see the Promised Land but could not enter, those missing the command of baptism may only see the promised kingdom. The omission of baptism excludes from entrance into the Millennial Kingdom, but not from eternal life. He is aware that to many of his readers this may seem severe or even impossible. By his own reckoning "Whitefield and Wesley will be excluded for want of immersion."[59] And Joshua because of his obedi-

---

55. Robert Govett, *Will All Believers Enter the Millennial Kingdom? A Reply to the Rev. R.A. Purdon's Attack in "The Last Vials"* (London: Nisbet, 1865) 4.

56. Govett, *Will All Believers Enter the Millennial Kingdom?*, 5.

57. Robert Govett, *Will All Believers Enter the Millennial Kingdom?*, 53. See also *The Rainbow: A Magazine of Christian Literature, with Special Reference to the Revealed Future of the Church and the World* 1 (1864) 562.

58. Govett, *Entrance into the Kingdom*, 310–11.

59. Ibid., 312.

ence (unlike Moses) was not only able to see the Promised Land, but entered into the promise.

Purdon was not the only person Govett publicly refuted on the subject of exclusion. The usual line of attack against Govett was with the use of scriptural texts which speak of God's grace. Those who refuted Govett's claims held to the notion of grace now exercised by God toward the believer, as set against justice which will one day be brought to bear. Added to this position was their opinion that the privileges afforded believers by God's grace would negate responsibility such that the consequences would be silenced on the Day of Judgment. Govett vigorously opposed this as a costly mistake because he was confident that a future day was coming in which God would render to each according to his work. Christ's inquiry will be, "How have my servants behaved themselves?" This very argument is found in *The Collection of Scriptures Not Shaken by Gen. Goodwyn's Observations* published in 1870. General Henry Goodwyn had published a tract which Govett perceived was intended to silence a number of Scriptures used by him in proof that not all believers will enter the Millennial Kingdom. Govett's response was a 59-page tract replete with a comprehensive list of scriptural proofs pertaining to the believer's promises of eternal life, as well as numerous other scriptures which speak directly to exclusion from the Millennial Kingdom.[60]

In the same year Govett published a book which he hoped would be especially beneficial to the church. Its subject was as usual the Coming Kingdom, but it begins with his statement that there are few subjects which penetrate so deeply into the doctrine and practice of the New Testament as that of the Kingdom of Heaven (or, the Kingdom of God) and proceeds to describe the Kingdom in two states: the "Kingdom in mystery," and the "Kingdom in manifestation."[61] Govett goes into depth on the distinctions, but they can be summed up by the parable of the wheat and the tares as found in Matthew 8, since it presents both states of the kingdom in question. The parable becomes allegorical in Govett's mind with the harvest representing the period of judgment, which ends the "Kingdom in mystery." Then occurs the placing of the wheat and tares in their requisite portion, during the Kingdom in manifestation. During the first period mercy reigns, and the tares and the wheat are allowed by God to run "to seed" because it is the "season of grace." But, after a period of time the end of the age comes when the angels will gather out of God's kingdom all "stumbling-blocks," and then

---

60. Robert Govett, *The Collection of Scriptures Not Shaken by Gen. Goodwyn's Observations* (London: Nisbet, 1870) 58–59.

61. Robert Govett, *The Kingdom of God Future* (London: Nisbet, 1870) 1–3.

the parable closes with an affirmation that the righteous will shine as the sun in the Kingdom of their Father.[62] Govett adds, "Hence we notice the mistake of the antimillenarian He would prove, if he could, that there is but one class of prophecy, not two ... He does not discern between the earthly promises made to the Jew, and the heavenly ones made to the church."[63]

In 1872 Govett published several more tracts and books on the Coming Kingdom. One in particular was a short tract produced in the form of a letter to the congregation at the close of a period of absence from them. The tone of the letter reminds them of the days becoming spiritually dark and that faith seems to be dying out in many hearts—perhaps a reflection of the crisis of faith which permeated the Victorian era. He portrays a picture of Israel as it tempted God in the desert. It is a somber picture he paints which communicates a danger found in the heart of the believer, should the believer return to the ways of the world. The congregation is reminded that their conduct should reflect their holding firm to the faith concerning the day of reward. They are to labor to enter the future millennial rest.[64]

In the same year Govett published a commentary on the book of Galatians. When he arrives at Galatians 6:7, in which is stated that God is not mocked and that what a man sows he will also reap, Govett reminds his readers that there will be a coming day wherein there will be a rendering to each (believer and unbeliever) according to works. The award to each will be impartial and strict.[65] Also in the same year Govett published another commentary, this time on 2 Timothy. In the second chapter he finds the verses to be occupied with the "day of glory" (entrance into the Millennial Kingdom) and the means by which to attain the rewards. Following these verses are those which pertain to the salvation which is in Christ, presented in two parts: eternal salvation, and the glory which is given according to works. Added to salvation which is gratuitous, and bestowed on those believing, there is reward also in the Millennial Kingdom "prepared for doers and sufferers for Christ."[66] Yet again, in 1872, Govett published a tract on the coming Millennial Kingdom: *The Promises*

---

62. Govett, *The Kingdom of God Future*, 8.

63. Ibid., 9–10. See also Robert Govett, *The Wheat and the Tares* (Norwich: Fletcher and Son, 1874).

64. Robert Govett, *Seek the Sabbath Rest to Come* (Norwich: Fletcher and Son, 1872). See also Robert Govett, *Christians! Seek the Rest of God in His Millennial Kingdom* (Norwich: Fletcher and Son, 1873).

65. Robert Govett, *Moses or Christ? Being the Argument of the Epistle to the Galatians* (London: Wheeler, 1872) 219.

66. Robert Govett, *The Last Days; and the First Resurrection; or, Thoughts on Paul's Last Epistle* (Norwich: Fletcher and Son, 1872) 33.

to Abraham Never Yet Fulfilled referred to the promises to Abraham and their fulfillment in the Coming Kingdom. It depicts Abraham living once more in the Millennial Kingdom and God shown to be the God of Abraham from that time and for evermore. But, Govett exclaims, Abraham alive in spirit here below is still Abraham dead, and Abraham divided. And a divided Abraham is not the man to whom the promise was made. According to Govett's findings, only when Abraham is alive before man in body and soul, can he enjoy the land of promise. Only then is God seen to be his God. Jesus, in his words, "I am the God of Abraham," presents the promise of resurrection. A better age is before the believer and it is to come by way of resurrection—a better resurrection.[67]

In 1876 Govett wrote once again about a better resurrection in *Christ's Resurrection and Ours*. On this occasion the book expounded what was contained in 1 Corinthians 15 and spoke of Christ's resurrection and the false denial of the believer's resurrection. In Govett's day the denial of resurrection found favor in the eyes of Swedenborg and the Spiritists. He refutes the position of the Swedenborgians and the Spiritists who asserted that "death *is* resurrection" and that the soul coming forth from the corpse is the only rising again that is ever to be experienced. The spirit state is man's final one.[68] But this position is one that suggests that it is prompted by God's delay in the promised resurrection. Govett argues that a day is coming that will reward the works of faithful believers. He answers the question of why the apostle Paul does not distinctly mention the Kingdom in these verses by stating that it relates to the "order" of the resurrections. The first resurrection introduces the Kingdom. The Kingdom of Christ is that which is granted to Christ as the "Worthy One." As he was raised first, he is coming back to raise believers. His presence begins as soon as his descent downward from heaven ceases and the Kingdom of God is ushered in. But here, in this book, Govett's description of the Kingdom becomes more complex. He asserts that the Kingdom of God has two aspects—its first (imperfect), and its second, final state. The first phase is the Kingdom when it is given into the hands of Christ, who is to subdue all to his Father. During that thousand-years it is called "the kingdom of the Christ and God" as described in Ephesians 5:5. It is not meant to last forever. Its design is to glorify and reward Christ, along with his working and suffering people. After that is the eternal state and the Kingdom of God is introduced.[69] Govett is aware that believers have

---

67. Robert Govett, *The Promises to Abraham Never Yet Fulfilled* (Norwich: Fletcher and Son, 1872) 18–19.

68. Govett, *Christ's Resurrection and Ours*, 2.

69. Ibid., 134.

a curiosity about the spirit and the body connected to the physical state of the believer in heaven. In 1 Thessalonians 4, Paul speaks of the Rapture of both the living and the dead, but he did not speak of their bodies or of the glorification of their bodies. Govett held that in 1 Corinthians 15, the apostle Paul settles the difficulty by stating that a change takes place on the bodies of both the living and the dead who rise, in order to fit them for their eternal glory. To this Govett wants to add his perceptive thoughts on the subject of resurrection and the state of the church's limited understanding.

> Scripture distinguishes resurrection where ordinary theology confounds it. Till within the last fifty years prophecy was not studied, nor had the distinction between the first and the second resurrection been observed and accepted. For till then Romish ideas on prophecy held their ground. The Reformers were content to consider the primary question—How sinners were to be saved? Until that was settled to the satisfaction of the soul, there was no room for the doctrine of the resurrection of the righteous apart from that of the wicked. Rome, by its doctrine of infused righteousness, had made a man's salvation turn on his perfection of inward holiness; instead of on the perfect work of Christ outside him.[70]

It may be ascertained from this particular book and these historical thoughts that Govett felt the doctrine of the resurrection pertaining to the thousand-years was naturally overlooked or set aside, and consequently, that the book of Revelation was dismissed as a mystery that none could penetrate. Therefore, it was commonly concluded that resurrection became one great act at the same moment for all alike—the saved and the lost.

In the final decade of his life Govett was still deeply concerned with the subject of resurrection. He wrote two books which projected as much critical demand upon the subject of resurrection as his previous works. The first of these was *The Presence of Christ in its Effects on the Church and the World* (1893).[71] It was intended as his platform to debate Ethelbert W. Bullinger, Church of England clergyman and dispensationalist, who had written some remarks concerning 2 Thessalonians 2. It also was used to debate the Scottish theologian John Eadie and his remarks on 1 Thessalonians 4. Govett applies Paul's words in the two epistles written to the Thessalonians to support his position on resurrection and the exclusion of some believers. His sum-

---

70. Ibid., 141–42.

71. Robert Govett, *The Presence of Christ in its Effects on the Church and the World: Being the Argument of the Epistles to the Thessalonians, with Notice of Dr. Bullinger's Theory of the Hinderers, and Dr. Eadie on the First Resurrection* (Norwich: Fletcher and Son, 1893).

mation of Paul's argument was that it was designed to correct two mistakes made by the Thessalonian believers. Their first error was that the believers who had previously died would not take part in the Millennial Kingdom of Christ. The second error was taken up in the second epistle and involved an erroneous understanding by the Thessalonians that the living believers would have to go through the Tribulation on earth which had already begun. Govett also found error in the church, but the error he found was in Bullinger's interpretation of 2 Thessalonians 2:6–7. Bullinger finds that the verses pertain to Satan and his hindrances. To publicly debate a scholar of the stature of Bullinger was no small endeavor. Bullinger had previously published a lexicon on the New Testament and was well respected as a linguist and scholar.[72] But Govett found Bullinger's translation and meaning of these two critical verses to be unacceptable. The hindrance, as Bullinger interprets the verses, was "the Well of the Bottomless Pit," the hinderer being the Devil. Govett disagreed. His interpretation was that the hindrance is Christ's "true-hearted ones (the Church)"; the hinderer is the "Holy Spirit." The hindrance—the church—is removed from earth by force.[73] The point of Govett's argument is that these verses are portraying Christ preparing his true church for resurrection.

He then turns to Eadie's views on 1 Thessalonians. In his commentary Eadie writes concerning 4:16 that "to identify the resurrection asserted in this verse with the First Resurrection of Revelation 20:6 is quite unwarranted."[74] Eadie preferred viewing the prophecy found in the books of the Thessalonians as symbolic. Govett held that the believers are to rise literally in the "first resurrection." But Govett affirmed a "second resurrection" as well—a resurrection of which Eadie was confused. Eadie, based on his reading of 4:15, thought that the "first resurrection" was confined to the martyrs. Govett responded to this assertion with "that is a mistake."[75] Govett was convinced that the verse pertained to a second resurrection which was to precede the "Day of the Lord," and the "Kingdom of God." It is the resurrection not *of* the dead, but a select resurrection *from among* the dead which referred to martyrs. Furthermore, Eadie held that the first resurrection is

72. See Ethelbert W. Bullinger, *A Critical Lexicon and Concordance to the English and Greek New Testament*, 2nd ed. (London: Longmans, 1886).

73. Robert Govett, *The Presence of Christ in its Effects on the Church and the World: Being the Argument of the Epistles to the Thessalonians, with Notice of Dr. Bullinger's Theory of the Hinderers, and Dr. Eadie on the First Resurrection* (Norwich: Fletcher and Son, 1893) 113–15.

74. John Eadie, and William Young, *A Commentary on the Greek Text of the Epistles of Paul to the Thessalonians* (London: Macmillan, 1877) 167.

75. Govett, *The Presence of Christ in its Effects*, 117.

that of souls and that the apostle does not say where the souls of the dead are, but Govett retorts that spiritual life is not spoken of in this verse.[76] He contends that it refers to Christ's martyrs who had spiritual life before they suffered literal death.[77]

In the second of these books, *Christ's Judgment of His Saints at His Return* (1895),[78] Govett recounts the consequences to the churches mentioned in the book of Revelation, and compares them to remarks made by Paul in the book of Ephesians. He also challenges Benjamin Newton, former member of the Brethren and close friend to Darby, in an appendix referring to remarks he made about 2 Thessalonians 1.[79] Newton believed that in Christ's return there would be no "secrecy."[80] Govett responded: "Christ our Lord comes first in secret *for* his saints: 1 Thessalonians 4. Then he comes in glorious manifestation on high *with* his saints."[81] This particular distinction had for some years been a point of contention in journals involving Govett.[82]

As Govett's life progressed, his thoughts on the reward of the believer and his place in the Coming Kingdom progressed as well. The complexities of his thoughts on the subject amazed many. He challenged whoever he believed to be in error on what was to him a crucial subject vital to the church. But he always rebutted their views with respect. Often they were respectful in return such as a writer in *The Rainbow* who said, "We owe so much to Mr. Govett for his interesting communications that I should be sorry to be, or to appear, captious in contesting his interpretations, but the question mooted is really so essential a one that I should be glad to be allowed a few words in reply to his remarks upon my criticism."[83] His comprehensive views on the Coming Kingdom brought about many rebuffs. Some were not so kind.

76. Eadie, *A Commentary on the Greek Text*, 168.

77. Govett, *The Presence of Christ in its Effects*, 118.

78. Robert Govett, *Christ's Judgment of His Saints at His Return: And Solution of the Main Argument Against Secret Presence* (Norwich: Fletcher and Son, 1895).

79. The appendix is titled: "Solution of the Main Argument Against the Secret Presence of Christ; or, a Note on 2 Thessalonians 1:3–10."

80. Benjamin W. Newton, *Occasional Papers on Scriptural Subjects*, no. 2 (London: Houlston and Wright, 1861) 47.

81. Govett, *Christ's Judgment of His Saints at His Return*, 68.

82. See "What is the Millennium, and How Cometh It?" (A letter Signed: A Lover of truth), *The Earthen Vessel, and Christian Record* 23 (1867) 235–40; Robert Govett, "Will the Rapture be Visible or Secret?," *The Rainbow: A Magazine of Christian Literature, with Special Reference to the Revealed Future of the Church and the World* 1 (1864) 257–65.

83. *The Rainbow: A Magazine of Christian Knowledge, with Special Reference to the Revealed Future of the Church and the World* 1 (1864) 520.

Yet, this was the price he was willing to pay for such an important subject to the church. The consequence of exclusion from the Kingdom was too great a verdict to be pronounced with no possibility for appeal. To be a believer adjudicated before Christ and found lacking had eternal consequence. And so, he wrote and spoke on the subject throughout his pastorate. In addition to pastoring and writing his numerous books and tracts, he frequently wrote on the subject of the Coming Kingdom in religious journals in order to reach a wider audience. His thoughts on the subject made him a popular, if not controversial, contributor.

Journal Reactions

This section on journals is included to provide another perspective on Govett's theological thoughts and the reactions of those who read him. Govett wrote articles for journals extensively to communicate his theological views. Appearing in them allowed a more immediate form of engagement with the relevant religious topics as they emerged. It also allowed for a "back and forth" dialogue between Govett and those who chose to disagree with him; something which carried over on occasion into several consecutive issues of a journal. This process sometimes provided for a transfer of articles into tracts, but frequently allowed for a deeper understanding of what Govett was attempting to convey to his readers on his favorite subjects. As previously noted, journals were numerous in Govett's day and a common source of reading material. What was thought regarding Govett's books could also be determined in the journals since his books were regularly reviewed and often met with enthusiastic approval. This, no doubt, tended to increase the sales of his many books.

In the 1840s and 1850s Govett did not engage in expressing his theological views in the religious journals; perhaps because he was content to write books and tracts. During those two decades he was quite busy growing an independent church congregation that soon outgrew its borrowed space, building a new church building, and writing over fifty books and tracts. But in the 1860s his correspondence with the religious journals began in earnest. 1865 was a prolific year for journal articles written by Govett and his focus was almost exclusively *The Rainbow*.[84] He had written in the magazine's first issue in 1864,[85] and in 1865 Govett received his first cor-

---

84. *The Rainbow: A Magazine of Christian Literature, with Special Reference to the Revealed Future of the Church and the World.*

85. See Robert Govett, "The Emperor," *The Rainbow: A Magazine of Christian Literature, with Special Reference to the Revealed Future of the Church and the World* 1 (1864)

respondent reply. The reply was not over the subject of exclusion but over a subject often confused in Govett's prophetic position: that of justification. An individual by the name of Nemo had written to the *The Rainbow*, contradicting Govett's position on justification and his interpretation of a related passage of Scripture. To this Govett responded with, "It is certain, therefore, that through faith in Christ the believer is justified by works of law, and only by faith is he so justified. He is not, cannot, be justified by his own works of law."[86] Nevertheless, just one month later the attacks on his position on entrance into the Kingdom began in earnest. A letter was submitted to *The Rainbow*, by someone who identifies himself as "the author of *For Ever*," engaging Govett on his reply to Arthur A. Rees. Rees had submitted a letter concerning whether all believers will partake of the Millennial Kingdom. For him the question of admittance into the Kingdom is either limited to martyrs, prophets, and apostles, or will be extended to all those who are "washed in the blood of the Lamb." He added, "If Mr. Govett can show that the temporal Kingdom of Christ is intended for the select few I have named, and for them alone, let him do so, and let *The Rainbow* cease to be published; the millennium can then have no practical and personal interest for the general Christian world."[87] He had misunderstood Govett on two points: Govett's distinction between the first and second resurrection, and his position on exclusion from the first.

In contrast to the objection which appeared in February, in the March issue of *The Rainbow* a letter appeared written to the editor and signed "A Lover of Practical Truth," Norwich. This writer sided with Govett concerning exclusion. He stated, "Now, believing the doctrine advanced by Mr. Govett in the main points to be true, I believe, that so far from its depreciating the blessed work of Christ, it is a truth which touches the secret walk with Christ, and if rightly secured, it brings the Christian to frequent confession of sin and prayer, and thus the heart is brought into closer communion and fellowship."[88] These are the sentiments Govett had hoped to evoke from the church. Conceivably this may have been written by a member of his own

---

169-74. See also Robert Govett, "Will the Rapture be Visible or Secret?," *The Rainbow: A Magazine of Christian Literature, with Special Reference to the Revealed Future of the Church and the World* 1 (1864) 257-65.

86. *The Rainbow: A Magazine of Christian Literature, with Special Reference to the Revealed Future of the Church and the World* 2 (1865) 44-45.

87. "Will All Believers Partake the Bliss of the Millennial Kingdom?," *The Rainbow: A Magazine of Christian Literature, with Special Reference to the Revealed Future of the Church and the World* 2 (1865) 89.

88. "A Practical Truth," *The Rainbow: A Magazine of Christian Literature, with Special Reference to the Revealed Future of the Church and the World* 2 (1865) 140.

congregation.[89] Yet, despite this one letter of agreement, there was more controversy which followed Govett and his futurist views. In the April 1865 issue of *The Rainbow*, Govett's 1852 tract *The Pope Not the Man of Sin: Being an Answer to the Publications of Dr. Cumming, Dr. Morison, and the Rev. E. B. Elliott on the Subject*,[90] was brought into debate. The tract was brought to the magazine's notice because of Govett's position opposing the belief that the Pope was not the Antichrist which resulted in a vigorous debate on the subject between himself and the editor, Edward Nangle, of the *Achill Missionary Herald*.[91] Nangle's magazine opposed the futurist position and held to the then common "Protestant interpretation" that the Pope and nobody else is the man of sin.[92] Govett, as a futurist, refused to accept that position. *The Rainbow* agreed with him and begged those who supported the so-called Protestant interpretation, to read Govett's tract. The magazine gave Govett high praise: "The volume is remarkable for all the higher qualities of polemical writing . . . Mr. Govett's knowledge of the Scriptures is something extraordinary . . . We wish we were able to place a copy of Mr. Govett's masterly work into the hands of every Protestant minister in England."[93]

---

89. There is no record showing how Govett's books and tracts may have been made available to his congregation. But a letter written to his congregation from Mundsley, 29 September, 1864, while on holiday, demonstrates that Govett was interested in involving his congregation on the progress of his public writings. He mentions that he is engaged in writing out for the press "those sermons on prophecy which you desired might be printed." Norwich Records Office files FC76/60.

90. Robert Govett, *The Popes Not the Man of Sin: Being an Answer to the Publications of Dr. Cumming, Dr. Morison, and the Rev. E. B. Elliott, on that Subject* (London: Nisbet, 1852). See also, Robert Govett, *The Saint's Rapture to the Presence of the Lord Jesus, with Appendix in Refutation of Dr. Cumming's Tract Entitled "The Pope the Man of Sin"* (London: Nisbet, 1852); John Cumming, *Apocalyptic Sketches. Lectures on the Book of Revelation*, 2nd series (Philadelphia: Lindsay and Blakiston, 1854). See also Govett's handwritten sermon numbered 305, entitled "Antichrist," from 2 Thess 2:1–12. Preached on 22 July 1855. Schoettle Publishing archives.

91. The *Achill Missionary Herald and Western Witness* was begun in July 1837 (later changed to *The Irish Church Advocate*). Published monthly in Dublin it was intended as a support to the missions work of the Achill Mission being carried out on the western island of Ireland known as Achill. The newspaper was begun by Rev. Edward Nangle who served as its first editor. See *The Achill Mission, and the Present State of Protestantism in Ireland. Being a Statement Delivered by the Rev. Edward Nangle at a Meeting of the Protestant Association in Exeter Hall, December 28, 1838* (London: Protestant Association, 1839) 13.

92. The entire correspondence between Nangle and Govett was later published in: Robert Govett, *The Man of Sin: Is He the Pope; being the Controversial Correspondence in the Achill Herald Between Edward Nangle and R. Govett* (London: Nisbet, 1866).

93. "Literature," *The Rainbow: A Magazine of Christian Literature, with Special Reference to the Revealed Future of the Church and the World* 2 (1865) 191–92.

Then in May of 1865 Govett's articles began appearing simultaneously with those of his critics opposing his articles from previous months. Arthur A. Rees in his letter to *The Rainbow*, asks several questions directed to Govett over his position on exclusion from the Kingdom. He asks if repentance, however tardy, would not obliterate their loss of reward in the Kingdom. He concludes his letter with, "Deeply sorry am I to differ from one so unquestionably devout and learned as my friend, and I would affectionately entreat him to reconsider whether his extreme literality of interpretation and his stiff Euclidian logic may have led him to overstretch the truth."[94] In the same issue Govett wrote an article entitled "What is Meant by Christ's Coming?" in which he attempts to clear-up the misunderstanding of what is meant by Christ's coming in context with the events which lead up to his appearing and the signs which precede it. Going ever deeper into the theology of Christ's appearance and the millennial reign he concludes that when Christ comes his feet will stand upon the mount of Olives (which he takes from Zechariah 14:54), as he also sat upon it at his departure.[95]

In June Govett's position on exclusion from the Kingdom came up again. S. H. Errington sided with him in a letter written to *The Rainbow* in which he agrees with Govett on his assessment that there are true believers who will be excluded from the Kingdom.[96] Sam C. Colman was another who wrote to the magazine in agreement with Govett on exclusion citing a descriptive phrase "positive punishment" (i.e., that reward will be withheld from some believers at the Judgment) to be correct. Colman draws his conclusion from Luke 12:43–48, and Hebrews chapters 3 and 4 respectively.[97] Concurrently Govett wrote a letter to a correspondent in *The Rainbow* regarding his position on believer's exclusion in the Kingdom. He argues against the correspondent who assumed that there is no exclusion for believers from the Kingdom, and only diminished reward in the Kingdom and eternity to follow. To counter his opposition Govett used as an example the seven churches mentioned in Revelation chapters 2 and 3, stating that Christ calls for repentance from believers and utters threats against those who will not manifest actual, visible,

---

94. Arthur A. Rees, "Questions for Mr. Govett," *The Rainbow: A Magazine of Christian Literature, with Special Reference to the Revealed Future of the Church and the World* 2 (1865) 233.

95. Robert Govett, "What Is Meant by Christ's Coming?," *The Rainbow: A Magazine of Christian Literature, with Special Reference to the Revealed Future of the Church and the World* 2 (1865) 217–22.

96. S. H. Errington, "Do All Believers Enter 'the Kingdom,'" *The Rainbow: A Magazine of Christian Literature, with Special Reference to the Revealed Future of the Church and the World* 2 (1865) 276.

97. *The Rainbow: A Magazine of Christian Literature, with Special Reference to the Revealed Future of the Church and the World* 2 (1865) 287–88.

and active repentance. "Christ does not teach that the Kingdom belongs to all who are vitally members of the church; but He divides the church itself, in reference to the day of reward and its promises, into two classes—the overcomers, and the overcome."[98]

For the remainder of 1865 the correspondence which appeared in *The Rainbow* took exception to Govett's position on exclusion. In July a correspondent refuted Govett's assertion that some believers will be excluded from the Kingdom, claiming that to make such a statement that some will be "cast into outer darkness" is a sort of purgatory.[99] In the August issue an unidentified reader also took exception to Govett's position on believer's exclusion from the Kingdom calling it a "reckless assertion."[100] In September a writer identifying himself in the Greek as "brotherly love," took exception to Govett's exclusionary opinions concerning the Kingdom. Of particular concern to this writer was the question of whether there could be unprofitable Christians within the church of God–as Govett supposes.[101] In November negative letters continued. A letter, written by someone who identified himself as "a pastor," disagreed with Govett's assessment of the Coming Kingdom. He contended that Govett's position appeared too "meritorious." He stated that, "The great error of Mr. Govett, as to 'Eternal Life and the Kingdom,' is, that he, 'puts asunder' what 'God has joined together.'" He believes that Govett would agree with him on eternal matters such as what is found in Jude 1 which affirms that "in him our blessings are not only great, but they are eternal and secure. We are preserved in Jesus as well as called." It is specifically the matter of Govett's position on the thousand-years that he finds he must refute. The correspondent also had difficulty with what happens to a believer who is excluded. "Is he not resurrected?" And if he is resurrected to stand before the judgment seat of Christ, and is thus excluded, "where do the 'unkingdomized' go who are excluded?" He ends his lengthy letter with a reference to Govett's great grandfather William Romaine.[102] "In short, we contend for truth, ably expressed in the title of the book written by Mr. Govett's great grandsire, Romaine (that sweet preacher

---

98. Ibid., 278.

99. *The Rainbow: A Magazine of Christian Literature, with Special Reference to the Revealed Future of the Church and the World* 2 (1865) 322.

100. *The Rainbow: A Magazine of Christian Literature, with Special Reference to the Revealed Future of the Church and the World* 2 (1865) 379–80.

101. "Believers and the Kingdom," *The Rainbow: A Magazine of Christian Literature, with Special Reference to the Revealed Future of the Church and the World* 2 (1865) 422–24.

102. It is interesting to note that he makes the Romaine connection, which begs the question as to whether it was well known.

of truth . . . because his note was always Jesus), and whilst declaring we are 'blessed in Jesus,' press 'the life, walk, and triumph of faith.'"[103] Throughout the year Govett continued to write about the subject of exclusion despite the objections to his position. Once again in November a correspondent by the name of Joseph Bryan Jr., wrote a letter to *The Rainbow* looking into the interpretation of Revelation 17:9–10 which Govett expounded upon in a previous issue. Govett's was one of three interpretations given, none of which Bryan agreed with and concluded by stating, "may we have less of theory, and still less of any private interpretations, and more of the jealous adherence to the simple and obvious meaning of the Word of God."[104]

It was in 1866 that Govett's complete correspondence with Nangle on the subject of the Antichrist was published,[105] and the reviews on the subject of the Antichrist and the disputants once again began in earnest. The April issue of the *Baptist Magazine* reviewed Govett's tract. It was noted that the tract was not only a compendium of the arguments that were used but of the Preterist and Futurist schools of prophetical interpretation to which Nangle[106] and Govett respectively belonged. The value of the tract was that it settled "as far as the examination of the evidence can settle anything— the question discussed in its pages."[107] Also in April, *The Earthen Vessel* reviewed Govett's tract on the debated question of who or what is intended by the Scriptural term "the Man of Sin." The review notes that the two were well-matched for controversy given that "they are learned, devoted, and earnest in their work."[108]

1867 was again a prolific year for Govett's articles in *The Rainbow*.[109] His topic was primarily that of the Coming Kingdom and rebuttals of other

---

103. "Eternal Life and the Kingdom," *The Rainbow: A Magazine of Christian Literature, with Special Reference to the Revealed Future of the Church and the World* 2 (1865) 523–26.

104. *The Rainbow: A Magazine of Christian Literature, with Special Reference to the Revealed Future of the Church and the World* 2 (1865) 519–21.

105. Robert Govett, *The Man of Sin: Is He the Pope; being the Controversial Correspondence in the Achill Herald Between Edward Nangle and R. Govett* (London: Nisbet, 1866).

106. *The Baptist Magazine* identifies Nangle and Govett as belonging to the Preterist and Futurist schools of prophetical interpretation respectively. See "Reviews," *The Baptist Magazine* 58 (1866) 243.

107. "Reviews," *The Baptist Magazine* 58 (1866) 243.

108. "New Books," *The Earthen Vessel, and the Christian Record* 22 (1866) 123.

109. See Robert Govett, "The First Resurrection and Kingdom of Christ. Answer to Mr. Grant's Third Volume," *The Rainbow: A Magazine of Christian Literature, with Special Reference to the Revealed Future of the Church and the World* 4 (1867) 118–23; Robert Govett, "The Twenty-Four Elders," *The Rainbow: A Magazine of Christian Literature,*

author's works on the subject. In 1868 Govett's booklet entitled *Sowing and Reaping*[110] was reviewed in *The Voice Upon the Mountains*.[111] The reviewer began by acknowledging that all who know Govett are aware that he is a man of tremendous ability who is "able to do full justice" to any subject he takes in hand. The booklet is the subject of reward received at the Judgment according to the works of the believer. Govett focused upon Galatians 6:7–8 which reads, "Do not be deceived: God cannot be mocked. A man reaps what he sows. The one who sows to please his sinful nature, from that nature will reap destruction; the one who sows to please the Spirit, from the Spirit will reap eternal life." He maintained that the passage relates to both a sowing to the flesh and a sowing to the spirit on the part of "true believers." The unregenerate sow to the flesh alone. The reviewer agreed with Govett that it can be proven by Scripture that at the Judgment, when the Lord comes again, believers will be judged according to their service and receive rewards apportioned to their individual sowing on earth. Nevertheless, the reviewer parts company with Govett when he states that some believers will be "excluded" from the Kingdom; choosing instead to believe that the unworthy believer will be confined to a place different from that of the "good and faithful servant."[112]

Govett's 1853 book *Entrance into the Kingdom, or Reward According to Works* and his subsequent publications were gaining in popularity as evidenced by their regular and lengthy reviews in a number of prophetic journals,[113] and his position on exclusion from the Kingdom for some

---

with Special Reference to the Revealed Future of the Church and the World 4 (1867) 170–74; Robert Govett, "Millenarian Arguments—The Second Adam," *The Rainbow: A Magazine of Christian Literature, with Special Reference to the Revealed Future of the Church and the World* 4 (1867) 193–200; Robert Govett, "Millenarian Arguments, the Second Joseph and the Prophet Like Moses," *The Rainbow: A Magazine of Christian Literature, with Special Reference to the Revealed Future of the Church and the World* 4 (1867) 256–66; Robert Govett, "Millenarian Arguments. The Promises and Threats of the Law," *The Rainbow: A Magazine of Christian Literature, with Special Reference to the Revealed Future of the Church and the World* 4 (1867) 353–60; Robert Govett, "Answer To the Rev. B. Young on the Millennium," *The Rainbow: A Magazine of Christian Literature, with Special Reference to the Revealed Future of the Church and the World* 4 (1867) 403–12; Robert Govett, "Answer to the Rev. B. C. Young on the Millennium," *The Rainbow: A Magazine of Christian Literature, with Special Reference to the Revealed Future of the Church and the World* 4 (1867) 506–11.

110. Govett, *Sowing and Reaping* (London: Nisbet, 1868).

111. *The Voice upon the Mountains. A Journal of Prophetic Testimony and Evangelistic Effort* 2 (1868) 148–49.

112. Ibid.

113. See, for example, "Reviews," *The Quarterly Journal of Prophecy* 15 (1863) 187–201; "Reviews," *The Voice of Truth; or, Strict Baptist Magazine* 2 (1864) 213; "Reviews,"

believers continued to be fiercely debated. While many would publicly agree with Govett on the subject of varied rewards for the believer at the Judgment, the thought that some would be excluded from reward was a theological deviation. Govett's assumption that only "true believers" enjoy the Millennial Kingdom, and that the justified but marginal believers are excluded, was beyond the theological sensibility of most. Therefore it opened up a debate that continued for years and created the occasion for a series of articles printed in *The Voice Upon the Mountains* over three consecutive issues beginning in November 1868. The first of these articles was written by Frederick Newman, Eynesbury, St Neots, titled appropriately "Entrance into the Kingdom."[114] Like Govett he affirms that there is exclusion of believers from the Coming Kingdom. In his article Newman refutes *The Voice Upon the Mountains* which printed that it believed that there would not be exclusion, but rather places in the Kingdom apportioned according to works.[115]

In its December 1868 issue *The Voice Upon the Mountains* published an article written by J. T. Molesworth, an attorney from Clifton, Bristol, opposing Frederick Newman's theological position of exclusion of believers in the Coming Kingdom. He did so on the grounds that God makes no provision in his Word for believers to be separated from Christ.[116] There were principally two objections to the doctrine of exclusion. The first was that it was inconsistent with grace, and the second objection was that exclusion would cause a severance of the body of Christ—one member with Christ in glory, another not. Molesworth's argument against exclusion rests upon these objections, but is not based upon an examination of the passages alleged by Govett and others. In the very next issue Govett refutes both the editor of the magazine and Molesworth.[117] Govett does agree with Molesworth on at least one point, and that is on the subject's importance—believing that the doctrine is second only to the doctrine of salvation, by the grace of God, through faith in the Lord Jesus Christ. One of the proofs Govett uses in his argument is that

The Baptist Magazine 58 (1866) 243–45; "Reviews and Criticisms," *The Gospel Herald; or, Poor Christian's Magazine* NS 38, no. 6 (1869) 45–46.

114. Frederick Newman, "Entrance into the Kingdom," *The Voice upon the Mountains. A Journal of Prophetic Testimony and Evangelistic Effort* 2 (1868) 146–47.

115. These statements were made in the September 1867 and October 1867 issues of *The Voice upon the Mountains*. See *The Voice upon the Mountains: A Journal of Prophetic Testimony and Evangelistic Effort* (September 1867), 175. See also, *The Voice Upon the Mountains. A Journal of Prophetic Testimony and Evangelistic Effort* (October 1867), 190.

116. J. T. Molesworth, "Exclusion from the Kingdom," *The Voice upon the Mountains: A Journal of Prophetic Testimony and Evangelistic Effort* 2 (1868) 156–57.

117. Robert Govett, "Exclusion from the Kingdom," *The Voice upon the Mountains: A Journal of Prophetic Testimony and Evangelistic Effort* 3 (1869) 8–10.

Christ supposes that sin will be committed by true believers, and as such, Christ has appointed exclusions in the church age as testimony of a future exclusion by Christ from the Kingdom to come.[118]

As Govett argued his position on exclusion he found himself simultaneously engaged in other eschatological topics of heightened concern to theologians. As an example, he argued about the topics of death and Hades, as well as the coming Antichrist. It was in 1843, early in Govett's pastorate that he wrote *A Treatise On Hades, or the Place of Departed Spirits*.[119] In it he lays out the distinction Scripture makes between the grave and Hades. As previously noted, it encompassed an early analysis of his doctrine of exclusion. He wrote on the subject a number of times during his writing career which always invited criticism. For example, in the August issue of *The Rainbow*, Purdon debated Govett on a number of issues related to the Antichrist and quotes him referring to the descent of the Antichrist into Hades where his soul remains.[120] Later, in 1881, when Govett published his exposition of the Gospel of John in two volumes, he articulated in depth his understanding of the believer's relationship to Hades in which he referenced exclusion. His explanation of the meaning of chapter 5 clearly explains that there are two distinct resurrections; one at the beginning of the millennial reign for the true "believer," but those believers who do not qualify based upon their works will be held in Hades to be resurrected in the second resurrection. He states:

> And entry on that millennial glory is not to be granted to simple faith; but to the fruits of faith, or good works. It is never said—"Blessed are they *that believe; for theirs is the kingdom of heaven.*" For that is a different day to this; and its principle is the rewarding each according to works. Hence we have the distinction between two judgments, and two resurrections.[121]

Leonard Strong, former Brethren missionary, when residing in Torquay, wrote a letter that appeared in the January 1869 issue of *The Voice Upon the Mountains* regarding Govett's position on Hades. Strong was not in favor of any believer being placed in Hades, citing that Christ distinctly declares that none of his assembly, or church, which he was "about to

---

118. See 1 Cor 5–6.

119. Robert Govett, *A Treatise On Hades, or the Place of Departed Spirits* (Edinburgh: Johnstone, 1843).

120. *The Rainbow: A Magazine of Christian Literature, with Special Reference to the Revealed Future of the Church and the World* 2 (1865) 371.

121. Govett, Robert, *Exposition of the Gospel of St. John, vol. I–II* (London: Bemrose and Sons, 1881) 211.

build," should go to Hades, where the souls of the former saints had gone. Strong introduces the martyred Stephen as an example of being the first Christian who died and was said to have "fallen asleep," and his spirit to be received by Jesus.[122]

It was in the same January 1869 issue of *The Voice Upon the Mountains* that Govett gave his response to Molesworth's article which denied the doctrine of exclusion. Molesworth's objections were many but among them is this: that the teaching casts eternal life, completed sanctification, perfected capacity for and desire after fellowship with the Father and the Son into inaction through one-thousand years.[123] This is precisely Govett's point. Exclusion is something to be avoided. Entrance into the Kingdom must be "pursued" by works. It is a prize that is granted by Christ only upon evidence of good works. In the February issue Molesworth followed up once again with another article opposing exclusion.[124] Irrespective of which magazine, whenever Govett wrote about exclusion he met with a few supporters, but many more who opposed him. For example, while Molesworth opposed him in the February issue of *The Voice Upon the Mountain*, Herbert Bennett, South Molton, followed suit in the same issue.[125]

The criticism of Govett's doctrines continued into 1871 when during that year the controversy over eternal punishment reached a peak in dissenting print culture. The *Methodist Quarterly* remarks that "the controversy now agitating the Christian Church as to Eternal Punishment is creating a literature of its own."[126] That same year Govett entered into the discussion with his book *Eternal Suffering of the Wicked*[127] which was reviewed by the *Methodist Quarterly* and found to display considerable mental aptitude in perceiving the weak points in an argument.[128] W. Maude did not agree. He scathingly challenged the merits of Govett's book. Maude wrote a two-part article in *The Rainbow* which brought into question Govett's interpretation

---

122. *The Voice upon the Mountains: A Journal of Prophetic Testimony and Evangelistic Effort* 3 (1869) 11.

123. Robert Govett, "Exclusion from the Kingdom," *The Voice upon the Mountains: A Journal of Prophetic Testimony and Evangelistic Effort* 3 (1869) 21.

124. J. T. Molesworth, "Exclusion from the Kingdom," *The Voice upon the Mountains: A Journal of Prophetic Testimony and Evangelistic Effort* 3 (1869) 21–22.

125. *The Voice upon the Mountains: A Journal of Prophetic Testimony and Evangelistic Effort* 3 (1869) 22.

126. "Eternal Punishment," *The Methodist Quarterly: A Journal of Theological and General Literature* 5 (1871) 267.

127. Robert Govett, *Eternal Suffering of the Wicked* (London: Nisbet, 1871).

128. "Eternal Punishment," *The Methodist Quarterly: A Journal of Theological and General Literature* 5 (1871) 268.

of Scripture as it pertained to the eternal suffering of the wicked. In condescending tone the first article is titled "Mr. Govett Versus the Bible," and laments that such a good and earnest "Christian man" could be found to fight in so bad a cause.[129] While Maude finds that he can agree most heartedly with Govett that all human souls survive continuously from the hour of death to the hour of resurrection, he goes farther than Govett is willing to go. As pertains to the people of God, Maude affirms that they are held in Hades where divine life is perfected up until the "day of Jesus Christ." But he particularly parts company with Govett when it comes to Govett's understanding of the resurrection and that *all* men shall exist, body and soul united, from the hour of judgment to eternal ages. And then he seeks to rebuke Govett for "garbling" the words of the Lord. "Disingenuousness, acrimony, and dishonesty are so scandalously exhibited . . . better things might have been hoped for from Mr. Govett."[130] Later in the same year the publisher permitted a second article by Maude to run in response to the fifth chapter of Govett's book. It dealt with the character of God. In his assessment of Govett's chapter he once again disagrees with Govett who finds that punishment of the wicked is literal and eternal. Because God has love and God *is* love, Maude cannot believe that God would inflict eternal torment on any of his creatures.[131] In October of 1871 Govett responded to Maude's erudite rebukes. But the rebuttal was not permitted to take place in *The Rainbow*. It took place instead in the *Baptist Magazine*. In the forum Govett was far more gracious in reminding the readers that good will come of Maude's "answer" to his book. But he finds it unfair that the editor of *The Rainbow* would not allow him to refute in his pages the aspersions which Maude "throws on him." "As far as I know myself, I am honest in this matter; and would not, if I could, steal a victory by fraud and falsehood. Nor do I believe that orthodoxy needs it: the Word of God is fully on its side, as I hope to prove."[132]

Always looking at the Word of God as the basis for his arguments, Govett turned almost exclusively to the writing of his books and tracts after the 1860s to prove his doctrinal causes. No apparent reason can be found

---

129. W. Maude, "Mr. Govett Versus the Bible. An Examination of the 'Eternal Suffering of the Wicked,'" *The Rainbow: A Magazine of Christian Literature, with Special Reference to the Revealed Future of the Church and the World* 3 (1871) 371.

130. Ibid., 379.

131. W. Maude, "The Character of God (Mr. Govett Versus the Bible)," *The Rainbow: A Magazine of Christian Literature, with Special Reference to the Revealed Future of the Church and the World* 3 (1871) 405.

132. Robert Govett, "Eternal Punishment. Mr. Govett's Reply to Mr. Maude," *The Baptist Magazine* 63 (1871) 648.

for this. It may simply be that the journal articles from later decades are no longer extant. Nevertheless, it can be verified that from the beginning of the 1870s to the close of his life he published eighty-three known books and tracts. One of his most comprehensive writings of that period was his two-volume commentary on the gospel of John. In this commentary Govett reiterated his regard for the import of the thousand-year reign. He was conscious of the argument of others who questioned why it was not Scripturally true that resurrection and the day of judgment would not be to the benefit of all believers to enjoy the thousand-years. But Govett was keenly aware that such a belief would be in contradiction with John 3:3–5, and other texts of the other Gospels. Govett wrote, "All believers will indeed be raised by Christ at His coming; but whether they enjoy the thousand-years or no depends, not on their faith, but on their works."[133] It was a conviction that many could not accept. The majority of his critics were far more comfortable with an image of God who was loving and forgiving of all his creation—especially his children. Perhaps it was inevitable that upon Govett's death his writings would be relegated to the ranks of bizarre or the extreme; and perhaps the early signs of this began in 1871 when the editor of *The Rainbow* would not permit Govett to defend himself against personal attack in the magazine—a magazine in which his views had previously appeared so frequently. No explanation was given. Thereafter, his views began to rapidly disappear from the journals. Even more telling was the reaction he received from the editor of *The Voice Upon the Mountains* just a few years prior. The circumstance was revealed in 1883 when Govett had published four letters he had sent to Molesworth.[134] Presumably the letters were originally written around the time that the two men were contesting exclusion in 1868 and 1869 in the *Voice Upon the Mountains*. In the first paragraph of the first letter to Molesworth, Govett remarks that the discussion on the subject in the magazine was being forced to end. Govett had received notice from the editor that a continuance of the topic would endanger "the very existence" of his periodical. It was noted that hundreds withdrew from the periodical when the discussion began, and others threatened to follow their example. Recognizing the basis of this reaction Govett asks a hypothetical question in his first letter: "How is this? Why will not Christians listen to an argument on this point wholly drawn from Scripture?" His simple reply to his own question was that "they do not like it." They wish to assume that the New Testament teaches that all believers will enter the Millennial Kingdom

---

133. Govett, Robert, *Exposition of the Gospel of St. John, Vol. I–II* (London: Bemrose and Sons, 1881) 268.

134. Robert Govett, *Entrance into the Millennial Kingdom: Four Letters To J. T. Molesworth, Esq.* (Norwich: Fletcher and Son, 1883).

without fail.[135] Even his congregation seemed to grow weary, as its numbers declined in the last decade of the nineteenth century.[136] A newspaper article written about Surrey Chapel and its pastors recounts that in the early days of Govett's ministry it was not uncommon to see the 1500-seat Surrey Road Chapel filled to "the utmost." It further states that, "As time passed the congregation from various causes dwindled somewhat, a tendency which became still more marked as extreme old age grew upon the minister. Eight or nine years ago there still remained an average congregation of about 200. Within the last year [1900] it was rare to see more than sixty worshipers."[137] But old age alone does not explain the decline in attendance in this venerable preacher's church. The crisis of faith in the waning years of the Victorian era accounts for much of the decline, but it does not explain the rapid decline in Govett's popularity so soon after his death. Some explanation for this may be found in the emerging and competing premillennial theologies which began to dominate in the evangelical communities in America. Crawford Gribben noted that innovative eschatology was "bolted on to the theories of biblical inerrancy" but which had gained new spokesmen in America.[138] Dispensationalism was having an impact in America, but probably the greatest factor in favor of dispensationalism was the publication in 1909 of the Scofield Reference Bible with footnotes expounding a Darbyite interpretation. It accustomed its readers to seeing the biblical text through dispensationalist eyes.[139] A new "fundamentalism" was forming and Govett was denied a part. The outcome was a slow and eventual disappearance of Govett from the scene of theological debate.

---

135. Robert Govett, *Entrance into the Millennial Kingdom: Four Letters to J. T. Molesworth, esq.* (Norwich: Fletcher and Son, 1883) 1.

136. For a record of the decline in baptisms at Surrey Chapel see Norfolk Records Office Catalog Reference FC 76/89.

137. "Surrey Chapel and Its Pastor: A Unique Ministry," no date or title of newspaper is known. Found in Norwich Records Office file FC 76/59, part 2 of 2.

138. Gribben, *Trans-Atlantic World*, 92.

139. Bebbinton, *Evangelicalism in Modern Britain*, 192.

CHAPTER 6

Govett's Afterlife in Context

SUSTAINED INTEREST IN PROPHECY—ESPECIALLY that involving the futurist position, dispensationalism, and associated eschatological events—provided a steady flow of articles and books during the period in which Govett was completing his university education and beginning his ministry. With the prophecy conferences of Henry Drummond at Albury Park, Surrey, and those of Lady Powerscourt in County Wicklow still present as a backdrop to the lingering debate over eschatology, Joshua William Brooks (1790–1882), vicar of Clarborough, Nottinghamshire, compiled a comprehensive dictionary of hundreds of authors of prophecy and over two-thousand books dating back to the Reformation.[1] His significant contribution indicates that it was not only the dissenters who had a profound interest in the end-times. The work was greatly aided by Robert Watt's two-volume *Bibliotheca Britannia* published in 1824,[2] as well as the contributions of several theologians including Edward Bickersteth. The dictionary provided references that pertained to many prophetic topics with a significant number written about the Apocalypse described in the books of Daniel and Revelation. It is important to note, however, that the three-volume work *La Venida del Mesias en Gloria y Magestad* (1790) by the Jesuit writer Emmanuel Lacunza (1731–1801), pen-name "Juan Josafat Ben Ezra—a converted Jew," is also included in Brooks's dictionary. It is this work that was later translated by Edward Irving under the English title *The Coming of the Messiah in Glory and Majesty* (1827),[3]

---

1. Joshua William Brooks, *A Dictionary of Writers on the Prophecies, with the Titles and Occasional Description of Their Works* (London: Simpkin, Marshall, 1835).

2. Robert Watt, *Bibliotheca Britannia: General Index to British and Foreign Literature*, 2 vols. (Edinburgh: Hurst, Robinson, 1824).

3. See Edward Irving, *The Coming of Messiah in Glory and Majesty: By Juan Josafat*

and, some, such as Timothy Stunt,[4] say influenced Darby in the development of his system of "Dispensationalism." In point of fact, much of what Darby represents as his own thinking can be traced to Lacunza's published work. And while there is no direct evidence that Darby used any of the writings of Morgan Edwards (1722–1795), who had written on the subject of a pretribulation Rapture in 1742, it is clear that there are similarities between their eschatological systems.[5] Lacunza's conclusions are also similar to the thoughts of Edwards. Jonathan Burnham, for one, suggests that Darby was not the first theologian to advance pretribulational millennialism and points to Edwards as his predecessor.[6] Edwards wrote of a distinct rapture that would occur three and a half years before the start of the Millennium. This was the same position held by Darby as late as 1845.[7] Yet, Edwards was not the first to write on the pretribulational Rapture of the church. One of the earliest to take up the subject after the Reformation was Nathaniel Homes (1599–1678) in his comprehensive work *The Resurrection Revealed, or the Dawning of the Day-Star* (1653).[8] Emergence of interest in this eschatological topic caused its republishing, by Brooks's publisher, in 1833. And while he never used the phrase "pretribulational rapture" he occasionally suggested an understanding of millennialism that alludes to it, while not fully embracing it. As such,

---

Ben-Ezra. Translated from the Spanish, with a Preliminary Discourse by E. Irving. (A Critique of the Work Composed by Juan Josafat Ben-Ezra, Entitled "the Coming of Messiah in Glory and Majesty," by M. R. P. Fr. Paul, of the Conception, of the Order of the Barefooted Carmelite) (London: Thames Ditton, 1827).

4. Stunt, *From Awakening to Secession*, 180.

5. Edwards first wrote about his pretribulation beliefs while a student at Bristol Baptist College, Bristol, England, as an assignment. It was originally written in Latin and later translated into English in 1788. See Morgan Edwards, *Two Academical Exercises on Subjects Bearing the Following Titles: Millennium, Last-novelties* (Philadelphia: Dodson and Lang, 1788); Tim LaHaye, Thomas Ice, and Ed Hindson, *The Popular Handbook on the Rapture* (Eugene, OR: Harvest House, 2011) 70. See also Thomas R. McKibbens Jr. and Kenneth L. Smith, *The Life and Works of Morgan Edwards* (New York: Arno, 1980).

6. Jonathan Burnham, "The Controversial Relationship Between Benjamin Wills Newton and John Nelson Darby," DPhil thesis, University of Oxford, 1999, 129.

7. Tim LaHaye, Thomas Ice, and Ed Hindson, *The Popular Handbook on the Rapture* (Eugene, OR: Harvest House, 2011) 71–72. See also John Nelson Darby, *Notes on the Book of Revelations; to Assist Inquiries in Searching into that Book* (London: Central Tract Depôt, 1839) 53.

8. Nathaniel Homes, *Apokalypsis Anastaseōs: The Resurrection Revealed, or, the Dawning of the Day-Star about to Rise and Radiate a Visible Incomparable Glory . . .* (London: Ibbitson, 1653). See also Nathaniel Homes, *The Resurrection Revealed Raised Above Doubt & Difficulties in Ten Exercitations* (London: Printed for the author, 1661).

his understanding of Christ's return was decidedly "spiritualized." In his chapter on "The Personal Appearing of Christ to His Church at Her Restoration on Earth," Homes states that while he had dealt with the topic of Christ's return in previous chapters it was important to devote an entire chapter to the Lord's appearing which Scripture represents as being "at least *in the clouds*, at the time of the Restoration of his church and at the beginning of the Millennium."[9] He was not prepared to declare that Christ would fully reside upon the earth; rather he chose to believe that Christ would reign spiritually with the saints. He defended his rapture position with Scripture references to include Zechariah 12:10. Upon this text Homes declares that "Every word almost of this text intimates, that this coming is meant of a time after his [Christ's] ascension, and yet before the ultimate day of doom . . . to set up his church into a most glorious estate on earth, before the day of judgment, and to make her reign with him on earth."[10] It appears, therefore, that the pretribulational Rapture was a subject of interest—in various forms—for some time before Govett began his writing career.

It was early in the 1840s when Govett inserted himself into the eschatological debate.[11] For the balance of his life he remained persistently engaged in that debate: chapter 5 documented the diverse and contested aspects of the debate over events surrounding Christ's return and the scriptural promises to his church; and it is in this environment Govett often found himself at odds with clergy and respected scholars. His unique, if not scandalous, thoughts on both baptism and the dividing of the church at the occasion of the Rapture brought both criticism and admiration from his peers. But it was the views he held on the future life that caused most difficulty for him. Even so, he was resolute in his conviction. Over his life he continued to develop his views on the subject. Toward the end of his life, his writings on the future life and the "last things" became perceptibly more developed and increasingly complex. Early on, such as in *The Locusts, the Euphratean Horsemen and the Two Witnesses; or, the Apocalyptic Systems of the Revds. E. B. Elliot, Dr. Cumming and Dr. Keith, Proved Unsound* (1852), while debating Edward Elliott, Church of England clergyman, and John Cumming, Presbyterian minister, Govett speaks of events in the book

9. Homes, *The Resurrection Revealed*, 247.

10. Ibid., 250.

11. See Robert Govett, *The Revelation of St. John, Literal and Future: Being an Exposition of that Book: To Which Are Added Remarks in Refutation of the Ideas that the Pope is the Man of Sin, and that Popery is the Apostasy Predicted by St. Paul, with a Special Reference to Doctor O'Sullivan on the Apostasy* (London: Hamilton, Adams, 1843).

of Revelation from a futurist position and engages in a discussion of "future reward," delineating it from earthy reward. But he does not attempt to include a discussion of believer's exclusion.[12] By 1860, when he published *Esau's Choice: A Sermon Preached February 26th, 1860* (1860), Govett is prepared to use Old Testament stories as metaphors to defend his position of exclusion. Using Esau as an example of one who forfeited his birthright and could receive no satisfaction from his father to recover it, he equates the story to the requirements of faithfulness of believers in the New Testament. Govett says, "You will bargain away your interest in future glory for present worldly advantages. Your hopes of the kingdom being faint, and your ideas of it feeble, you will like Esau, sell at a price ruinously low; establishing to God's eyes also, your profaneness."[13] Whereas in his sermon on Esau in 1860 he declared a warning about not giving away one's reward for earthly pleasure, in *Sowing and Reaping* (1868) Govett probes the issue more deeply by asking a question metaphorically, "What kind of seed are you sowing? Is it the world's or God's?"[14] Here, in this tract, he once again finds that the reaping corruption from sowing to the flesh is the same as being shut out of the Millennial Kingdom.[15]

The depth of his conviction and ability to delineate his thoughts on the subject were especially apparent in the writings in the last decade of his life.[16] It was in his commentary on the book of Philippians,[17] published in 1894, that his readers received a fully developed picture of the peril that awaits the casual Christian at the Rapture. Govett articulates one verse in particular which speaks perceptively to this future event and helps present his unique understanding of pretribulational events.

In Philippians 3:11, Paul outlines his heightened hope of attaining to the resurrection "by any means possible." This "hapax legomai" specifies a different kind of "resurrection." Seizing upon the importance of this single

12. Robert Govett, *The Locusts, the Euphratean Horsemen and the Two Witnesses; or, the Apocalyptic Systems of the Revds. E. B. Elliot, Dr. Cumming and Dr. Keith, Proved Unsound* (London: Nisbet, 1852).

13. Robert Govett, *Esau's Choice: A Sermon Preached February 26th, 1860* (Norwich: Fletcher and Son, 1860) 13.

14. Robert Govett, *Sowing and Reaping* (London: Nisbet, 1868) 13.

15. Govett, *Sowing and Reaping*, 16.

16. See Robert Govett, *Will All Believers Have Part in the Thousand Years?* (Norwich: Fletcher and Son, 1895); *Christ's Judgment of His Saints at His Return: and Solution of the Main Argument Against Secret Presence* (Norwich: Fletcher and Son, 1895); *The Faith and Obedience of Abraham: A Pattern to Believers* (Norwich: Fletcher and Son, 1900).

17. Robert Govett, *The Fourth Kingdom of Man and His City: Being the Argument of the Epistle of the Philippians* (Norwich: Fletcher and Son, 1894).

verse, Govett identifies the significance of the phrase "if by any means" as referring to something that is very desirable; but also cautions is something that is encompassed with difficulty and danger. As such, there will be its loss on the part of any who did not strive to attain it. Govett, invariably seeking to prove his case through Scripture, calls attention to the trustworthiness of the meaning of this phrase. He finds, for instance, in Acts 27 that the apostle Paul is aboard a ship warning his fellow voyagers of dangers ahead because of the stormy time of the year for travel hoping "if by any means they could reach Phoenix, and winter there." Govett then references two additional instances of usage[18] to further his argument of the phrase expressing desirability and difficulty, while at the same time communicating determination to break through all difficulties in order to achieve it.[19] Immediately following the initial phrase "if by any means," Paul expands its context. Govett explains its meaning to his readers by acknowledging that it is generally, but wrongly, believed that there is only one resurrection; a conclusion which is historically apparent in Govett's contributions to print culture. The assumption made by some was that both the righteous and the ungodly would appear together and receive the judgment of Christ at the same time. Govett countered with his customary appeal to Scripture to affirm that there are two resurrections, one-thousand years apart. The first resurrection is to be for honor and reward; the second, mainly for judgment and condemnation. After the completion of the thousand-years of blessing, the rest of the dead will be assembled before the throne of judgment. In that judgment the books containing the deeds of the wicked are opened and they are judged.

The first resurrection, according to Govett's understanding, is of necessity a resurrection from among the dead. Those whom God "favors" arise, but the main body of the dead remain in the grave until the day of reward (the thousand-years) is over. The compelling controversy looming over many of his writings surfaced with what Govett next believed: "and this rest of the dead consists of two portions." The two portions are those believers not accounted worthy of the Millennial Kingdom, and all unbelievers who are condemned after the Kingdom.[20] Therefore, when the Great White Throne of Judgment, spoken of in Revelation 20:11, takes place at the close of the thousand-years there are two classes of people that will be discovered. One class consists of those condemned according to their works whose names do not appear in the Book of Life, and the other class those whose names did appear. And, while those whose names were

---

18. See Rom 1:10; 11:14.
19. Govett, *The Fourth Kingdom*, 75–76.
20. Ibid., 78.

not written in the Book of Life are cast into the "lake of fire," those whose names appear are entitled to enter the "City of God."[21] Christ is the first example of the special resurrection spoken of by Paul in Philippians 3:11. He has won this place by his perfect righteousness.[22] With this Govett adds to the developing complexity of thought by concluding that Christ being made an example to the church was raised according to Acts 26:23, "as the first to rise from the dead, to proclaim light to his own people and to the Gentiles." In likeness to Christ's first example there will come another resurrection of honor. Those who believe and are saved, but not accounted worthy of it, have to wait a thousand-years before they enter by means of the provided inheritance. In summation of Govett's belief, the first resurrection is a desirable resurrection to be sought. Entry into it demands faith. But, faith alone, faith without works, is not enough. Those who enter the Kingdom of millennial glory enter as "the righteous," not as believers only. To this Govett quotes Jesus in Luke 14:14 who said, "you will be repaid at the resurrection of the righteous." Here then is Govett's unequivocal position; believers are separated at the Rapture, some to receive entry and some to remain in Hades until the thousand-years has been completed; making exclusion from the Millennium a serious adjudication for the believer. This was Govett's unwavering stance for nearly a half century and one he staunchly held upon his death in 1901.

As he promulgated his unique doctrine of the Millennial Kingdom, his persistence in going against the established views on eschatology was, in his opinion, simply a necessary trial of life that could benefit his appearing before Christ at the Rapture. His confidence in the favorable outcome of his earthly condemnations is alluded to in his writings, but he chose especially to reveal it in his Philippians commentary in which he notes that the apostle Paul expressed his certainty of the "prize" in his last letter to Timothy. Paul encouraged Timothy (2 Timothy 4:7–8) with his statement that "henceforth there is laid up for me the crown of righteousness."[23] While Paul sometimes expressed uncertainty of reward for himself, Govett never expressed any doubt over his own entrance into the Coming Kingdom even though his teachings on exclusion isolated him from the mainstream of theological thought. Govett's confidence came from his certainty that his obedient conduct as a Christian would yield reward in the life to come as Scripture pronounced. His peers chiefly determined him to be in error on the subject while curiously maintaining their respect for his learning and

21. See Rev 21:27.
22. See Acts 26:27.
23. Govett, *The Fourth Kingdom*, 80.

scholarship. He was sometimes seen as an enemy of orthodoxy, sometimes just misunderstood, occasionally dismissed, but paradoxically sought-after by the many journals in which his writings appeared. Typical of the praise was a review by the editor of the *Last Vials* who wrote, "There is a London paper called the *Morning Advertiser*, which we believe is edited by the same person who lately wrote an 'overwhelming' article against the doctrine of the Second Coming. He was immediately taken up by a variety of periodicals, and praised to the heavens as the ablest controversialist of the day, and as the victorious champion of all who 'hate his appearing!' His work was torn to pieces by Mr. Govett, who vouchsafed an answer to it; but in fact, it did not contain one argument which was worth of being answered."[24]

There were a few popular authors who appeared to share some of Govett's convictions regarding the consequences to the church at the Rapture, but none that dared go so far. For example, Joseph A. Seiss, an American theologian, in his book *The Parable of the Virgins* (1862) suggests that there is loss in the coming age for actions committed or neglected in this life, but does not suggest exclusion.[25] But in *The Apocalypse* (1900) he does reveal a form of exclusion of the church by stating that even the professing church will be overtaken by his appearing unaware and left behind.[26] G. H. Pember in *Earth's Earliest Ages* (1884) suggests an exclusion of believers at the Rapture by citing examples both from the Old Testament and the New Testament. He notes Christ's disciples standing on the Mount of Olives as they beheld the cloud receiving their Master out of their sight, but were not yet prepared to follow Him.[27] Pember also wrote elsewhere, "It is possible for a Christian to suffer loss, and to be saved only so as through fire, instead of having an entrance richly supplied into the eternal Kingdom of our Lord and Savior."[28] Later, G. H. Lang in his book *The Epistle to the Hebrews* (1951) speaks to the question of judgment for believers upon Christ's return, and while not as concise as Govett in articulating the consequences alludes to the loss of reward while not mentioning exclusion from the Kingdom.[29]

---

24. *The Last Vials* 23, no. 1 (1868) 6–7.

25. Joseph A. Seiss, *The Parable of the Ten Virgins: In Six Discourses. And a Sermon on the Judgment of the Saints* (Philadelphia: Lutheran Book House, 1862) 189.

26. Joseph A. Seiss, *The Apocalypse: Lectures on the Book of Revelation* (New York: Cook, 1900) 175.

27. G. H. Pember, *Earth's Earliest Ages; and Their Connection with Modern Spiritualism and Theosophy*, 5th ed. (London: Hodder and Stoughton, 1884) 195.

28. G. H. Pember, *The Great Prophecies Concerning the Gentiles, the Jews, and the Church of God* (London: Hodder and Stoughton, 1881) 328. Later, G. H. Lang and D. M. Panton republished Pember's work (London: Oliphants, 1941).

29. G. H. Lang, *The Epistle to the Hebrews: A Practical Treatise for Plain and Serious*

The debate about this unique, yet troublesome, doctrine of exclusion declined soon after Govett's death. There was one author, however, who earnestly endeavored to keep his memory and teaching alive. D. M. Panton, Govett's friend and successor at Surrey Chapel, picked up Govett's mantle in his own books on the afterlife which meticulously followed the pattern of eschatology taught to him by his mentor including the doctrine of exclusion.[30] But Panton's broader method of communicating was through *Dawn* which he founded in 1924 and edited until his death in 1955. From its inception Panton systematically published portions of Govett's commentary on the Gospel of John. He continued this monthly pattern until April 1929 when it appears that the inclusion of Govett's work in his magazine abruptly ceased without explanation. A pastor and scholar long admired for his knowledge of Scripture had been effectively placed onto the sideline of evangelical debate. It is unclear why his work was seldom considered relevant or referenced so soon after his death. Nevertheless, there are a few historic channel markers that can guide our response to this problem. One such guide is an insightful article that appeared in the *Journal of Sacred Literature* (1852) early in Govett's ministry, but remained relevant in its evaluation a half century later. John Kitto, the editor of the magazine, made these remarks concerning Govett's book *The Saints' Rapture to the Presence of the Lord Jesus, with Appendix in Refutation of Dr. Cumming's Tract Entitled "The Pope the Man of Sin."*[31]

> We are pleased to see any new emanation from the pen of Mr. Govett. We are familiar with his "Isaiah Unfulfilled," and often consult it with advantage. Moreover, his tracts and smaller works, which are rapidly multiplying, have attracted many readers, and Mr. G's pulpit at Norwich becomes the centre of a holy influence. We are not, however, prepared to say that the views of this excellent man are always clear. They are more often characterized by originality and enterprise than by that patient spirit of investigation which avails itself of the labors of those who have gone before, that spirit which elucidates as well as confirms.[32]

Readers (London: Paternoster, 1951).

30. See David M. Panton, *The Apocalypse of the Lord (Revelation XIX)* (London: Thynne, 1922). David M. Panton, *Earth's Last Pentecost* (London: Thynne, 1922). David M. Panton, *Rapture* (London: Thynne, 1922).

31. Robert Govett, *The Saints' Rapture to the Presence of the Lord Jesus, with Appendix in Refutation of Dr. Cumming's Tract Entitled "The Pope the Man of Sin"* (London: Nisbet, 1852).

32. *Journal of Sacred Literature* 3, no. 5 (1852) 218.

Kitto's appraisal of Govett took two tracks of thought. First, he compliments Govett for his interpretation of Scripture and his ability to communicate it. This was typical of the accolades he was to commonly receive throughout his ministry. For example, in the July 1880 issue of Spurgeon's *The Sword and the Trowel*, Govett is described as "an aged disciple, and a profound student of the Scriptures."[33]

Kitto's second point, that Govett was most often motivated by the pursuit of "originality" and "enterprise" in his writings, was insightfully phrased for so early in his writing ministry. Originality and boldness (or "enterprise") would remain hallmarks of his writing. He was widely read because of his frequent appearances in journals, but those who fully agreed with his premillennial conclusions were much fewer in number. *The Sword and the Trowel* alludes to this in 1881 when it states "Mr. Govett, of Norwich, is known and valued by a select circle of judicious and instructed Christians, who make up for the smallness of their number by the heartiness of their esteem."[34] There were many who could not agree with him because his conclusions did not concur with their own. And it was usually the case that when others opposed him in writing he quickly responded; not so much to defend himself as to defend biblical "truth." The frequency of Govett's appearances in Victorian era print made him the target of many rebuttals. But once he died his name slowly drifted from prominence. Perhaps this was due to his close association with a very unorthodox and contentious view of the Rapture. Whatever the cause, his original doctrine soon followed him into obscurity. And with a lack of prolific and exuberant writers to carry on the message, after a half century of debate, his principle belief slipped from scholastic and theological purview. More than this, near the close of the nineteenth century, a series of events took place on both sides of the Atlantic that served to insure that Govett's legacy was certain not to return to the mainstream of premillennial discussion. The mood of evangelicalism was changing and nowhere was this more apparent than in America.

New Expectations

It is in America in the latter half of the nineteenth century where the center of the dispensational system of theology shifts and ossifies. This occurred at the expense of what Govett had to say on the subject. As a

---

33. *The Sword and the Trowel; a Record of Combat with Sin and of Labor for the Lord* (1880) 407.

34. *The Sword and the Trowel; a Record of Combat with Sin and of Labor for the Lord* (1881) 480.

result, it ultimately led to his vanishing from conversation and scholarship. James Inglis, American pastor and editor of *Waymarks in the Wilderness, and Scriptural Guide*, in 1864, wrote to his subscribers that "No reader of the Bible can have failed to notice the space which the prophetic Scriptures occupy. When, in addition to this, we observe how prophecy is interwoven with the whole fabric of almost every book in the volume, whether narrative, didactic, or poetical in its character, it seems strange that the study of prophecy should ever have been discountenanced."[35] This reflective thought took place in a world of religious transition in which the focus of debate was shifting from Europe to North America. That movement was extremely complex as it extended over centuries and was filled with disillusionment as well as successes.[36] As such, our attention must shift for a moment to the start of the nineteenth century which saw events take place that were profound enough to inestimably change the religious landscape of both the British Isles and eventually North America. Samuel Taylor Coleridge described this time as "an age of anxiety from the crown to the hovel, from the cradle to the coffin."[37] It summarized the social uncertainty and upheaval that accompanied the start of the century. It was during the uncertainty of this time of unrest that many turned to a renewed interest in prophecy and speculation about the future of the world.[38] It was also at the dawn of this new century that a movement was spawned that was soon dubbed "dispensationalism" which brought a resurgence of the futurist, premillennial interpretation of Scripture and gave rise to a preoccupation with "pretribulationism."[39] Jürgen Moltmann boldly asserted that the dawn of the new century had become "the Christian era." For Christianity, the evangelization of the world seemed to be in reach.[40] The prophetic parameters shared by many modern evangelicals were finally established.[41] In Ireland, where pretribulationism was given a new birth,

35. James Inglis, ed., *Waymarks in the Wilderness, and Scriptural Guide* (New York: J. Inglis & Co., 1864), 1.

36. Mark A. Noll, *Old Religion in a New World: The History of North American Christianity* (Grand Rapids: Eerdmans, 2002) 1.

37. Samuel Taylor Coleridge, *A Book I Value: Selected Marginalia* (Princeton: Princeton University Press, 2003) 172.

38. Mark S. Sweetnam and Crawford Gribben, "J. N. Darby and the Irish Origins of Dispensationalism," *Journal of the Evangelical Theological Society* 52, no. 3 (2009) 571.

39. George Eldon Ladd, *The Blessed Hope: A Biblical Study of the Second Advent and the Rapture* (Grand Rapids: Eerdmans, 1956) 35.

40. Jürgen Moltmann, *The Coming of God: Christian Eschatology* (Minneapolis: Fortress, 1996) 3.

41. Crawford Gribben and Timothy C Stunt, eds., *Prisoners of Hope? Aspects of Evangelical Millennialism in Britain and Ireland, 1800–1880* (Waynesboro, GA:

there was increased pessimism after the 1798 Rebellion and the 1801 Act of Union which caused the nation to become religiously introspective and created a unique moment in time for the reception of Darby's developing dispensational ideas. In America, evangelicals in the South were forced to rethink their optimistic postmillennial hopes with the collapse of the Confederacy and the shattering impact of Reconstruction. Their millennial exuberance slowly gave way to eschatological uncertainty while the theology of some of the religious leaders began to reflect that shift in thinking.[42] James P. Boyce (1827–1888), for example, who had studied at Princeton Theological Seminary under the tutelage of Charles Hodge and who later became the president of the Southern Baptist Theological Seminary, was forced to reconsider his postmillennial position as he moved a considerable distance from traditional postmillennialism to an emphasis on the imminence of the second coming.[43] But the development of premillennial, pretribulational thought in America was not a repeat or merely an extension of British religious experience.

What influenced America and became assimilated into religious thought arrived on the heels of circumstances and events that were unique to a new nation. Mark Noll in *The Old Religion in a New World* isolates four of many aspects of the American religious environment which were especially important to this process. The first was the sheer spaciousness of America. The huge expanse of North America gave churches breathing room to develop their own religious visions and the possibility of producing new versions of Christianity. The second aspect pertained to race and ethnicity. North America witnessed a confluence of the various British nations. During the migrations of the 1830s, Northern Europeans migrated across the ocean in large numbers soon followed by Eastern and Southern Europeans. Thirdly, pluralism and its subsequent diversity presented itself in an impressive pattern of churches, religious agencies, modes and forms of Christian worship which gave occasion for a pattern best described as a "denominationalism" which appeared to exceed what had previously been experienced in Great Britain. And, finally, there was an absence of confessional conservatism as evidenced by a liberalism defined in the nineteenth century as an affinity for populism, individualism, and democratization.[44]

Paternoster, 2004) 11.

42. Gribben, *Evangelical Millennialism*, 94.

43. Crawford Gribben, *Writing the Rapture: Prophecy Fiction in Evangelical America* (Oxford: Oxford University Press, 2009) 51.

44. Mark A. Noll, *The Old Religion in a New World: The History of North American Christianity* (Grand Rapids: Eerdmans, 2002) 12–25.

All of these factors were present by the second half of the nineteenth century—a time in which the millennial movement in the United States became prevalent. At the same time Govett continued his work to disseminate scriptural truth in England with no apparent concern for publishing his work in the United States. His many works were all exclusively published in England by English publishers. The millennial movement in America had no particular name at first but functioned as a remedial to denominationalism with a distinct identity. Ernest R. Sandeen in his work *The Roots of Fundamentalism* associates the movement with all of the characteristics of a new sect. Many of its leaders were drawn from Episcopal, Presbyterian, and Baptist ministers of the abilities of men such as James H. Brookes, Arthur T. Pierson, and Nathaniel West.[45] Millennialism spread through such men who were respected for their zeal and knowledge of Scriptures while their millennial followers came together in the summer at annual conferences—one of the most popular of which were the Niagara meetings. There were also meetings in the winter to include the occasional Bible and Prophetic Conference such as that held in New York City in 1878. Periodicals including *Truth* (started by Brookes) and *Watchword* further helped to spread the movement. And, while millennialism in America began with a single focus upon the imminent return of Christ it broadened to include other issues that became crucial to the followers and created distinctions that separated them from other evangelical denominations. In the face of extremes and fanaticism that sprang up around the doctrine of Christ's imminent return, such as that of William Miller and the Millerites, the millennialists sought to present a reasoned handling of eschatology. In the light of American nationalism, they offered a sober and pessimistic view of the future of all human society, so that by late in the nineteenth century criticism of millenarianism moderated and the movement began to receive a measure of respectability. Still, millenarianism failed to appeal to more than a minority of American evangelicals, while those who resisted its teaching eventually became more tolerant.[46] Dispensationalism and millennialism were forging new ground in America, while in Great Britain Govett and others continued to go over the same theological ground with their debates on the Antichrist, the visible return of Christ, and, of course, the exclusion of believers at the Rapture. What gave millennialism a boost in popularity were the visits of dispensationalism's founder to America. Darby visited the United States and Canada seven times between 1862 and 1877 residing in and traveling

---

45. Ernest R. Sandeen, *The Roots of Fundamentalism: British and American Millennialism, 1800–1930*, 2nd ed. (Grand Rapids: Baker, 1978) xix.

46. Sandeen, *The Roots of Fundamentalism*, xx.

through those countries for seven out of the sixteen years. He was primarily devoted to strengthening the cause of the Brethren movement and to teaching his distinctive dispensationalism. Aiding Darby in the endeavor of spreading dispensationalism was the *Waymarks in the Wilderness* begun in 1862 and edited by James Inglis, and James H. Brookes's *Maranatha*[47] published in 1870. The journal sought to promote a form of Darby's dispensational premillennialism.[48] In general Darby found the church in America more "worldly" than anywhere else he had travelled.[49] And he was appalled by the worldliness of American Christians' overwhelming focus upon their denominations.[50] It was America's undiminished adherence to denominationalism that created resistance to Darby's teaching. James Inglis in an issue of the *Waymarks in the Wilderness* clarified matters concerning Darby feeling that the Americans took what they wanted from his theology and refused to forsake their denominations. Nevertheless, Inglis asserted that Americans appreciated Darby's doctrine of grace and his doctrine of the secret Rapture with the imminent return of Christ.[51]

Anticipating the imminent Second Coming of Christ may have been the primary focus of the millenarian movement in America but it was not its sole aim. However, in England, it remained an almost singular priority for Govett. While they awaited Christ's return in America, their aim also became one of awakening a church to the reality of pending judgment and to call sinners to repentance before it was too late. In this light millenarian leaders met with increased success toward the end of the nineteenth century and into the first decade of the twentieth century as conservative leaders, particularly those within the Baptist and Presbyterian denominations, began to increase their cooperation with each other. This increased cooperation between the millenarians and the conservatives occurred primarily because they perceived a common enemy in the form of "Modernism" which was viewed as a threat to the basic assumptions of their world views.[52] In this new alliance these conservatives joined in the conferences that sprang up during the last quarter of the nineteenth century, of which

47. James H. Brookes, *Maranatha: or the Lord Cometh* (St. Louis: Bredell, 1870).

48. Harriet A. Harris, *Fundamentalism and Evangelicals* (Oxford: Oxford University Press, 1998) 23.

49. Sandeen, *The Roots of Fundamentalism*, 71.

50. See Timothy P. Weber, "Dispensational and Historic Premillennialism as Popular Millennialist Movements," in Craig L. Blomberg and Sung Wook Chung, eds., *A Case for Historic Premillennialism: An Alternative to "Left Behind" Eschatology* (Grand Rapids: Baker, 2009).

51. Sandeen, *The Roots of Fundamentalism*, 101.

52. Ibid., xxi.

the Niagara Bible Conference held initial preeminence. It was likely the first of the major Bible conferences that proliferated in various cities. The first of these conferences originated with a group of men associated with the millenarian periodical *Waymarks in the Wilderness*, including James Inglis (its editor), George S. Bishop, L. C. Baker, and George C. Needham who held an informal private conference in New York City in 1868. Needham had recently emigrated from Ireland and claimed that the idea came from conferences that originated in Ireland earlier in the century; presumably the Powerscourt Prophetic Conferences in the early 1830s which were influential in the formation of Darby's eschatology.[53] Eventually younger men took over the leadership and after reorganizing in Chicago in 1875 the conference met each summer for one or two weeks. From 1883 to 1897 the conferences met at Niagara-on-the-Lake, Ontario. It is asserted that virtually everyone of any significance in the history of the American millenarian movement during this period attended the Niagara Conference.[54] However, Govett is never mentioned as having been issued an invitation. Yet, it was at the Niagara Bible Conferences where Darby's concept of the church and his theology could be received without concern for denominational prejudice since there was an attempt to ignore such partiality. A new form of exposition emerged in which the Scriptures were read, preached and vigorously discussed. The Niagara Bible Conference became the prototype for hundreds of Bible conferences; and while it was not overwhelmingly dispensational at the outset it quickly moved in that direction. Darby-fashioned pretribulationists such as Presbyterians Nathaniel West, James A. Brookes, and the Baptist A. J. Gordon all argued for the doctrine of Christ's premillennial second coming to be included among the fundamental doctrines. By 1878 their position prevailed and led the way to other conferences that excluded all other views.[55]

The interdenominational Niagara Bible Conference introduced the word "fundamentals" into evangelical discourse with a fourteen-page creed advocating biblical inerrancy and premillennial eschatology. In 1910 doctrinal norms for the clergy of the northern Presbyterian Church (U.S.A.) were drafted which insisted upon belief in the so-called five points centering upon the inerrancy of Scripture, the virgin birth, atoning death, and physical resurrection of Jesus Christ, and the supernatural character of the New Testament miracles. Then between 1910 and 1915 a series of tracts in twelve

---

53. Ibid., 132–33.

54. Ibid., 134.

55. Gary J. Dorrien, *The Remaking of Evangelical Theology* (Louisville: Westminster John Knox, 1998) 15.

volumes was published entitled *The Fundamentals: A Testimony to the Truth*, which attempted to answer the mounting evangelical concern over higher criticism, the decline of traditional belief, Darwinism, and especially the propagation of new religious beliefs. By 1920 Curtis Lee Laws, minister and editor of the Northern Baptist Convention newspaper *The Watchman-Examiner*, published the word "fundamentalist" for the first time. This was followed in the same year by a pre-convention caucus of three-thousand delegates of the Northern Baptist Convention who met to restate, reaffirm, and reemphasize the fundamentals of the New Testament faith. Laws wrote in the *Watchman-Examiner*: "The movement itself will never die, because always there will be men brave enough to contend earnestly for the faith delivered once for all the saints."[56]

The most famous of the Bible conferences was not Niagara but the conference at Northfield, Massachusetts, originating in 1880, which was linked to Dwight L. Moody (1837–1899). The first conference was attended by some three hundred persons, among whom was a delegation from Britain including his friend and Baptist preacher F. B. Meyer,[57] and was mainly for a "convocation for prayer."[58] When Moody convened the first Northfield conference he had chosen speakers who were predominantly leaders of the millenarian conferences. Moody himself did not reject millenarianism or object to the presence of millenarians on the speakers list. They were nearly always dominant throughout the years of the conference's existence which gave a national platform from which to teach and to establish themselves as reputable Protestant leaders. These same leaders appeared with nonmillenarian conservatives which helped to strengthen the relationships between millenarians and conservatives within the Baptist and Presbyterian denominations. But even Moody could go too far. There were limits to teachings that conservatives and millenarians alike would accept. Thus, Moody was criticized on occasion for extending invitations to those in Britain and America whose views ran too far to the left or right of perceived orthodoxy.[59] This may explain why there is no record of Moody extending an invitation to Govett. Yet, while there is no indication from Moody's writings that he knew of Govett, Moody is respectfully remembered in Govett's *Exposition of the Gospel of St. John* as "one who gathered in where others have

---

56. Peter A. Huff, *What Are They Saying About Fundamentalism?* (Mahwah, NJ: Paulist, 2008) 40–41. See also, Robert A. Ashworth, "The Fundamentalist Movement Among the Baptists," *The Journal of Religion* 4, no. 6 (1924) 611–31.

57. Albert Shaw, ed., *The American Monthly Review of Reviews* 21 (1900) 173.

58. Arthur T. Pierson, *Forward Movements of the Last Half Century* (New York: Funk & Wagnalls, 1900) 155.

59. Sandeen, *The Roots of Fundamentalism*, 175–76.

sown. He has pressed souls to decision who formerly have been instructed about Christ, but had not actually received him."[60]

All of these factors created a climate in which extreme views on the subject of the imminent return of Christ were regarded with skepticism. Prophetic teaching that tended to unite was preferred by both millenarians and denominational conservatives and served to keep the numbers of attendees at the Bible conferences growing. In this climate Govett's general commentaries, such as *The Apocalypse: Expounded by Scripture*, were accepted and promoted,[61] but his doctrine of exclusion—for which he was most often know—was neither presented nor endorsed.

But one more historical event would occur that changed the course of dispensationalism and restrained Govett's contributions of a half century. That event was the publication of the *Scofield Reference Bible* in 1909. It was not written in isolation, but was a byproduct of the millenarian surge that had preceded it for several decades in America. Its author was Cyrus I. Scofield (1843–1921) and his early Christian life was inextricably shaped by the lives of leaders who were helping to define and promote the American dispensational experience. One such leader who was essential to the life of Scofield and to the implementation of the Reference Bible was James H. Brookes (1830–1897).

Brookes was pastor of Washington and Compton Avenue Presbyterian Church in St. Louis, Missouri, and was the man who discipled Scofield in his early years as a Christian.[62] Scofield was also in attendance at Moody's 1879 crusade in St. Louis, Missouri, and it was during this time that he made a commitment to Christ.[63] It was Brookes who became an early convert to dispensationalism in America, a widely read author on the subject, and a leader of the Niagara conferences.[64] Scofield became attracted to the Niagara conferences and although he was not a major speaker at these conferences he was increasingly in demand across the country and less available to the church

---

60. Robert Govett, *Exposition of the Gospel of St. John* (London: Bemrose & Sons, 1881) 1:170.

61. See, for instance, Nathaniel West, *The Thousand Year Reign of Christ* (Grand Rapids: Kregel, 1993) 251; George C. Needham, *Prophetic Studies of the International Prophetic Conference (Chicago, November, 1886)* (Chicago: Revell, 1886) n.p.

62. Sweetnam, "Theological Roots," 76.

63. Colin Standish and Russell R. Standish, *The Perils of Ecumenism* (Rapidan: Hartland, 2003) 213. See also Joseph M. Canfield's account in *The Incredible Scofield and His Book*, rev. ed. (Vallecito: Ross, 2004) 198–99.

64. Yaakov Ariel, *An Unusual Relationship: Evangelical Christians and Jews* (New York: New York University Press, 2013) 62.

he pastored in Dallas, Texas. Moody also had a connection to Scofield.[65] In 1895 Scofield accepted the pulpit of Moody's home church in Northfield, Massachusetts. And when Moody died four years later it was Scofield that presided over the funeral. Soon after, in 1901, he and several other summer conference circuit veterans started their own conference venue at Sea Cliff, New York. Among the speakers of this new conference was Arno C. Gaebelein, editor of *Our Hope*. It was at the Sea Cliff Bible Conference that for the first time Scofield mentioned to Gaebelein his idea to develop and publish a study Bible. Gaebelein encouraged him and over the span of seven years helped Scofield give theological shape to the Bible's marginal notes.[66] It was in this latter part of Scofield's life that he was taken up with the effort to publish the Scofield Reference Bible[67] whose credibility was enhanced by the publisher being the New York office of the Oxford University Press. The outstanding features of Darby's redemptive-historical theology were popularized by Scofield despite occasional questions about character, his divorce, and old allegations of financial irregularities.[68] His intent was to produce a Bible with reference notes that faithfully explain the Bible's teaching without undue intrusion of distinctive theological ideas.[69] The publication of Scofield's Reference Bible had great impact upon the spread of dispensationalism in America, as well as the development of competing systems of thought. As dispensationalism grew, however, there was less room for variant forms and those who espoused them—such as Govett—found their published work less acceptable. Yet, as popular as the Scofield Reference Bible was to become, it had its early detractors.

The appearance of the Scofield Reference Bible was not without criticism from within the evangelical community. For instance, Philip Mauro (1859–1952) expressed his concern for the "modern system" of dispensationalism and the acceptance of the recently published Scofield Reference Bible which was exerting great influence upon orthodox Christians. He warns in his book *The Gospel of the Kingdom: With an Examination of Modern Dispensationalism* that "the main vehicle of the new system of doctrine

65. Standish, *The Perils of Ecumenism*, 213.

66. R. Todd Mangum, "Cyrus Ingerson Scofield: A Controversial Life," in R. Todd Mangum and Mark S. Sweetnam, *The Scofield Bible: Its History and Impact on the Evangelical Church* (Colorado Springs: Paternoster, 2009) 15.

67. *The Scofield Reference Bible* (New York: Oxford University Press, 1909).

68. See Joseph M. Canfield, *The Incredible Scofield and His Book*, rev. ed. (Vallecito: Ross, 2004).

69. R. Todd Mangum, "The Theology of the Scofield Reference Bible," in R. Todd Mangum and Mark S. Sweetnam, *The Scofield Bible: Its History and Impact on the Evangelical Church* (Colorado Springs: Paternoster, 2009) 93.

referred to has usurped the place of authority that belongs to God's Bible alone."[70] But complicating the matter was the fact that Mauro held differing beliefs than that of the dispensationalists. In his writings he observes that the Kingdom of Heaven began at Pentecost and continues to the resurrection of the saints, and is to be followed immediately by the Kingdom of the Son of Man. The latter, he claimed, is also the Kingdom of God, but it is not the Kingdom of Heaven.[71] In part, his disagreement with Scofield was that in his Bible the corrupt words of mortal man are printed on the same page with the holy Word of God, made for sale, entitled the Bible, and distinguished by a man's name. Although in close fellowship with the Brethren movement for many years he had turned from much of their teachings and now found dispensationalism to be in error.[72] He was particularly offended by how the advertisements surrounding the promotion of the Scofield Reference Bible exclaimed that there can be "no adequate understanding or rightly dividing the Word of God except from the standpoint of dispensational truth."[73] Mauro declared that it is mainly due to this "cleverly executed work that dispensationalism owes its popularity."

Nevertheless, Scofield's Bible came along at a time when much debate was intensifying over various points of interpretation and chronology in dispensationalism. This was especially true regarding the doctrine and timing of the secret rapture. Debate was so intense between Robert Cameron's postribulationist party and the Scofield-Gaebelein pretribulationist party that it led to the demise of the Niagara Bible Conference series in 1901. It was also at the turn of the century that pretribulationism surfaced as the dominant view of the dispensationalists. And it was the huge success of the Scofield Reference Bible, published in 1909, that kept it that way.[74] Paul Reiter remarks that the final product of the Niagara cooperation was the Scofield Reference Bible.[75] The new Bible featured a system of annotations and cross-references with classic dispensational divisions that emphasized a Darbyite understanding of Scripture. Scofield's notes accentuated the im-

70. Philip Mauro, *The Gospel of the Kingdom: With an Examination of Modern Dispensationalism* (Boston: Hamilton Bros., 1928) 5.

71. Philip Mauro, *After This or the Church, the Kingdom, and the Glory* (New York: Revell, 1918) 73.

72. Gordon P. Gardiner, *Champion of the Kingdom: The Story of Philip Mauro* (Brooklyn: Bread of Life, 1961).

73. Mauro, *The Gospel of the Kingdom*, 6.

74. Dorrien, *The Remaking of Evangelical Theology*, 31.

75. Paul R. Reiter, "A History of the Development of the Rapture Positions," in Gleason L. Archer, ed., *Three Views on the Rapture: Pre-, Mid-, or Post-Tribulation* (Grand Rapids: Zondervan, 1996) 24.

minent Second Coming of Christ and the pretribulationist secret Rapture of the church. And while Govett's numerous works spoke in great detail on the subject of the Rapture there is no evidence that Scofield relied upon them or was specifically aware of his writings as Scofield never referenced them by name; although it is not likely that he would have been ignorant of Govett's existence since his name appeared in pretribulation-oriented print culture in America from time to time.

From 1909 until the mid-century pretribulational dispensationalism continued to advance under its institutional base and the leadership of men like James M. Gray at Moody Bible Institute, Ruben A. Torrey at the Bible Institute of Los Angeles, Harry A. Ironside at Moody Memorial Church, and Lewis Sperry Chafer at the Evangelical Theological College (later named Dallas Theological Seminary). In contrast, post-tribulational theology after the fall of the Niagara conferences lacked institutional base and leadership, or extensive literature to counter the teachings of the pretribulationalists.[76] Twentieth-century evangelicals continued to adhere to premillennial options, at a popular level at least, and particularly within North America. The eschatological preferences of Anglo-American fundamentalists reiterated the basic themes of nineteenth-century futurism. At the same time the dispensational approach was provided with classic expression in the Scofield Reference Bible.[77] Pretribulational dispensationalism under the classical approach taught in the Scofield Reference Bible continued its advance and adherents had their pick of institutions through which to learn its theology. Scofield himself entered into the field of education. He became interested in developing an institute on the East Coast, filling a role similar to Moody's institute in the Midwest. It was opened in 1914 and was called the Philadelphia School of the Bible.[78] As the entrenched classical dispensationalism model of millennialism took deeper root in America other variant forms fell into disfavor. By 1924 this process was aided by the identification of an ideological center for its training in the founding of the Evangelical Theological College (later named Dallas Theological Seminary). Its founder was a Scofield acolyte, Lewis Sperry Chafer. Chafer was an ordained Presbyterian minister who did more than anyone else to provide a steady theological foundation.[79] He provided the movement with its first systematic theology.[80] It was an expansive, eight volume work that took ten

---

76. Reiter, "A History of the Development of the Rapture Positions," 24.
77. Gribben, "Evangelical Eschatology and the Puritan Hope," 384.
78. Canfield, *The Incredible Scofield and His Book*, 328.
79. Gribben, *Trans-Atlantic World*, 104.
80. Lewis Sperry Chafer, *Systematic Theology* (Dallas: Dallas Seminary Press, 1947).

years to complete. But with its development classical dispensationalism was set upon a firm theological foundation which left diminishing room for common ground with those prophetic systems that strayed from the prescribed theological path. Govett and his increasingly controversial Rapture theory was no exception.

The eclipsing of Govett from conversation and scholarship so soon after his death could have been anticipated if for no other reason than from a pragmatic perspective. It was reported in several obituary articles that he became more reclusive in the latter part of his life.[81] He was a man who showed no interest in international travel or personal promotion of his theology. Without this exposure one could not expect him to retain the small amount of influence that he once held. This became especially evident as the center of the emerging dispensational movement shifted across the Atlantic to America and as dispensationalism was codified at Bible conferences which he did not attend and did not participate in as a speaker. And as publications proliferated in the latter part of the nineteenth century in America he did not contribute.

An Occasional Remembrance

Ernest Sandeen in his extensively researched book *The Roots of Fundamentalism* recalls something of Govett's contribution to the writings on the Rapture by noting that he was a "perpetual controversialist and author of more than twenty books and tracts." Sandeen suspects that Govett's doctrines were influenced by Darby and other Brethren teachers, while conceding that Govett presented himself as one who defined his own position.[82] This is an example of what has commonly resulted from the disappearance of Govett as author. And as he has been largely ignored for over a century, with the preponderance of his works no longer known, he is easily characterized as one who merely sought to stir debate. A simple knowledge of the reviews of Govett's writings would quickly correct the assessment. For example, Govett's tract, *The Kid in Milk*, was reviewed in *The Voice Upon the Mountains*, the title of his work being taken from Exodus 23:19, "thou shalt not boil a kid in its mother's milk."[83] The journal was impressed with his handling of the text in which Govett finds that the Lord's Word is intended

---

81. See Norfolk Records Office file FC76/59 parts 1 and 2.
82. Sandeen, *The Roots of Fundamentalism*, 88.
83. Robert Govett, *The Kid in Milk: or, the Second Covenant on Sinai* (London: printed by the inmates of the Girls' Industrial Orphan Home, 1868); *The Voice upon the Mountains: A Journal of Prophetic Testimony and Evangelistic Effort* 2 (1868) 73.

to edify the soul and nourish it in faith.[84] In fairness, respected scholars such as Sandeen have had little to draw upon in framing conclusions concerning Govett's true contributions to pretribulational dispensationalism. Sandeen is not alone. When Panton ceased publishing Govett's work in *Dawn* at the end of the second decade of the twentieth century, his work was largely relegated to the archives of his former church, Surrey Chapel, and to the personal libraries of a few adherents, mostly in England.

Occasionally Govett's contributions to print culture have focused exclusively on his biblical scholarship and with it he appears to get a less biased assessment of his contributions. Wilbur M. Smith, for instance, in *A Preliminary Bibliography for the Study of Biblical Prophecy* (1952), believed that Govett's 629-page abridgement of the four-volume work *The Apocalypse: Expounded by Scripture* (1861–1865) brought to his interpretation "a more thorough knowledge of the Scriptures in their bearing on the last book of the Bible than any other writer of his generation."[85] One writer that followed the biblical interpretations of Govett, including his doctrine of exclusion, was the Chinese church leader Watchman Nee (1903–1972). His books span from the mid-1920s until his death.[86] In the translator's preface to *Come, Lord Jesus: A Study of the Book of Revelation* it gives the following credit: "In the study of prophecy our brother followed the approach of such people as G. M. Pember, Robert Govett and D. M. Panton, though he no doubt had his own original views and interpretations."[87] Isolating upon Govett's doctrine of exclusion, Wilbur E. Smith in the preface to his book *The Real Thing: An Exhortation for the Christian Life* (2010) writes that in desiring a deeper Christian faith God had directed him to several seemingly forgotten teachers of old, including Govett. He speaks of discovering the doctrine of exclusion and suggests to his readers that if they are unfamiliar with it they should become acquainted with the writings of Robert Govett among several others. He cautions that "few, if any, churches in America

---

84. Ibid., 73.

85. Wilbur M. Smith, *A Preliminary Bibliography for the Study of Biblical Prophecy* (Boston: Wilde, 1952) 28.

86. Watchman Nee has an interesting connection with Govett's church, Surrey Chapel. Archival records indicate that Govett's church supported missions work in China. Under D. M. Panton's leadership support apparently continued as there is a letter held in the archives of Schoettle Publishing Co. written by Margaret Barber, a British missionary in south China, to Panton dated 2 April 1926, in which she cautions that Nee is in "great danger" because he has a "mental apprehension of God's Truth which unless lived out will be his peril."

87. Watchman Nee, *Come, Lord Jesus: A Study of the Book of Revelation* (New York: Christian Fellowship, 1976) n.p.

would invite Robert Govett or G. H. Pember . . . to preach from their pulpit, were they alive today."[88]

Still, it is far more common to find Govett ignored and the doctrine of exclusion, while seldom assigned to Govett as its originator, dismissed. Charles C. Ryrie, former professor of Systematic Theology at Dallas Theological Seminary, author of the book *Dispensationalism Today*,[89] former president of Philadelphia College of the Bible (now Cairn University), is also author of an article in *Israel My Glory* entitled "Why I Am a Pretribulation Rapturist." Ryrie defines five views of the Rapture. One of those five is the "partial rapture" view. His tone is filled with sarcasm and intentionally dismissive: "If you're a good Christian, you go first. If not, you'll languish in a sort of Protestant purgatory and then be raptured as you shape up."[90] His remarks tell of the limited tolerance many dispensational authors have toward opposing views of a pretribulation rapture. In 2004 Tim LaHaye, coauthor of the Left Behind series, edited a book entitled *The Popular Encyclopedia of Bible Prophecy* in which an explanation of the "partial rapture" theory appeared. Similar to Ryrie, the coauthors of the article were also dismissive of the notion of partial rapture, stating that it fails to be convincing "for numerous other reasons," and concluding with an assessment that warning Christians in their personal lives to be cautious concerning the Rapture has nothing to do with determining who might or might not be excluded. The coauthors emphatically state that the "ultimate resolution of this issue rests upon a proper understanding of the doctrine of salvation and a clear exegesis of the biblical passages about the rapture."[91] Such an assessment clearly disregards the solemn debate which took place in the nineteenth century over these crucial theological positions. They give no mention of Govett who, based upon his historical track record, would have vehemently disagreed with their dismissive conclusions. A further example is John Whitcomb who also dismisses the concept of a "partial rapture": "If that is the qualification God has for us then none of us can be raptured, for

---

88. Wilbur E. Smith, *The Real Thing: An Exhortation for the Authentic Christian Life* (Grove City: Livingwalk, 2010) 46.

89. Charles C. Ryrie, *Dispensationalism Today*, 2nd edition (Chicago: Moody Bible Institute, 1965). The forward is written by Frank E. Gaebelein, son of A. C. Gaebelein influential dispensational leader who encouraged Scofield in the writing of the Scofield Reference Bible.

90. Charles C. Ryrie, "Why I Am a Pretribulation Rapturist," *Israel My Glory* (2012) 30.

91. Elmer Towns and Richard Mayhue, "Partial Rapture," in Tim LaHaye and Ed Hindson, eds., *The Popular Encyclopedia of Bible Prophecy* (Eugene, OR: Harvest House, 2004) 261–62.

none of us is worthy."[92] These challenges to beliefs are not new to dispensationalism. Throughout the twentieth century longstanding and universally held dispensational positions were challenged, clarified, and changed. In 1999 Herbert Bateman served as general editor of *Three Central Issues in Contemporary Dispensationalism*, a book in which articles were written by faculty members of Dallas Theological Seminary. Bateman contends that dispensationalism is still under systematization and development because it is driven by Scripture and a desire to determine the infallibility of the text. But he shifts the paradigm away from the arguments of the later half of the nineteenth century and the first half of the twentieth century to a new emphasis. What now unites the new dispensational thinkers is the basic unifying issue that Israel is not the church.[93]

The mounting differences within dispensationalism have created concern as tensions within dispensationalism have increased in recent history. The tension, in part, has been caused by confusion brought about by the increase in dispensationally oriented fictional writings which demonstrate a lack of concern for strict accuracy. Mark Sweetnam notes that this occurs in the "often-complex discussion of the prophetic framework implied in the novels."[94] Critics have paid too little attention to the warning given by one of the leading historians of the Plymouth Brethren—one of the most dispensationally based movements. F. Roy Coad cautioned in 1966 against oversimplification: "We shall rarely find in practice that our fellows will fall neatly into our mental categories . . . we shall be the better Christians if we refrain from extending the orderliness of disciplined minds to the placing of neat little labels on our fellow men."[95] In such a theologically confusing time, Scofield's Philadelphia School of the Bible renamed itself in 2012 to Cairn University and removed any mention of dispensationalism from its published purpose statement designed to inform incoming students. Paul S. Boyer, in his book *When Time Shall be No More* (1992) tells his readers that the conviction that the course of history and the sequence of events found in the Bible which will announce the end of the world have received

---

92. John C. Whitcomb, *The Rapture and Beyond* (Waxhaw: Kainos, 2012) 19.

93. Herbert W. Bateman, IV, ed., *Three Central Issues in Contemporary Dispensationalism: A Comparison of Traditional and Progressive Views* (Grand Rapids: Kregel, 1999) 307–8.

94. Mark Sweetnam, "Tensions in Dispensational Eschatology," in Kenneth G. C. Newport and Crawford Gribben, eds., *Expecting the End: Millennialism in Social and Historical Context* (Waco: Baylor University Press, 2006) 173.

95. Frederick Roy Coad, "Prophetic Developments with Particular Reference to the Early Brethren Movement," *Occasional Paper Number 2* (Pinner, Middlesex: Christian Brethren Research Fellowship, 1966).

little scholarly attention.⁹⁶ But this viewpoint can no longer be maintained in light of the success of the *Left Behind* series and the growing collection of rapture-based fictional books and apocalyptic-oriented movies. In their wake critics and commentators have reacted to the phenomenon in increasing numbers. Nevertheless, they have tended to do so with less than strict accuracy.⁹⁷ Given the continued shifts in dispensational thinking and the current digression of accuracy often portrayed in fictional writing it is improbable that Spurgeon's prediction uttered in 1881 will come to pass: "The day will come when the idols of the hour will perish, and the writings of such men as R. Govett will be prized as much fine gold."⁹⁸ In Spurgeon's mind it was only a matter of time before Govett would be prized.

As late as 1 February 1966, the Reverend M. Guthrie Clark, St John's Vicarage, Parkstone-Poole, Dorset, inquired in an advertisement in the *Eastern Daily Times* "I am investigating the career and ministry of the late Robert Govett . . . but it is proving very difficult to get information. As far as I am aware no memoir was ever published, and his books do not shed much light on the details of his life."⁹⁹ No record of communication exists beyond this enquiry and no evidence that Reverend Clark ever made his findings known to the public.

One hundred years after Spurgeon's predictions that Govett's writings would someday be prized, Lewis Schoettle, founder of Schoettle Publishing Company in Hiawassee, Georgia, has attempted to revive the interest in Govett's writings by republishing nearly all of his original books and combining a number of his tracts on various subjects into books.¹⁰⁰ The publishing company has also republished the works of G. H. Pember, D. M. Panton, and G. H. Lang, among others, that deal with the subject of partial rapture. Since the 1980s, Schoettle has catered to a small but enthusiastic group of readers from within evangelical circles. In higher education, a few university libraries have also purchased Govett's books.¹⁰¹

96. Paul S. Boyer, *When Time Shall be No More: Prophecy Belief in Modern American Culture* (Cambridge, MA: Belknap, 1992) ix.

97. Sweetnam, "Tensions in Dispensational Eschatology," 173.

98. *The Sword and the Trowel; a Record of Combat with Sin and of Labor for the Lord* (1881) 480.

99. "Robert Govett," *Eastern Daily Times* (1 February 1966).

100. Schoettle Publishing on occasion combined tracts into books. See, for example, *Govett on the Parables* (Miami Springs: Schoettle, 1989).

101. For example, in 1989 Schoettle combined a series of fourteen Govett tracts and sold them as a book titled *Kingdom Studies*. According to the website "WorldCat" *Kingdom Studies* can be found in the library collection of nine universities and seminaries in America. The most widely known of Govett's books, *Entrance into the Kingdom; or, Reward according to Works*, according to the "Copac" website (http://copac.ac.uk/),

Retrospectively, at Govett's memorial service several clergy spoke to a full chapel. One of them had these remarks: "Should his life be ever written one of the most interesting things in it would be the letters full of praise and full of approval, that he had received from Charles Haddon Spurgeon."[102] Undoubtedly he was a great man in the Word of God, and he was brave in his determination at any cost to carry its precepts into effect."[103] Nevertheless, just three decades after Govett's death a letter to the editor of a local Norwich newspaper in 1937 contained this lament, "Today he is all but forgotten, but there was a time when he was a notable figure in our city. Who then was he?"[104] This thesis has answered that question.

---

exists in seven universities in Great Britain (holdings were all published prior to 1900). In America, the book exists in the collections of 37 university libraries (see WorldCat website: http://www.worldcat.org/).

102. Three of the letters remain. See Norfolk Records Office file FC76/59 part 1 of 2.

103. "The Rev. R. Govett," obituary article. Newspaper not identified. Norfolk Records Office file FC76/59 part 1 of 2.

104. "The Founder of Surrey Chapel," Newspaper not identified (20 August 1937). Norfolk Records Office file FC76/59 part 1 of 2.

CHAPTER 7

Conclusion

THIS STUDY HAS EXAMINED Robert Govett, nineteenth-century author and pastor, in light of his contribution to the debate about the "last things" in the print culture of the Victorian era. In order to place Govett's life into context this work provides a succinct historic overview of the rise in evangelicalism and religious dissent in England from the sixteenth century to the turn of the twentieth century. It traces the shifts from post to premillennial thinking and encompasses the debate over millennialism as it shifts in popularity from the historicist to the futurist interpretation of Revelation. The work provides a biography of Govett's life drawn from original documents maintained primarily in government archives in Norwich, England, and Schoettle Publishing in Georgia, USA. The work also traces Govett's engagement with print culture over the span of a half-century with concentration upon the doctrines of baptism and the Rapture. It also introduces the development of dispensationalism, its later spread in America during the second half of the nineteenth century into the twentieth century, and that spread's direct impact upon the disappearance of Govett's writings and contributions on both sides of the Atlantic.

This study has been informed by a thorough engagement with Govett's voluminous published output. At the same time it has demonstrated that while Govett had initial appeal in print culture he was never more than a minor figure in comparison to the popularity of some preachers and theologians of his day. This was mostly due to the perception that he was a rather eccentric figure because of his developing idiosyncratic theological position on eschatology. At the same time, this study has demonstrated the complexity of an accurate understanding of Dissenting culture in the Victorian period, as well as the vitality of debate. Govett's work has contributed to a furthering of understanding that there existed in his day a theological complexity that has often tended to be presented in very monolithic ways by historians.

Particular attention has been drawn to events and correspondence leading up to what was the single-most pivotal event in Govett's life—his conclusion in 1844 that adult baptism, in the context of faith in Christ, was scripturally correct and that infant baptism was theologically invalid. This conviction, along with his own baptism, which appears to have been swiftly reached, caused the immediate removal of his right to preach in the Church of England and began a compendium of tracts on the subject and an interest in conveying its importance that lasted throughout the remainder of his life. As a scriptural imperative the doctrine was also determined by Govett to be inexorably connected to the faithful believer's entrance into the Coming Kingdom of Christ. Govett declared baptism to not only be an act performed as the visible sign of a believer's commitment of faith in Christ, but just as importantly, as a necessary requirement for entrance into his Coming Kingdom. The event of the Rapture which allows for entrance was to be "pretribulational" and "premillennial" and was in keeping with the dispensational theology he embraced.

It is not known when Govett first embraced a belief in a dispensational system of theology. But it is apparent that from his earliest writings, such as *Isaiah Unfulfilled* (1841)[1] and *The Revelation of St. John* (1843),[2] his frame of theological reference was decidedly dispensational and his understanding of Scriptural prophecy was both literal and future. Some contemporary scholars have suggested that Govett adopted his dispensational understanding of Scripture from Darby and Brethren leaders, but there is no indication in his writings that this was the case.[3] To the contrary, there is ample proof that Govett found much wrong with Darby's theological conclusions. For instance, Govett opposed Darby's stance on imputed righteousness, as did *The Voice of Truth*, which reported that Darby held that the "imputed righteousness of Christ is nowhere to be found in Scripture, nor is it necessary to

---

1. Robert Govett, *Isaiah Unfulfilled: Being an Exposition of the Prophet; with New Version and Critical Notes to which are Added Two Dissertations One on the "Sons of God" and "Giants" of Genesis VI and the Other a Comparative Estimate of the Hebrew and Greek Texts* (London: Nisbet, 1841).

2. Robert Govett, *The Revelation of St. John, Literal and Future: Being an Exposition of that Book: To which are Added Remarks in Refutation of the Ideas that the Pope is the Man of Sin, and that Popery is the Apostasy Predicted by St. Paul, with a Special Reference to Doctor O'Sullivan on the Apostasy* (London: Hamilton, Adams , 1843).

3. See, for example, Ernest R. Sandeen, *The Roots of Fundamentalism*, 88.

a sinner's justification."[4] Govett also interjected himself into the controversy that developed between Benjamin Wills Newton and Darby over Brethren commitments to "open" or "closed" Communion, by publishing *Open or Strict Communion? Judgment Pronounced on the Question by the Lord Jesus Himself*. He notes: "Our standard still is the rule of our Master—who has taught us to prefer mercy to sacrifice, and the edification of his disciples before the exactitude of any ceremony whatever."[5] Govett strongly opposed any scriptural conclusions held by others when he determined the presence of biblical error and he sought to communicate the error in order that the church would not be deceived. A telling look into Govett's lifelong pursuit of biblical understanding and communication of its truth can be found in a letter written to a friend in 1900. The letter contained an explanation of the Lord's Supper as found in Paul's writings. He explained that he "began prayerfully to study the New Testament thereon. And having now arrived at some conclusions which seem to me clear and Scriptural, I commend them to your prayerful regard. To me now the subject of the Lord's Supper is full of momentous import and blessing."[6]

But Govett's most ardent defense of Scripture occurred with his understanding of the Rapture. He developed a theological perspective of exclusion for believers which was to occur at the Rapture. By his own assertion, this theological perspective originated with him. It is a position that he held and continually honed throughout his life. How or why these thoughts of the Rapture began to unfold in his mind are not known and can only be observed as a cogently definable doctrine by examining his early writings. The earliest of these writings appear in a series of tracts on the parables published in 1845 and 1846. The doctrine of exclusion is alluded to in many of these early tracts, such as *The Parable of the Hid Treasure Explained* (1845).[7] It surfaces with more definition in *All Believers Interested in the Parable of*

---

4. "Reviews," *The Voice of Truth; or, Strict Baptist Magazine* 2 (1864) 138. See also Robert Govett, *Address to the Christians Commonly Called Plymouth Brethren on Liberty of Ministry and Gift* (Norwich: Fletcher, 1847).

5. Robert Govett, *Open Or Strict Communion? Judgment Pronounced on the Question by the Lord Jesus Himself* (Norwich: Fletcher, 1845) 36. See also, Jonathan Burnham, "The Controversial Relationship Between Benjamin Wills Newton and John Nelson Darby," DPhil thesis, University of Oxford, 1999.

6. The letter was turned into a fifteen-page tract entitled *The Lord's Supper as Presented by the Apostle Paul: A Letter to a Friend* (R. Govett, A.D. 1900). No publisher information is given. Source: bound publications archived in the "Govett Room," Surrey Chapel, Norwich.

7. Robert Govett, *The Parable of the Hid Treasure Explained* (Hull: Anderson, 1845).

the Virgins (1846),[8] and is then precisely articulated in 1850 with the publishing of *Reward According to Works*.[9]

His futurist understanding of prophecy provided ample opportunity, for one so inclined to write in multiple venues, to speak to controversial matters such as the debate over the Antichrist, whether the Rapture was to be understood as "secret" and "invisible," or whether there was a Hell that exacted eternal punishment. Concerning the latter, Govett's book *Eternal Suffering of the Wicked* was referenced as part of a two-part series on eternal punishment in the *Methodist Quarterly*.[10] The articles were based upon a total of five books and one magazine article that had been recently published on the subject.[11] It is clear from the articles that there existed at the time a controversy over eternal punishment which was creating a substantial amount of literature and polarization over the subject. The articles describe Govett to be a believer in literal fire as the mode of punishment for those condemned to Hell. One also describes him as one who "displays a complete mastery of the Scriptures . . . and his treatment of the various subjects displays considerable mental aptness in perceiving the weak points in an argument."[12] His articles and tracts were written to refute the historicist position that declared the Antichrist to be associated with the Roman Catholic Church. Govett opposed their position on grounds that the appearing of the Antichrist was yet future. According to Kenneth Newport a major point among Protestant historicist interpreters concerned the identity of Antichrist. It was upon this point that nearly all Protestant commentators agreed and was a view that was quickly developed. This view, combined with the year-day principle (which held that one day in prophetic time periods is equal to a literal year), paved the way for very precise prophetic

---

8. Robert Govett, *All Believers Interested in the Parable of the Virgins: Matthew XXV, 1* (Norwich: Fletcher, 1846) 39. See also Robert Govett, *Supplement to the Ten Virgins* (Norwich: Fletcher, 1846).

9. Robert Govett, *Reward according to Works* (Norwich: Fletcher and Son, 1850).

10. Robert Govett, *Eternal Suffering of the Wicked* (London: Nisbet, 1871).

11. In addition to Robert Govett's work, the article relied upon the following publications: M. Rander, *For Ever, an Essay on Eternal Punishment* (London: Wesleyan Conference Office, 1871); T. R. Birks, *The Victory of Divine Goodness* (London: Rivington, 1870); James William Barlow, *Eternal Punishment and Eternal Death, an Essay* (London: Longman, 1865); Henry Constable, *The Duration and Nature of Future Punishment*, 3rd ed. (London: Longman, 1870); *The Rainbow, a Magazine of Christian Literature, with Special Reference to the Revealed Future of the Church and the World* 6 (1869).

12. "Eternal Punishment," *The Methodist Quarterly: A Journal of Theological and General Literature* 5 (1871) 268. See also "As to the Meaning of 'Life' and 'Death,'" *The Methodist Quarterly: A Journal of Theological and General Literature* 5 (1871) 278–97.

calculations."[13] Postmillennialists, then, looked with general confidence to the future as they waited and expected to see the purposes of God being worked out through the medium of human agents.[14]

As Govett engaged the historicists and postmillennialists his arguments were always centered in his interpretation of Scripture rather than opinions gleaned from others. He was equally comfortable drawing proof from the Old Testament as he was from the New Testament. He was skilled in the use of the original biblical languages, and equally comfortable relating the thoughts of the early divines and the writings of contemporaries. Yet, while he busied himself in what appeared to be a constant flow of writing, his writings never achieved the fame or stature of one such as Darby.[15] The principle reason for this is due to the fact that Govett intentionally chose to remain a pastor and believed his first obligation was to his congregation. He did not travel and speak in an effort to garner support for his theological findings. He traveled only as demand dictated to mount a pulpit to deliver a sermon and usually only within relatively short distances from Norwich. There is no evidence that he ever traveled outside of England, although his writings were known and valued by some in America. For instance, his name was mentioned in an American publication of the proceedings of the International Prophetic Conference held in Chicago, 1886. He is listed among other prominent English authors of prophecy, including Michael P. Baxter, editor of the *Christian Herald*.[16]

Govett was a very prolific writer, but appears to have written from the isolation of his parsonage. This was especially true during the last years of his life. Although many of his theological positions were controversial he never sought personal fame; although it was evident that others recognized his abilities and thus he was called upon to speak periodically in various evangelical churches—among them Baptist churches. Perhaps because of this it is sometimes reported that Govett was a Baptist. On a number of reported occasions Govett was invited to speak at special events and services. One such occasion was the memorial service and burial of Mrs. Keen, the wife of a Baptist pastor formerly of Waltham Abbey, who passed away on 16 September

---

13. Kenneth G. C. Newport, *Apocalypse and Millennium: Studies in Biblical Eisegesis* (Cambridge: Cambridge University Press, 2000) 10.

14. Newport, *Apocalypse and Millennium*, 14.

15. Govett's known volume of published books and tracts included a total of: 29 in the 1840s; 23 in the 1850s; 22 in the 1860s; 37 in the 1870s; 32 in the 1880s; 12 in the 1890s; as well as a number of books and tracts that cannot be specifically dated to include: 11 ca. 1840s; 2 ca. 1870–1895; and 15 whose dates cannot be verified.

16. George C. Needham, *Prophetic Studies of the International Prophetic Conference (Chicago, November, 1886)* (Chicago: Revell, 1886) n.p.

1853. At her request Govett officiated at her funeral.[17] On another occasion an announcement was published in *The Gospel Herald* notifying its readers of the anniversary of the Baptist church, Gildencraft, Norwich. The article mentions Govett as participating with an address in the first year anniversary of this new independent Baptist church in Norwich.[18]

Nevertheless, Govett remained unaffiliated with any denomination once he left the Church of England. The *Eastern Daily Press* in an obituary article reported that Govett's congregation never affiliated itself with any existing denomination and preferred to be known merely as Christians. In the early days of the congregation, when they met in temporary space in the Victoria Hall they were sometimes alluded to as "the saints assembled at the bazaar," and among the general population of the city the congregation was on occasion spoken of as "Govettites."[19] But the misapplied affiliation to the Baptists may further be due to the doctrinal direction of his writings. Spurgeon's *The Sword and the Trowel* remarked, "Although Mr. Govett would decline the name of Baptist, we venture to say for the sake of brevity that a more thorough Baptist commentary [*Exposition of the Gospel of St. John*] was never written."[20] He also maintained a cordial relationship with Spurgeon— a relationship that appears to have originated with Spurgeon. On at least one occasion Govett received an invitation to teach as a guest lecturer at his training school.[21] Govett's writings often appeared in Spurgeon's magazine and in a review of his tract entitled, *Christ Superior to Angels: A Comment on the Epistle to the Hebrews*, the editors of *The Sword and the Trowel* wrote: "We may differ from some of Mr. Govett's opinions, but we never differ from himself. This work is a valuable exposition of the epistle to the Hebrews, full of spiritual weight, light, and saviour. Our friend received his gospel, not of man, neither was he taught it, but he searched the Word for himself under the illumination of the Holy Ghost."[22] And, while there is no indication that Spurgeon himself agreed with all the fine points of Govett's eschatology, their

---

17. "Recent deaths," *The Baptist Magazine*, series 4, vol. 45 (1853) 703–6. See also "Death—Mrs. Keen," *The Primitive Church Magazine, Advocating the Constitution, Faith, and Practice of the Apostolic Churches* 9, no. 119 (1853) 378.

18. "Anniversary of the Baptist Church, Gildencraft, Norwich," *The Gospel Herald; or, Poor Christian's Magazine* 30–NS7 (1861) 267.

19. Norwich Records Office file FC76/94. *Eastern Daily Press* (21 February 1901).

20. *The Sword and the Trowel; a Record of Combat with Sin and of Labor for the Lord* (1881) 480.

21. Letter to Govett from Spurgeon dated 1879. Norfolk Records Office file FC76/59 (1 of 2).

22. *The Sword and the Trowel; a Record of Combat with Sin and of Labor for the Lord* (1885) 548.

was enough commonality in their premillennialism that they could agree on the need for the pursuit of holiness.[23]

This study has also established that criticisms of Govett's theological positions were treated harshly on occasion and directed toward him with a tone of personal attack. Govett's responses often appeared measured and a tone of respect for his opponent was typically present in his remarks. For instance, in his reply to Mr. Purdon in *The Rainbow*, he hoped "that we may have grace not to write bitterly of one another in the controversies which arise. Truth and love are sisters; let us not, in the fight for truth, plunge our sword into the bosom of love. The adversary will have vantage ground against us if he can say that we are just like any other men, and cannot keep our tempers when once we differ."[24]

Harsh attacks regarding Govett's polemics did not dissuade him from continuing his lifelong endeavor to communicate biblical truths. The importance of the Rapture and his concern that some Christians might fail to receive entry into the Millennial Kingdom continued to be of paramount concern to Govett. It was this doctrine of exclusion that caused the greatest difficulty for many theologians and religious leaders who were dispensationally oriented and might otherwise have accepted his teachings. Nowhere was this more true than in America. While dispensationalism became prominent among a growing number of evangelical fundamentalists in American religious circles, it was on the decline in Great Britain, a decline caused by a number of factors including the impact of higher criticism and a cultural crisis of faith which became more acute toward the close of the Victorian era. An indicator of this shift of concern over Govett's writings on the subject of exclusion can be observed from two perspectives. First, of the many obituary articles and remembrances which appeared in the press over a number of years subsequent to Govett's death, there is no specific mention of his doctrine of exclusion. The general mention of the "millenarian controversies" is present in some of the articles, his interest in matters of the Apocalypse is also mentioned, and more than a few of his prophetic books are named, but there is no mention of controversy over his unique pretribulational position on the Rapture.[25] At the same time, in America, dispensationalism was on the rise. It soon had a clear pattern of belief and direction. It grew in popularity due to a number of factors including Darby's visits to America and Canada and the personal promotion of his

23. Peter John Morden, "Communion with Christ and His People: The Spirituality of C. H. Spurgeon (1834–92)," PhD thesis, Spurgeon's College, 2010, 245.

24. *The Rainbow: A Magazine of Christian Literature, with Special Reference to the Revealed Future of the Church and the World* 2 (1865) 187.

25. See Norwich Records Office file FC76/94 and FC76/59.

CONCLUSION 219

theological system, the influence of the prolific Bible conferences with their pretribulational and dispensational leanings, and the growing number of colleges and seminaries founded upon the same leanings. Govett remained of interest as a scholar while dispensational interest increased during the latter years of the nineteenth century. And while there is no evidence that Govett ever traveled outside of Great Britain there is ample indication that during his lifetime he was well known in America. For example, Nathaniel West makes reference to him in his work originally published in 1889 entitled *The Thousand Years; Studies in Eschatology in Both Testaments* in which he lists Govett alongside several other reliable theologians concerning Old Testament prophecy.[26] Furthermore, Spurgeon's *The Sword and the Trowel* (1881) commends its American brethren to get a copy of Govett's two-volume work on the Gospel of St John.[27]

Yet, as dispensationalism emerged into the twentieth century, less room was allowed on both sides of the Atlantic for the notion that believers could be excluded from the Millennial Kingdom. And as so much of Govett's life work was intermingled with the doctrine of exclusion, it was inevitable that his writings would become ignored. The "partial rapture," as Govett's theory of exclusion was to become known, became merely one of the marginalized renderings on the subject of the Rapture. But the memory of the partial rapture endured after Govett had been forgotten: *Kept from the Hour* (1956), by Gerald B. Stanton, devotes a chapter on partial rapture but makes no mention of the originator of the idea.[28]

By the 1950s, long after Govett was forgotten, the debate and interest over the Rapture had been rekindled and its controversies heightened by a scathing attack upon pretribulationalism in Alexander Reese's book *The Approaching Advent of Christ* (1937) which had the effect of giving new life to the post-tribulational argument.[29] Robert H. Gundry in *The Church and the Tribulation* (1973) described Stanton's postulations as being "out of date, not to mention embarrassingly bombastic."[30] Also in the mid-1950s George E. Ladd published *The Blessed Hope* (1956). Ladd was a premillen-

26. Nathaniel West, *The Thousand Year Reign of Christ* (Grand Rapids: Kregel, 1993) 251.

27. *The Sword and the Trowel; a Record of Combat with Sin and of Labor for the Lord* (1881) 480.

28. See Gerald B. Stanton, *Kept from the Hour: A Systematic Study of the Rapture in Bible Prophecy* (Grand Rapids: Zondervan, 1956).

29. See Alexander Reese, *The Approaching Advent of Christ: An Examination of the Teaching of J. N. Darby and His Followers* (Grand Rapids: International, 1937).

30. See Robert H. Gundry, *The Church and the Tribulation* (Grand Rapids: Zondervan, 1973) 9.

nialist but did not support a pretribulation rapture. He points out that the reason why pretribulationism has held such an important place in prophetic teaching is that it has been thought to be inseparable from premillennialism and from biblical doctrine of the Second Coming of Christ.[31] In 1957 John F. Walvoord, former President of Dallas Theological Seminary, published *The Rapture Question* in which he brings into question the hermeneutical argument regarding post-tribulationalist's tendency to depart from normal literal interpretation, in contradiction to the approach of premillennialists.[32] In 1958 an extensive 633-page book on biblical eschatology was written by J. Dwight Pentecost entitled *Things to Come* in which he, like Walvoord, contends that the pretribulation Rapture rests upon the literal method of interpretation. He treats the partial rapture theory in some detail, mentioning Govett "as one" holding the view, but no credit for its origination.[33] Others followed in defense of the post-tribulational position including J. Barton Payne who wrote *The Imminent Appearing of Christ*.[34] Extremists and hoax controversialists eventually entered the discussion, such as Dave MacPherson who wrote a series of books on the pretribulational Rapture claiming it to have a "bizarre origin" and finding it heretical.[35] The debate over pretribulationalism and its scriptural accuracy continues and the viewpoints on the occasion of the Rapture are met with mixed acceptance. All the while, the memory of Govett wanes.

Reflections

In 1883 there appeared a hopeful note of remembrance in *The Sword and the Trowel* that read: "We only express our heart when we say that we venerate and admire this author and preacher, whose works will be more appreciated by future generations than by this frivolous age."[36] It is interesting to note

---

31. George E. Ladd, *The Blessed Hope: A Biblical Study of the Second Advent and the Rapture* (Grand Rapids: Eerdmans, 1956) 137.

32. See John F. Walvoord, *The Rapture Question* (Findlay: Dunham, 1957).

33. J. Dwight Pentecost, *Things to Come: A Study in Biblical Eschatology* (Findlay: Dunham, 1957) 158.

34. See J. Barton Payne, *The Imminent Appearing of Christ* (Grand Rapids: Eerdmans, 1962).

35. See Dave MacPherson, *The Unbelievable Pre-Trib Origin: The Recent Discovery of a Well-Known Theory's Beginning, and its Incredible Cover-up* (Kansas City: Heart of America Bible Society, 1973); *The Incredible Cover-up* (Medford: Omega, 1975); *The Great Rapture Hoax* (Fletcher: New Puritan Library, 1983); *The Rapture Plot* (Simpsonville: Millennium III, 1994).

36. *The Sword and the Trowel; a Record of Combat with Sin and of Labor for the Lord*

that around the time of the appearance of this article Govett's own church attendance was already beginning to diminish in number. Several attempts over the years were made in an attempt to restore appreciation of Govett. As late after Govett's death as 20 August 1937 an article concerning him was written to the editor in the *Eastern Daily Press*. He is identified only as E. H. B. His intent was to keep the memory alive of one who was a "notable figure in the city."[37] And then on 8 January 1952, a letter was written to the same newspaper remembering the great preachers of the 1800s in Norwich, of "which there were many." The writer noted that Govett drew crowds from across the City of Norwich by his preaching.[38] Yet, the occasional effort to keep Govett's memory alive has been unsuccessful.

This study ends where it began—at the occasion of Govett's death and the mention of his passing in the local press. A month after Govett's death *The Christian* posted these posthumous remarks: "In an unfading hope of the Lord's return—a hope which he had himself by grace kindled in their hearts—the brethren of Surrey Road Chapel laid their beloved pastor to rest. It was the closing of a life that was garnered as a shock of ripened grain, and that had diffused much light and grace to the glory of God."[39] Govett has been forgotten; his legacy and contributions to church history hidden for a time, requiring only rediscovery.

(1883) 512.

37. See Norfolk Records Office file FC76/59 (1 of 2), *Eastern Daily Press* (20 August 1937).

38. See Norfolk Records Office file FC76/59 (1 of 2), *Eastern Daily Press* (8 January 1952).

39. Norfolk Records Office, catalog reference FC76/59. *The Christian* (28 March 1901).

Bibliography

Archival Sources

Middlesex County, will, Martha Romaine, proved 2 February 1853.
Middlesex County, will, Robert Govett, Sr, proved 26 October 1858.
Norfolk County, will, Robert Govett the younger, proved 3 June 1901. Norfolk Records Office, catalog reference FC76/59. 175 files relating to Govett dating from 1836.
Norfolk Records Office, catalog reference FC76/89.
Norfolk Records Office, catalog reference FC76/91.
Norfolk Records Office, catalog reference FC76/92.
Norfolk Records Office, catalog reference FC76/95.
Sermons. Govett's handwritten sermons archived at Norfolk Records Office and Schoettle Publishing Co., Georgia.

Primary Sources

A Letter to Mr. Robert Govett on the Subject of His Tract, "Address to the Christians, Commonly Called Plymouth Brethren, on Liberty of Ministry and Gift." Bristol: J. Wright, 1848.

Govett's Books and Tracts 1840s
(listed in date order)

Govett, Robert, ed. *Calvinism by Calvin; being the Substance of Discourses.* London: Nisbet, 1840.
———. *Isaiah Unfulfilled: Being an Exposition of the Prophet ; with New Version and Critical Notes to Which Are Added Two Dissertations one on the "Sons of God" and "Giants" of Genesis VI and the Other a Comparative Estimate of the Hebrew and Greek Texts.* London: Nisbet, 1841.
———. *Gospel Analogies and Other Sermons.* London: Hamilton, Adams, 1843.

———. *The Revelation of St. John, Literal and Future: Being an Exposition of That Book: to Which Are Added Remarks in Refutation of the Ideas That the Pope is the Man of Sin, and That Popery is the Apostasy Predicted by St. Paul, with a Special Reference to Doctor O'Sullivan on the Apostasy*. London: Hamilton, Adams, 1843.

———. *A Treatise on Hades, or the Place of Departed Spirits*. Edinburgh: Johnstone, 1843.

———. *The Gifts of The Holy Ghost and Miracle Essentially Connected with Justification by Faith*. Norwich: Fletcher, 1844.

———. *Not Water Baptism But the Gifts of the Holy Spirit the Baptism of Christ*. Norwich: Fletcher, 1844.

———. *Open or Strict Communion? Judgment Pronounced on the Question by the Lord Jesus Himself*. Norwich: Fletcher, 1845.

———. *The Parable of the Drag-Net (Matt xiii 47–50) Explained*. Hull: Anderson, 1845.

———. *The Parable of the Hid Treasure Explained*. Hull: Anderson, 1845.

———. *Sin after Baptism; or a Long Neglected Command of the Lord Jesus, Recommended to Believers*. Norwich: Fletcher and Son, 1845.

———. *All Believers Interested in the Parable of the Virgins: Matthew XXV, 1*. Norwich: Fletcher, 1846.

———. *At Any Rate, Infant Baptism Is Not Forbidden*. Norwich: Fletcher and Son, 1846.

———. *Infant Baptism and the Abrahamic Covenant*. Norwich: Fletcher, 1846.

———. *The Order of Reward or the Parable of the Labourers in the Vineyard (Matthew XX 1) Explained*. Norwich: Fletcher and Son, 1846.

———. *The Parable of the Leaven Explained*. Norwich: Josiah Fletcher, 1846.

———. *The Parable of the Mustard Seed Explained*. : Fletcher, 1846.

———. *The Parable of the Pearl of Great Price (Matt XIII 45–46) Explained*. Norwich: Fletcher, 1846.

———. *The Parable of the Sheep and the Goats*. Norwich: Fletcher and Son, 1846.

———. *The Parable of the Talents Explained*. Norwich: Fletcher and Son, 1846.

———. *The Prophecy on Olivet or Matthew XXIV & XXV Expounded*. Norwich: Fletcher, 1846.

———. *Supplement to the Ten Virgins*. Norwich: Fletcher, 1846.

———. *Wine and Its Bottles or Rite and Doctrine: A Truth for the Times*. Norwich: Fletcher and Son, 1846.

———. *Address to the Christians Commonly Called Plymouth Brethren on Liberty of Ministry and Gift*. Norwich: Fletcher, 1847.

———. *The Baptismal Services of the Church of England Considered*. Norwich: Fletcher and Son, 1847.

———. *The Groaning Creation Delivered*. Norwich: Fletcher and Son, 1847.

———. *The Principal Arguments from Scripture in Favour of Infant Baptism*. Norwich: Fletcher and Son, 1847.

———. *On the Use of Money: or, the Unjust Steward*. Norwich: Fletcher, 1848.

———. *Vegetarianism: A Dialogue*. London: Campbell, 1849.

Govett's Books and Tracts 1850s

(listed in date order)

Govett, Robert. *Are Oaths Lawful for a Christian?* Norwich: Fletcher, 1850.

———. *Babylon Mystical and Babylon Literal or the Vision of Ephah*. Norwich: Fletcher and Son, 1850.

———. *Babylon Mystical and Babylon Literal: Or the Vision of the Ephah. Zechariah V, 5*. Norwich: Fletcher, 1850.

———. *The Best Mode of Presenting the Gospel*. Norwich: Fletcher, 1850.

———. *The Christian and Politics*. Norwich: Fletcher, 1850.

———. *The Church Government of the New Testament*. Norwich: Fletcher and Son, 1850.

———. *The Church of Old in its Unity, Gifts, and Ministry, or, an Exposition of 1 Corinthians XII, XIII, XIV*. Norwich: Fletcher and Son, 1850.

———. *The Future Apostasy*. Norwich: Fletcher and Son, 1850.

———. *Gospel Hymns*. Norwich: Fletcher and Son, 1850.

———. *Parents Addressed*. Norwich: Fletcher, 1850.

———. *Reward According to Works*. Norwich: Fletcher and Son, 1850.

———. *Warrant of Scripture concerning New Testament Priesthood*. Norwich: Fletcher, 1850.

———. *The Locusts, the Euphratean Horsemen and the Two Witnesses; or, the Apocalyptic Systems of the Revds. E. B. Elliot, Dr. Cumming and Dr. Keith, Proved Unsound*. London: Nisbet, 1852.

———. *The Popes Not the Man of Sin: Being an Answer to the Publications of Dr. Cumming, Dr. Morison, and the Rev. E. B. Elliott, on that Subject*. London: Nisbet, 1852.

———. *The Saints' Rapture to the Presence of the Lord Jesus, with appendix in Refutation of Dr. Cumming's Tract Entitled "The Pope the Man of Sin."* London: Nisbet, 1852.

———. *Warrant of Scripture that Believers are Not Equal. A lecture, Etc.* Norwich: Fletcher, 1852.

———. *Entrance into the Kingdom. or Reward According to Works*. Norwich: Fletcher and Son, 1853.

———. *Warrant of Scripture that Believers are Not Equal: a lecture delivered at the Assembly Rooms, Norwich, Oct. 28th, 1852, on the Proceedings of a Body Entitling Itself 'The Conference of Norfolk Norwich, Norwich Steam Press, Nonconformists.'* Norwich: Fletcher, 1853.

———. *"Your Children Holy:" or, Were Infants Baptized in Apostles' Days?* Norwich: Fletcher and Son, 1857.

———. *Infant Sprinkling No Baptism: Being a Refutation of Mr. C. Paget's "Godly Practice of Infant Baptism."* London: Houlston and Wright, 1858.

———. *The Three Witnesses that Jesus is the Son of God*. Norwich: Fletcher, 1858.

Govett's Books and Tracts 1860s
(listed in date order)

Govett, Robert. *Esau's Choice: A Sermon Preached February 26th, 1860*. Norwich: Fletcher and Son, 1860.

———. *Eternal Punishment: A Sermon Preached Jan. 23rd, 1859*. Norwich: Fletcher and Son, 1860.

———. *The Lamp and Its Stand*. London: Educational Trading, 1860.

———. *The Righteousness of God: What is It?* London: Nisbet, 1860.

———. *Salvation Certain: A Sermon Preached February 26th, 1860*. Norwich: Fletcher and Son, 1860.
———. *The Septenary Arrangement of Scripture: Reissued from Dr. Kitto's "Journal of Sacred Literature."* London: Campbell, 1860.
———. *The Apocalypse: Expounded by Scripture*. Vols. 1–4. London: Nisbet, 1861–65.
———. *The Cherubim: What Do They Mean? Extracted from "The Apocalypse Expounded by Scripture."* London: Nisbet, 1861.
———. *The Sermon on the Mount Expounded*. London: Nisbet, 1861.
———. *To Members of the Church of England: Are the Members of It All Elect, Regenerate, Forgiven?* London: Baptist Tract Society, Elliot Stock, 1864.
———. *To Members of the Church of England: Is the Church of England a Church of Christ?* London: Baptist Tract Society, Elliot Stock, 1864.
———. *To Members of the Church of England: Its Way of Salvation: Can You be Saved by It?* London: Baptist Tract Society, Elliot Stock, 1864.
———. *The Righteousness of Christ, the Righteousness of God, a Refutation of the Views Generally held by the Christians Commonly Called "Plymouth Brethren" on That Subject*. London: Elliot Stock, 1864.
———. *Will All Believers Enter the Millennial Kingdom? A Reply to the Rev. R. A. Purdon's Attack in "The Last Vials."* London: Nisbet, 1865.
———. *The Man of Sin: Is He the Pope?; being the Controversial Correspondence in the Achill Herald between Edward Nangle and R. Govett*. London: Nisbet, 1866.
———. *Sowing and Reaping*. London: Nisbet, 1868.
———. *Christadelphians, Not Christians*. London: Nisbet, 1869.
———. *English Derived from Hebrew. With Glances at Greek and Latin*. London: Partridge, 1869.
———. *The Gifts of the Holy Ghost and Miracle [sic]: Essentially Connected with Justification by Faith*. London: Nisbet, 1869.
———. *Have We the Gifts of the Spirit? Two Letters to Indoctus*. London: Nisbet, 1869.
———. *The Jews, the Gentiles, and the Church of God, in the Gospel of Matthew*. London: Nisbet, 1869.
———. *The Kid in the Milk: Or, the Second Covenant of Sinai*. London: Girls' Industrial Home, 1869.
———. *The Observance of Lent*. Norwich: Fletcher and Son, 1869.

Govett's Books and Tracts 1870s
(listed in date oder)

Govett, Robert. *The Collection of Scriptures Not Shaken by Gen. Goodwyn's Observations*. London: Nisbet, 1870.
———. *We Have Not the Spirit's Gifts: Let Us Seek Them: Another Letter to Indoctus*. London: Nisbet, 1870.
———. *Eternal Suffering of the Wicked*. London: Nisbet, 1871.
———. *Are Dissenters from the "Church of England" Guilty of Schism?* Glasgow: MacLehose, 1872.
———. *Are Oaths Lawful for a Christian?* Norwich: Fletcher and Son, 1872.
———. *The Believer's Standings in Grace and Under Responsibility: or, Sins before Faith and Sins after Faith*. London: Nisbet, 1872.

———. *The Last Days; and the First Resurrection; or, Thoughts on Paul's Last Epistle*. Norwich: Fletcher and Son, 1872.
———. *Moses or Christ? Being the Argument of the Epistle to the Galatians*. London: Wheeler, 1872.
———. *The Promises to Abraham Never Yet Fulfilled*. Norwich: Fletcher and Son, 1872.
———. *The Resurrection of Christ the Foundation of the Faith*. Norwich: Fletcher and Son, 1872.
———. *Seek the Sabbath Rest to Come*. Norwich: Fletcher and Son, 1872.
———. *Baptist and Justification: or, Thoughts on Rom. VI. 1–7*. Norwich: Fletcher and Son, 1873.
———. *The Bride's Bath*. Norwich: Fletcher and Son, 1873.
———. *Christians! Seek the Rest of God in His Millennial Kingdom*. Norwich: Fletcher and Son, 1873.
———. *The Church the Body of Christ, and House of God, in Relation to Baptism*. Norwich: Fletcher and Son, 1873.
———. *Exclusion of Believers for Doctrine, Unscriptural*. Norwich: Fletcher and Son, 1873.
———. *"He That Is Baptized with the Spirit Needs No Baptism of Water."* 2nd ed. Norwich: Fletcher and Son, 1873.
———. *How Long Is Baptism to Be Observed?* Norwich: Fletcher and Son, 1873.
———. *Noah's Ark and Baptism*. Norwich: Fletcher and Son, 1873.
———. *The Resurrection: Events of the First Day*. Norwich: Fletcher and Son, 1873.
———. *Types of the Righteousness of Christ*. Norwich: Fletcher and Son, 1873.
———. *Baptist an Act of Faith, of Obedience, and of Salvation*. Norwich: Fletcher and Son, 1874.
———. *The Brazen Serpent*. Norwich: Fletcher and Son, 1874.
———. *Is the Law the Christian's Rule of Life?* Norwich: Fletcher and Son, 1874.
———. *Of Whom Does the Church Consist?* Norwich: Fletcher and Son, 1874.
———. *Spiritism a Foe of Christianity: Death and Resurrection*. Norwich: Fletcher and Son, 1874.
———. *The Trinity, the Christ, and Antichrist: or, Thoughts on the First Epistle of John*. Norwich: Fletcher and Son, 1874.
———. *The Wheat and the Tares*. Norwich: Fletcher and Son, 1874.
———. *Babylon Mystical and Babylon Literal, or the Vision of the Ephah. Zachariah V,5*. Norwich: Fletcher and Son, 1875.
———. *Is Sanctification Perfect Here below? Or Romans VI–VIII Expounded: With Special Reference to the Views of Messrs. Pearsall Smith and Darby*. Norwich: Fletcher and Son, 1875.
———. *The Passage through the Red Sea a Type of Baptism*. Norwich: Fletcher and Son, 1875.
———. *Are "The Brethren" Right? Or, Scripture Testimony Concerning the Spirit and His Gifts*. Norwich: Fletcher and Son, 1876.
———. *Christ's Resurrection and Ours: Or, I Corinthians XV. Expounded*. Glasgow: James MacLehose, 1876.
———. *Mysterious Disappearance, and Its Explanation*. Norwich: Fletcher and Son, 1876.

———. *How Interpret the Apocalypse? As Naturalists? or As Supernaturalists? A Refutation of the Historic Interpretation, with Especial Reference to the Rev. G. Guinness' "Approaching End of the Age."* Norwich: Fletcher and Son, 1879.

Govett's Books and Tracts 1880s
(listed in date order)

Govett, Robert. *Baptism and the Kingdom.* Norwich: Fletcher and Son, 1880.
———. *The Best Mode of Presenting the Gospel.* Norwich: Fletcher and Son, 1880.
———. *The Consequences of Jesus Being Son of David.* Norwich: Fletcher and Son, 1880.
———. *The Gift and the Prize.* Norwich: Fletcher and Son, 1880.
———. *Is God the Father of All Men?* Norwich: Fletcher and Son, 1880.
———. *Israel's History, the Church's Warning.* Norwich: Fletcher and Son, 1880.
———. *King Solomon and the Apostle Paul: or, the Earthly Calling and the Heavenly.* Norwich: Fletcher and Son, 1880.
———. *The Millennial Kingdom One of Reward.* Norwich: Fletcher and Son, 1880.
———. *Mount Sinai and Zion.* Norwich: Fletcher and Son, 1880.
———. *The Race and the Crown, I Corinthians IX, 24-27.* Norwich: Fletcher and Son, 1880.
———. *Rome's Way of Justification, Compared with God's.* Norwich: Fletcher and Son, 1880.
———. *The Sabbath and the Lord's Day.* Norwich: Fletcher and Son, 1880.
———. *Stephen's Accusation, Defence, and Martyrdom.* Norwich: Fletcher and Son, 1880.
———. *Tracts on the Kingdom.* Norwich: Fletcher and Son, 1880.
———. *The Unjust Steward; or the Use of Money. Luke XVI, 1-13.* Norwich: Fletcher and Son, 1880.
———. *The Visible Glory of God.* Norwich: Fletcher and Son, 1880.
———. *A Word to Antimillenarians.* Norwich: Fletcher and Son, 1880.
———. *Exposition of the Gospel of St. John, Vol. I-II.* London: Bemrose and Sons, 1881.
———. *The Gospel's "Righteousness of God" Is the Righteousness of Christ.* Norwich: Fletcher and Son, 1881.
———. *Entrance into the Millennial Kingdom: Four Letters to J. T. Molesworth, Esq.* Norwich: Fletcher and Son, 1883.
———. *Christ Superior to Angels, Moses, Aaron: A Comment on the Epistle to the Hebrews.* London: Nisbet, 1884.
———. *The New Jerusalem: Our Eternal Home.* Norwich: Fletcher and Son, 1884.
———. *The Scapegoat, or, the Two Goats of the Day of Atonement.* Norwich: Fletcher and Son, 1884.
———. *Leading Thoughts on the Apocalypse.* Norwich: Fletcher and Son, 1885.
———. *The New Life and Birth, Part II.* Norwich: Fletcher and Son, 1885.
———. *The New Life, with its New Birth and Kingdom: Part I-II.* Norwich: Fletcher and Son, 1885.
———. *Not Law, but Grace, or the Effects of Law in the Spiritual World: An Argument Against Mr. Drummond's Book.* Norwich: Fletcher and Son, 1885.
———. *God's Election.* Birmingham: Caswell, 1886.

———. *The Secret Presence and Rapture Defended, a Letter to Pastor Frank White.* Norwich: Fletcher and Son, 1887.
———. *The Three Eatings, Supplement to John VI.* Norwich: Fletcher and Son, 1888.
———. *Gospel Hymns.* Compiled by Robert Govett. 5th ed. Norwich: Fletcher and Son, 1889.
———. *What Is the Church? Or the Argument of Ephesians.* Norwich: Fletcher and Son, 1889.

Govett's Books and Tracts 1890s
(listed in date order)

Govett, Robert. *Christ the Head; the Church His Body: Its Dangers, Duties, Glories: or, the Argument of Colossians.* Norwich: Fletcher and Son, 1890.
———. *The Faith and Obedience of Abraham: A Pattern to Believers.* Norwich: Fletcher and Son, 1890.
———. *The Righteousness of God, the Salvation of the Believer: or, the Argument of the Romans.* Norwich: Fletcher and Son, 1891.
———. *The Two-Foldness of Divine Truth.* Norwich: Fletcher and Son, 1892.
———. *The Presence of Christ in Its Effects on the Church and the World: Being the Argument of the Epistles to the Thessalonians, with Notice of Dr. Bullinger's Theory of the Hinderers, and Dr. Eadie on the First Resurrection.* Norwich: Fletcher and Son, 1893.
———. *The Fourth Kingdom of Man and His City: Being the Argument of the Epistle of the Philippians.* Norwich: Fletcher and Son, 1894.
———. *Further Light on Romans V.12 to VI.11: or, Adam and Christ the Two Great Heads of Men.* Norwich: Fletcher and Son, 1894.
———. *Christ's Judgment of His Saints at His Return: And Solution of the Main Argument against Secret Presence.* Norwich: Fletcher and Son, 1895.
———. *Keswick Teaching: The Command Indicated by It, But Not Obeyed, Supplied and Enforced from Scripture.* Norwich: Fletcher and Son, 1895.
———. *Will All Believers Have Part in the Thousand Years?* Norwich: Fletcher and Son, 1895.
———. *The Order and Connexion of Circumcision and the Passover Under Moses, and of Immersion and of the Lord's Supper under Christ, or, the Union of Faith and Obedience Called for by God.* Norwich: Fletcher and Son, 1896.
———. *The Two Heads of Men: Adam, Head of Sin and Death, Christ, Head of Righteousness and Life.* Norwich: Fletcher and Son, 1896.

Govett's Books and Tracts 1900s
(listed in date order)

Govett, Robert. *The Faith and Obedience of Abraham: A Pattern to Believers.* Norwich: Fletcher and Son, 1900.
———. *Two Views of the Supper of the Lord in 1 Corinthians X and XI.* Norwich: Fletcher and Son, 1900.

Govett's Undated Tracts
(listed in date order)

Govett, Robert. *An Appeal to Evangelical Clergymen and Churchmen.* 2nd ed. London: Yapp, ca. 1845.

———. *Advice to the Debtor.* Norwich Gospel Tracts 1. Norwich: Fletcher and Son, ca. 1844–1850.

———. *Can a Churchman Be Saved?* Tracts to Churchmen 2. Norwich: Fletcher and Son, ca. 1844–1850.

———. *The Churchman's Creed.* Tracts to Churchmen 1. Norwich: Fletcher and Son, ca. 1844–1850.

———. *The Crucified Three: Or, the Savior and the Robbers.* Norwich Gospel Tracts 3. Norwich: Fletcher and Son, ca. 1844–850.

———. *The Gospel of the Passover.* Norwich Gospel Tracts 5. Norwich: Fletcher and Son, ca. 1844–1850.

———. *Have You Been Saved?* Tracts to Churchmen 3. Norwich: Fletcher and Son, ca. 1844–1850.

———. *How to be Saved.* Norwich Gospel Tracts 4. Norwich: Fletcher and Son, ca. 1844–1850.

———. *The Runaway Slave.* Norwich Gospel Tracts 2. Norwich: Fletcher and Son, ca. 1844–1850.

———. *Should a Man Promise What He Cannot Perform?* Tracts to Churchmen 4. Norwich: Fletcher and Son, ca. 1844–1850.

———. *Why Does the Church of England Baptize Infants?* Tracts to Churchmen 5. Norwich: Fletcher and Son, ca. 1844–1850.

———. *Resting and Wrestling.* Tracts on the Kingdom 14. Norwich: Fletcher and Son, ca. 1870–1895.

———. *Unwatchful Believers of the Church Will Be Left in the Future Great Tribulation.* Tracts on the Kingdom 13. Norwich: Fletcher and Son, ca. 1870–1895.

———. *Baptism An Act of Faith, of Obedience, and of Salvation.* 3rd ed. Norwich: Fletcher and Son, nd.

———. *Baptism in Relation to the Coming Kingdom and to Eternal Life.* Part 1. London: Holness, n.d.

———. *Baptism, the Kingdom of God, and Eternal Life.* Norwich: Tilney, n.d., posthumous.

———. *Christians! Seek the Rest of God in the Millennial Kingdom.* Norwich: Fletcher and Son, n.d.

———. *Ifs of the New Testament Addressed to Believers.* 2nd ed. Birmingham: Caswell, n.d.

———. *May a Christian Be a Soldier?* 3rd ed. Norwich: Tilney, n.d.

———. *The Millennium Cannot Come in Gospel Times.* London: Nisbet, n.d.

———. *Mr. Darby's Sentiments concerning Communion.* Birmingham: White and Pike, n.d.

———. *The Mystery of Godliness.* Norwich: Fletcher and Son, n.d.

———. *Should a Christian be a Teetotaller?* Norwich: Fletcher and Son, n.d.

———. *The Son of God (in Matthew): A Word about Swedenborgianism.* No. 1. Norwich: Fletcher and Son, n.d.

———. *The Son of God (in John): A Word About Swedenborgianism*. No. 2. Norwich: Fletcher and Son, n.d.
———. *The Spirits in Prison*. Norwich: Fletcher and Son, n.d.
———. *To Believers among Wesleyans*. Norwich: Fletcher and Son, n.d.
———. *The Whole Counsel of God*. Norwich: Fletcher and Son, n.d.

Journals/Magazines (Archival)

The American Monthly Review of Reviews 21 (1900) 173.
"Anniversary of the Baptist Church, Gildencraft, Norwich." *The Gospel Herald; or, Poor Christian's Magazine* 30–NS 7 (1861) 267.
"As to the Meaning of 'Life' and 'Death.'" *The Methodist Quarterly: A Journal of Theological and General Literature* 5 (1871) 278–97.
"The Ascent From the Pit." *The Last Vials: Being a Series of Essays Upon the Subject of the Second Advent* 3–28th year (1873) 33–48.
Ashworth, Robert A. "The Fundamentalist Movement among the Baptists." *The Journal of Religion* 4, no. 6 (1924) 611–31.
"Believers and the Kingdom." *The Rainbow: A Magazine of Christian Literature, with Special Reference to the Revealed Future of the Church and the World* 2 (1865) 422–25.
Bennett, Herbert. "Exclusion from the Kingdom." *The Voice upon the Mountains: A Journal of Prophetic Testimony and Evangelistic Effort* 3 (1869) 22.
"Birk's Elements of Prophecy." *The Churchman's Monthly Review and Chronicle* (1843) 633–59.
"Books Wanted to Purchase." *The Publishers "Circular and Booksellers" Record of British and Foreign Literature* 74 (1901) 428.
"Catholic Convert Club." *Bengal Catholic Expositor* 3, no. 24 (1840) 355–58.
Collins, Wilkie. "The Unknown Public." *Household Words: A Weekly Journal* 439 (1858) 217–22.
"Contemporary Literature." *The Westminster Review*, American ed., 116 (1881) 250–56.
Cox, John. "Divine Testimony and Human Inference." *Primitive Church Magazine, Advocating the Constitution, Faith, and Practice of the Apostolic Churches* 11, no. 124 (1854) 108–12, 148–52.
Darby, John N. "The House of God—The Body of Christ—The Baptism of the Holy Ghost." *The Present Testimony, and Original Christian Witness Revived: In Which the Church's Portion and the Hope of the Kingdom, Etc.* 11 (1859) 40–67.
"Death—Mrs. Keen." *The Primitive Church Magazine, Advocating the Constitution, Faith, and Practice of the Apostolic Churches* 9, no. 119 (1853) 376–78.
"Discourses on the Millennium." *The Christian Observer* 17, no. 11 (1818) 744–55.
Errington, S. H. "Do All Believers Enter 'the Kingdom.'" *The Rainbow: A Magazine of Christian Literature, with Special Reference to the Revealed Future of the Church and the World* 2 (1865) 275–76.
"Eternal Life and the Kingdom." *The Rainbow: A Magazine of Christian Literature, with Special Reference to the Revealed Future of the Church and the World* 2 (1865) 523–26.
"Eternal Punishment." *The Methodist Quarterly: a Journal of Theological and General Literature* 5 (1871) 267–77.

"Free Church Movement in Hackney." *The Harbenger: A Magazine of the Countess of Huntingdon's Connexion* (1859) 271.

Govett, Robert. "Answer to the Rev. B. Young on the Millennium." *The Rainbow: A Magazine of Christian Literature, with Special Reference to the Revealed Future of the Church and the World* 4 (1867) 403–12.

———. "Answer to the Rev. B. C. Young on the Millennium." *The Rainbow: A Magazine of Christian Literature, with Special Reference to the Revealed Future of the Church and the World* 4 (1867) 506–11.

———. "The Body and its Ministry." *The Voice upon the Mountains: A Journal of Prophetic Testimony and Evangelistic Effort* 2 (1868) 4–5. Govett's Argument is Continued in two more issues of the journal: 2 (1868) 26–27; 2 (1868) 41–42.

———. "The Christadelphian Ecclesia." *The Voice upon the Mountains: A Journal of Prophetic Testimony and Evangelistic Effort* 2 (1868) 52–55.

———. "Christadelphianism. Is Satan a Real Person?" *The Voice upon the Mountains: A Journal of Prophetic Testimony and Evangelistic Effort* 2 (1868) 65–67.

———. "The Emperor." *The Rainbow: A Magazine of Christian Literature, with Special Reference to the Revealed Future of the Church and the World* 1 (1864) 169–74.

———. "Exclusion from the Kingdom." *The Voice upon the Mountains: A Journal of Prophetic Testimony and Evangelistic Effort* 3 (1869) 8–10.

———. "The First Resurrection and Kingdom of Christ: Answer to Mr. Grant's Third Volume." *The Rainbow: A Magazine of Christian Literature, with Special Reference to the Revealed Future of the Church and the World* 4 (1867) 118–23.

———. "Millenarian Arguments. The Promises and Threats of the Law." *The Rainbow: A Magazine of Christian Literature, with Special Reference to the Revealed Future of the Church and the World* 4 (1867) 353–60.

———. "Millenarian Arguments—The Second Adam." *The Rainbow: A Magazine of Christian Literature, with Special Reference to the Revealed Future of the Church and the World* 4 (1867) 193–200.

———. "Millenarian Arguments: The Second Joseph and the Prophet Like Moses." *The Rainbow: A Magazine of Christian Literature, with Special Reference to the Revealed Future of the Church and the World* 4 (1867) 256–66.

———. "Parable of the Drag-net." *The Voice upon the Mountains: A Journal of Prophetic Testimony and Evangelistic Effort* 3 (1869) 36.

———. "The Pardon of Sin Under Law." *The Sword and the Trowel* (1889) 566–71.

———. "The Twenty-Four Elders." *The Rainbow: A Magazine of Christian Literature, with Special Reference to the Revealed Future of the Church and the World* 4 (1867) 170–74.

———. "What Is Meant by Christ's Coming?" *The Rainbow: A Magazine of Christian Literature, with Special Reference to the Revealed Future of the Church and the World* 2 (1865) 217–22.

———. "Will the Rapture Be Visible or Secret?" *The Rainbow: A Magazine of Christian Literature, with Special Reference to the Revealed Future of the Church and the World* 1 (1864) 257–65.

Hone, William. "The Late Mr. William Hone." *Notes and Queries* 93 (1851) 106.

Hutchinson, P. "Govett Family." *Notes and Queries: A Medium of Inter-communication* 3rd series, 12 (1867) 274.

"Index." *Index to the British Catalogue of Books, Published During the Years 1837 to 1857 Inclusive* (1858) 245.

Journal of Sacred Literature. New Series 3, no.5 (1852) 218.

Lea, E. G. "Mr. Govett on the Antichrist." *The Rainbow: A Magazine of Christian Literature, with Special Reference to the Revealed Future of the Church and the World* 2 (1865) 425–26.

"Literature." *The Rainbow: A Magazine of Christian Literature, with Special Reference to the Revealed Future of the Church and the World* 2 (1865) 191–92.

"Literature." *The Rainbow: A Magazine of Christian Literature, with Special Reference to the Revealed Future of the Church and the World* 7 (1870) 526–28.

Lloyd, George. "Letter to the Editor." *The Voice upon the Mountains: A Journal of Prophetic Testimony and Evangelistic Effort* 2 (1868) 85.

The London Catalogue of Books Published in Great Britain. 1831 to 1855 (1855) 86, 209.

Molesworth, J. T. "Exclusion from the Kingdom." *The Voice upon the Mountains: A Journal of Prophetic Testimony and Evangelistic Effort* 2 (1868) 156–57.

———. "Exclusion from the Kingdom." *The Voice upon the Mountains: A Journal of Prophetic Testimony and Evangelistic Effort* 3 (1869) 21–22.

"New Books." *The Earthen Vessel, and the Christian Record* 22 (1866) 122–24.

"New Books Published in London During March." *Appleton's Literary Bulletin a Monthly Record of New Books, English and American* 1, no. 3 (1843) 95.

"New Works and New Editions Published in March." *A Monthly List of All New Books Published in Great Britain*. Sold by Mr. C. Muquardt, no. 18 (1844) 81.

Newman, Frederick, "Entrance into the Kingdom." *The Voice upon the Mountains: A Journal of Prophetic Testimony and Evangelistic Effort* 2 (1868) 146–47.

"Notes and News." *The Academy. A Weekly Review of Literature, Science, and Art* 19 (1881) 278.

"Notice of Books." *The Journal of Sacred Literature and Biblical Record* 5 (1864) 478.

"Notice of Books." *The Sword and the Trowel* (1889) 34–40.

"Notice of Books." *The Sword and the Trowel* (1885) 546–53.

"Notices and Books." *The Voice upon the Mountains: A Journal of Prophetic Testimony and Evangelistic Effort* 2 (1868) 162.

"Notices and Books." *The Voice upon the Mountains: A journal of Prophetic Testimony and Evangelistic Effort* 2 (1868) 148–49.

"Notice of Books." *The Voice upon the Mountains: A Journal of Prophetic Testimony and Evangelistic Effort* 3 (1869) 36.

"A Practical Truth." *The Rainbow: A Magazine of Christian Literature, with Special Reference to the Revealed Future of the Church and the World* 2 (1865) 140–41.

Purdon, R. A. "Expostulation." *The Rainbow: A Magazine of Christian Literature, with Special Reference to the Revealed Future of the Church and the World* 2 (1865) 139–40.

———. "The Great Popish League." *The Last Vials: Being a Series of Essays Upon the Subject of the Second Advent* 1, tenth series (1855) 1–16.

———. "The Marks of Antichrist." *The Rainbow: A Magazine of Christian Literature, with Special Reference to the Revealed Future of the Church and the World* 2 (1865) 370–72.

———. "The Restoration of the Gentiles." *The Last Vials: Being a Series of Essays Upon the Subject of the Second Advent* 6, tenth series (1855) 1–16.

"Questions for Mr. Govett." *The Rainbow: A Magazine of Christian Literature, with Special Reference to the Revealed Future of the Church and the World* 2 (1865) 329.

"Recent Deaths." *The Baptist Magazine* series 4, vol. 45 (1853) 703–6.

Rees, Arthur A., "Questions for Mr. Govett." *The Rainbow: A Magazine of Christian Literature, with Special Reference to the Revealed Future of the Church and the World* 2 (1865) 233.
"Reviews." *The Baptist Magazine* 58 (1866) 243–45.
"Reviews." *The Quarterly Journal of Prophecy* 13 (1861) 395–407.
"Reviews." *The Quarterly Journal of Prophecy* 15 (1863) 187–201.
"Reviews." *The Voice of Truth; or, Strict Baptist Magazine* 2 (1864) 183–86.
"Reviews." *The Voice of Truth; or, Strict Baptist Magazine* 2 (1864) 138–39.
"Reviews." *The Voice of Truth; or, Strict Baptist Magazine* 2 (1864) 213.
"Reviews and Criticisms." *The Gospel Herald; or, Poor Christian's Magazine* 38–36, NS (1869) 45–46.
"Reviews and Criticisms." *The Gospel Herald; or, Poor Christian's Magazine* 38–36, NS (1869) 143.
"Scottish Natural Science." *North British Review* 55 (1858) 70–100.
Strong, Leonard, "The Present Mysteries of the Kingdom of Heaven." Edited by T. George Bell. *The Voice upon the Mountains: A Journal of Prophetic Testimony and Evangelistic Effort* 3 (1869) 33–35.
"Systems of Interpretation." *The Churchman's Monthly Review and Chronicle* (1843) 264–78.
The Sword and the Trowel; a Record of Combat with Sin and of Labor for the Lord (1880) 407.
The Sword and the Trowel; a Record of Combat with Sin and of Labor for the Lord (1881) 480.
"Thoughts for the Day. II. The Emperor." *The Last Vials* 23, no. 1 (1868) 6–11.
The Voice upon the Mountains: A Journal of Prophetic Testimony and Evangelistic Effort (1867) 190.
The Voice upon the Mountains: A Journal of Prophetic Testimony and Evangelistic Effort (1867) 175.
"What Is the Millennium, and How Cometh It?" (A Letter Signed: A Lover of truth). *The Earthen Vessel, and Christian Record* 23 (1867) 235–40.
"Will All Believers Partake the Bliss of the Millennial Kingdom?" *The Rainbow: A Magazine of Christian Literature, with Special Reference to the Revealed Future of the Church and the World* 2 (1865) 89–90.
Wilson, P. E. "A Comment on a Commentator." *The Church of England Temperance Chronicle* 10, no. 1 (1882) 15.

Newspapers

Eastern Daily Press.
The Christian.
The Hull Packet and East Riding Times.
The Morning Chronicle.
The Observer.
The Times.
Trewman's Exeter Flying Post or Plymouth and Cornish Advertiser.

Secondary Sources

Books and Tracts

Agbaje, John O. B. *Prophetic Force: A Demystification of Eschatology.* Bloomington, IN: Authorhouse, 2012.

Alger, William R. *A Critical History of the Doctrine of a Future Life.* New York: Widdleton, 1867.

Alliborne, S. Austin. *Critical Dictionary of English Literature and British and American Authors Living and Deceased from the Earliest Accounts to the Latter Half of the Nineteenth Century.* Vol.1 Philadelphia: Lippincott, 1874.

Altholz, Josef L. *The Religious Press in Britain, 1760–1900.* New York: Greenwood, 1989.

———. "The Warfare of Conscience with Theology." In *Religion in Victorian Britain*, edited by Gerald Parsons, 150–69. Manchester: Manchester University Press, 1988.

Altick, Richard D. *The English Common Reader: A Social History of the Mass Reading Public, 1800–1900.* Chicago: University of Chicago Press, 1957.

Ariel, Yaakov. *An Unusual Relationship: Evangelical Christians and Jews.* New York: New York University Press, 2013.

Arnold, Matthew. *The Poetical Works of Matthew Arnold.* New York: Crowell, 1897.

Arnold, Thomas K. *Remarks on the Rev. E. B. Elliott's "Horae Apocalypticae."* London: F. & J. Rivington, 1845.

Bainton, Roland H. *The Reformation of the Sixteenth Century.* Boston: Beacon, 1985.

Bank, David, and Theresa McDonald. *British Biographical Index.* 2nd Cumulated and Enlarged Edition. Münich: Saur, 1998.

Barkun, Michael. *Millennialism and Violence.* London: Cass, 1996.

Bass, Clarence B. *Backgrounds to Dispensationalism: Its Historical Genesis and Ecclesiastical Implications.* Grand Rapids: Eerdmans, 1960.

Bateman, Herbert W., IV, ed. *Three Central Issues in Contemporary Dispensationalism: A Comparison of Traditional and Progressive Views.* Grand Rapids: Kregel, 1999.

Bayne, A. D. *A Comprehensive History of Norwich: Including a Survey of the City and Its Public Buildings.* London: Jarrold and Sons, 1869.

Baxter, Richard. *The Glorious Kingdom of Christ, Described and Clearly Vindicated.* London: Printed by T. Snowden, for Thomas Parkhurst, 1691.

Baxter, Michael P. *Forty Coming Wonders; Between 1890 and 1901, as Foreshadowed in the Prophecies of Daniel and Revelation.* London: Christian Herald Office, 1887.

———. *Louis Napoleon the Destined Monarch of the World.* Philadelphia: Claxton, 1867.

———. *The Wonders of Prophecy Between 1896 and April 23, 1908: As Foreshow in the Prophecies of Daniel and Revelation.* London: Christian Herald Office, 1894.

Bebbington, David W. *The Dominance of Evangelicalism: The Age of Spurgeon and Moody.* Leicester: InterVarsity, 2005.

———. "Evangelicalism." In *The Blackwell Companion to Nineteenth-Century Theology*, edited by David Fergusson, 235–50. Chichester: Wiley-Blackwell, 2010.

———. *Evangelicalism in Modern Britain: A History from the 1730s to the 1980s.* London: Unwin Hyman, 1989.

———. *Patterns in History: A Christian View.* Downers Grove, IL: InterVarsity, 1979.

———. *Victorian Nonconformity.* Gwynedd: Headstart History, 1992.

Bellett, J. G. *Assembly Writers Library*. Vol. 11, *The Works of J.G. Bellett*. Glasgow: Gospel Tract, 1985.

Berman, Bob. "End of the World: 2012." *Astronomy Magazine* 35, no. 12 (2007) 14–19.

Bethell, Christopher. *A General View of the Doctrine of Regeneration in Baptism*. 2nd edition London: Printed for J. G. & F. Rivington, 1836.

Birks, Thomas R. *First Elements of Sacred Prophecy: Including an Examination of Several Recent Expositions and of the Year-Day Theory*. London: Painter, 1843.

———. *Memoirs of the Rev. Edward Bickersteth, Late Rector of Watton, Herts*. Vol. 1. London: Seeleys, 1951.

Blakeney, R. P. *The Book of Common Prayer in its History and Interpretation*. 3rd ed. London: Miller, 1870.

Boase, Frederic. *Modern English Biography*. Vol. 1, *A–H*. Truro, UK: Netherton and Worth, 1892.

———. *Modern English Biography*. Vol. 2, *I–Q*. Truro: Netherton and Worth, 1897.

Bogue, David, *Discourses on the Millennium*. London: Hamilton, 1818.

Boyer, Paul S. *When Time Shall be No More: Prophecy Belief in Modern American Culture*. Cambridge, MA: Belknap, 1992.

Brackney, William H. *The Baptists*. Westport, CT: Praeger, 1994.

Briggs, J. H. Y. *The English Baptists of the Nineteenth Century*. Didcot: Baptist Historical Society, 1994.

Bromley, G. W., ed. *Zwingli and Bullinger*. Philadelphia: Westminster, 1979.

Brookes, James H. *Maranatha: or the Lord Cometh*. St. Louis: Bredell, 1870.

Brooks, Chris, and Andrew Saint. *The Victorian Church: Architecture and Society*. Manchester: Manchester University Press, 1995.

Brooks, Joshua William. *A Dictionary of Writers on the Prophecies, with the Titles and Occasional Description of Their Works*. London: Simpkin, Marshall, 1835.

Brown, David. *Christ's Second Coming: Will It Be Pre-Millennial?* Edinburgh: Johnstone, 1846.

Brown, Stewart J. *Providence and Empire: Religion, Politics, and Society in the United Kingdom 1815–1914*. Harlow: Longman, 2008.

Bullinger, Ethelbert W. *A Critical Lexicon and Concordance to the English and Greek New Testament*. 2nd ed. London: Longmans, 1886.

Burnham, Jonathan D. *A Story of Conflict: The Controversial Relationship between Benjamin Wills Newton and John Nelson Darby*. Carlisle: Paternoster, 2004.

Calvin, John. *Institutes of the Christian Religion, 1536 Edition*. Translated and annotated by Ford Lewis Battles. Grand Rapids: Eerdmans, 1986.

Campbell, Thomas. *The Complete Poetical Works of Thomas Campbell, With A Memoir of His Life*. Boston: Phillips, Sampson, 1857.

Canfield, Joseph M. *The Incredible Scofield and His Book*. Rev. ed. Vallecito: Ross House, 2004.

Carter, Grayson. *Anglican Evangelicals: Protestant Secessions from the Via Media, c. 1800–1850*. Oxford: Oxford University Press, 2001.

Case, Shirley Jackson. *The Millennial Hope: A Phase of War-Time Thinking*. Chicago: University of Chicago Press, 1918.

Chadwick, Owen. *The Mind of the Oxford Movement*. Stanford: Stanford University Press, 1960.

———. *The Spirit of the Oxford Movement, Tractarian Essays*. Cambridge: Cambridge University Press, 1990.

Chafer, Lewis Sperry. *The Kingdom in History and Prophecy.* New York: Revell, 1915.
———. *Systematic Theology.* 8 vols. Dallas: Dallas Seminary Press, 1947.
Clark, G. Kitson. *The Making of Victorian England.* Cambridge, MA: Harvard University Press, 1962.
Cleall, Charles. *A Jewel of a Church: Laleham Parish Church—an Historical Guide.* England: n.p., 2001.
Clouse, Robert G., et al., eds. *The Meaning of the Millennium: Four Views.* Downers Grove, IL: InterVarsity, 1977.
Coad, Frederick Roy. "Prophetic Developments with Particular Reference to the Early Brethren Movement." *Occasional Paper Number 2.* Pinner, Middlesex: Christian Brethren Research Fellowship, 1966.
Codling, Rosamunde. *Book of Thanksgiving, 150 Years at Surrey Chapel, Norwich: 1854–2004.* Norwich: Surrey Chapel, 2004.
Cohn, Norman. *The Pursuit of the Millennium.* Rev. ed. Oxford: Oxford University Press, 1970.
Colenso, John William. *The Pentateuch and Book of Joshua Critically Examined.* London: Longman, Roberts and Green, 1862.
Coleridge, Samuel Taylor. *A Book I Value: Selected Marginalia.* Princeton: Princeton University Press, 2003.
Collini, Stefan, Richard Whatmore, and Brian Young, eds. *History, Religion, and Culture: British Intellectual History 1750–1950.* Cambridge: Cambridge University Press, 2000.
Collins, John J., Bernard McGinn, and Stephen J. Stein. *The Encyclopedia of Apocalypticism.* New York: Continuum, 1998.
Constable, Henry. *The Duration and Nature of Future Punishment.* 3rd ed. London: Longman, 1870.
Corfield, Penelope J. "Millennialism: 'The End Is Nigh.'" *History Today* 57, no. 3 (2007) 37–39.
Corrie, George Elwes, ed. *Sermons by Hugh Latimer.* Vol. 1. Cambridge: Cambridge University Press, 1844.
Couch, Mal, ed. *Dictionary of Premillennial Theology: A Practical Guide to the People, Viewpoints, and History of Prophetic Studies.* Grand Rapids: Kregel, 1996.
Craik, Henry. *An Amended Translation of the Epistle to the Hebrews.* London: Bagster and Sons, 1847.
Crenshaw, Curtis I., and Gunn Grover. *Dispensationalism Today, Yesterday, and Tomorrow.* Memphis: Footstool, 1985.
Cross, F. L., and E. A. Livingstone, eds. *The Oxford Dictionary of the Christian Church.* New York: Oxford University Press, 2005.
Crowther, M. A. "Church Problems and Church Parties." In *Religion in Victorian Britain*, edited by Gerald Parsons, 4–27. Manchester: Manchester University Press, 1988.
Crutchfield, Larry V. *The Origins of Dispensationalism: The Darby Factor.* Lanham, MD: University Press of America, 1992.
Cruttwell, Charles Thomas. *Six Lectures on the Oxford Movement and its Results on the Church of England.* London: Skeffington & Son, 1899.
Cumming, John. *Apocalyptic Sketches: or, Lectures on the Book of Revelation; Delivered in the Large Room, Exeter Hall, in 1847–1848.* London: Hall, 1848.
Cunningham, Valentine. *Everywhere Spoken against: Dissent in the Victorian Novel.* Oxford: Clarendon, 1975.

Daley, Brian A. *The Hope of the Early Church: A Handbook of Patristic Eschatology.* Cambridge: Cambridge University Press, 1991.

Dallimore, Arnold A. *George Whitefield: God's Anointed Servant in the Great Revival of the Eighteenth Century.* Wheaton: Crossway, 1990.

———. *George Whitefield: The Life and Times of the Great Evangelist of the Eighteenth-Century Revival.* Vol. 1. London: Banner of Truth, 1970.

Daniels, Ted. *Millennialism: An International Bibliography.* New York: Garland, 1992.

Darby, John Nelson. *The Believer's Place in Christ: 2 Corinthians V.* London: Weston, 1905.

———. *Catalogue of the Library of the Late John Nelson Darby: Comprising Important Works Relating to Theology, History, Geography, Archaeology, Voyages and Travels: Benedictine and Best Editions of the Fathers of the Church: Rare Editions of the Scriptures: Bibliography, Dictionaries.* London: Dryden, 1984.

———. *The Correspondents of John Nelson Darby 1800-1882: With a Geographical Index and a Chart of His Travels Through His Life.* Ramsgate: Hodgett, 1995.

———. *To Him that Overcometh.* New York: Loizeaux Bros., 1910.

———. *The Hope of the Christian.* London: Weston, 1903.

———. *The Judgment Seat of God and of Christ.* Addison: Bible Truth, 1990.

———. *Lectures on the Second Coming.* London: Morrish, 1909.

———. *Man's Constitution and Eternal, Conscious Punishment of the Wicked.* Morganville: Present Truth, 2001.

———. *Notes of Readings on the Epistles to the Corinthians.* London: Morrish, 1825.

———. *Notes on the Book of Revelations; to Assist Inquiries in Searching into that Book.* London: Central Tract Depôt, 1839.

———. *Notes on the Gospel of Luke.* Glasgow: Allan, 1869.

———. *The Watching Servant: Notes of an Address.* Belfast: Words of Truth, 1985.

———. *The Watching Servant or the Coming of the Lord That which Characterizes the Christian Life.* Belfast: Words of Truth, 1985.

Davies, Douglas. *Theology of Death.* London: T. & T. Clark, 2008.

Davis, John Jefferson. *Christ's Victorious Kingdom: Postmillennialism Reconsidered.* Grand Rapids: Baker, 1986.

Davis, Philip. *The Victorians: 1830–1880.* New York: Oxford University Press, 2002.

Dever, Mark. *The Church: The Gospel Made Visible.* Nashville: B&H, 2012.

Dickens, Charles. *Great Expectations.* Vol. 1. New York: Gregory, 1861.

———. *Our Mutual Friend.* Chicago: Belford, Clarke, 1884.

Dickerson, Matthew, "Who Gets Left Behind? How End Times Theories Shape the Ways We View Our Earthly Abode." *Christianity Today* 55, no. 6 (2011) 38–41.

Dillow, Joseph C. *The Reign of the Servant Kings: A Study of Eternal Security and the Final Significance of Man.* Hayesville: Schoettle, 1992.

Dorrien, Gary J. *The Remaking of Evangelical Theology.* Louisville: Westminster John Knox, 1998.

Douglas, J. D., ed. *The New International Dictionary of the Christian Church.* Exeter: Paternoster, 1974.

Draper, John William. *History of the Conflict Between Religion and Science.* New York: Appleton, 1898.

Duffield, George. *Dissertations on the Prophecies Relative to the Second Coming of Jesus Christ.* New York: Dayton & Newman, 1842.

Duke of Manchester, George. *The Times of Daniel, Chronological and Prophetical. Examined with Relations to the Point of Contact Between Sacred and Profane Chronology.* London: Darling, 1845.

Eadie, John, and William Young. *A Commentary on the Greek Text of the Epistles of Paul to the Thessalonians.* London: Macmillan, 1877.

Ede, Janet, and Norma Virgoe. *Religious Worship in Norfolk: The 1851 Census of Accommodation and Attendance at Worship.* Norwich: Norfolk Record Society, 1998.

Ellegård, Alvar. *Darwin and the General Reader: The Reception of Darwin's Theory of Evolution in the British Periodical Press, 1859–1872.* Stockholm: Almqvist & Wiksell, 1958.

Elliott-Binns, L. E. *Religion in the Victorian Era.* 2nd ed. London: Lutterworth, 1966.

Elliott, Edward Bishop. *Horae Apocalypticae, or a Commentary on the Apocalypse, Critical and Historical: Including Also an Examination of the Chief Prophecies of Daniel.* London: Seeley, Burnside & Seeley, 1846.

Erickson, Millard J. *Contemporary Options in Eschatology: A Study of the Millennium.* Grand Rapids: Baker, 1977.

Erdman, David, ed. *The Complete Poetry and Proses of William Blake.* Berkeley: University of California Press, 1982.

Estep, William R. *Anabaptist Story: An Introduction to Sixteenth-Century Anabaptism.* 3rd ed. Cambridge: Eerdmans, 1996.

Euler, Carrie. *Couriers of the Gospel: England and Zurich, 1531–1558.* Zurich: TVZ, 2006.

Evans, Austin Patterson. *An Episode in the Struggle for Religious Freedom: The Sectaries of Nuremberg, 1524–1528.* New York: Columbia University Press, 1924.

Fairbairn, James. *Fairbairn's Crests of the Families of Great Britain and Ireland.* London: New Orchard, 1986.

Feinberg, Charles L. *Millennialism: The Two Major Views: The Premillennial and Amillennial Systems of Biblical Interpretation Analyzed and Compared.* Chicago: Moody, 1982.

Ferguson, Everett. *Baptism in the Early Church: History, Theology, and Liturgy in the First Five Centuries.* Grand Rapids: Eerdmans, 2009.

Fleming, Robert, *The Rise and Fall of Papacy.* Edited by Thomas Thomson. London: Johnstone, 1848.

Fletcher and Son. *List of Books and Tracts by R. Govett, published by Fletcher and Son, Norwich.* Norwich: Fletcher and Son, n.d.

Floyd, Richard D. *Church, Chapel and Party: Religious Dissent and Political Modernization in Nineteenth-Century England.* New York: Palgrave MacMillan, 2008.

Foster, Charles. *Israel in the Wilderness; or Gleanings from the Scenes of the Wanderings, with Essays on the True Date of Korah's Rebellion.* London: Bentley, 1865.

Foster, Joseph. *Alumni Oxonienses: The Members of the University of Oxford, 1715–1886: Their Parentage, Birthplace, and Year of Birth, with a Record of Their Degrees.* Vol. 1. Liechtenstein: Kraus Reprint, 1968.

———. *Men-at-the-bar: A Biographical Hand-List of the Members of the Various Inns of Court.* London: Reeves and Turner, 1885.

Frith, John. "A Mirror or Looking Glass, Wherein You May Behold the Sacrament of Baptism." In *The Works of the English Reformers: William Tyndale and John Frith*, edited by Thomas Russell, 3:284–96. London: Palmer, 1831.

Froom, Le Roy Edwin. *The Prophetic Faith of Our Fathers: The Historical Development of Prophetic Interpretation*. Vol. 1, 1946–54. Washington, DC: Review and Herald, 1946.

———. *The Prophetic Faith of Our Fathers: The Historical Development of Prophetic Interpretation*. Vol. 3. Washington, DC: Review and Herald. 1946.

———. *The Prophetic Faith of Our Fathers: The Historical Development of Prophetic Interpretation*. Vol. 4. Washington, DC: Review and Herald. 1954.

Gardiner, Gordon P. *Champion of the Kingdom: The Story of Philip Mauro*. Brooklyn: Bread of Life, 1961.

Gash, Norman. *Aristocracy and People: Britain 1815–1865*. Cambridge, MA: Harvard University Press, 1979.

Giebelhausen, Michaela. *Painting the Bible: Representation and Belief in Mid-Victorian Britain*. Aldershot: Ashgate, 2006.

Gilbert, Alan D. *Religion and Society in Industrial England: Church, Chapel and Social Change, 1740–1914*. London: Longman, 1976.

Gilbert, Richard. *The Clerical Guide, or Ecclesiastical Directory: Containing a Complete Register of the Dignities and Benefices of the Church of England*. London: J. G. & F. Irvington, 1836.

Glabach, Wilfried E. *Reclaiming the Book of Revelation: A Suggestion of New Readings in the Local Church*. New York: Lang, 2007.

Goodby, J. Jackson. *Bye-Paths in Baptist History*. London: Stock, 1871.

Goode, William. *The Doctrine of the Church of England as to the Effects of Baptism in the Case of Infants*. 2nd ed. London: Hatchard and Son, 1850.

Grass, Tim. *Gathering to His Name: The Story of the Open Brethren in Britain and Ireland*. Milton Keynes: Paternoster, 2006.

———. *The Lord's Watchman: A Life of Edward Irving (1732–1834)*. Eugene, OR: Pickwick, 2012).

Gray, Thomas. *An Elegy Written In a Country Churchyard*. Philadelphia: Lippincott, 1883.

Gribben, Crawford. "Evangelical Eschatology and the Puritan Hope." In *The Emergence of Evangelicalism: Exploring Historical Continuities*, edited by Michael A. G. Haykin and Kenneth J. Stewart, 375–93. Nottingham: InterVarsity, 2008.

———. *Evangelical Millennialism in the Trans-Atlantic World, 1500–2000*. New York: Palgrave Macmillan, 2011.

———. "Millennialism." In *Drawn into Controversies: Reformed Theological Diversity and Debates within Seventeenth-Century British Puritanism*, edited by Michael A. G. Haykin and Mark Jones, 83–98. Göttingen: Vandenhoeck & Ruprecht, 2011.

———. *The Puritan Millennium: Literature and Theology, 1550–1682*. Dublin: Four Courts, 2000.

———. *Writing the Rapture Prophecy Fiction in Evangelical America*. Oxford: Oxford University Press, 2009.

———. "Wrongly Dividing the Word of Truth: The Uncertain Soteriology of the Scofield Reference Bible." *Evangelical Quarterly* 74 (2002) 3–25.

Gribben, Crawford, and Andrew R. Holmes, eds. *Protestant Millennialism, Evangelicalism, and Irish Society, 1790–2005*. Hampshire: Palgrave Macmillan, 2006.
Gribben, Crawford, and Mark S. Sweetnam, eds. *Left Behind and the Evangelical Imagination*. Sheffield: Sheffield Phoenix, 2011.
Gribben, Crawford, and Timothy C. Stunt, eds. *Prisoners of Hope? Aspects of Evangelical Millennialism in Britain and Ireland, 1800–1880*. Waynesboro, GA: Paternoster, 2004.
Guinness, H. Grattan. "Appendix D: Containing Answers to Futurist Objections." In *The Approaching End of the Age Viewed in the Light of History, Prophecy, and Science*, 699–761. 8th ed. London: Hodder and Stoughton, 1882.
Gundry, Robert H. *The Church and the Tribulation*. Grand Rapids: Zondervan, 1973.
Hall, William. *The History of Infant Baptism: In Two Parts*. Vol. 1. 4th ed. London: Printed for F. C. & J. Rivington, 1819.
Hamilton, Floyd Eugene. *The Basis of Millennial Faith*. Grand Rapids: Eerdmans, 1952.
Hamilton, Frank. *The Bible and the Millennium: Being a Compilation of the Two Books, the Old Testament & Messiah's Reign on Earth and the New Testament & the Millennium*. Ventnor: Hamilton, 1900s.
Hammond, W. A. *The Catechism of the Church of England, or an Instruction to Be Learned of Every Person before He Be Brought to Be Confirmed by the Bishop*. London: Printed For J. G. F. & J. Rivington, 1844.
Harnack, Adolph. *What Is Christianity? Lectures Delivered in the University of Berlin During the Winter Term 1899–1900*. 2nd ed. New York: Putnam's Sons, 1908.
Harris, Harriet A. *Fundamentalism and Evangelicals*. Oxford: Oxford University Press, 1998.
Harris, Khim. *Evangelicals and Education: Evangelical Anglicans and Middle-Class Education in Nineteenth-Century England*. Milton Keynes: Paternoster, 2004.
Hart, Darryl G. *Deconstructing Evangelicalism: Conservative Protestantism in the Age of Billy Graham*. Grand Rapids: Baker Academic, 2004.
Hastings, James. *A Dictionary of the Bible*. Vol. 4/1. Honolulu: University Press of the Pacific, 2004.
Haykin, Michael, and Kenneth Stewart, eds. *The Emergence of Evangelicalism: Exploring Historical Continuities*. Nottingham: InterVarsity, 2008.
Hermann, Mary. *Catholic Devotion in Victorian England*. Oxford: Clarendon, 1995.
Hexham, Irving, Stephen Rost, and John W. Morehead II, eds. *Encountering New Religious Movements: A Holistic Evangelical Approach*. Grand Rapids: Kregel, 2004.
Hill, Charles E. *Regnum Caelorum: Patterns of Millennial Thought in Early Christianity*. Grand Rapids: Eerdmans, 2001.
Hillerbrand, J. Hans, ed. *Encyclopedia of Protestantism*. Vol. 1. New York: Routledge, 2004.
Hilton, Boyd. *The Age of Atonement: The Influence of Evangelicalism on Social and Economic Thought, 1795–1863*. Oxford: Clarendon, 1988.
Himmelfarb, Gertrude. *The Spirit of the Age: Victorian Essays*. New Haven: Yale University Press, 2007.
Hindmarsh, D. Bruce. "The Antecedents of Evangelical Conversion Narrative: Spiritual Autobiography and the Christian Tradition." In *The Advent of Evangelicalism: Exploring Historical Continuities*, edited by Michael A.G. Haykin and Kenneth J. Stewart, 327–44. Nashville: B&H Academic, 2008.

Hirst, Julie. *Jane Leade: Biography of a Seventeenth-Century Mystic.* Aldershot: Ashgate, 2006.
Hodder, Edwin. *The Life and Work of the Seventh Earl of Shaftesbury, K.G.* London: Cassell, 1887.
Hodges, Zane C. *Grace in Eclipse: A Study of Eternal Rewards.* Dallas: Redencion Viva, 1985.
Hodgett, L. J. L. *The Correspondents of John Nelson Darby 1800–1882: With a Geographical Index and a Chart of His Travels Through His Life.* Ramsgate: Hodgett, 1995.
Hoekema, Anthony A. *The Bible and the Future.* Grand Rapids: Eerdmans, 1979.
Homes, Nathaniel. *Apokalypsis Anastaseōs: The Resurrection Revealed, or, the Dawning of the Day-Star About to Rise and Radiate a Visible Incomparable Glory.* London: Ibbitson, 1653.
———. *The Resurrection Revealed Raised Above Doubt & Difficulties in Ten Exercitations.* London: Printed for the author, 1661.
Hopkins, Hugh Evan. *Charles Simeon of Cambridge.* Grand Rapids: Eerdmans, 1977.
Hopkins, Mark. *Nonconformity's Romantic Generation: Evangelical and Liberal Theologies in Victorian England.* Milton Keynes: Paternoster, 2004.
Hoppen, K. Theodore. *The Mid-Victorian Generation 1846–1886.* Oxford: Oxford University Press, 1998.
Houghton, Walter E. *The Victorian Frame of Mind, 1830–1870.* New Haven: Yale University Press, 1957.
Houghton, Walter E., and Jean Harris Slingerland. *The Wellesley Index to Victorian Periodicals, 1824–1900.* London: Routledge, 1966.
Huff, Peter A. *What Are They Saying about Fundamentalism?* Mahwah, NJ: Paulist, 2008.
Ingham, Richard. *A Handbook on Christian Baptism: Its Subjects.* London: Stock, 1871.
Inglis, James, ed. *Waymarks in the Wilderness, and Scriptural Guide.* New York: Inglis, 1864.
Ironside, H. A. *A Historic Sketch of the Brethren Movement.* Neptune: Loizeaux Bros., 1942.
Irving, Edward. *Preliminary Discourse to the Work of Ben-Ezra, Entitled the Coming of Messiah in Glory and Majesty: To Which Is Added an Ordination Charge and Also Introductory Essay to Horne's Commentary on the Psalms.* London: Bosworth & Harrison, 1859.
Ischebeck, G. *John Nelson Darby.* Witten: Bundes, 1929.
Jalland, Pat. *Death in the Victorian Family.* Oxford: Oxford University Press, 1996.
Jeremias, Joachim. *Infant Baptism in the First Four Centuries.* Eugene, OR: Wipf and Stock, 2004.
Jewson, C.B. *Simon Wilkin of Norwich.* Norwich: University of East Anglia, 1979.
Jones, David Ceri. "Calvinistic Methodism and the Origins of Evangelicalism in England." In *The Advent of Evangelicalism: Exploring Historical Continuities*, edited by Michael A. G. Haykin, and Kenneth J. Stewart, 103–28. Nottingham: Apollos, 2008.
Jowett, Paul K. *Infant Baptism & the Covenant of Grace.* Grand Rapids: Eerdmans, 1978.
Jurgen-Goertz, Hans. *The Anabaptists.* Oxon: Routledge, 1996.
Kalla, Krishen L. *The Mid-Victorian Literature and Loss of Faith.* New Delhi: Mittal, 1989.
Kellogg, Samuel H. *Are Premillennialists Right?* New York: Revell, 1923.

Kelly, William, ed. *Collected Writings of J. N. Darby*. Vols. 1–34. London: Stow Hill Bible and Tract Depot, 1956.

———. *John Nelson Darby: As I Knew Him*. Belfast: Words of Truth, 1986.

King, Andrew, and John Plunkett, eds. *Popular Print Media 1820–1900*: Vol. 1. Abingdon: Routledge, 2004.

King, Joseph. *Ten Decades: The Australian Centenary Story of the London Missionary Society*. London: London Missionary Society, 1895.

Kitto, John, ed. *The Cyclopaedia of Biblical Literature*. Vol. 1. New York: American Book Exchange, 1882.

Knight, Mark, and Emma Mason. *Nineteenth-Century Religion and Literature: An Introduction*. Oxford: Oxford University Press, 2006.

Kromminga, Diedrich Hinrich. *The Millennium, in the Church: Studies in the History of Christian Chiliasm*. Grand Rapids: Eerdmans, 1945.

———. *The Millennium, Its Nature, Function and Relation to the Consummation of the World*. Grand Rapids: Eerdmans, 1948.

LaHaye, Tim, Thomas Ice, and Ed Hindson. *The Popular Handbook on the Rapture*. Eugene, OR: Harvest House, 2011.

Lacunza Y Diaz, Manuel. *The Coming of Messiah in Glory and Majesty. Being an Abridgement of a Work Translated from the Spanish by E. Irving*. London: Seeley, 1827.

Ladd, George E. *The Blessed Hope: A Biblical Study of the Second Advent and the Rapture*. Grand Rapids: Eerdmans, 1956.

———. *Crucial Questions about the Kingdom of God*. Grand Rapids: Eerdmans, 1952.

Landes, Richard. "The Fear of an Apocalyptic Year 1000: Augustinian Historiography, Medieval and Modern." In *The Apocalyptic Year 1000: Religious Expectation and Social Change*, edited by Richard Landes, Andrew Gow, and David C. Van Meter, 243–55. Oxford: Oxford University Press, 2003.

Lane, Anthony N. S. "Dual-Practice Baptism View." In *Baptism: Three Views*, edited by David F. Wright, 139–92. Downers Grove, IL: InterVarsity, 2009.

Lane, Christopher. *The Age of Doubt: Tracing the Roots of Our Religious Uuncertainty*. New Haven: Yale University Press, 2011.

Lang, G. H. *The Epistle to the Hebrews: A Practical Treatise for Plain and Serious Readers*. London: Paternoster, 1951.

———. *Firstborn Sons, Their Rights and Risks: An Inquiry as to the Privileges and Perils of the Members of the Church of God*. London: Roberts, 1936.

———. *The Parabolic Teaching of Scripture*. Grand Rapids: Eerdmans, 1956.

———. *The Presence of the Future*. Grand Rapids: Eerdmans, 1974).

Larsen, Timothy. *Contested Christianity: The Political and Social Contexts of Victorian Theology*. Waco: Baylor University Press, 2008.

———. *Crisis of Doubt, Honest Faith in Nineteenth-Century England*. Oxford, Oxford University Press, 2006.

———. *A People of One Book: The Bible and the Victorians*. Oxford: Oxford University Press, 2011.

Latourette, Kenneth Scott. *A History of Christianity*. Vol. 2, *Reformation to the Present*. Revised edition. New York: Harper & Row, 1975.

Lea, Thomas D. "A Survey of the Doctrine of the Return of Christ in the Ante-Nicene Fathers." *Journal of the Evangelical Theological Society* 29 (1986) 163–77.

Leafe, G. Harry. *Running to Win! A Positive Biblical Approach to Rewards and Inheritance.* Houston: Scriptel, 1992.
Ledbetter, Kathryn. *Tennyson and Victorian Periodicals: Commodities in Context.* Aldershot: Ashgate, 2007.
Lee, Sidney, ed. *Dictionary of National Biography.* Vol. 10. London: Smith, Elder, 1908.
———. *Dictionary of National Biography.* Vol. 13. London: Smith, Elder, 1909.
Lewis, Donald M., ed. *The Blackwell Dictionary of Evangelical Biography, 1730–1860.* Vols. 1–2. Oxford: Blackwell, 1995.
Lightman, Bernard. "Robert Elsmere and the Agnostic Crisis of Faith." In *Victorian Faith in Crisis: Essays on Continuity and Change in Nineteenth-Century Religious Belief*, edited by Richard J. Helmstadter and Bernard Lightman, 283–311. Stanford: Stanford University Press, 1990.
Lindbergh, Carter. *The European Reformations.* 2nd ed. Chichester: Wiley-Blackwell, 2010.
Lindsey, Hal. *The Late Great Planet Earth.* Grand Rapids: Zondervan, 1970.
Littell, Franklin H. *The Anabaptist View of the Church: A Study in the Origins of Sectarian Protestantism.* Paris: Baptist Standard Bearer, 2000.
Livingston, James C. *The Ethics of Belief: An Essay on the Victorian Religious Conscience.* Tallahassee: American Academy of Religion, 1974.
———. *Matthew Arnold and Christianity: His Religious Prose Writings.* Columbia: University of South Carolina Press, 1986.
———. *Religious Thought in the Victorian Age: Challenges and Reconceptions.* New York: T. & T. Clark, 2006.
Lowth, R. *Isaiah.* London: Routledge, 1995.
Luther, Martin. *Luther's Small Catechism Developed and Explained.* 6th ed. Philadelphia: Lutheran Publication Society, 1893.
MacArthur, John. *You Call Me Lord? Making Jesus Saviour and Lord.* London: Pickering, 1989.
MacPherson, Dave. *The Unbelievable Pre-trib Origin: The Recent Discovery of a Well-Known Theory's Beginning, and Its Incredible Cover-Up.* Kansas City: Heart of America Bible Society, 1973.
Mackenzie, Robert. *The 19th Century: A History.* London: Nelson and Sons, 1880.
Mallock, William Hurrell. *Lucretius on Life and Death, in the Metre of Omar Khayyam, to Which Are Appended Parallel Passages from the Original.* London: A. & C. Black, 1900.
Mangum, R. Todd, and Mark S. Sweetnam. *The Scofield Bible: Its History and Impact on the Evangelical Church.* Colorado Springs: Paternoster, 2009.
Marsden, George M. *The Evangelical Mind and the New School Presbyterian Experience: A Case Study of Thought and Theology in Nineteenth-Century America.* New Haven: Yale University Press, 1970.
———. *Fundamentalism and American Culture.* New York: Oxford University Press, 2006.
———. *Fundamentalism and American Culture: The Shaping of Twentieth-Century Evangelicalism: 1870–1925.* New York: Oxford University Press, 1980.
———. *Understanding Fundamentalism and Evangelicalism.* Grand Rapids: Eerdmans, 1991.
Marsh, Joss. *Word Crimes: Blasphemy, Culture, and Literature in Nineteenth-Century England.* Chicago: University of Chicago Press, 1998.

Martin, J. Wesley. *The Coming Kingdom: A Study in Prophecy and History*. London : Thynne & Jarvis, 1924.
Martin, Regis. *The Last Things: Death, Judgment, Heaven, Hell*. San Francisco: Ignatius, 1998.
Masselink, William. *Why Thousand Years? Or Will the Second Coming Be Pre-Millennial?* Grand Rapids: Eerdmans, 1953.
Mauro, Philip. *After This or the Church, the Kingdom, and the Glory*. New York: Revell, 1918.
———. *The Gospel of the Kingdom: With an Examination of Modern Dispensationalism*. Boston: Hamilton Bros., 1928.
McGinn, Bernard, ed. *Apocalyptic Spirituality*. Quoted in *Prisoners of Hope? Aspects of Evangelical Millennialism in Britain and Ireland, 1800–1880*, edited by Crawford Gribben and C. F. Timothy, 19. Waynesboro, GA: Paternoster, 2004.
McGrath, Alister E. *Darwinism and the Divine: Evolutionary Thought and Natural Theology*. Chichester: Wiley-Blackwell, 2011.
———. *Historical Theology: An Introduction to the History of Christian Thought*. 2nd ed. Chichester: Wiley & Sons, 2013.
———. *Science and Religion: A New Introduction*. 2nd edition. Chichester: Wiley-Blackwell, 2010.
McKibbens, Thomas R., Jr., and Kenneth L. Smith. *The Life and Works of Morgan Edwards*. New York: Arno, 1980.
Mellor, Anne K. *Mary Shelley: Her Life, Herr Fiction, Her Monsters*. New York: Methuen, 1988.
Melnyk, Julie. *Victorian Religion: Faith and Life in Britain*. Westport, CT: Praeger, 2008.
Miller. Andrew, *The Brethren ("Commonly So-Called") a Brief Sketch of Their Origin, Progress and Testimony*. London: Morrish, 1879.
Milton, Anthony. *Catholic and Reformed the Roman and Protestant Churches in England Protestant Thought, 1600–1640*. Cambridge: Cambridge University Press, 1995.
Moltmann, Jürgen. *The Coming of God: Christian Eschatology*. Translated by Margaret Kohl. Minneapolis: Fortress, 1996.
Moorman, John R. H. *A History of the Church of England*. 3rd edition. London: A. & C. Black, 1986.
Morris, Leon. *The Biblical Doctrine of Judgment*. Grand Rapids: Eerdmans, 1960.
Murray, George Lewis. *Millennial Studies, a Search for Truth*. Grand Rapids: Baker, 1948.
Murray, Iain Hamish. *The Puritan Hope: A Study in Revival and the Interpretation of Prophecy*. London: Banner of Truth Trust, 1984.
Nantais, David E., and Michael Simone. "Apocalypse When?" *America Magazine* 189, no. 4 (2003) 18–25.
Nee, Watchman. *Come, Lord Jesus: A Study of the Book of Revelation*. New York: Christian Fellowship, 1976.
Neff, David. "Signs of the End Times: Our Pursuit of Justice in the Present Foreshadows the Perfect Justice of an Age to Come." *Christianity Today* 55, no. 8 (2011) 46–49.
Newman, Francis William. *Phases of Faith*. Leicester: Leicester University Press, 1970.
Newport, Kenneth G. C. *Apocalypse and Millennium: Studies in Biblical Eisegesis*. Cambridge: Cambridge University Press, 2000.
———. "Premillennialism in the Early Writings of Charles Wesley." *Wesleyan Theological Journal* 32, no. 1 (1997) 85–106.

———. *The Sermons of Charles Wesley: A Critical Edition with Introductions and Notes.* Oxford: Oxford University Press, 2001.

Newport, Kenneth G. C., and Crawford Gribben, eds. *Expecting the End: Millennialism in Social and Historical Context.* Waco, TX: Baylor University Press, 2006.

Newton, Benjamin W. *Occasional Papers On Scriptural Subjects.* No. 2. London: Houlston and Wright, 1861.

Nietzsche, Friedrich. Translated by Thomas Wayne. *Ecce Homo & the Antichrist.* New York: Algora, 2004.

———. *The Gay Science.* Translated by Walter Kaufmann. Mineola: Dover, 2006.

Nockles, Peter B. *The Oxford Movement in Context: Anglican High Churchmanship 1760–1857.* Cambridge: Cambridge University Press, 1996.

Noll, Mark A. *Old Religion in a New World: The History of North American Christianity.* Grand Rapids: Eerdmans, 2002.

———. *The Rise of Evangelicalism: The Age of Edwards, Whitefield and the Wesleys.* Downers Grove, IL: InterVarsity, 2003.

North, John S., and Brent Nelson, eds. *The Waterloo Directory of English Newspapers and Periodicals, 1800–1900.* Waterloo: North Waterloo Academic, 2003.

O'Connor, Benjamin. "An Introduction to the Oxford Movement." In *Authority, Dogma, and History: The Role of the Oxford Movement Converts in the Papal Infallibility Debates,* edited by Kenneth L. Parker, and Michael J. G. Pahls, 9–43. Palo Alto: Academica, 2009.

Oliphant, Margaret. *The Life of Edward Irving, Minister of the National Scottish Church, London.* Vol. 1. London: Hurst and Blacket, 1862.

Oliver, W. H. *Prophets and Millennialists: The Uses of Biblical Prophecy in England from the 1790s to the 1840s.* Auckland: Auckland University Press, 1978.

Orme, William. *Remarkable Passages in the Life of William Kiffin.* London: Burton and Smith, 1823.

Panton, D. M. *The Apocalypse of the Lord (Revelation XIX).* London: Thynne, 1922.

———. *Earth's Last Pentecost.* London: Thynne, 1922.

———. *The Judgment Seat of Christ.* 1922. Repr., Hayesville: Schoettle, 1984.

———. *The Panton Papers: Current Events and Prophesy.* New York: Chalmers, 1928.

———. *Rapture.* London: Thynne, 1922.

Palmegiano, E. M. *Perceptions of the Press in Nineteenth-Century British Periodicals: A Bibliography.* New York: Anthem, 2012.

Parker, Kenneth L., and Michael J. G. Pahls, eds. *Authority, Dogma, and History: The Role of the Oxford Movement Converts in the Papal Infallibility Debates.* Palo Alto: Academica, 2009.

Patterson, Mark, and Andrew Walker. "Our Unspeakable Comfort: Irving, Albury, and the Origins of the Pre-tribulation Rapture." In *Christian Millennialism: From the Early Church to Waco,* edited by Stephen Hunt, 98–115. Bloomington: Indiana University Press, 2001.

Payne, John Barton. *Erasmus: His Theology of the Sacraments.* Richmond: Knox, 1970).

———. *The Imminent Appearing of Christ.* Grand Rapids: Eerdmans, 1962.

Pearce, Robert, and Roger Stearn. *Government and Reform: 1815–1918.* London: Hodder & Stoughton, 1994.

Pember, George H. *The Antichrist Babylon and the Coming of the Kingdom.* London: Hodder & Stoughton, 1886.

———. *The Church the Churches and the Mysteries: or Revelation and Corruption.* New York: Revell, 1901.

———. *Earth's Earliest Ages; and Their Connection with Modern Spiritualism and Theosophy.* 5th ed. London: Hodder and Stoughton, 1884.

———. *The Great Prophecies Concerning the Gentiles, the Jews, and the Church of God.* London: Hodder and Stoughton, 1881.

———. *The Great Prophecies of the Centuries Concerning Israel and the Gentiles.* London: Hodder & Stoughton, 1895.

Pentecost, J. Dwight. *Things to Come: A Study in Biblical Eschatology.* Findlay: Dunham, 1957.

Pettingill, William L., *Nearing the End, Simple Studies Concerning the Second Coming of Christ and Related Events.* Chicago: Van Kampen, 1948.

Pierson, Arthur T., *Forward Movements of the Last Half Century.* New York: Funk & Wagnalls, 1900.

———. *George Mueller of Bristol and His Witness to a Prayer-hearing God.* London: Pickering and Inglis, 1899.

———. *The New Acts of the Apostles, or the Marvels of Modern Missions, a Series of Lectures upon the Foundation of the "Duff Missionary Lectureship."* London: Nisbet, 1894.

Piggin, Stuart. "Preaching the New Birth and the Power of Godliness and Not Insisting So Much on the Form. Recent Studies on (Mainly English) Evangelicalism." *Journal of Religious History* 33, no. 3 (2009) 366–76.

Phillips, John. *Exploring Galatians: An Expository Commentary.* Grand Rapids: Kregel, 2004.

Philpot, Joseph Charles. *A Letter to the Provost of Worcester College, Oxford: On Resigning His Fellowship, and Seceding from the Church of England.* 6th ed. London: Fowler, 1835.

———. *The Kingdom of God Hidden and Revealed.* Pensacola: Chapel Library, 1990.

———. *Letters and Memoir of Joseph Charles Philpot.* Grand Rapids: Baker, 1981.

———. *Mr. J. C. Philpot's Review: Of "Apocalyptic Sketches," "Signs of the Times," and "The Coming Struggle."* Grand Rapids: Zion Baptist Church, 1980.

Philpot, Joseph Charles, and Sarah L. Philpot. *Letters: With a Brief Memoir of His Life and Labors.* London: Gadsby, 1987.

Philpot, Joseph Charles, and William Tiptaft. *The Seceders: The Story of J. C. Philpot and William Tiptaft.* London: Banner of Truth Trust, 1964.

Philpot, Joseph Charles, William Tiptaft, and Joseph Henry Philpot. *The Seceders (1829–1869).* London: Farncombe & Sons, 1930.

Pickering, Hy. *Chief Men among the Brethren: One Hundred Records and Photos.* London: Pickering & Inglis, 1931.

Piggott, J. R. *Palace of the people: The Crystal Palace of Sydenham, 1854–1936.* London: Hurst, 2004.

Pink, Arthur W. *The Redeemer's Return.* Swengel: Bible Truth Depot, 1918.

Priestley, J. *Tracts in Controversy with Bishop Horsley.* London: Printed by R. and A. Taylor for the London Unitarian Society, 1815.

Prosser, Peter. E. *Dispensationalist Eschatology and its Influence on American and British Religious Movements.* New York: Mellen, 1999.

Rall, Harris Franklin. *Modern Premillennialism and the Christian Hope.* New York: Abingdon, 1920.

Ramsey, George H. "A Brief Memoir of the Late Editor." *Dawn* 32, no. 6 (1955) 161.
Rander, M. *For Ever, an Essay on Eternal Punishment*. London: Wesleyan Conference Office, 1871.
Rappaport, Helen. *Queen Victoria: A Biographical Companion*. Santa Barbara: ABC-CLIO, 2003.
Rawcliffe, C., R. Wilson, and C. Clark. *Norwich Since 1550*. London: Hambledon & London, 2004.
Reardon, Bernard M. G. *Religious Thought in the Victorian Age: A Study from Coleridge to Gore*. London: Longman, 1980.
Reese, Alexander. *The Approaching Advent of Christ. an Examination of the Teaching of J.N. Darby and His Followers*. London: Marshall, Morgan & Scott, 1937.
Reiter, Paul R. "A History of the Development of the Rapture Positions." In *Three Views on the Rapture: Pre-, Mid-, or Post-Tribulation*, edited by Gleason L. Archer, 9–44. Grand Rapids: Zondervan, 1996.
Robert, Robert. *The Twelve Lectures on the Teaching of the Bible in Relation to the Faiths of Christendom; to which are Added Five Additional Lectures, on the Devil, Judgment to Come, the Promises to the Fathers, the Covenant with David, and the Signs of the Times*. 5th ed. Birmingham: Roberts, 1869.
Robinson, Edward. *Greek and English Lexicon of the New Testament*. Boston: Crocker and Brewster, 1836.
Romaine, William. *Letters From the Late Rev. William Romaine, M.A., Rector of St. Andrews Wardrobe, and St. Ann Black Friars; and Lecturer of St. Dunstan's in the West, To a Friend, On the Most Important Subjects, During a Correspondence of Twenty Years*. New Brunswick: Walker, 1809.
Robins, Colin. *Romaine's Crimean War: The Letters and Journal of William Govett Romaine, Deputy Judge-Advocate to the Army of the East 1854-6*. Stroud: Sutton for the Army Records Society, 2005.
Romilly, Joseph. *Graduati Cantabrigienses: Sive Catalogus Exhibens Nomina Eorum*. London: Deighton, Bell, 1856.
Rowell, Geoffrey. *Hell and the Victorians; A Study of the Nineteenth-Century Theological Controversies concerning Eternal Punishment and the Future Life*. Oxford: Clarendon, 1974.
Royle, Edward. *Radicals, Secularists and Republicans: Popular Freethought in Britain, 1866–1915*. Manchester: Manchester University Press, 1980.
———. *Victorian Infidels: The Origins of the British Secularist Movement, 1791–1866*. Manchester: Manchester University Press, 1974.
Russen, David. *Fundamentals without foundation: Or, a True Picture of the Anabaptists in Their Rise, Progress and Practice, to Which Is Added a Letter from the Reverend Mr. James Brome to the Author*. London: Printed For R. Bassett, 1703.
Ryrie, Charles Caldwell. *The Basis of the Premillennial Faith*. New York: Loizeaux Bros., 1953.
———. *Dispensationalism Today*. 2nd ed. Chicago: Moody, 1965.
———. "Why I Am a Pretribulation Rapturist." *Israel My Glory* (2012) 30–33.
Sandeen, Ernest R. *The Roots of Fundamentalism: British and American Millenarianism, 1800–1930*. 2nd ed. Grand Rapids: Baker, 1978.
Sant, Henry. *J. C. Philpot, the Faith That Unites to the Lamb: His Call by Grace and Concept of the Nature of Saving Faith*. Southampton: Huntingtonian, 2003.

Saucy, Robert L. *The Case for Progressive Dispensationalism: The Interface between Dispensational & Non-Dispensational Theology.* Grand Rapids: Zondervan, 1993.

Schaff, Philip. *History of the Christian Church.* Vol. 7. New York: Charles Scribner's Sons, 1907.

Scofield, C. I. "Biblical Notes and Queries." *Record of Christian Work* 18, no. 1 (1899) 31–32.

Secor, Philip B. *Richard Hooker and the Via Media.* Bloomington: Author-House, 2006.

———. *Richard Hooker: Prophet of Anglicanism.* Kent: Burns & Oates, 1999.

Seiss, Joseph A. *The Apocalypse: A Series of Special Lectures on the Revelation of Jesus Christ, with Revised Text.* New York: Cook, 1900.

———. *The Parable of the Ten Virgins: In Six Discourses. And a Sermon on the Judgment of the Saints.* Philadelphia: Lutheran, 1862.

Shagan, Ethan H. *Popular Politics and the English Reformation.* Cambridge: Cambridge University Press, 2003.

Shantz, Douglas H. "Millennialism and Apocalypticism in Recent Historical Scholarship." In *Prisoners of Hope? Aspects of Evangelical Millennialism in Britain and Ireland, 1800–1880,* edited by Crawford Gribben and C. F. Stunt, 18–43. Waynesboro, GA: Paternoster, 2004.

Shelley, Mary. *The Last Man: In Three Volumes.* London: Colburn, 1826.

Shenton, Tim. *An Iron Pillar. The Life and Times of William Romaine.* Darlington: Evangelical, 2004.

Shuff, Roger. *Searching for the True Church: Brethren and Evangelicals in Mid-Twentieth Century England.* Carlisle: Paternoster, 2005.

Smith, Mark, and Stephen Taylor, eds. *Evangelicalism in the Church of England, c. 1790-c.1900.* Woodbridge: Boydell, 2004.

Smith, Sir William, and J. M. Fuller, eds. *A Dictionary of the Bible Comprising its Antiquities, Biography, Geography, and National History.* Vol. 1/1. 2nd ed. London: Murray, 1893.

Smith, Wilbur E., *The Real Thing: An Exhortation for the Authentic Christian Life.* Grove City: Livingwalk, 2010.

Smith, Wilbur M. *A Preliminary Bibliography for the Study of Biblical Prophecy.* Boston: Wilde, 1952.

Smolinski, Reiner. "Caveat Emptor: Pre- and Postmillennialism in the Late Reformation Period." In *Millenarianism and Messianism in Early Modern European Culture, Volume III, The Millenarian Turn: Millenarian Contexts of Science, Politics and Everyday Anglo-American life in the Seventeenth and Eighteenth Centuries,* edited by James E. Force and Richard H. Popkin, 145–69. Dordrecht: Kluer Academic, 2001.

Snowden, James Henry. *The Coming of the Lord: Will It Be Premillennial?* New York: Macmillan, 1919.

Spurgeon, C. H. *Commentary on Matthew: The Gospel of the Kingdom.* Edinburgh: Banner of Truth Trust, 2010.

St. Aubyn, Giles. *Souls in Torment: Victorian Faith in Crisis.* London: Sinclair-Stevenson, 2011.

Standish, Colin, and Russell R. Standish. *The Perils of Ecumenism.* Rapidan: Hartland, 2003.

Stanton, Gerald B. *Kept from the Hour: A Systematic Study of the Rapture in Bible Prophecy.* Grand Rapids: Zondervan, 1956.

Stennett, Joseph. *An Answer to Mr. David Russen's Book, Entitul'd, Fundamentals Without A Foundation, or a True Picture of the Anabaptists, &c. Together with Some Brief Remarks on Mr. James Broome's Letter Annex'd to that Treatise.* London: Brown, Crouch, and Baker, 1704.

Stephen, Leslie, and Sydney Lee, eds. *Dictionary of National Biography.* Vol. 2. London: Smith, Elder, 1908.

———. *Dictionary of National Biography.* Vol. 6. London: Smith, Elder, 1908.

Stephens, John, "The Ministration of Private Baptism of Children in Houses." In *The Book of Common Prayer: With Notes, Legal and Historical*, 2:1305-1421. London: Harrison and Son, 1850.

Stewart, Kenneth J. "A Millennial Maelstrom: Controversy in the Continental Society in the 1820s." In *Prisoners of hope? Aspects of evangelical millennialism in Britain and Ireland, 1800-1880*, edited by Crawford Gribben and Timothy C. F. Stunt, 122-49. Waynesboro, GA: Paternoster, 2004.

Stunt, Timothy C. F. *From Awakening to Secession: Radical Evangelicals in Switzerland and Britain, 1815-35.* Edinburgh: T. & T. Clark, 2000.

———. "Influences in the Early Development of J. N. Darby." In *Prisoners of hope? Aspects of evangelical millennialism in Britain and Ireland, 1800-1880*, edited by Crawford Gribben and Timothy C. F. Stunt, 44-68. Waynesboro, GA: Paternoster, 2004.

———. "Trinity College, John Nelson Darby and the Powerscourt Milieu." In *Beyond the End: The Future of Millennial Studies*, edited by Joshua Searle and Kenneth G. C. Newport, 47-74. Sheffield: Sheffield Phoenix, 2012.

Sumner, Arthur, T. H. Darlow, and H. F. Moule, eds. *Historical Catalogue of Printed Editions of the English Bible: 1525-1961.* London: British & Foreign Bible Society, 1968.

Sumner, John B. *Apostolic Preaching Considered in Examination of St. Paul's Epistles.* New York: New York Protestant Episcopal, 1830.

Sweetnam, Mark S. "Defining Dispensationalism: A Cultural Studies Perspective." *Journal of Religious History* 34 (2010) 191-212.

———. "Tensions in Dispensational Eschatology." In *Expecting the End: Millennialism in Social and Historical Context*, edited by Kenneth G. C. Newport and Crawford Gribben, 173-92. Waco: Baylor University Press, 2006.

Sweetnam, Mark S., and Crawford Gribben. "J. N. Darby and the Irish Origins of Dispensationalism." *Journal of the Evangelical Theological Society* 52, no. 3 (2009) 569-77.

Syle, Louis Du Pont. *From Milton to Tennyson; Masterpieces of English Poetry.* Boston: Allyn and Bacon, 1894.

Tan, Paul Lee. "Partial Rapture." In *Dictionary of Premillennial Theology: A Practical Guide to the People, Viewpoints, and History of Prophetic Studies*, edited by Mal Couch, 347-48. Grand Rapids: Kregel, 1996.

Tatford, Frederick A. *Will There Be a Millennium?* Eastbourne: Prophetic Witness, 1969.

Telford, John, ed. *The Letters of the Rev. John Wesley.* 8 vols. London: Epworth, 1931.

Temple, Frederick, et al. *Essays and Reviews.* London: Parker, 1860.

Thiselton, Anthony C. *Life after Death, a New Approach to the Last Things.* Grand Rapids: Eerdmans, 2012.

Tjoa, Hock Guan. *George Henry Lewis, a Victorian Mind.* Cambridge, MA: Harvard University Press, 1977.

Todd, James Henthorn. *Six Discourses on the Prophecies Relating to Antichrist in the Apocalypse of St. John. Preached Before the University of Dublin, at the Connellon Lecture.* London: F. & J. Rivington, 1846.
Towns, Elmer, and Richard Mayhue. "Partial Rapture." In *The Popular Encyclopedia of Bible Prophecy*, edited by Tim LaHaye and Ed Hindson, 260–62. Eugene, OR: Harvest House, 2004.
Trench, George F. *After the Thousand Years: The Glorious Reign of Christ as Son of Man in the Dispensation of the Fulness of Times.* London: Morgan and Scott, 1890.
Trueman, Carl R. *Histories and Fallacies: Problems Faced in the Writing of History.* Wheaton, IL: Crossway, 2010.
Turner, Frank M. *John Henry Newman: The Challenge of Evangelical Religion.* New Haven: Yale University Press, 2002.
———. "The Victorian Crisis of Faith and the Faith That Was Lost." In *Victorian Faith in Crisis: Essays on Continuity and Change in Nineteenth-Century Religious Belief*, edited by Richard J. Helmstadter and Bernard Lightman, 9–38. Stanford: Stanford University Press, 1990.
Turner, W. G. *John Nelson Darby: A Bibliography.* London: Hammond, 1926.
Tuveson, Ernest L. *Redeemer Nation: The Idea of America's Millennial Role.* Chicago: University of Chicago Press, 1968.
Van Asselt, W. J. "Chiliasm and Reformed Eschatology in the Seventeenth and Eighteenth Centuries." In *Christian Hope in Context*, edited by A. van Egmond and D. van Keulen, 11–29. Studies in Reformed Theology 4. Zoetermeer: Meinema, 2001.
Vann, J. Don, and Rosemary T. VanArsdel, eds. *Periodicals of Queen Victoria's Empire: An Exploration.* Toronto: University of Toronto, 1996.
Veitch, T. S. *The Story of the Brethren Movement, a Simple and Straightforward Account of the Features and Failures of a Sincere Attempt to Carry Out the Principles of Scripture During the Last 100 Years.* London: Pickering & Inglis, 1933.
Waddington, Barbara, ed. *The Dairy and Letters of Edward Irving.* Eugene, OR: Pickwick, 2012.
Wale, Burlington B. *The Closing Days of Christendom as Foreshadowed in Parable and Prophecy.* 2nd ed. London: Partridge, 1883.
Walker, Charles C. *Rome and the Christadelphians: Being a Reply to "Christadelphianism" by J. W. Pointer.* Birmingham: Christadelphian, 1923.
Wall, William. *The History of Infant Baptism: In Two Parts.* 2 vols. 4th ed. London: Printed for F.C. and J. Rivington, 1819.
Walton, Robert C. *Zwingli's Theocracy.* Toronto: University of Toronto Press, 1967.
Walvoord, John F. *The Millennial Kingdom: A Basic Text in Premillennial Theology.* Grand Rapids: Zondervan, 1959.
———. *The Rapture Question.* Findlay: Dunham, 1957.
———. *The Rapture Question.* Grand Rapids: Zondervan, 1979.
Ward, W. R. *Early Evangelicalism: A Global Intellectual History, 1670–1789.* Cambridge: Cambridge University Press, 2006.
———. *Religion and Society in England 1790–1850.* New York: Schocken, 1973.
Ward, William S. *Index and Finding List of Serials Published in the British Isles 1789–1832.* Lexington: University of Kentucky Press, 1953.
Weber, Timothy P. "Dispensational and Historic Premillennialism as Popular Millennialist Movements." In *A Case for Historic Premillennialism: An Alternative*

to "Left Behind" Eschatology, edited by Craig L. Blomberg and Sung Wook Chung, 1–22. Grand Rapids: Baker, 2009.
Welchman, Edward. *The Thirty-Nine Articles of the Church of England, Confirmed by Text of Holy Scripture, and Testimonies of the Primitive Fathers: To which are Added, Short Notes, in Illustration of the Articles.* London: SPCK, 1842.
Wheeler, Michael. *Death and the Future Life in Victorian Literature and Theology.* Cambridge: Cambridge University Press, 1990.
———. *Heaven, Hell and the Victorians.* Abridged ed. of *Death and the Future Life in Victorian Literature and Theology.* Cambridge: Cambridge University Press, 1994.
Whitcomb, John C. *The Rapture and Beyond.* Waxhaw: Kainos, 2012.
Williams, Edward. *An Essay on the Equity of Divine Government and the Sovereignty of Divine Grace.* London: Burditt, 1809.
Williams, George H., Angel M. Nergal, and Juan de Valdés, eds. *Spiritual and Anabaptist Writers.* London: Westminister, 1957.
Wills, Gregory A. "A Fire That Burns within: The Spirituality of John Gills." In *The Life and Thought of John Gill (1697-1771) a Tercentennial Application*, edited by Michael A.G. Haykin, 191–210. Leiden: Brill, 1997.
Wilson, Bryan R. *Sects and Society; A Sociological Study of the Elim Tabernacle, Christian Science, and Christadelphians.* Berkeley: University of California Press, 1961.
Wilson, Daniel. *Expository Lectures on St. Paul's Epistle to the Colossians.* London: Hatchard and Son, 1845.
Wilson, John, ed. *The Watchmen of Ephraim.* London: Mackintosh, 1869.
White, Andrew Dickson. *A History of the Warfare of Science with Theology in Cristendom.* London: King, 1876.
White, W. *White's 1845 Norfolk: A Reprint of the 1845 Issue of History, Gazetteer, and Directory of Norfolk.* Newton Abbot: David & Charles, 1969.
Wordsworth, William. *The Excursion.* London: Moxon, 1836.
———. *The Prelude.* Vol. 3 of *The Complete Poetical Works of William Wordsworth.* Boston: Houghton Mifflin, 1919.
Yates, Nigel, *Anglican Ritualism in Victorian Britain 1830–1910.* Oxford: Oxford University Press, 1999.

Dissertations

Burnham, Jonathan David. "The Controversial Relationship between Benjamin Wills Newton and John Nelson Darby." DPhil thesis, University of Oxford, 1999.
Crutchfield, Larry V. "The Doctrine of Ages and Dispensations as Found in the Published Works of John Nelson Darby (1800-1882)." PhD diss., Drew University, 1985.
Jue, Jeffrey K. "Heaven upon Earth: The Apocalyptic Thought of Joseph Mead (1586-1638)." PhD thesis, University of Aberdeen, 2003.
Kelly, Thomas J. "Trapped Between Two Worlds: Edward Nagle, Achill Island, and Sectarian Competition in Ireland, 1800–1862." PhD diss., Trinity College Dublin, 2004.
Morden, Peter John. "Communion with Christ and His People: The Spirituality of C. H. Spurgeon (1834-92)." PhD thesis, Spurgeon's College, 2010.

Nebeker, Gary Lynn. "The Hope of Heavenly Glory in John Nelson Darby." PhD. diss., Dallas Theological Seminary, 1997.
Robertson, Arthur K. "The New Testament Doctrine of Sanctification as Found in the Published Writings of John Nelson Darby, 1800–1882." PhD diss., New York University, 1975.
Rosscup, James E. "Paul's Teaching on the Christian's Future Reward with Special Reference to 1 Corinthians 3:10–17." PhD thesis, University of Aberdeen, 1976.
Seip, David. "Pauline Theology on Future Reward for Christians: With Particular Reference to Forfeiture." MTh diss., University of Aberdeen, 2000.
———. "Robert Govett: His Understanding of the Millennium and Its Reward, with Emphasis upon His Impact on the Early Development of Dispensationalism." ThM thesis, Westminster Theological Seminary, 2009.
Travis, Stephen H. "The Place of Retribution in the Thought of Paul." PhD diss., University of Cambridge, 1970.
Turner, Layne H. "The Use of Eternal Rewards as a Motivation in the New Testament." ThD diss., Dallas Theological Seminary, 1991.
Ward, John P. "The Eschatology of John Nelson Darby." PhD diss., University of London, 1976.

www.ingramcontent.com/pod-product-compliance
Lightning Source LLC
Chambersburg PA
CBHW050348230426
43663CB00010B/2035